Frommer's®

Moscow & St. Petersburg

4th Edition

by Angela Charlton

WILEY

John Wiley & Sons, Inc.

Published by:

JOHN WILEY & SONS, INC.

111 River St.

Hoboken, NJ 07030-5774

ISBN 978-1-118-16715-1 (paper); ISBN 978-1-118-22629-2 (ebk); ISBN 978-1-118-24097-7 (ebk); ISBN 978-1-118-23953-7 (ebk)

Editor: Stephen Bassman
Production Editor: Lindsay Conner
Cartographer: Elizabeth Puhl
Photo Editor: Richard Fox
Production by Wiley Indianapolis Composition Services

Front cover photo: Monument of Yuri Dolgoruki in front of St. Basil Cathedral in Moscow © Igor Sinitsyn / Imagebroker.net / PhotoLibrary
Back cover photo: Portrait Hall at The Hermitage (Winter Palace) in St. Petersburg © Cindy Miller Hopkins / DanitaDelimont.com / Alamy Images

Manufactured in the United States of America

5   4   3   2   1

CONTENTS

18 USEFUL RUSSIAN TERMS & PHRASES 315

LIST OF MAPS

ABOUT THE AUTHOR

Angela Charlton moved to Russia in the early 1990s and spent most of the ensuing decade in the former Soviet Union working as a journalist. She was the Moscow correspondent for the Associated Press for six years, and she also studied in St. Petersburg and worked in Kiev. She is currently a journalist based in Paris.

HOW TO CONTACT US

In researching this book, we discovered many wonderful places—hotels, restaurants, shops, and more. We're sure you'll find others. Please tell us about them, so we can share the information with your fellow travelers in upcoming editions. If you were disappointed with a recommendation, we'd love to know that, too. Please write to:

Frommer's Moscow & St. Petersburg, 4th Edition
John Wiley & Sons, Inc. • 111 River St. • Hoboken, NJ 07030-5774
frommersfeedback@wiley.com

AN ADDITIONAL NOTE

FROMMER'S STAR RATINGS, ICONS & ABBREVIATIONS

Every hotel, restaurant, and attraction listing in this guide has been ranked for quality, value, service, amenities, and special features using a star-rating system. In country, state, and regional guides, we also rate towns and regions to help you narrow down your choices and budget your time accordingly. Hotels and restaurants are rated on a scale of zero (recommended) to three stars (exceptional). Attractions, shopping, nightlife, towns, and regions are rated according to the following scale: zero stars (recommended), one star (highly recommended), two stars (very highly recommended), and three stars (must-see).

In addition to the star-rating system, we also use seven feature icons that point you to the great deals, in-the-know advice, and unique experiences that separate travelers from tourists. Throughout the book, look for:

special finds—those places only insiders know about

fun facts—details that make travelers more informed and their trips more fun

kids—best bets for kids and advice for the whole family

special moments—those experiences that memories are made of

overrated—places or experiences not worth your time or money

insider tips—great ways to save time and money

great values—where to get the best deals

The following abbreviations are used for credit cards:

AE   American Express   DISC   Discover   V   Visa

DC   Diners Club   MC   MasterCard

TRAVEL RESOURCES AT FROMMERS.COM

Frommer's travel resources don't end with this guide. Frommer's website, **www.frommers. com**, has travel information on more than 4,000 destinations. We update features regularly, giving you access to the most current trip-planning information and the best airfare, lodging, and car-rental bargains. You can also listen to podcasts, connect with other Frommers. com members through our active-reader forums, share your travel photos, read blogs from guidebook editors and fellow travelers, and much more.

THE BEST OF MOSCOW & ST. PETERSBURG

Russia breathes superlatives: the world's biggest country; its largest supplier of natural gas and one of the largest oil producers; home of the planet's longest railroads, busiest subway system (Moscow's), and its deepest, oldest lake (Baikal, in Siberia). It even boasts balmy beach resorts (on the Black Sea), though the Kremlin and the snowcapped cupolas of its cathedrals seem truer reflections of this northern nation's might and mysticism.

What the country lacks in climatic warmth, Russians make up for with their bottomless generosity and heartfelt hospitality. Survivors of despots from Ivan the Terrible to Stalin, Russians place high value on keeping their home world safe from the perils of without and stocking their larders with homemade jams, pickles, and desserts. The past two decades have been rough on most Russians, but have sharpened their adaptation skills. Today's Russian university graduates know more languages, more about financial markets, and more about social networking than many of their Western counterparts.

There is much for travelers to experience in Russia's two most popular cities. The rigorous traditions of the Bolshoi Theater's dance company coexist with some of Europe's most cutting-edge DJs. Hip restaurants fashion mouthwatering delicacies that put a twist on traditional Russian meat pies and cabbage soup. St. Petersburg's Hermitage Museum is a fortress of fine art from around the world, and just down the street, the Russian Museum overflows with underrated works by local artists from throughout the centuries. Celebrate Russia's contributions to the exploration of the universe by trying on a spacesuit at the Star City training village or wandering Moscow's Cosmonautics Museum, a tribute to the tireless scientists and engineers who sent the first man—and woman—into space.

Russia's tourism infrastructure, alas, is still catching up with the rest of the nation's societal and economic changes, but Moscow and St. Petersburg are well on their way. Take along some pluck and flexibility and have a look at the best Russia has to offer.

most memorable RUSSIAN EXPERIENCES

o **Viewing Red Square at Night** (Moscow): The crimson-and-ivy-colored domes of St. Basil's Cathedral rise in a dizzying welcome to this most majestic of Russian plazas. The red stars on the Kremlin towers twinkle above one side of the square, making the medieval fortress seem festive instead of forbidding. Lenin's Mausoleum in nighttime shadow is appropriately eerie. Stand on the rise in the center of the square and feel a part of Russia's expanse. See p. 103.

o **Experiencing White Nights in St. Petersburg:** Two weeks of festivities in late June celebrate the longest day of the year, when the northern sun never dips below the horizon. The White Nights are more than just a party; they're a buoyant, carefree celebration of summer—liberation after the city's long hibernation. Watch at midnight as residents picnic with their kids or play soccer in the courtyards. Then take a nighttime boat ride through the canals as the sunset melts into a languorous sunrise, and you'll never want to go south again. See p. 258.

o **Steaming Your Stress Away at the Banya:** Thaw your eyelashes in January or escape snow flurries in May in the traditional Russian bathhouse, something between a sauna and a Turkish hammam. The pristine Sandunovsky Baths in Moscow are a special treat, with Greek sculptures and marble baths. Watch expert banya-goers beat themselves with birch branches, plunge into icy pools, exfoliate with coffee grounds, and quaff beer, or tea, while waiting for the next steam. **Sandunovsky Baths (Sandunovskiye Banyi)** are at 14 Neglinnaya, Moscow (© **495/625-4631**). See p. 123.

o **Watching the Drawbridges Open Along the Neva River** (St. Petersburg): An unforgettable outing during White Nights (p. 258), or anytime, involves perching yourself on the quay at 2am to watch the city's bridges unfold in careful rhythm to allow shipping traffic through the busy Neva. Just be careful not to get caught on the wrong side of the river from your hotel.

o **Taking the Trans-Siberian Railroad:** This winding link between Europe and Asia illustrates Russia's continent-spanning scale. Seven days from Moscow to Beijing, or from Moscow to Vladivostok on the Pacific Coast, the journey provides time for reflection on history, geography and destiny, and making acquaintances. Lake Baikal and the Altai Mountains form stunning interruptions in Siberia's swath of pine and birch forests.

o **Picnicking at Kolomenskoye** (Moscow): This architectural reserve hosts the breathtaking 16th-century Church of the Assumption and the wooden house where Peter the Great sought refuge before assuming the throne. The surrounding lawns and groves beckon visitors to stretch out with caviar or cucumber sandwiches and a thermos of strong Russian tea. The hilly paths wind through apple orchards. Historic folk festivals are staged here throughout the year. See p. 118.

o **Paying Your Respects at Novodevichy Cemetery and Convent** (Moscow): The intricately original graves of the Russian eminences buried here—writers Anton Chekhov and Nikolai Gogol, Soviet leader Nikita Khrushchev, and Stalin's suicidal wife among them—are allegories more than headstones. The tranquil grounds of the convent above witnessed bloody palace intrigues, and many a powerful woman in Russian history was exiled there. Today its restored cathedrals and adjacent pond exude a quiet serenity. See p. 107.

- **Sipping Baltika Beer at Patriarch's Ponds** (Moscow): This prestigious neighborhood inspired writer Mikhail Bulgakov (*Master and Margarita*). It's still a prime spot to sink onto a bench with a bottle of local beer (Baltika is a popular choice) or other beverage and watch Moscow spin by. Whimsical statues of characters from Ivan Krylov's fables will entertain kids, and the pond is a skating rink in winter. See p. 117.

- **Taking Tea at a Luxury Hotel:** A cup of steaming tea from an antique samovar is a treat for anyone, and even those on tight budgets should find something affordable at top-end hotels. To accompany the tea, try jam-filled *bliny* (thin Russian pancakes), fruit- or meat-filled *pirozhki* (pies), or caviar on toast. For more information, see the listings for Moscow's Le Royal Meridien National (p. 60) or Metropol (p. 57) or St. Petersburg's Grand Hotel Europe (p. 194).

- **Sampling Wild Mushrooms:** Mushroom-picking in the countryside is a national pastime, and homemade mushroom dishes are heavenly, though not without risks. Restaurant-approved mushrooms are nearly as good and are sure to be safe: succulent cepes in soup; chanterelles sprinkled on pork chops; or *zhulien*, any wild mushroom baked with cheese and sour cream. See chapters 5 and 12.

- **Enjoying a Night Out at the Mariinsky Theater** (formerly known as the Kirov; St. Petersburg): Russia's premier ballet and opera house set the standard for companies worldwide, and it continues to produce top-class performers. Even seats on the fourth-level balcony offer views of the opulent 18th-century interior. The Bolshoi Theater in Moscow is closed for renovations, though its company is performing on a still-impressive stage nearby. See p. 259.

best LUXURY HOTELS

- **Ritz-Carlton** (Moscow; © **495/225-8888**; www.ritzcarltonmoscow.ru): This eye-catching new addition to Moscow's top-end hotel scene has outdone its predecessors. Its Classicist style and high-tech glass architecture are the perfect symbols for the wealth and success of today's Moscow. See p. 60.

- **Baltschug Kempinski** (Moscow; © **800/426-3135**; www.kempinski-moscow. com): The hotel's views of St. Basil's Cathedral, Red Square, and the Kremlin are so picturesque that TV networks set up here for their stand-ups. The brunch is fit for a czar, and the understated elegance of the rooms complements the facade's pastel ornamentation. See p. 68.

- **Grand Hotel Europe** (St. Petersburg; © **812/329-6000**; www.grandhoteleurope. com): This baroque confection in central St. Petersburg charmed Tchaikovsky and U.S. presidents, among other rarefied guests. The winter garden stays lush even during St. Petersburg's dimmest months. The harpist and plush furniture of the mezzanine cafe provide respite from a day of touring. See p. 194.

- **Corinthia Nevsky Palace** (St. Petersburg; © **812/380-2001**; www.corinthia. ru): Bursting with amenities too rare in Russia's second city, this thoroughly modern hotel is housed in a 19th-century landmark on central Nevsky Prospekt. Its heated garage, aromatherapy sessions, and sunbathing terrace compete with its in-house theatrical museum for customer raves. See p. 193.

- **Le Royal Meridien National** (Moscow; © **495/258-7000**; www.national.ru): The National (a Royal Meridien hotel) has hosted legions of foreign and Russian dignitaries, including Vladimir Lenin before he moved into the Kremlin across the street. Now Russia's capitalist multimillionaires make it their home away from home. See Hotel National p. 60.

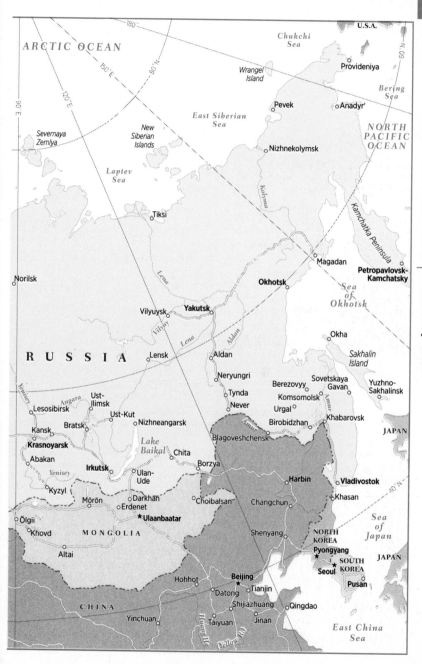

best AFFORDABLE ACCOMMODATIONS

- **Nevsky Hotels** (St. Petersburg; ✆ **812/703-3860**; www.hon.ru): A local company has a network of renovated buildings around town, including some with views of St. Petersburg's greatest monuments. A range of room sizes, prices, and services is available, with the best deals a bit beyond the tourist-beaten path. See p. 195.

- **Moscow Apartments** (Moscow; ✆ **495/662-2224**; www.moscowapartments. net): An appealing option if you're traveling with a family or staying for several days, this company offers basic, serviced apartments in a variety of locations. Bumping into neighbors allows a peek at Russian life. See p. 76.

- **Kristoff** (St. Petersburg; ✆ **812/571-6643**): This tidy hotel offers a glimpse of Russian life that bigger hotels can't, since it occupies two floors of an apartment building. It's in a charming, lively neighborhood most tourists don't see, but isn't far from the main sights. See p. 199.

- **Suharevka Hotel** (Moscow; ✆ **910/ 420-3446**): Shirred curtains and houseplants make this locale feel like grandma's house, but with a bustling Moscow edge. Both a hostel and hotel, it's one of the best deals in a costly town. See p. 73.

best DINING EXPERIENCES

- **Best Aristocratic Atmosphere:** Plunge into the refined opulence of 19th-century Russia at **Cafe Pushkin** (Moscow; 26a Tverskoi Bulvar; ✆ **495/739-0033**) as you spear a bite of suckling pig or sip fine tea from a silver samovar—24 hours a day. It opened in 2000, but the three-story restaurant's careful design and popularity make it seem like an imperial-era landmark. See p. 83.

- **Best Comfort Food:** One of the most reliable, reasonable Russian menus in Moscow is at the basement restaurant/bar **Uncle Vanya** (Moscow; 16 Pyatnitskaya; ✆ **495/232-1448**). Literary and musical memorabilia line the walls, and the placemats teach you the Russian alphabet. Favorites are the buckwheat kasha and their dumplings (*pelmeni* or *vareniki*) with meat, potato, or berry fillings. See p. 92.

- **Best Fusion:** Leading restaurateur Anton Novikov has capitalized on Russia's growing obsession with Asian cuisine without surrendering to it at two restaurants; the latest is **Nedalny Vostok** (Moscow; 1 Ostozhenka; ✆ **495/202-3341**). The menu is relentlessly fresh; recent options included Caesar salad with tuna and salmon sashimi, and Sechuan scallops with cauliflower puree and grilled sausage. The prices mirror Novikov's success, and ego.

- **Best Fresh Fish:** The spare stone arches of St. Petersburg's **Restoran** (St. Petersburg; 2 Tamozhenny Pereulok; ✆ **812/327-8975**) evoke another era, but its elegant lines and innovative chef keep things thoroughly modern. The unobtrusive salad bar offers marinated Russian specialties. The fish is so fresh you can forget any fears and indulge. See p. 217.

- **Best Georgian Fare:** The generous cuisine of Georgia, in the herb- and sheep-covered Caucasus Mountains, is best sampled at **Genatsvale** (Moscow; 12/1 Ostozhenka; ✆ **495/695-0401**). Exposed wood and lace curtains provide the perfect home-style setting for cheese-filled *khachapuri* loaves or lamb marinated in pomegranate juice. Georgia's southern climes inspire spicy vegetable dishes sorely lacking in Russian cuisine. St. Petersburg's Georgian restaurants also shine. See p. 90.

o **Best Literary Dive:** Just a small streetlight above the entrance marks the bohemian vegetarian basement cafe **Idiot** (St. Petersburg; 82 Moika Canal; ✆ **812/315-1675**), named after a Fyodor Dostoyevsky novel. Mulled wine warms visitors in the winter months; lightly fermented *kvas* cools you in July. Pick a book in English from the cafe's eclectic library to peruse while you sip. See p. 216

o **Best Kitschy Theme Dining:** Three elaborate and pricy Moscow restaurants plumb the stereotypes and cuisines of Russia's neighbors. **Shinok** (Moscow; 2 Ulitsa 1905 Goda; ✆ **495/988-2656**), a Ukrainian farm with a chicken coop, is hidden on one of the city's hippest streets. Aromatic borscht is served here 24 hours. **Prisoner of the Caucasus** (Moscow; Kavkazkaya Plennitsa; 36 Prospekt Mira; ✆ **495/280-5111**) offers grilled lamb and garlicky eggplant. Waiters are decked out as mountain warriors. **White Sun of the Desert** (Moscow; Beloye Solntse Pustyni; 29/14 Neglinnaya St.; ✆ **495/625-2596**) offers central Asian cuisine like lamb pilaf and spicy dumplings. See p. 93, 93, and 88, respectively.

o **Best Quickie Meal: Yolki-Palki** is a Russian chain with basic sit-down service in a country kitchen setting. It's also kid-friendly, a rarity on Russia's otherwise up-to-date dining scene. See p. 87.

best VIEWS

o **Lookout Point at Sparrow Hills** (Moscow): With the Stalin Gothic skyscraper of Moscow State University at your back, the capital spreads out beneath you in its enormity. Watch newlyweds pose and embrace at the lookout, leaving empty champagne bottles on the ledge. See p. 122.

o **Resurrection Gate Entrance to Red Square** (Moscow): Get ready to gasp when the beveled onion domes of St. Basil's Cathedral greet you at this cobblestone hilltop square. Resurrection Gate, itself resurrected in the 1990s, forms a perfect frame. See p. 103.

o **Strelka** (St. Petersburg): If you stand on this spit of land on Vasilevsky Island, you'll get a panorama of nearly every major landmark and monument in St. Petersburg, while the Neva River laps at your feet. It's also a window onto the classical conformity of the city's architecture. See p. 161.

o **The Sail Up to the Petrodvorets Palace** (Peterhof): The dense forests along the Baltic shore suddenly part and the gilded palace emerges, atop cascading fountains and sculpted gardens. Any boat from St. Petersburg to the imperial summer residence offers this vista. Hydrofoils leave from the Winter Palace/Hermitage in the warmer months. See chapter 16.

best ARCHITECTURE

o **The Kremlin** (Moscow): This red-brick fortress encloses a complex of 15th-century cathedrals that serve as Russia's best-preserved window into that era, with their gold domes and pointed arches. Surrounding them are palaces where Russia's presidents and their Soviet and czarist predecessors have reigned, from the flowered columns of the Grand Kremlin Palace to the classical triangular Senate Building. See p. 99.

o **Palace Square** (St. Petersburg): The Russian baroque Winter Palace looks across this square—the stage for the Russian Revolution—toward the Alexander Column (celebrating the victory over Napoleon) and the curved facade of the General Staff building. Though its parts were erected at different times, Palace Square demonstrates the ensemble architecture that gives this planned city its consistency. See p. 227.

o **Stalin Gothic Skyscrapers** (Moscow): These seven towers raised in the 1940s and 1950s soar above the capital, looking grandiose from afar and eerie up close. Two of the towers house private apartments, two house government buildings, two are hotels, and one is Moscow State University. See p. 287.

o **Kolomenskoye Museum Reserve** (Moscow): The towering tented spires of the 16th-century Church of the Ascension share this reserve with the quirky wooden house in which Peter the Great once stayed, among other architectural treasures. See p. 118.

o **Moscow's Metro Stations** (Moscow): The spotless marble and granite floors of the subway are as remarkable as the intricate artwork and regal columns that adorn the stations. Favorites include the bronze statues at Ploshchad Revolutsii, the aviation mosaics at Mayakovskaya, and any stop on the opulent Circle Line. See the map on the inside front cover of this guide.

best MUSEUMS

o **State Hermitage Museum** (St. Petersburg; 1 Palace Sq.; ✆ 812/710-9079): The museum holds one of the world's best and biggest collections of fine art, from Egyptian carvings to Rembrandt to Impressionist masterpieces. A controversial hall holds so-called trophy art seized from the Germans after World War II. The museum is located in the Winter Palace, stormed in 1917 by revolutionaries arresting Czar Nicholas II's government. See p. 223.

o **Armory Museum** (Moscow; Kremlin; ✆ 495/921-4720): Fabergé eggs, coronation robes, royal carriages, and jewels have filled what was once the czarist weapons storehouse. The Armory, the Kremlin's main museum, also holds an impressive collection of armor and weaponry. Admission is limited to four sessions per day. See p. 102.

o **Tretyakov Gallery** (Moscow; 10 Lavrushinsky Pereulok; ✆ 495/230-7788): The largest collection of Russian art, this museum is treasured by locals but under-appreciated by visitors. Chagall and Kandinsky share space with penetrating medieval icons. Vrubel's Style Moderne and Levitan's smoky landscapes are pleasant discoveries. See p. 114.

o **Peter and Paul Fortress** (St. Petersburg; Hare's Island or Zaichy Ostrov): This island fort holds the cathedral where the remains of Russia's last royal family are interred, as well as a former mint and several small galleries. It was here that Peter the Great started his project to build this northern capital. See p. 229.

o **Museum of Cosmonautics** (Moscow; 111 Prospekt Mira; ✆ 495/683-7914): Housed beneath a sculpture of a rocket shooting off into the cosmos, this museum traces the formidable industry that put the Soviets head-to-head with the United States in the Space Race. Exhibits include moon rocks and the evolution of spacesuits. See p. 112.

- **Literary Museums:** Moscow and St. Petersburg have wonderful small museums devoted to Pushkin, Tolstoy, Dostoyevsky, Bulgakov, Gorky, and scores of other Russian writers, though signage is often in Russian only. See p. 118 and 238.

best GIFTS TO BRING HOME

See chapters 7 and 14 for shopping listings.

- **Linens:** Delicately embroidered tablecloths, pillowcases, and women's or children's traditional tunics made from local linen are great buys.
- **Lacquer Boxes:** Different schools produce different styles of boxes, usually in black wood decorated with images from Russian folk tales.
- **Vodka:** Russky Standart and Flagman are two top-quality choices rarely available outside Russia.
- **Nesting Dolls:** *Matryoshka* dolls can be tacky or tasteful, and kids love them. Adults like the political ones portraying Russian or U.S. leaders stacked inside each other.
- **Stones from Siberia:** Malachite, charoite, and rhodonite are set into jewelry hard to find anywhere else in the world.

best ODDBALL ATTRACTIONS

- **Lenin's Mausoleum** (Moscow): The red-and-black granite mausoleum on Red Square is no longer the pilgrimage site it once was, and its future is in question—which is all the more reason to go see USSR founder Vladimir Lenin's embalmed body now. A visit allows you access to the graves of other Soviet leaders along the Kremlin wall. See p. 106.
- **Art MUSEON** (Moscow, behind the Central House of Artists; 10 Krymsky Val): A collection of Lenin heads and other Soviet monuments toppled in the early 1990s lay abandoned in Gorky Park until the pieces were unofficially resurrected and lined up in a garden behind Moscow's modern art museum. The place is a fitting commentary on Russia's political tumult. See p. 110.
- **Kunstkamera** (St. Petersburg; 3 Universitetskaya Naberezhnaya): Peter the Great's museum of 18th-century scientific curiosities is not for viewing after lunch. Among exhibits of the foremost technical developments of his day, the museum boasts pickled animals and human heads. See p. 233.
- **Star City Space Museum** (outside Moscow): This long-secretive site has trained cosmonauts since the Space Race and now welcomes select tourists. Sample "astronaut food" or the gyrating chairs meant to make your stomach lurch as in a real rocket blastoff.

MOSCOW & ST. PETERSBURG IN DEPTH

Russia fills out Europe's right flank and reaches across the top of Asia to wade in the Pacific, making it European, Asian, Arctic, and none of the above. Its struggle for identity, association, and empire has defined it since the Vikings formed the state of Rus nearly 1,200 years ago. Blood and repression have marred this struggle, right up to today. Russia's leaders have been expert at inflicting ugliness on their people, and Russians have become expert at tolerating it.

Yet the country has survived and thrived, producing some of the world's best science, music, and literature. More remarkably, Russians are among the most festive and giving people on the planet, always ready to put their last morsel of food and last drop of drink on the table to honor an unexpected late-night guest with toasts, more toasts, and laughter. Moscow has dominated the country's political, economic, and cultural life for most of the past 900 years; St. Petersburg, during the two centuries when it assumed the role of Russia's capital, thrust the country at long last into the modern world. The two distinct, yet distinctly Russian, cities remain the pride of this unfathomably vast country.

RUSSIA TODAY

For tourists, there's never been a better time to visit Russia than today. Politics aside, it's a confident global power that's more open to outsiders now than it's been for much of its history.

For Russians, the picture is more nuanced. Today's Russia is the product of Vladimir Putin, who rose to the presidency in 2000 and remains the country's most powerful politician. Under his watch, the country has become a calmer and richer place than it was under his predecessor Boris Yeltsin—and markedly more free for the Russians who inhabit it. Putin allowed the sale of land for the first time since Lenin's days, slashed income taxes, and presided over the greatest growth in Russia's economy in decades.

Putin, a former KGB agent, was able to do all this largely because he disabled his political opposition and quashed much public dissent.

Pro-Kremlin parties rule parliament and few legislators are left to question the policies of Putin or his protégé Dmitry Medvedev, who was elected president in 2008 but remains in Putin's shadow. Feisty television stations were shuttered under Putin, for what prosecutors called financial reasons and journalists called political ones. Russia's richest man, Mikhail Khodorkovsky, was sentenced in 2005 to prison on tax evasion charges that he says were punishment for his support of opposition parties; his Yukos oil empire was dismantled by the state. The killings of vocal Kremlin critics such as journalist Anna Politkovskaya cast a further shadow over Putin's administration.

Russia's relations with Western governments have suffered as a result, especially as Moscow has sought to reassert its influence beyond its borders in ways not always transparent or democratic. Millions of Russians, though, adore Putin for restoring a sense of stability and national pride that the decline of the Soviet Union had shattered. And foreign investors remain hungry for a piece of Russia's petroleum riches amid mounting concerns about worldwide energy supplies.

Small-scale crime has decreased under Putin, thanks partly to his increased use of KGB-style security services. Many Russians welcomed this new order after the 1990s, when residents and business owners were widely victimized by organized crime. But recent years have also seen an alarming rise in racist attacks, largely targeting Muslim migrant workers from Central Asia or ethnic groups from the Caucasus Mountains, perceived as threatening Slavic Russians' jobs and identity. And Putin's security policies failed to solve the bigger problems of corruption and terrorism. The Russian army continues to battle insurgents in Chechnya, where casualty figures are a secret. Chechen suicide bombers have targeted Moscow. Car bombings and other violence plague southern provinces surrounding Chechnya.

Putin handed the presidency to his chosen successor Dmitry Medvedev in elections in 2008, which lacked any serious opponents. Putin moved across town to the prime minister's office, and continues to hold the reins of power, even though Medvedev is officially the nation's public face. Putin is widely believed to want the presidency back in the next elections scheduled for 2012.

Although Russia as a whole is a graying country with a relatively low standard of living, Moscow and St. Petersburg are glaring exceptions. Both cities, especially the capital, experienced a genuine economic boom in the first decade of the 21st century that brought them in line with some of the world's richest cities. The worldwide economic slump of 2008–09 hit Russia particularly hard. Banks were squeezed, economic growth plunged into negative territory, and wage arrears spiked. But the country weathered the crisis more deftly than in the past, and the ruble's exchange rate and inflation remain under control.

Russians who for centuries were cut off from or suspicious of foreigners are finally free to reach out to the rest of the world, and vice versa, which is evident at the uninhibited pickup scenes in Moscow and St. Petersburg bars. Visitors are no longer assigned "minders," as they were in the not-so-distant past, and Russians no longer need permission to leave their country. Surly service is giving way to smiling efficiency, as more and more Russians travel abroad and bring home higher expectations of service and options at home. New restaurants open in Moscow almost daily, and fashions are as fresh as in Milan. Cash machines are ubiquitous and English is increasingly widespread. Russia has, at last, opened its doors to the world.

CHECHNYA

Chechnya is an uncomfortable subject, and objective information is nearly impossible to come by. Even calling the blood spilling that continues there a "war" can provoke hours of debate. The fate of this region and the surrounding Northern Caucasus Mountains is the most controversial subject in today's Russia—and in many ways, the most important.

Chechens make up one of nearly 100 ethnic groups with no relation to Slavic Russians scattered through the slopes and valleys of the Caucasus. Russians fought for dominance over the region in the 18th and 19th centuries, and technically "won" in 1859; but Chechens in particular continued to bristle at Russian rule, and guerrilla bands repeatedly attacked Russian colonizers. During the Russian Revolution and ensuing civil war, the Bolsheviks won over many Chechens with promises of greater autonomy and religious freedom. These promises were quickly forgotten, however, and Chechens staged uprisings against Soviet rule.

Stalin was so panicked by Chechen hostility toward Moscow that he accused the entire Chechen population of collaborating with the Nazis and exiled them all to concentration camps in Kazakhstan in 1944. They were allowed to return home only under Khrushchev's thaw 13 years later, to find Chechnya "Sovietized," with an ethnically diverse population, a university, and a busy airport. The Chechens assimilated back into their homeland, which was by then a province within the Soviet Union. But the indignity of exile remains seminal in Chechens' modern memory, and pent-up rage over that and other Russian offenses simmered for decades. The late-1980s independence movements in other Soviet republics fueled the ambitions of a few Chechens, led by Dzhokhar Dudayev, to establish their own sovereign state. But Chechnya remained a republic within Russia when the Soviet Union collapsed. Dudayev encouraged resistance against Russian police, and amid increasing violence in the region, then-President Boris Yeltsin ordered troops into Chechnya in December 1994.

Neither side seemed ready for what happened next. The Russian army turned out to be so demoralized and financially crippled that its troops succumbed in battle after battle to ragtag

LOOKING BACK: RUSSIAN HISTORY

In The Beginning

Early tribes of nomadic Scythians first settled what are now Russian lands in the 7th century B.C., but it wasn't until the 6th century A.D. that Slavic tribes from southeastern Europe advanced into the neighborhood. It was not the Slavs, however, but the Viking Rurik from nearby Scandinavia who established the first Russian state, based in Novgorod, in the 9th century A.D. The population remained primarily Slavic, though its leaders claimed descent from Rurik for the next 700 years.

The young state's power base soon shifted to Kiev, now the capital of Ukraine. The era of Kievan Rus, as it was called, saw the flowering of a major European entity, whose territories stretched across present-day Belarus, Ukraine, and much of western Russia. As Kievan Rus, the country gained a religion and an official language and developed the distinctive architectural styles seen across the region today.

Chechen bands. The Russian populace was horrified by the war and the deaths of underfed, underpaid teenage conscripts in pointless firefights. Even Dudayev's death in 1996 didn't improve the Russian forces' lot, and in August that year the two sides signed a peace deal allowing Chechnya greater autonomy. Yet the Chechens proved unprepared to govern themselves, and the republic sank into lawlessness. Reconstruction funds were blatantly embezzled, and kidnapping for ransom became the engine of the Chechen economy (in addition to siphoning oil from pipelines leading out of the Caspian Sea). Nearly no outsiders dared enter the region, whether federal official, journalist, or aid worker.

In August 1999, Chechen bands raided the neighboring Russian republic of Dagestan and seized several villages, pledging to create a regionwide Islamic state. Soon afterward, apartment bombings in Moscow and two other cities killed 300 civilians and terrified the nation. Yeltsin sent troops back to Chechnya, and his new prime minister, Vladimir Putin, successfully "sold" the war to the Russian people, who by then were eager for determined leadership and an end to Chechen crime and terrorism. Putin's popularity soared amid early successes for Russian troops, and within months he had replaced Yeltsin as president.

And the fight rages on. Warlords in Chechnya and surrounding regions stage sporadic terrorist attacks, primarily in the Caucasus but occasionally in the nation's capital: They were blamed for the 2011 bombing at Domodedovo Airport and the hostage-taking in a Moscow theater in 2002, both of which left scores of dead. The Chechens' funding is believed to come from various Islamic extremist groups. A generation ago most Chechens were casual in their observance of Islamic custom, but wars have changed that. Many now sport long beards, forego alcohol, and adhere to sharia law. Chechnya's Kremlin-backed president, Ramzan Kadyrov, is widely feared, and his militias are believed to act with impunity against perceived threats. International pressure has failed to persuade Putin to rethink his Chechnya policy.

Kievan Rus cast its lot with the Orthodox Christian world in 988, during the reign of Vladimir. Orthodoxy became the foundation of Russian life for nearly 800 years, and remains a crucial part of the Russian identity, even after 70 years of Soviet state-enforced atheism. In the 9th century, two monks, Cyril and Methodius, developed what became known as the Cyrillic alphabet, which Russia still uses today. Largely an agricultural economy, Kievan Rus developed substantial trade with Byzantium and Scandinavia, using the resulting riches to build the cathedrals and fortresses that protected and symbolized the empire.

Internecine battles gradually weakened Kievan Rus, and the invasion of its eastern lands by Genghis Khan's Mongol hordes in 1237 made things worse. Moscow, meanwhile, had matured from a hilltop village into a substantial principality by 1147, the official year of its founding, and became the seat of Russian authority in 1326. The Russian state remained feeble, however, and fell to repeated invasion by Mongol Tatars from the east. The Tatars kept Russia's princes under their thumbs until Ivan III (Ivan the Great) came to power in the late 1400s and refused to pay the Mongols any more tribute. His reign saw Muscovite-controlled lands spread north to

Unorthodox Beginnings

Whether legend or fact, the story of how Russians chose Orthodox Christianity hardly sounds holy: Grand Prince Vladimir I of Kievan Rus was deciding which of the world's religions would best suit his burgeoning state. He rejected Judaism for its prohibition of pork, a crucial Russian food source; and dismissed Islam because no Russian (even in the 10th c.) would heed a ban on liquor—a lesson Mikhail Gorbachev learned a millennium later after launching a disastrous anti-alcohol campaign. Prince Vladimir finally settled on Orthodox Christianity, allegedly because of his envoys' rave reviews of the Hagia Sophia cathedral in Constantinople.

the Arctic and east to the Urals. It was Ivan the Great who launched construction of the Kremlin's magnificent cathedrals and its current walls.

His grandson Ivan IV was the first Russian crowned "czar" (a variation on "Caesar") but became better known as Ivan the Terrible. He further strengthened the state and was considered an enlightened leader until the death of his wife plunged him into paranoia and despotism. He instituted Russia's first secret police force, persecuted former friends as enemies, and killed his own son and pregnant daughter-in-law in a fit of rage. The country and his dynasty were devastated by the time Ivan IV died in 1584.

The ensuing decades were wrought with bloody, corrupt struggles for succession that came to be known as the "Time of Troubles." Boris Godunov (1598–1605) was the most legendary of this era's leaders, a *boyar* (nobleman) elected in an unusual experiment with democracy called the *zemsky sobor* (national assembly), which was made up of nobles, church leaders, and commoners. Godunov's death left a power vacuum that led to the appearance of the first False Dmitry, a Polish-backed prince who claimed to be Ivan the Terrible's son Dmitry, whose death 15 years earlier remained shrouded in mystery. The False Dmitry and his Polish entourage made it to the Kremlin but he was soon executed by angry opponents. Remarkably, another

DATELINE

7th c. B.C. Scythian tribes settle lands in what is now Russia.	1547 Ivan IV (The Terrible) named first czar of all Russians.
862 Viking Rurik establishes state at Novgorod.	1605-13 "Time of Troubles."
888 Monks Cyril and Methodius invent Cyrillic alphabet.	1613 Mikhail Romanov crowned czar.
988 Prince Vladimir adopts Orthodox Christianity for Russian lands.	1703 Peter the Great founds St. Petersburg, and later moves the capital there from Moscow.
1326 Russian capital moved to Moscow. Muscovite prince achieves first major defeat of Mongols at Kulikovo Pole.	1755 Russia's first university, Moscow University, established.
	1780s Catherine the Great expands Russian lands to Crimea, Georgia, deeper into Siberia.
1480 Ivan III (the Great) ejects Mongol Tatars, freeing Russia from "the Mongol Yoke."	1805-07 First war with Napoleon.

Polish-backed False Dmitry was among the several ill-fated leaders to take over the Kremlin in the ensuing years.

At last the 16-year-old Mikhail Romanov, a distant relative of Ivan the Terrible, was elected czar in 1613 by another national assembly. It took him 2 years to establish himself securely and put an end to the Time of Troubles. Ultimately, Mikhail was able to establish a new dynasty, one that would last until Czar Nicholas II was executed by Bolsheviks 300 years later.

The Window to Europe

Although Russians through the ages have debated whether to look to western Europe or to their Slavic roots for inspiration, Peter the Great had no doubts: Europe on the verge of the Enlightenment held the future. His early years were fraught with hostilities within the royal family, and once he attained the throne, he abandoned the medieval Moscow Kremlin. Peter traveled to western Europe and upon his return moved to a swamp on the Baltic Sea, ultimately transforming it into a grand capital of columned, Italian-designed palaces along broad avenues and sculpted canals. St. Petersburg's beauty came at a great price: Thousands of people died fulfilling Peter's sometimes impossible building orders, and the damp climate just below the Arctic Circle weakened and sickened many of its new residents.

Peter's policies dragged Russia out of its insularity and planted it firmly in the world of European diplomacy and modern thought. Yet he was as authoritarian as any Russian leader, and even had his own son sentenced to death. Russia's next exceptional leader was Catherine the Great (1762–96), a German princess who married into the Romanov family and conspired to oust her husband to attain the throne. She greatly expanded Russia's territory to the east and south, and her foreign policies won her and Russia great respect in the rest of Europe. Russia's aristocracy came to speak French better than Russian, a trend that continued for generations.

Russia's love affair with France collapsed under Napoleon, who gave Russia its biggest military challenge in centuries. The French made it into Moscow in 1812—but only after the Russians had set fires in the city, stripped it bare, and fled, leaving

1812 Napoleon reaches Moscow but leaves in defeat.	1880s–1903 Series of pogroms against Russian Jews.
1814 Triumphant Russians reach Paris.	1904–05 War with Japan.
1825 Decembrist uprising by progressive generals quashed by Nicholas I.	1905 Striking workers revolt, forcing czar to allow first elected parliament.
1853–56 Crimean War pits Russia against Britain, France, and Turkey.	1914 Russia joins World War I against Germany; St. Petersburg residents change the city's name to the less-German-sounding Petrograd.
1850s Caucasus Wars end with Russian armies subduing Chechnya and other mountain regions.	
1861 Czar Alexander II abolishes serfdom.	1916 Royal favorite Rasputin murdered.
1881 Czar Alexander II assassinated by revolutionaries.	1917 February Revolution; Czar Nicholas II abdicates; in October, Vladimir Lenin's Bolsheviks storm

continues

A "Bistro" Meal—And Make It Snappy!

The term "bistro" is purported to have come from hungry Russian soldiers descending on Paris in 1814, who demanded their meals fast—*bystro* in Russian—from harried servers in Montmartre's cafes.

Napoleon's army without food and shelter on the eve of winter. The *Grande Armée* retreated, and the Russians' victorious drive into Paris 2 years later was immortalized in poems, songs, and children's rhymes.

Russia's Artistic Apex

Until the 19th century, Russia's artistic developments were little known abroad and underappreciated at home. That changed after the Napoleonic Wars, as Russia's confidence in its place in Europe led to greater support and recognition of local composers, writers, and choreographers in the emerging art of ballet. Alexander Pushkin became Russians' best-loved poet, with his direct, melodic use of the Russian language—and his liberal political leanings, which ran him afoul of the czars. Fyodor Dostoyevsky's fiction delved into innermost existential depths in response to repression from without. Pyotr Tchaikovsky's symphonies gave voice to the terror and triumph of war with France. Writer Leo Tolstoy, playwright Alexander Griboyedov, and artist Isaak Levitan were among the legions of cultural heroes who found success in their uniquely Russian ways of expression.

Readying For Revolution

Much of Russia's 19th century was defined by pre-revolutionary struggle, as radicals studied the revolutions in the United States and France, and the czars sought to stamp out dissent even where it didn't exist. The Decembrist uprising of 1825, led by reformist generals in the royal army, was quashed by Czar Nicholas I, who then bolstered the censors and the secret police. Czar Alexander II freed the serfs at last in

	St. Petersburg's Winter Palace and depose provisional government.
1917–19	Civil war ravages Russia, ending in victory for Lenin; capital moved back to Moscow.
1922	Union of Soviet Socialist Republics (USSR) officially founded, eventually growing to 15 republics.
1924	Death of Lenin.
1930s	Stalin's collectivization kills millions; purges of party and military leadership take place.
1939	Nazi-Soviet nonaggression pact divides eastern Europe into spheres of influence.

1941	Hitler's army invades the Soviet Union; Nazi siege of Leningrad begins, lasting 900 days.
1943	Battle at Stalingrad proves turning point in World War II.
1945	Soviet army liberates Auschwitz; Hitler defeated; war ends; Yalta conference.
1948	Soviets develop atomic bomb.
1953	Death of Stalin.
1956	Nikita Khrushchev denounces Stalin's policies in a secret Politburo speech; Hungarian uprising crushed.

1861, but society remained starkly unequal and most of the population was still poor and uneducated. The thriving merchant class helped fuel Russia's industrial advances in the late 1800s. Alexander II grew increasingly conservative and suspicious of opposition in his later years; he was assassinated in 1881 by anarchists. The next 2 decades were marred by a series of pogroms against Russia's substantial and influential Jewish population; Jews were massacred and their property was seized. Since Catherine the Great's time, Jews other than select professionals were banished from St. Petersburg and elsewhere in the empire to the Pale of Settlement, a swath of land in what is now Poland, Belarus, Ukraine, Lithuania, and western Russia.

Alexander II's grandson Nicholas II—the last of the Romanov czars—assumed the throne in 1894 with few plans for reform. From 1904 to 1905, Russia fought a war with Japan over territory in the Far East, which left the czarist navies humiliated and laid bare the weaknesses of the imperial government. Nicholas stifled an uprising of striking workers in January 1905 on what is known as Russia's Bloody Sunday. Under increasing pressure from the population and his court, the czar allowed the creation of a limited parliament, Russia's first ever, elected in 1906.

All this was setting the stage for 1917. Fighting the Germans in World War I had further weakened Nicholas's shaky hold on the country, and with revolution in the air, he abdicated in February 1917. An aristocrat-led provisional government jockeyed for power with the revolutionary parties of Vladimir Lenin and Leon Trotsky. Lenin's more extremist Bolshevik Party, claiming support among exploited workers and peasants, emerged the victor. Nicholas, his wife Alexandra, and their five children were exiled to Siberia and then executed in 1918, as civil war engulfed the nation. Years of chaos, famine, and bloodshed followed, before the Union of Soviet Socialist Republics was born.

Soviet Russia

After Lenin died in 1924, Josef Stalin, a former seminary student from Georgia, worked his way to the top of the Communist Party leadership. Stalin reversed Lenin's late attempts at liberalization, instead ushering in a campaign to collectivize all land

1961	Soviets send first man into space (Yuri Gagarin); Berlin Wall built.
1962	Cuban Missile Crisis.
1968	"Prague Spring" quashed by Soviet troops.
1979	Soviet forces invade Afghanistan; war against U.S.-funded Islamic guerrillas lasts 10 years.
1985	Mikhail Gorbachev appointed General Secretary of the Communist Party; launches *glasnost* and *perestroika*.
1986	Chernobyl nuclear reactor explodes in world's worst nuclear accident.
1989	Berlin Wall falls.
1990	Baltic states declare independence; Boris Yeltsin elected president of the Russian Federation, the biggest Soviet republic.
1991	Hard-liners attempt a coup against Gorbachev but fail; Leningrad residents vote to change the city's name back to St. Petersburg; Yeltsin and the leaders of Ukraine and Belarus declare the USSR defunct; Gorbachev resigns.
1993	Opposition lawmakers revolt against Yeltsin, who attacks them with tanks.

continues

into state hands—no small task in a nation so vast. The brutal drive, combined with a drought, led to famine that left 5 to 10 million dead. Stalin crafted a dictatorship by gradually purging his rivals, real and imagined. His repression reached a peak in the late 1930s and decimated the party and military leadership. Millions were executed or exiled to prison camps across Siberia and the Arctic, referred to by their Russian initials GULAG, or State Agency for Labor Camps.

Stalin tried to head off war with Germany through a secret pact with Hitler, known as the Molotov-Ribbentrop Pact after the foreign ministers who signed it. The pact promised Soviet food supplies to the Nazis and set out a plan for dividing eastern Europe between the two powers. Hitler invaded anyway, plunging the Soviet Union into a war that would cost the country 27 million lives, more losses than any other nation suffered in World War II. The Great Patriotic War, as Russians call it, brought the 900-day siege of Leningrad (see the sidebar "The Siege of Leningrad," p. 223) as well as gruesome battles at Stalingrad and Kursk that helped break the back of Hitler's forces.

Genuine grief mixed with nervous relief gripped the country when Stalin died in 1953, as many feared that life without this frightening father figure would be even worse than with him. Nikita Khrushchev's eventual rise to power brought a thaw; political prisoners were released and there was a slight relaxation of censorship amid continued postwar economic growth. But he also put down protests in Hungary in 1956 and nearly provoked nuclear war in the 1962 Cuban Missile Crisis. Khrushchev was eventually ousted by more conservative colleagues in a bloodless coup. Soviet space successes during this time—including sending the first satellite, first man, and first woman to space—awed the world and fueled the Cold War arms race.

Khrushchev's replacement, Leonid Brezhnev, is largely remembered for the era of stagnation that marked the Soviet Union in the 1960s and 1970s—but it was also an era of peace and stability that had been so elusive for Russians for so long. This era ended with the Soviet invasion of Afghanistan in 1979, leading to an inconclusive, unpopular 10-year war with U.S.-backed Islamic guerrillas. Brezhnev's death brought two quick successors in the early 1980s, Yuri Andropov and Konstantin Chernenko, who both died in office before the relatively young Mikhail Gorbachev took over.

1994 Yeltsin sends troops into Chechnya to quash rebellion; 20 months later, Russian troops withdraw in humiliation and Chechnya enjoys semiautonomy.	2006 Critical journalist Anna Politkovskaya and former spy Alexander Litvinenko killed, casting shadow on Putin's Kremlin.
1998 Russia's reviving economy hit by global financial crisis; government defaults on debt and ruble crashes.	2008 Dmitry Medvedev elected president; Putin becomes prime minister.
1999 Russian army reenters Chechnya and remains there today.	2012 Presidential elections scheduled.
Dec. 31, 1999 Yeltsin unexpectedly resigns, appointing Prime Minister Vladimir Putin his successor.	

rasputin: MYSTIC, SINNER, HEALER, OR SPY?

In 1907, Czar Nicholas II and his empress Alexandra, desperate to help their hemophiliac son and only male heir, Alexy, turned to a wandering healer named Grigory Rasputin. The decision was to have consequences for the whole country. The facts around Rasputin's life remain clouded in contradiction and controversy, but his influence on the royal household in the years leading up to the Russian empire's demise are indisputable. Nicholas and Alexandra remained loyal to him for his apparent success in easing Alexy's suffering, which they were trying to keep from the Russian public. But Rasputin's personal life—including energetic sexual exploits and drunken binges—sullied his reputation as an Orthodox mystic, especially among the czar's advisers and aristocracy. Some claim Rasputin was a member of the *khlisty* sect, who believed in salvation through sin (the name comes from the Russian word for "whip").

The royal couple's increasing alienation from Russian reality was blamed on Rasputin's twisted advice, and he was accused of acting as a German spy during World War I. Nicholas's inner circle grew so worried about Rasputin's influence on national policies that they murdered him in 1916. Even his death is steeped in legend: His killers reported that they poisoned him, shot him, and beat him before tossing him into an icy canal—and that he was still kicking underwater. Alexandra, devastated, ordered his remains dragged out a few days later. Within 2 years, Nicholas's rule had collapsed and his whole family had been executed.

The Soviet Collapse & Aftermath

Gorbachev's name became synonymous with the policies of *glasnost* (openness) and *perestroika* (restructuring) that he tried to apply to the Soviet system. But he underestimated how deeply the country's economy and political legitimacy had decayed. The reforms he cautiously introduced took on a momentum that ultimately doomed him and the Soviet Union. After the fall of the Berlin Wall in 1989 and the peaceful revolutions around the Communist bloc of eastern Europe, Gorbachev aligned with hard-liners at home to cling to power and keep the USSR together.

The hard-liners thought he wasn't doing enough, however, so they tried to overthrow him in a desperate, poorly executed coup attempt in August 1991. They were defeated by defiant generals and a buoyant Boris Yeltsin, then president of the Russian part of the USSR, who was cheered on by thousands of pro-democracy demonstrators. Three months later, Gorbachev resigned and the Soviet Union's 15 republics splintered into 15 new countries.

When Yeltsin freed the ruble from its state controls, he wiped out millions of people's savings, and his popularity plummeted. Yeltsin and his administration couldn't keep up with the economic transition from a planned economy to the free market, and crime, corruption, and poverty flourished. The 1990s saw a few Russians make exorbitant sums by buying up state property on the cheap, while workers at thousands of schools, hospitals, and factories lost their jobs or went months, even years, without pay.

Politically, Yeltsin grew increasingly intolerant, like so many Russian leaders before him. He faced a showdown with opposition parliament deputies in 1993 that he ended by sending in tanks, after his opponents tried to seize the country's main television

SELECTED LIST OF RUSSIAN leaders

Rurik 862–79   Viking prince who founded state of Rus, based in northern city of Novgorod and populated by eastern Slavs.

Vladimir I 978–1015   Prince who chose Orthodox Christianity as the Russian state religion, launching widespread cathedral construction. Oversaw emergence of Kievan Rus as major European state.

Ivan III (The Great) 1462–1505   Ended 3 centuries of Mongol dominance over Russian lands, expanded Russian territories east and north, ordered construction of the Kremlin's greatest cathedrals.

Ivan IV (The Terrible) 1533–84   First Russian crowned "czar." Initially a reformer, he later introduced Russia's first secret police force and terrorized political opponents.

Boris Godunov 1598–1605   *Boyar* (nobleman) elected czar by a national assembly amid a power vacuum in the Kremlin. His death led to another crisis of succession.

Mikhail I 1613–45   Son of noble Romanov family, elected czar. Romanov dynasty would stay in power for the next 300 years, until Soviet rule. His coronation ended the "Time of Troubles."

Peter I (The Great) 1698–1725   Moved Russian capital to St. Petersburg, a city he built on a delta on the Baltic Sea. Turned Russia westward, introducing

European architectural styles, art, and attitudes to his isolated nation. Founded Russian navy.

Elizabeth I 1741–61   Built many of Petersburg's greatest palaces, including the Winter Palace that houses the Hermitage.

Catherine II (The Great) 1762–96   A German princess who married into the Romanov dynasty and became one of Russia's most influential leaders. Expanded Russian territory south and west, oversaw construction of many crucial St. Petersburg buildings and institutions.

Alexander I 1801–25   Led Russian army against Napoleon, eventually driving the Grande Armée back to Paris.

Nicholas I 1825–55   Suppressed uprising by reformist generals (later dubbed "Decembrists") soon after his coronation; maintained hard line against dissent.

Alexander II 1855–81   Abolished serfdom, freeing the majority of the population and allowing land ownership. Later grew more conservative and was assassinated by an anarchist.

Alexander III 1881–94   Reactionary leader whose reign was fraught with revolutionary activity that he sought to suppress.

Nicholas II 1894–1917   Russia's last czar. Resisted increasing calls for reforms until 1906, after disastrous war with

tower. Meanwhile, separatist-led violence in the southern province of Chechnya prompted Yeltsin to send in troops in 1994. This led to a deeply unpopular war that exposed the shoddy state of the Russian army, which withdrew in defeat 2 years later. Chechnya's status remained murky, however, and the region fell to lawlessness. A series of apartment bombings in Moscow and other Russian cities in 1999 was blamed on Chechens, and offered a pretext for a new war. (See box, p. 12).

This second war was championed by Vladimir Putin, who had just been named prime minister. This time, terrorism-scarred Russians supported the war, and the man leading it. Putin's law-and-order image from his years as a KGB agent worked in his favor, as did Russians' weariness of the capricious, ailing Yeltsin. On December 31,

Japan and striking workers led to creation of Russia's first parliament. Led Russia against Germany in World War I; abdicated amid revolutionary activity in 1917; was executed along with his wife and five children in 1918.

Vladimir Lenin 1917–24 Founder of Soviet state. After years abroad studying Marxist theory and plotting revolution, returned to Russia to lead Bolsheviks. Led "red" Communist forces during civil war; established Soviet secret police. His embalmed body is on Red Square.

Josef Stalin 1924–53 Seminary-student-turned-dictator who forcibly collectivized Soviet land, purged Soviet leadership of purported enemies in "The Great Terror," and executed or repressed millions of Soviet citizens for real and imagined crimes. Led the Soviet Union to victory in World War II at the cost of 27 million lives.

Nikita Khrushchev 1955–64 Congenial leader who denounced many of Stalin's policies and oversaw period of "thaw" in arts and political life. Nearly came to nuclear conflict with U.S. in Cuban Missile Crisis. Deposed by conservative Communist Party colleagues.

Leonid Brezhnev 1964–82 Long-serving leader who came to embody stagnation of late Soviet period. Oversaw crackdown on "Prague Spring," expulsion of dissidents. Launched war in Afghanistan.

Yuri Andropov 1982–84 Influential former KGB chief who sought to stem corruption and introduce minor reforms.

Konstantin Chernenko 1984–85 Conservative Brezhnev protégé who escalated Cold War military spending.

Mikhail Gorbachev 1985–91 Last Soviet leader. Reformer who introduced *glasnost* and *perestroika* but later tried to rein in the independence movements spawned by these policies. Briefly ousted by hard-liners in failed coup attempt; 3 months later the Soviet Union collapsed.

Boris Yeltsin 1991–99 First Russian president. Orchestrated end of USSR, freed prices, and oversaw privatization of state companies. Launched war in Chechnya; sent tanks against recalcitrant lawmakers; opened Russia to foreign investors.

Vladimir Putin 2000–08 Second Russian president. Former KGB agent who assumed power when Yeltsin resigned. Oversaw economic boom, suppressed free media, and squeezed out political rivals.

Dmitry Medvedev 2008–present Chosen Russian president after being anointed by Putin in an election with no serious opponents. Real power rests with Putin, named prime minister after Medvedev's election.

1999, the eve of the new millennium, Yeltsin unexpectedly resigned and handed power to his protégé Putin.

ART & ARCHITECTURE

Russian art and architecture remain a mystery to most outsiders, even as the country itself has opened up to the world. Knowing just a little about the evolution of Russian fine and applied arts, and about the political movements that often drove them, will make your trip less overwhelming and more eye-opening.

For a millennium, from Russia's 9th-century conversion to Orthodox Christianity until the 19th century, Russian art was almost exclusively defined by **icon painting.**

This Byzantine practice of painting saints or biblical scenes on carved wooden panels was guided rigidly by church canon, so the icons appear much more uniform and repetitive than western European religious art of the Renaissance, for example. The best advice for a novice viewer is to pick one or two icons in a room and study their lines and balance—don't look for realism or classic proportion, or expect to be uplifted. They're meant to be somewhat haunting and introspective.

Some Russian icon painters managed to infuse originality into their work, but it takes a trained eye to notice the distinctions. Andrei Rublev was the most famous and most controversial medieval icon painter, and brought the genre to a new level in the 14th century. His works are best appreciated at Tretyakov Gallery in Moscow (p. 114) and Trinity Monastery at Sergiev Posad (p. 158). Spaso-Andronnikov Monastery in Moscow (p. 109), where he lived and worked, has none of his original work but does contain an informative exhibit about him. For tips on purchasing Russian icons, see the box "Russian Orthodox Icons" on p. 131.

Russian art fell out of favor after Peter the Great transferred the capital to St. Petersburg in the early 1700s and adorned it with French and Italian masterpieces, or imitations thereof. It wasn't until the mid–19th century that the Slavophile movement brought real success to Russian painters. The **Wanderers,** or *peredvizhniki,* broke from the St. Petersburg Academy of Arts and its Western-style traditions to focus on portraying Russian village life. Standouts of this period include Ivan Kramskoi and Ilya Repin, whose works are well displayed at Tretyakov Gallery (p. 114) and at the Russian Museum in St. Petersburg (p. 234).

The late 19th century saw Russia's version of the **Arts and Crafts** movement, relying on traditional Russian applied arts. Russian artists also embraced what they call Style Moderne, or **Art Nouveau.** Stunning interpretations of this style can be found in Mikhail Vrubel's *Dream Princess* mosaic around the top of the Metropol hotel's facade (p. 57) and in a related, room-size mosaic by him in Tretyakov Gallery.

The political upheaval of the early 20th century was a major engine of Russian artistic growth. Vibrant colors, angular shapes, and the intensity of urban life replaced the bucolic rural scenes, and the Russian **Avante-Garde** movement flourished. Kasimir Malevich and Mikhail Larionov explored the genres of Futurism, Rayonism (Russia's only truly abstract art), and Suprematism. Belarusian Marc Chagall produced surreal and surprising paintings during this period. Many of these works are on display at Tretyakov Gallery in Moscow (the old and new wings) and at the Russian Museum in St. Petersburg.

Calendar Confusion

Russia used the Julian calendar until February 1918, well after the rest of Europe switched to the Gregorian calendar, which at that point was 13 days ahead. When the Bolsheviks stormed the Winter Palace, it was still October 1917 in Russia but was already November in the rest of Europe; hence, for the next 7 decades, the Soviets celebrated "Great October Revolution Day" on November 7. The Russian Orthodox calendar ignored the switch, and Russians still celebrate Christmas on January 7 instead of December 25. Some also celebrate the "Old" New Year on January 13 and 14, as well as the traditional New Year's bash on December 31 and January 1.

THE GREAT russian spying TRADITION

You've heard of the KGB, that ultimate of Cold War villains. Yet it represents just one chapter in Russia's rich history of spying, snooping, informing, rooting out conspiracies, and all-around paranoia. Most of this activity has been aimed not at outsiders, but at Russians themselves. Ivan the Terrible (1533–84) was the first Russian leader to establish a secret office to spy on his subjects, and his successors kept up the tradition. Undercover agents and counterespionage thrived amid the revolutionary activity of the late 19th century. When the Soviets took over, they formalized the secret police into a pillar of the government that became notorious for torturing or murdering suspects or sending them to prison based on flimsy or nonexistent evidence.

Soviet spy agencies were labeled with a succession of double-speak acronyms. Felix Dzerzhinsky, considered the father of Soviet espionage, established the Cheka, an abbreviation for the Extraordinary Commission for the Struggle against Counter-revolution, Speculation and Sabotage, in 1917. Later, the NKVD (People's Committee for Internal Affairs) ruled over labor camps and prisons for political enemies under Stalin. It then became the MGB (Ministry of State Security), before morphing into the better-known KGB (Committee of State Security). Its many departments snooped on every aspect of Russians' lives, from workplace tardiness to personal correspondence. The system shrank considerably after the Soviet collapse, but the *"gebeshniki,"* or "state security guys," enjoyed a bit of a comeback under Vladimir Putin, an ex-KGB operative who ran the post-Soviet intelligence agency, the FSB (Federal Security Service), in the late 1990s before becoming president. While the FSB is in charge of domestic snooping, foreign spies are tracked by the honestly named Foreign Intelligence Service (SVR).

Early Soviet leaders initially harnessed the creativity of free-thinking artists for propaganda purposes, and the posters, sculptures, and public spaces designed by Russian artists in the 1920s are among the world's most stirring artworks. The **Constructivists,** including Vladimir Tatlin, Alexander Rodchenko, and Varvara Stepanova, incorporated technological and industrial themes and energy into their work. Their works are only beginning to emerge from museum storehouses, and some are on display at Tretyakov Gallery and at St. Petersburg's Russian Museum. Russia's Avante-Garde contributed more to world art than is usually appreciated, largely because the Soviet government so effectively erased or discredited their work by the 1930s, championing instead the bold images but less daring ideas of Socialist Realism.

The **propaganda poster** came to replace the icon as Russia's chief canvas for most of the Soviet era, until freedom from artistic constrictions in the late 1980s and 1990s produced a wave of bold, experimental art. Today, Russia's artists seem to be casting about for a new role.

Russian architecture, too, was church-centric and followed Orthodox stricture for centuries. Churches were built in the shape of a Greek cross, with few windows and steep roofs. The onion domes became a prominent feature in the 11th century. The **iconostasis,** a screen in front of the altar with a careful hierarchy of icons, is the key object to look for inside a church.

Medieval architects took more risks than their icon-painting colleagues. The cathedrals in the Kremlin are the most coherent examples of the slow encroachment of

STALIN'S seven sisters

By the end of your first day in Moscow, you're bound to have noticed at least one of these sky-scraping, turreted castles to Communism. Seven of them cut into the city skyline, immediately differentiating the city from any other in the world. Initiated under Stalin, Moscow's "Seven Sisters" emerged in the 1950s and came to embody an architectural style dubbed "Stalin Gothic" that was emulated in buildings throughout the Communist world.

The buildings are immediately recognizable by their tapered towers, glass spires, and solid stone enormity. Architecturally, they combine features of Russian 17th-century churches, Western Gothic cathedrals, and American skyscrapers of the 1930s. Many were built by German prisoners of war. The grandest example is the main building of **Moscow State University,** lording over the city from the peak of Sparrow Hills. Containing 32km (20 miles) of corridors, this 5,000-room building is best viewed at a distance, ideally from the lookout platform above the Moscow River. Another impressive sister is the **Kotelnicheskaya apartment building** (1 Kotelnicheskaya Naberezhnaya), which housed the Communist elite in decades past and now includes some of the city's priciest real estate, even if its infrastructure is in need of an upgrade. A second apartment building, **Krasnaya Presnya Tower** at Kudrinskaya Square, once housed Soviet aviation elite. Two more of the Stalin Gothic buildings are hotels (**Hotel Ukraina,** 2/1 Kutuzovsky Prospekt; and **Hotel Leningradskaya,** near the Leningradsky Train Station at 21/40 Kalanchevskaya Ulitsa). The remaining two are government buildings (the **Foreign Ministry** on Smolenskaya Sq., and the **Transport Ministry** on the Garden Ring Rd. at Krasniye Vorota). Even modern developers have caught the Stalin Gothic bug: The biggest real estate project in recent years is the **Triumph Palace** apartment complex in northwest Moscow, one of Europe's tallest structures—you're sure to spot it on your way in from the airport.

The biggest castle of all—and the one that served as a boilerplate for the others—never reached fruition. The **Palace of Soviets** was intended to be the most elaborate ode to Communist power that Stalin could conceive, planned for the site of the razed Christ the Savior Cathedral (p. 107). The plans were sabotaged by infighting and later by World War II, and the site became a public swimming pool, and remained so until the end of the Soviet era. Today a new cathedral stands on the site, one so grandiose that some call it an Orthodox version of the Palace of Soviets. Original designs of the Palace of Soviets are among the exhibits at **Shchusev Museum of Architecture** at 5/25 Vozdvizhenka Ulitsa (© **495/291-2109;** metro: Biblioteka Imeni Lenina; admission 100 rubles. It's open Tuesday to Friday from 11am to 7pm, Saturday and Sunday from 11am to 6pm.

Italian influences upon Russian tradition in the 15th and 16th centuries. Venetian scallops edge the roofs, though the buildings include the *kokoshniki* (pointed arches) and *zakomari* (semicircular gables) typical of the era's architecture in Moscow. St. Basil's Cathedral in Moscow is one of the last churches to so boldly use beveled domes and the *shatyor,* or tent-roofed tower later banned by Orthodox leaders—no other church in Russia today looks quite like it.

Peter the Great's Western-looking ideas overturned Russian architecture, and the capital he built adhered to Enlightenment ideals and a relentless symmetry. The rococo Winter Palace (p. 223) and Smolny Cathedral (p. 232), as well as the neoclassical Mikhailovsky Palace and Admiralty (see the walking tour on p. 178), look almost nothing like the twisted domes of medieval Moscow. Visit any square in St. Petersburg and turn around 360 degrees, and you'll have a sense of how consistent and secular the city's designers were, even those who came well after Peter's death.

The Revivalist movement of the 19th century saw the return of traditional Russian church features such as the decorated cupolas seen in St. Petersburg's Church of the Savior on the Spilled Blood (p. 230). After the victory over Napoleon, the Empire style caught on for Russian aristocratic residences, proof of which can be found around the streets of Prechistenka and Ostozhenka in Moscow.

Early Soviet architecture was as creative and energized as the period's art, with architects such as Konstantin Melnikov forging functional, elegant buildings that made the Soviet idea (of a progressive, egalitarian state) seem the pinnacle of modernity. (His most famous house is near the Arbat at 6 Krivoarbatsky Pereulok.) Lenin's Mausoleum on Red Square (p. 106), for all its morbid function, is one of the last surviving examples of Constructivist architecture. The Moscow metro system was designed by the country's top architects and is an excellent place to view the juxtaposition of tradition (flowery capitals) with Soviet politics (statues of the proletariat). It's also one of the most beautiful subway systems in the world. (See p. 110 for more information.)

Later, the "Stalin Gothic" style appeared in dozens of towering buildings around Moscow (spreading as far as Warsaw and Prague), with turrets and spires on administrative or residential buildings. Two prime examples are the Ukraina hotel and Moscow State University. (See the box "Stalin's Seven Sisters.") Architecture after Stalin descended into the bleak, boxy towers that mar the skyline of any Russian city. Today's architectural trends are set by the nouveau riche Russians building multimillion-dollar "cottages" on the outskirts of Moscow and St. Petersburg. The guiding principle often seems to be "as big and extravagant as possible." They make for amusing viewing, though many are surrounded by tall walls and security systems to stop you from doing just that.

RUSSIA IN POP CULTURE

Depictions of Russians in Western pop culture tend toward stereotypes of the mafia thug, dubious spy, top model, or angry old lady. A much richer view comes through from Russians' own literature, films, plays, and ballets—all increasingly accessible in online bookstores or urban cinemas well beyond Russia's borders.

Books

Dense, fatalistic, philosophical, lyrical, haunting, bleak, passionate . . . . These stereotypes cling to Russian literature and often scare newcomers away. But even a little knowledge of the country's greatest authors will help you make sense of the many literary museums, monuments, and slogans you'll run across during your trip. Russians are extremely well-read, and take any opportunity to celebrate their literary traditions (and they may know more about your country's authors than you do).

Russian writing didn't really blossom until the 19th century, long after most European cultures had well-established literary traditions. In the early 1800s, serfdom was still enshrined in law, and literacy remained the luxury of the upper classes, who preferred to read European literature to demonstrate their Western mind-set. But a burst of nationalism following the victory over Napoleon began to change Russia's

THE RUSSIAN silver screen

An excellent way to prepare for your Russia trip would be to watch at least one movie from the Soviet era and one movie made since then. There are few better ways to glimpse how the country has changed over the past generation. Soviet filmmakers were heavily censored but free of commercial constrictions; post-Soviet filmmakers face the opposite problem, desperate for money but free to produce movies as political, tasteless, or shallow as the viewers will bear. The selection of Russian movies available abroad is limited, and those that are available are often too dense or tragic for Western audiences, but a few suggestions are listed below.

Russian film in the 20th century mirrored Russian politics more closely than any other medium. Vladimir Lenin quickly recognized the new "moving picture" as an excellent propaganda tool. But early filmmakers were crippled by the devastation to the country's basic infrastructure (including reliable electricity) wrought by World War I and the ensuing revolution and civil war, and by the loss of top performers and writers who fled abroad to escape the Communist regime. Eventually, a new artistic community emerged eager to define Soviet film as something

more experimental than the commercial products coming out of capitalist America. Sergei Eisenstein was the most well-known of this group, and his Battleship Potemkin, released in 1925, became an international classic. Short propaganda films known as agitki were carried to towns and villages from Siberia to central Asia to advertise the wonders of modern technology—and by extension, of Soviet rule. Communist Party leaders became increasingly restrictive, however, and the 1930s and 1940s saw few artistic breakthroughs. The thaw under Khrushchev led to some internationally acclaimed films, but was followed by 2 more decades of stagnation under Brezhnev, an era dominated by bland dramas and goofy comedies. Gorbachev's glasnost produced some of the best Russian films to date, though most are pretty grim, reflecting the uncertain state of the USSR and the whole Communist experiment.

Russian film today is on the upswing, and movie selections look more and more like those in stable European countries: sci-fi blockbusters packed with special effects, psychological crime dramas, romantic teen comedies, and esoteric art films honored at international festivals. Russian animation—for

literary habits, much as it affected Russian art of the same period. A growing class of students in universities and academies took up their pens. **Alexander Pushkin** is the most important of these, revered by Russians as the father of modern Russian literature for applying day-to-day language to poetic forms. This made his work more accessible than any other Russian writer's work before his. His death in a duel in 1837 at the age of 37 elevated him to icon status.

If Pushkin's romantic epics such as *Eugene Onegin* and *Ruslan and Ludmila* reflected the more hopeful, ironically playful side of Russian life, **Fyodor Dostoyevsky**'s work revealed its darker, more troubled side. *Crime and Punishment* traces the inner turmoil of a poor student who murders a pawnbroker. No character is really likable, but each is disturbingly believable. *Notes From Underground*'s account of a man expressing his free will by sinking into desperation leaves the reader ready to jump off a bridge.

Nikolai Gogol chose satire over solemnity, portraying the complacency and petty concerns of the rural gentry and urban clerical classes in short stories such as *The* both children and adults—has long been a strong genre that tends to be edgier than western animation, so if you have a chance to see some Russian animated shorts at a film festival near you, seize it.

A few favorite Soviet films:

The Cranes Fly (Letyat Zhuravli), 1957: Tale of a musician who goes to war, and the romantic turmoil he leaves behind.

Ballad of a Soldier (Ballada o Soldate), 1959: Tender and heartbreaking account of a soldier on leave in the few days before he's killed in World War II.

Solaris, 1972: Psychological science fiction journey by Andrei Tarkovsky; remade by Hollywood in 2003.

Seventeen Instants of Spring (Semnadstat Mgnovenii Vesny), 1973: Tale of a Soviet spy in wartime Germany carefully balancing his dual identity; Stirlitz became a hero and antihero for Soviet jokes for decades.

Moscow Doesn't Believe in Tears (Moskva Slezam ne Verit), 1979: Bittersweet tale of three young women from small towns who arrive in Moscow to pursue their dreams.

Nostalgia, 1984: Soviet-Italian chronicle of a couple's relationship, one of the most accessible films of Andrei Tarkovsky.

Repentance (Pokoyaniye), 1987: Surreal and tragicomic saga of Stalinist repression in his homeland of Georgia, suppressed by censors for years.

Little Vera (Verochka), 1988: Account of a young woman's coming of age amid the social drift, shortages, and alcoholism in provincial Gorbachev-era Russia.

And post-Soviet Russian films:

Burnt by the Sun (Utomlyonnoye Solntsem), 1994: Oscar-winning account of a sun-kissed summer and the cold-blooded, Stalin-era secret police.

Prisoner of the Caucasus (Kavkazky Plennik), 1996: Moving, nuanced portrait of Russians and Chechens during the first Chechnya War.

East-West (Vostok-Zapad), 1999: Russian-French film about a Russian-French couple whose marriage and lives fall apart after they're lured back to Stalin's repressive Soviet Union.

The Wedding (Svadba), 2000: Painfully authentic drama about small-town romance and limited opportunity.

Nightwatch (Nochnoi Dozor), 2003: Big-budget thriller featuring vampires, darkness, and strong special effects.

Nose and *The Overcoat* and in his novel *The Inspector-General.* **Mikhail Lermontov** carved a name for himself with *A Hero of Our Time* and other tales about the Caucasus Mountains and Russia's efforts to subdue warrior clans there.

Nineteenth-century writers also took on Russian politics, often incurring the wrath of czarist governments: Pushkin was exiled from St. Petersburg, and Dostoyevsky was jailed for taking part in a radical intellectual discussion group.

The next crucial figure in the Russian literary pantheon was **Leo Tolstoy.** His writing career spanned 6 decades, starting with *Sevastopol Sketches* about his time serving in the Crimean Wars. He won fame for *War and Peace,* his careful and complex account of the Napoleonic Wars, and for *Anna Karenina,* about the fall of a married woman suffocated by her bourgeois world. Tolstoy later abandoned the aristocratic, intellectual realm for a form of Christian anarchism and asceticism at his farm at Yasnaya Polyana outside Moscow.

Anton Chekhov countered Tolstoy's rejection of modern life with an unflagging faith in progress. Originally a doctor, Chekhov began writing short stories before discovering widespread success as a playwright. His preference for progress underpinned plays such as *The Seagull, The Three Sisters,* and *The Cherry Orchard,* in which stagnation and the emptiness of rural life are recurrent themes.

The political turmoil of the early 20th century fueled literary expression before Soviet ideology crippled it or sent it fleeing abroad. Some writers managed to produce masterpieces amid this repression and fear. **Anna Akhmatova** thrived in the heady years before the revolution, then spent decades producing subtle yet wrenching commentary on the transformation of her beloved hometown into Soviet Leningrad. The Communist leadership was notoriously fickle in its loyalties. **Vladimir Mayakovsky** was hailed as the voice of the revolution but by the late 1920s was ostracized. **Mikhail Bulgakov** staged several plays in the 1920s; his *Dog's Heart,* in which a bourgeois surgeon puts a dog's heart in a decidedly proletariat patient, became a much-loved film. However, most of his works were banned or censored, including his masterpiece *Master and Margarita,* a complex novel that invokes Pontius Pilate and has the devil stalking one of Moscow's most prestigious neighborhoods. **Vladimir Nabokov** fled Russia after the revolution but continued publishing in Russian and translating his own works into English. His stylized allegories on art and life include *The Luzhin Defense, Invitation to a Beheading,* and his most notorious novel, *Lolita.*

Of Russia's modern writers, **Alexander Solzhenitsyn** was the most iconic. Imprisoned in a labor camp in the 1950s for his dissident views, he emerged even more determined to fight the Soviet system. His *Gulag Archipelago* chronicled the network of labor camps in exhaustive and exhausting detail. He earned a Nobel Prize but was afraid to collect it; he was eventually exiled in 1974. He returned to post-Soviet Russia in 1994 and continued to write essays critical of Russia's direction and moral decay until his death in 2008.

Perhaps post-Soviet Russia's most successful writer is **Boris Akunin** (a pseudonym), who has tapped into a mass-market hunger for accessible historical fiction that satirizes Russian faults without ridiculing them. Following the antiestablishment myth-busting of the *perestroika* era, many authors have taken on a more nationalist tone in recent years, focusing on Russia's beauty instead of its flaws, though it's still nothing like the propaganda-infused writings of Soviet times.

An exception to this is **Tatyana Tolstaya,** a great-grandniece of Tolstoy's and acerbic commentator on Russian and Western life. **Viktor Pelevin**'s cynical and philosophical novels toy with fantasy and the dangerous combination of Russian fatalism and modern technology. Pelevin was the first to play with the concept of manipulating media via advertising instead of political propaganda. The concept has taken flight with **Sergei Minayev**'s recent and more rugged *Media Sapiens* series, a disturbing lesson in PR for the modern age.

Books about Russia tend to be either murky or politicized, depending on prevailing worldviews at publication time. *The Icon and the Axe* by Library of Congress director James Billington is a broad and readable history. For a peek into czarist life that reads like historical fiction, try Robert Massie's lively *Peter the Great* and *Nicholas and Alexandra.* The most renowned reference on the Stalin era is Robert Conquest's *Great Terror,* and his very anti-Soviet *Reflections on a Ravaged Century* is based on decades of meticulous research for his numerous books. For a view from the other side, try Karl Marx's *Das Kapital,* which still provides food for thought even for the most die-hard capitalist. John Reed's *Ten Days That Shook the World* is an intricate report on the 1917 revolution by an American radical journalist, who is the only foreigner buried along the Kremlin wall. For a chilling account of the nearly 3-year siege of Leningrad by Hitler's army, and the broader context of the young nation it wounded, Harrison Salisbury's *The 900 Days* is a must. *Moscow: An Architectural History* by Kathleen Berton gives insight into why St. Basil's Cathedral looks nothing like its contemporaries. Tamara Talbot Rice's *Concise History of Russian Art* is rather superficial but serves as a good introduction, covering early Kievan Rus up through the Soviet era. Osip Mandelstam's *Noise of Time* portrays life in St. Petersburg in the early 20th century, before the author's persecution and death in 1938.

Post-Soviet books about Russia tend to focus on the negative, painting a bleak or sinister picture of its economic, political, and environmental prospects. David Remnick is one of the more optimistic observers in *Resurrection* and its predecessor, *Lenin's Tomb,* about the fall of the USSR. Prostitution, narcotics, organized crime, and corrupt judges are laid bare in *The Exile: Sex, Drugs and Libel in the New Russia* by Mark Ames and Matt Taibbi.

The Performing Arts

You don't have to know a word of Russian to delight in its ballets and symphonies, and its operas are worth viewing for the spectacle and drama even if the language escapes you. Russians take great pride in their cultural heritage, and in the Soviet era nearly everyone, factory worker and collective farmer included, made regular visits to theater, concert hall, or opera house. The generous Communist subsidies that made such widespread cultural appreciation possible shriveled in the 1990s, but both performers and theatergoers are now climbing out of the post-Soviet slump and finding a balance between honoring the classics and testing new artistic directions.

Russia's rigorous **ballet** traditions have relaxed little in the past 200 years, and that commitment to physical perfection carries over into every form of dance represented in today's Russia. Even strippers often have classical training. The wave of departures by Russian ballet prodigies for richer Western companies has ebbed in recent years, and a new generation is carrying on the traditions of Baryshnikov, Nureyev, and Nijinsky in their homeland. Russia's reputation makes it a top destination for dance festivals, offering a great opportunity to see international superstars or smaller European and Asian companies.

For **classical music** fans, there's no better way to pay tribute to the homeland of Tchaikovsky, Rachmaninoff, Mussorgsky, Scriabin, Shostakovich, and Rimsky-Korsakov than to hear their works played in a Russian conservatory by their dedicated heirs. Russia's musicians—like its athletes and dancers—are trained from preschool age, with strict discipline and devotion to classicism. Even though musicians remain dreadfully underpaid and many have left for more lucrative jobs, theirs remains a highly selective profession. Any concert you hear in Russia is bound to be of top quality.

Devotees of playwright **Anton Chekhov** and the **Stanislavsky acting method** may appreciate a visit to the **Moscow Art Theater,** where both found fame. However, it's difficult to celebrate their contributions to theater traditions in Moscow or St. Petersburg without a good command of Russian. A relatively new phenomenon in the Russian performance scene is the musical; fans of the originals may find it amusing to watch the Russian-language version of *Chicago* or *The Hunchback of Notre Dame.*

What Russian **opera** lacks in subtlety, it makes up for in volume and visuals. Opera tickets generally cost less than ballet tickets, and seeing Mussorgsky's historical saga *Boris Godunov* is a dramatic way to dose up on Russian culture and see the interior of a monumental theater like the Mariinsky (Kirov) at the same time.

AIR, EARTH, FIRE ... vodka?

Russians call it a blessing and a curse. No Russian family is untouched by vodka, for better or for worse. Your trip to Russia will invariably involve at least a taste of the national drink. Even its name is fundamental: It's a diminutive of the Russian word for "water" *(voda)*.

EVOLUTION OF A SPIRIT Some credit (or blame) the Genoans for introducing the concept of distilled alcohol to Russia in the late 1300s, not long after western European alchemists discovered its wonders. Monks in Moscow's Kremlin were soon brewing "bread wine," using grain, which was ubiquitous in Russia, instead of grapes. Though it was initially intended as a medicine, the drink became so popular that Ivan III (The Great) introduced the first vodka monopoly soon afterward. His grandson Ivan IV (The Terrible) recognized its dangers as well as its power, and introduced the first of several unsuccessful attempts by Russian leaders to ban the drink.

Vodka was absorbed into Russian court ceremony, and by the 17th century, Russian merchants and nobles were exporting their vodkas across Europe. Recipes expanded to include vodkas scented with cherries, apples, pears, blackberries, acorns, caraway seeds, dill, and sage, and the drink gradually grew stronger. The Russian chemist Mendeleyev—the author of chemistry's Periodic Table of Elements—played a key role in establishing vodka standards used to this day. In his late-19th-century doctoral dissertation, he determined

what he considered the scientifically ideal proportion of alcohol to water (40%). Most vodkas today are 40% alcohol (80 proof), twice as strong as the 40-proof vodkas of the 16th and 17th centuries.

Czar Nicholas II tried to ban alcohol during World War I to keep the troops clearheaded, and Lenin kept the ban in place after taking over in 1917. Stalin reversed this policy, expanding state-run vodka production and including a glass of low-quality vodka in the daily rations for construction workers, road workers, and dock workers. Reviving a tradition that dated back to Peter the Great's time, the military brass added vodka to Red Army rations in World War II. The pendulum swung back in the 1980s under Mikhail Gorbachev, whose anti-alcohol campaign was disastrous to his reputation and to government coffers, which had enjoyed substantial revenues from state-run distilleries. Boris Yeltsin had no such distaste for vodka, personally or politically. His free-market reforms encouraged innovation and competition, but also flooded stores with cheap, poorly regulated, and often dangerous new spirits.

THE MAGIC BEVERAGE TODAY Today rules are tighter than in the 1990s, and rich Russians are demanding ever-purer and more innovative vodkas. Most vodkas are distilled from wheat, rye, or barley malt or some combination of the three, though village distillers prefer cheaper sources such as corn and

EATING & DRINKING

Dining in Russia can be delectable or dangerous, dismal or divine. Caviar and vodka are readily available, as are melt-in-your-mouth *bliny* (similar to crepes), wild mushrooms, and succulent lamb dumplings. The range and number of restaurant options keeps expanding. Hotel dining, alas, has changed little from the bland Soviet era, except in the top-end spots, where luxurious brunches recall the decadence of pre-revolutionary aristocracy.

potatoes. The traditional restaurant serving size is a *ryumka* (shot glass) of 50 grams (1.8 oz.). Rural Russians largely prefer the cheaper *samogon*, a milky homemade brew guaranteed to set your throat on fire. Bathtub distilleries are a common sight in villages, and are the butt of many a Russian joke, but the humor is tinged with tragedy. Making and drinking *samogon* is increasingly the only occupation available in Russian villages, with employment and opportunity nearly nonexistent outside the big cities. Alcohol poisoning is a leading cause of death.

Most Russians, however, know how to celebrate vodka without abusing it. To join in this national pastime, stick to the brands served in restaurants or sold in supermarkets. **Stolichnaya, Russky Standart,** and **Flagman** are safe and excellent choices. A 750-milliliter bottle of high-quality vodka purchased in a Russian store costs 30% to 50% less than it would abroad, though domestic Russian prices are rising rapidly. Other brands to try are the basic but good **Zelyonaya Marka** ("Green Brand"), and the wheat-based **Pshenichnaya.** Avoid purchasing from street kiosks—in return for their rock-bottom prices you often get a liquid of dubious quality.

HOW TO DRINK VODKA If you want to appreciate a good vodka the way Russians do, follow these guidelines:

○ Drink it well chilled and straight, preferably in 50-gram shots. No ice or vodka cocktails are allowed. Ignore anyone who tries to get you to mix it with beer.

○ Down it in one gulp. No sipping allowed.

○ Don't drink until someone proposes a toast. (If you're really eager, propose a toast yourself; your hosts will be stunned but impressed.)

○ Always chase it with something to eat. Russians prefer pickles, a clove of garlic, marinated herring, or a slice of lard, but really, whatever's on the table will do. Connoisseurs can neutralize the vodka's power just by sniffing a slice of the rich, brown bread ubiquitous at Russian meals.

If you pace yourself, vodka can be like a good wine, a pleasant accompaniment to a rich table but not necessarily the prelude to a dreadful hangover. If you do go overboard, the Russians have a surefire, if noxious, morning-after cure: Drink a potful of cabbage brine. The dread of that should be enough to keep you in check the night before.

For a closer view at vodka's role in Russian history, visit the **Vodka Museum** in St. Petersburg, at 5 Konnogvardeisky Bulvar (✆ **812/312-9178;** Metro: Nevsky Prospekt). The small exhibit includes paraphernalia for producing and imbibing, and they even offer you a free sample (Tues–Sun 11am–9pm).

Breakfast is served from about 7 to 10am, and although Russians at home usually eat heartily in the morning, hotels often offer just rolls and jam with tea or coffee. Lunch has traditionally been the major meal of the day, and includes appetizer, soup, main course of meat or fish, and dessert. It can be eaten any time after noon. The pace of today's Moscow and St. Petersburg has popularized the smaller, quicker "business lunch," served around noon to 2pm. Dinner can be anything from a light sandwich to another four- or five-course meal, and is usually not eaten before 7 or 8pm. These are rough guidelines, since most restaurants in Moscow and St. Petersburg serve continuously.

A foodie SHORTLIST

Russian restaurants now offer a choice unthinkable 10 years ago. Not all of it is worth paying for, however. While there are some outstanding restaurants at the top and bottom of the market, mid-range venues—particularly the international offerings (French, Italian, Chinese, Thai)—can be seriously disappointing for the prices charged. When you've had your fill of the Russian staples, do what the locals do and head for the long-established Caucasian eateries. Here are a few terms you should know:

o *Kutabi*: thin, crepelike bread filled with meat, herbs, or cheese.
o *Kharcho*: spicy beef soup.
o *Khachapuri*: oven-baked flat-bread with cheese.
o *Khashi*: be careful here, it's a meat stew, made mainly from pig's trotters and offal; unbelievably, it's traditionally a breakfast dish.
o *Khinkali*: meat-filled dumplings.
o *Lobio*: a side dish of kidney beans.
o *Lyulya kebab*: minced beef with herbs and spices.
o *Kazy*: Another one to watch out for, horsemeat sausage.
o *Manty*: meat-filled dumplings but not, the texture is closer to pasta than to dough.
o *Piti*: a slow-cooked stew with lamb and chickpeas.
o *Satsivi*: chicken in a spicy sour cream with walnut sauce. If you only eat one Georgian dish, make it this one.

Russia's lively restaurant scene is all the more impressive when you realize that the country had no casual restaurant culture at all before the 1990s. Dining out was reserved for special occasions, and always involved formalwear, endless courses, and some kind of entertainment.

It almost never included children, who were not considered mature enough for such an event. The food and service, especially in the Soviet era, were generally bleak. Even now, most Russians prefer to eat at home. If you're invited to someone's home, be prepared for an endless stream of food, most of it rich and well-salted. Alcohol will invariably be served, and to avoid offense it's a good idea to at least sip or sample everything, though you don't have to drain your glass. As a foreigner you will be the star of the show, doted upon and offered the best cuts of meat and the juiciest berries. And you will not be allowed to lift a finger to help; that would be an insult to your hosts, a suggestion that they are somehow inadequate at satisfying you.

Pelmeni, dumplings filled with ground beef, pork, or lamb and spices and boiled in broth (a bit like overstuffed ravioli), are a Siberian specialty. *Vareniki* are a larger, flatter version of these dumplings, filled with potatoes or berries. The Georgian version, *khinkali*, are larger and spicier; the central Asian version, *manty*, are steamed instead of boiled. *Piroshki* are small baked pies filled with ground meat, cabbage, or fruit, and are eaten with your hands; *pirogi* are large dessert pies. Buttery *bliny*, thin crepelike pancakes, are spread with jam or savory fillings such as ham and cheese and rolled up. Tiny round *olady* are the pancakes eaten with caviar. Russian soups done right are delightfully flavorful, such as the refreshing summer sorrel soup *zelyoniye shchi* or the hearty winter meat stew *solyanka*.

Vodka—whose name means "little water" in Russian—is ubiquitous and demands a complex ritual of imbibing if Russians are at your table. (See the following sidebar..) Local beers are improving rapidly; Baltika and Nevskoye are cheap and tasty choices.

Russian-made versions of Belgium's Stella Artois and Czech pilsner are also available. French and Californian wines are quite expensive. Simpler wines from the former Soviet republic of Georgia were once a staple, but were banned amid a diplomatic dispute. At business meals, wine or even vodka is common at lunch or dinner. If

> ## Impressions
>
> *If only there was vodka,*
> *and with it selyodka (herring),*
> *Then everything would be all right.*
> —Traditional Russian saying

you're feeling adventurous, try *kvas*, a thirst-quenching beverage made from fermented bread. Available only in summer, it's very mildly alcoholic, and Russians consider it something between a Coke and a beer.

Russians' drink of choice, however, is tea *(chai)*, ideally served from a samovar: a small pot of strong tea base *(zavarka)* sits brewing on top and is diluted to taste with the hot water from the belly of the samovar *(kipitok)*. Coffee *(kofye)* is often instant or resembles thick Turkish coffee, unless the menu specifically says espresso or cappuccino.

A service charge is usually included in the restaurant bill, but a nominal tip is welcome.

WHEN TO GO

Frost-tinged, wind-whipped, ice-glazed. Snow blankets much of Russia for much of the year, and Moscow and St. Petersburg usually see flurries in May and September. Warming global temperatures have made for some unusually mild Januarys in recent years, but it's still a northern nation. Understandably, September through May prices are lower and tourist sites less crowded. Hotel and airline rates spike around the New Year's holiday, the main event in the Russian calendar.

Most visitors favor summer, in both Moscow and subarctic St. Petersburg, with sunsets that linger until sunrise, balmy temperatures, and all-night activity that makes you forget it's 3am and you haven't slept. Russians shed layers, sunbathe on park benches, and let loose after their long hibernation. Festivals and open-air concerts make up for the summer departure of the major opera and dance companies such as the Bolshoi and Mariinsky (formerly the Kirov) theaters. Summer weather in both cities can be unpredictable, though, with spells of heavy heat (and rare air-conditioning) or drizzly cold. Bring layers and an umbrella no matter when you go.

Autumn is a few idyllic weeks in late September and early October when the poplars and oaks shed their leaves and the afternoon sun warms you enough to help you through the cooling nights. Spring, a few weeks in April, is slushy and succinct in Moscow and St. Petersburg.

If a winter wonderland is your fantasy, Russia in December won't disappoint. The northern sun shines softly low on the horizon, and snow masks garbage-strewn courtyards and muffles the sound of traffic. Cross-country skiing fans can wind through forests within Moscow city limits or skate-ski along the frozen Gulf of Finland in St. Petersburg. Skaters have frozen ponds galore for ice-season fun. The downside, other than a suitcase weighted with sweaters, is that many country palaces and other outdoor sites close for the winter.

THE BIGGEST party OF THE YEAR

Presents under a fir tree, a copious family feast, and a big man with a long white beard—for a Russian, these traditions conjure up not Christmas, but New Year's Eve. The atheist Soviet government wiped religious holidays off the official calendar, but they couldn't suffocate the midwinter holiday spirit. Stalin, recognizing the people's unwillingness to abandon Christmas traditions, encouraged their shift to the more secular New Year's holiday. Even today, a decade and a half after the collapse of Soviet Communism, New Year's remains the primary event on the Russian calendar. Russian Orthodox Christmas—celebrated on January 7, according to the Julian calendar in use before the revolution—has reassumed some of its former significance, but it's seen as a day for attending Mass and singing hymns instead of gift-giving and family celebration. Those rituals are reserved for December 31, when even the smallest children stay up to ring in the New Year.

Some restaurants and clubs are tapping into Western New Year's rituals with expensive all-night parties drenched in champagne, but the majority of Russians consider it an at-home, family event. The appetizers emerge in early evening, when relatives squeeze around the over-burdened table. For the next several hours, people eat, drink, tell stories, and dance to favorite songs. Father Frost, or Dyed Moroz, delivers gifts sometime around midnight. Because most Russians live in apartment buildings, the whole coming-down-the-chimney tradition plays no role here, and family members pull presents from cupboards or from under beds. In fairy tales, Dyed Moroz is assisted by a Snow Maiden, Snegurochka, and some families dress up as the two characters.

Menu items reflect the end of the pre-Christmas fast called for by Orthodox custom, 40 days of refraining from meat and dairy products: beef and pork roasts dripping with fatty sauces, cured meats, veal in aspic, salads packed with diced ham and egg and heaped with mayonnaise, buttery pancakes heaped with caviar. . . . To drink, men stick to vodka; women either join in or sip *nastoika,* a homemade liqueur made of vodka brewed with berries, herbs, or roots. Pre-revolutionary aristocrats introduced fine French champagne to their Christmas feasts; the Soviets spread the tradition to the masses with the production of cheap sparkling wine that is still a staple of the New Year's table. The most popular brand is Sovietskoye (all categories but the *brut* are quite sweet).

The New Year's celebrations peak with a midnight fireworks display over Red Square, broadcast nationwide. The crowds of mostly young revelers in the square are so dense that few of them notice the freezing temperatures. In St. Petersburg, the biggest fireworks are shot over the Neva River across from the Hermitage. Back at home, many families celebrate well into the night, or go outside to set off their own small firecrackers. The first day of the year is a day of rest and lots of leftovers.

If you visit Moscow or St. Petersburg over New Year's, be sure to check in advance online or through your travel agent for special holiday events at your hotel. If you can't get invited to a Russian home, try one of the elaborate parties at traditional Russian restaurants such as One Red Square, Baltschug Kempinski hotel, or Le National hotel (all have great views of the Moscow fireworks). Meal service starts at 10pm or later. Seats are expensive and must be booked well in advance. For English-language listings on New Year's parties, see *The Moscow Times* newspaper (www.themoscow-times.com) or *The St. Petersburg Times* (www.sptimes.ru). And practice saying "S Novym Godom!" ("Happy New Year!

Businesses and government agencies slow down considerably because of vacations the first 2 weeks of January, the first 2 weeks of May, and much of August. These are calmer times to visit Russia but can prove a nightmare if you have visa problems or other administrative needs. When a public holiday falls on a weekend, the nearest weekday is given off in compensation.

Weather

Moscow's Average Temperatures

	JAN	FEB	MAR	APR	MAY	JUNE	JULY	AUG	SEPT	OCT	NOV	DEC
Temp (°F)	16	18	28	42	54	60	63	60	50	39	28	21
Temp (°C)	-9	-8	-2	6	12	16	17	16	10	4	-2	-6

St. Petersburg's Average Temperatures

	JAN	FEB	MAR	APR	MAY	JUNE	JULY	AUG	SEPT	OCT	NOV	DEC
Temp (°F)	14	18	25	39	54	59	66	63	54	43	32	19
Temp (°C)	-10	-8	-4	4	12	15	19	17	12	6	0	-7

Calendar of Events

All dates below are official holidays unless noted. December 25 is not a holiday in Russia.

For other festivals and sports championships, see "The Performing Arts" in chapters 8 and 15, and "Spectator Sports" in chapters 6 and 13.

For an exhaustive list of events beyond those listed here, check http:events.frommers. com, where you'll find a searchable, up-to-the-minute roster of what's happening in cities all over the world.

JANUARY

New Year's Day. This is the major holiday of the Russian year, a family event centered around a fir tree, a huge feast, and gift-giving traditions transferred by Soviet leaders from Christmas to the more secular New Year's Day. Even the smallest children stay up to ring in midnight. Both January 1 and 2 are holidays.

Russian Orthodox Christmas. Ignored in Soviet times, this is now a primary religious holiday, with many people attending midnight Mass and more festive meals. January 7.

"Old" New Year. Not an official holiday, but celebrated nonetheless. It's left over from the pre-revolutionary days when Russia followed the Julian calendar, which was about 2 weeks behind the one used by the Western world. January 14.

FEBRUARY

Defenders of the Motherland Day (Armed Forces Day). With the military draft still mandatory, many Russians see this as a general "Men's Day," involving much vodka and stories of hazing and corrupt commanding officers. February 23.

Maslenitsa, or Butter Week. Not an official holiday. The week before Orthodox Lent is traditionally a time to eat lots of buttery *bliny* (crepelike pancakes) and other rich foods that believers will forego for the next 40 days. The origins of the holiday are pagan, and many towns stage raucous Maslenitsa festivals. It's not Carnival or Mardi Gras, but it's lively. End of February, beginning of March. (See Butter Week sidebar p. 37.)

International Women's Day. Begun by U.S. feminists in the 1920s, the holiday became a Soviet banner for gender equality. Today's Russian women lament that men get pampered 364 days a year and women get appreciated only on Vosmovo Marta (Mar 8). It's a sacred holiday and official day off work for everyone nonetheless, and every Russian male is expected to present flowers or chocolates to his wife, mother, daughters, and female colleagues. March 8.

APRIL

Orthodox Easter. The date varies, but it's usually 1 or 2 weeks after Catholic/Protestant Easter. The following Monday is a state holiday, though Good Friday is not. The day has taken on greater significance since the collapse of Soviet atheism, and on Easter morning, every Orthodox church has lines of people waiting to have their traditional Easter cakes blessed. The holiday feast is the richest on the Russian calendar, with eggs a major theme. End of April or early May.

Easter Arts Festival (Moscow). A weeklong event showcasing St. Petersburg's Mariinsky Company orchestra in Moscow and small choral ensembles performing in the city's cathedrals following Orthodox Easter. Bell ringing is a major part of the event. End of April or early May.

Labor Day/Spring Festival. May Day parades under red Communist banners still wend through Moscow's streets, though they're no longer allowed on Red Square, site of the tremendous Soviet-era demonstrations of Kremlin-enforced proletarian solidarity. May 1–2.

Victory Day. The Soviet Union lost more people than any other nation in World War II, and even 6 decades later the day commemorating Hitler's defeat is a major Russian holiday. Every Russian has a relative or friend who served in what they call the Great Patriotic War, and the sight of elderly veterans pinning on rusting medals for a day is a poignant reminder of one of the most impressive feats of the Soviet era. May 9.

JUNE

Russian Independence Day. On this day in 1990, the Russian Federation declared itself independent from the Soviet Union, a symbolic move inspired by nationalist movements in the Baltics and eastern Europe. Few Russians today know what the holiday commemorates. June 12.

White Nights. Two weeks around the summer solstice, St. Petersburg puts on concerts, film festivals, all-night boat tours, and other events to celebrate the northern light. It's peak tourist season. Late June or early July.

NOVEMBER

Day of Reconciliation and Accord. For 70 years this was called Revolution Day, marking the 1917 events that brought the Soviets to power. The post-Soviet government didn't have the heart to take away the holiday, so they renamed it. A dwindling number of Communist die-hards still gather around Red Square, visiting Lenin's tomb and lamenting the demise of his brainchild. November 7.

DECEMBER

Constitution Day. Marks the 1993 referendum that approved Russia's first post-Soviet constitution. December 12.

White Days Festival (St. Petersburg). The city boosters' efforts to lure tourists during the snowy months, this festival includes winter carnivals in the city parks and a dense program of dance, opera, and orchestral performances. See www.white days.com for more information. Last week in December.

RESPONSIBLE TRAVEL

In line with its reputation as a country of extremes, Russia offers some of the best and worst that nature has to offer: vast tracts of untouched Siberian forest and wildlife, and pollution-choked cities with little regard for recycling or emissions limits. Its attitude toward transport is similarly polar: Its trains and trolleybuses carry millions daily and have offered efficient, carbon-free travel for a century, and most Russians do not own cars. But those that do generally own the dirtiest kind: fuel-thirsty SUVs and Hummers, or Soviet-era models built when emissions were of no concern. One positive development is that the collapse in Russia's industry in the 1990s means office buildings and apartment towers took over factory grounds that used to cough pollution into downtown Moscow and St. Petersburg.

butter WEEK

Known as Maslenitsa in Russian, Butter Week began as a pagan festival celebrating the end of winter. The arrival of the Orthodox calendar didn't extinguish this week of revelry, but turned it into a pre-Lenten party, a sort of Russian version of Carnival or Mardi Gras. The name comes from the butter used for pancakes eaten throughout the week—pancakes whose golden warmth and roundness are meant to represent the sun and impending springtime. The butter also refers to the upcoming Lent, when Orthodox believers are expected to refrain from dairy products and other luxuries. To store up for this austere period, Russians indulge greedily in rich foods during Maslenitsa. Pancakes are stuffed with soft farmers' cheese, ham, or caviar. Eggy desserts grace the table, not to be seen again until Easter.

Maslenitsa was a major event in Moscow and St. Petersburg before the revolution, and after a Soviet-era lull, festivities are again staged at parks such as **Kolomenskoye** in Moscow (p. 118) and the **Summer Gardens** in St. Petersburg (p. 235), as well as in villages and country estates on the cities' outskirts. A key part of the ritual is the burning of one or several straw scarecrows representing winter. They're paraded around a snow-covered field and then set alight as onlookers cheer, chant, and dance. At Kolomenskoye, performers in embroidered costumes revive traditional songs and children's games, and build ice forts for mass snowball fights. Everyone is treated to honey from nearby hives, and tea and barrels of mead—a warm, fermented honey drink—are prepared just for the occasion.

Dates of Butter Week vary from year to year, since it's linked to Orthodox Easter, but it usually falls between late February and late March. The original rituals have been adapted to modern times, with the big parties usually held on Saturday and Sunday to accommodate work schedules. Each day of the week has a significance. Thursday, for example, is **Cleansing Day,** when Russians are expected to clean out their cupboards and lives for the coming spring. Sunday is **Forgiveness Day,** and even in Soviet times it was common for long-feuding siblings to phone each other on that day to mend their differences. According to some traditions, Monday morning is teeth-cleaning day, when men are expected to drink large amounts of vodka to cleanse the remnants of fatty foods from their teeth.

If you're visiting Russia during this season, tracking down a Maslenitsa party is a great way to boost your mood and distract you from the cold slushiness all around. Some Russian travel agencies arrange special Maslenitsa tours. Check with your hotel concierge for a calendar of Moscow Maslenitsa events; or check *The St. Petersburg Times* website (www.sptimes.ru) for St. Petersburg parties.

Navigating both cities with the environment in mind is challenging but possible. Nearly every site listed in this book can be reached by public transport. Bikes are available for rent in both cities.

In Moscow, try Veloprokat (www.veloprokat.ru site in Russian only; 6 Shestaya Radialnaya Ulitsa; ✆ **926/284-9232;** metro: Tsaritsino). It's in a garage. Bikes cost up from 800 rubles a day. They'll also deliver your bike to you for another 1,200 rubles.

In St. Petersburg, try Skat Prokat, for 500 rubles a day plus deposit. (www.skatprokat.ru; 3 Glinka Ulitsa, inside the Kitsport store; ✆ **812/325-7198**).

None of the car rental agencies in either city currently offer hybrids.

Few hotels or restaurants pay much heed to environmental concerns. An exception is the **Alexander Hotel in St. Petersburg** (p. 198). To be more certain about the provenance and contents of your food, try the open-air markets in either city (Izmailovsky Market in Moscow or Mikhailovsky Market in St. Petersburg is a good options). The older women camped out on the edge of the markets are often selling goods from their own gardens. For vegetarian dining suggestions, see p. 79.

Though caviar is a centerpiece of Russian cuisine, the Caspian Sea sturgeon that produce them are desperately endangered. If you are keen for a taste, favor the red caviar, or salmon roe, on many restaurant menus.

Recycling has yet to catch on in either city, as the excessive packaging we know in the West came only recently to Russia. An exception are Soviet-era machines that allow you to exchange empty aluminum cans for cash, though they are often out of order. Recycling bins around Moscow are marked with images of paper, glass, or plastic but are often filled with other debris.

The best way to stay "green" in both cities is to visit their extensive parks. **Losiny Ostrov** in Moscow was a former imperial hunting grounds and is the size of a city unto itself. It is believed to still host elk, wild boar, and beavers, and is an excellent place to get lost in the "wilderness" on a bike or cross-country skis (p. 121).

The St. Petersburg island **Krestovsky Ostrov** has sporting facilities near the main entrance but thins out into lush, peaceful forest farther back (p. 236). St. Petersburg's botanical gardens host some 12,000 plant species.

The Typhoon Experimental Meteorology Research Institute sets ecological standards for the country (www.typhoon.obninsk.ru/english/main.htm). See frommers.com/planning for more tips on responsible travel.

TOURS

Escorted General-Interest Tours

Russia's tourism industry is only beginning to tap the travel possibilities across the world's largest country. No roads exist across much of the territory, and hotels and services in small towns are often little better than Gulags. All this makes an escorted tour—with a group leader, including airfare, hotels, meals, admission costs, and local transportation—quite appealing. The chief benefit is that the tour company negotiates the hassle of getting a visa; it's also handy to have tour guides navigate museums and street signs labeled in Russian only. The main drawback of an escorted tour is its high cost.

Special-interest tours remain rare in Moscow and St. Petersburg, though some adventure and ecological tours take you to the wilds of the Russian Far East or the Trans-Siberian railway.

For general-interest tours to Russia's premier cities, **Escorted Russian Tours** (© 800/942-3301; www.escortedrussiantours.com) provides a range of offerings focusing on Moscow and St. Petersburg, as do the U.K.-based **Russian Gateway** (© 08-704-461-812; www.russiangateway.co.uk) and the Russian-based www.tourstorussia.com.

One popular excursion is a **cruise from St. Petersburg to Moscow.** It takes your boat about 10 days to wind through rivers and canals, with stops at the island monastery at Valaam, the fairy tale–like wooden village of Kizhi, lakes Ladoga and

Onega, and the Volga river towns of Yaroslavl and Kostroma. **Russian Tours** (www.rus-tours.com) and **Russiana** (www.russiana.co.uk) are two places to start.

For more information on escorted general-interest tours, including questions to ask before booking your trip, see www.frommers.com/planning.

Package Tours

Package tours are simply a way to buy the airfare, accommodations, and other elements of your trip (such as car rentals, airport transfers, and sometimes even activities) at the same time and often at discounted prices—kind of like one-stop shopping. Packages are sold in bulk to tour operators—who resell them to the public at a cost that usually undercuts standard rates.

Two tour companies to try are **Eastern Tours,** run by Russian émigrés and focusing on reasonably priced tours to Moscow, St. Petersburg, and Kiev (© **800/339-6967;** www.traveltorussia.com); and **Cosmos Tours,** which includes several Russian packages (© **800/276-1241;** www.cosmos.com). Be sure to read reviews of their tours by former clients on www.frommers.com or other independent websites.

Many of the mainstream packagers haven't caught on to Russia yet, so the choices are more limited. Russia-based packages are cheaper but riskier than those based in your home country; be sure to get as much insurance and guarantees as you can. Places to check include **Tour Vacations To Go** (© **800/680-2858;** www.tourvacationstogo.com) and **Budget Travel** (www.budgettravel.com). Russia-based agencies include **Russia Info-Center** (© **495/939-1605;** www.russia-ic.com) and www.homestay.ru, which offers high-end hotels as well as homestays.

Before you invest in a package tour, get some answers. Ask about the **accommodations choices** and prices for each. Then look up the hotels' reviews in a Frommer's guide and check their rates online for your specific dates of travel. You'll also want to find out what **type of room** you get. If you need a certain type of room, ask for it; don't take whatever is thrown your way. Request a nonsmoking room, a quiet room, a room with a view, or whatever you fancy.

Finally, look for **hidden expenses.** Ask whether airport departure fees and taxes, for example, are included in the total cost.

Academic Trips & Language Classes

"Russia cannot be understood with the mind/Or by an ordinary yardstick/She has a special status/All you can do is believe in Russia." So goes an oft-quoted verse by 19th-century Romantic poet Fyodor Tyutchev that has stood as a challenge to foreign scholars of Russia and Russian ever since. What better way to prove him wrong and expand your understanding than to take a language tour in Russia? It is certain to be intense and productive, as English speakers and familiar lettering are scarcer here than in Western Europe. Tours linked to reputable Russian universities are the least risky and most streamlined. **Study Russian** (© **495/939-0980;** www.studyrussian.com) offers language lessons in Moscow or St. Petersburg for all skill levels and can tailor them to your business specialty. Courses in Russian history or literature are also available. Visas and accommodations are arranged for you. The **Center for Russian Language** (© **495/939-1463;** www.ruslanguage.ru) arranges courses and accommodations at a dormitory; conditions are basic but comfortable and immersion is guaranteed.

MOSCOW NEIGHBORHOODS & SUGGESTED ITINERARIES

3

From the swirl of humanity on Red Square to the rush of the every-90-seconds Metro trains, Moscow whisks visitors into its ever-changing whirlwind. Nearly 900 years of history lurk underfoot in Russia's capital, and blinding digital billboards glitter overhead. Aromatic tea or seasoned vodka beckons from dining havens that have flourished since the collapse of the Soviet era, along with couture gowns and Ferraris, fast food and streetside software stalls.

THINGS TO DO   The crimson-walled **Kremlin** defines Moscow and the glories and horrors of Russian history, and forms the foundation of any journey here. From there, find silence and reflection before a portrait in the **Tretyakov Gallery,** or a fresco in **St. Basil's Cathedral.** Shed stress in a **bathhouse spa** steeped in the scent of pine and birch—or in a night club pulsing with Moscow's musical talent. And walk, walk, walk through the city's parks and tree-lined boulevards.

SHOPPING   What was once a Communist outpost is now one of the world's most capitalist cities, boasting wares for any taste or budget, 24 hours a day. Nesting dolls sold on the **Arbat** are just the beginning. Linens and modern art in craft stores south of the Moscow River contrast with the sprawling cacophony of **Izmailovsky Market,** a mother lode of Siberian gemstones, military memorabilia, and Uzbek ceramics.

RESTAURANTS & DINING   Suckling pig, garlic-drenched eggplant, Siberian dumplings, deviled eggs stuffed with caviar, sushi in a sandwich shop—anything is possible in today's Moscow when it comes to satisfying hunger. The options are rich and ever-changing on and off the central artery of **Tverskaya.** Away from main avenues, treasures can lurk, such as **Uncle Vanya** with its cheesy mushroom *julyen* and borscht, and restaurants specializing in unexpected dishes from Central Asia and the Caucasus Mountains.

NIGHTLIFE & ENTERTAINMENT   Moscow's entertainment scene never sleeps—or fails to astound. Even with the **Bolshoi Theater**'s main stage closed for renovation, a ballet or symphony performance in any city venue is certain to be top rate. DJs from around the world converge on the no-holds-barred dance floors of Russia's capital, experimenting with new sounds from the avant-garde **Colors Bar** to the time-tested **Propaganda.**

Neighborhoods in Brief

Moscow is divided into six districts, or *okrugs,* with most of the activity focused on the Central district. The best way to view the city is as a daisylike flower, with neighborhoods stretching like petals from the Kremlin out toward a series of concentric circles delineated by what Russians call "ring roads." (See the map on p. 44.) Most historical buildings and key sights are within the Boulevard Ring; museums are within the Garden Ring; and hotels, restaurants, and shopping for all budgets are found everywhere. The area between the Kremlin and the Boulevard Ring was known historically as the "Bely Gorod," or "White Town," because of the white stone walls that encircled it to fend off outsiders. The area between the Boulevard and Garden rings was called "Zemlyanoi Gorod," or "Earth Town," after its earthen ramparts.

THE PRIMARY DISTRICTS

At the center is **The Kremlin,** a village unto itself, with cathedrals, palaces, an enormous concert and congress hall, and of course the seat of presidential power—all surrounded by imposing red-brick walls that extend for 2.5km (1½ miles). On its east side is **Red Square,** the epicenter of the city and the country. The square abuts a small neighborhood called **Kitai-Gorod.** This is almost like an annex to the Kremlin, with a dense collection of churches, old merchants' courtyards, and administrative buildings clustered on quiet streets overlooking the Moscow River. Its name today translates as "Chinatown," but more likely comes from an old Russian term for battlements because of its proximity to the Kremlin. The area boasts many restaurants but few hotels.

The primary petal of Moscow's daisy is undoubtedly **Tverskaya Street,** shooting north from Red Square in the direction of Russia's other imperial city, St. Petersburg. Moscow's most important thoroughfare, Tverskaya throbs with commerce, cafes, and nightclubs, with the columns of City Hall overseeing it all. Tverskaya and its environs include key hotels and museums, and offer close-up views of Moscow's breakneck post-Soviet evolution. Hotels right on Tverskaya suffer from its 24-hour schedule; those on the side streets are calmer but farther from the action.

The more true-to-tradition **Petrovka** district slopes eastward from Tverskaya. It includes several old and new restaurants, boutiques, and (mostly upmarket) hotels, in addition to two monasteries and a historic bathhouse. Curving southeast from there is the **Ukrainian Quarter,** whose steep and crooked lanes unveil architectural treasures tucked behind embassies and run-down government buildings. Accommodations here are limited, but the area is great for wandering. As you continue to circle Red Square clockwise, you cross the Moscow River to the Zamoskvarechye neighborhood on the opposite bank. Moving northwest, you come to aristocratic Ostozhenka and Prechistenka streets and the **Arbat district,** centered around the pedestrian Arbat Street lined with souvenir shops and cafes. Touristy but colorful, the Arbat is surrounded by alleys rich in literary legend and by a few convenient, reasonably priced hotels.

Outside the **Garden Ring Road** lie many hotels, as well as former "country mansions" now museums or concert halls surrounded by urbanism. Basing yourself beyond the center means you'll need more travel time to see city sights, but if your hotel is close to a metro station, the distance shouldn't be a hindrance.

THE BOULEVARD RING

This is not a neighborhood, but as an urban geographical marker, it's as distinctive as they come: The innermost of Moscow's concentric circles is both a main traffic artery and one of the world's most oddly shaped parks. **The Boulevard Ring,** actually

Moscow

a partial circle tracing a hump through central Moscow, is a road split down the middle by a 9.7km-long (6-mile) green space. It's lined with paths and benches, and interrupted by a couple of playgrounds, a pond, several monuments, and busy intersections. If you have a free afternoon and the weather cooperates, wander one or more segments of the "bulvar"—an activity that Muscovites call the cheapest amusement in town.

The lines of the boulevard date back to the 14th century, when ramparts were erected to defend the city that had grown up between here and the Kremlin. White stone walls were installed in the 16th century, giving the settlements within the ramparts the nickname "Bely Gorod" or "White Town." Towers, chapels, and gates marked the spots where major intersections now throng with traffic and pedestrians, and the current names of some crossings reflect that era, such as Nikitsky Gates and Sretensky Gates. The ramparts were razed piece by piece in the 18th century and replaced with leafy alleys and wrought-iron lampposts much like those standing today. When Napoleon's army entered an abandoned and charred Moscow in 1812, soldiers chopped down many of the boulevard's trees for fuel. Today, it is lined with linden and poplar trees, and if you wander the ring in June, you may be sprinkled by white poplar tufts that Russians call their "summer snow."

A few key spots on the ring worth visiting are **Pushkin Square,** on either side of Tverskaya Street, a major gathering place and the most energized of the boulevard's intersections; the two **statues of author Nikolai Gogol,** one triumphant and prominent on Arbat Square, the other contemplative and intriguing in a courtyard on Nikitsky Bulvar; and **Chistiye Prudy (Clean Ponds),** actually a single pond on the east side of the ring that serves as an outdoor skating rink in winter and boating pond in summer.

"THE LAND BEYOND THE MOSCOW RIVER"

The neighborhood of Zamoskvarechye (Zamoss-kva-*reh*-cha), which translates as "the land beyond the Moscow River," abuts the very heart of Moscow, even though its name makes it sound like it's in the city's nether reaches. The area does feel different from the rest of town, however, making it well worth a wander at some point on your trip. Situated on a bell-shaped cluster of islands south of the Moscow River, it spreads from the embankment opposite the Kremlin's southern wall down to the Garden Ring. Settlements in Zamoskvarechye date back to at least the 13th century, when Mongol envoys camped here during visits to exact tribute from their Muscovite subjects. The Muscovites themselves eventually moved into the neighborhood, setting up fortified compounds to house the *streltsy* (palace guards), who served as a buffer protecting the Kremlin from raids from the south.

With the end of Mongol domination, the area began attracting craftsmen, who settled in walled compounds. Each housed a different guild—tanners, weavers, barrelmakers, sheepskin curers—and was run by a council of elected elders called a *mirsky soviet.* As the guilds flourished, they began building the neighborhood's churches, many of which remain standing. Their modest lines contrast with the designs of more resplendent cathedrals elsewhere in town.

Merchants trading in the Kitai-Gorod district across the river "discovered" Zamoskvarechye in the 19th century, building mansions there and sponsoring neighborhood artists and artisans—eventually creating the country's first art museum, Tretyakov Gallery. By the early 20th century, Zamoskvarechye had become a major industrial district, but its factories grew up alongside the homes and churches instead of subsuming them. The district was touched by uglier episodes in Russian history, too: Bolotnaya Ploshchad (Marshy Square) was once the site of public executions, though it now houses a tranquil park and a statue of painter Ilya Repin. The House on the Embankment (the enormous gray complex on Bersenevskaya Naberezhnaya) was transformed from a prestigious residence for the Communist elite into a house of terror during Stalin's purges. Overall, the neighborhood's character

Moscow Neighborhoods

The Kremlin **1**

Around Red Square **2**

Tverskaya Street
and Environs **3**

Petrovka and the
Ukrainian Quarter **4**

Zamoskvarechye **5**

Arbat District **6**

Common terms and abbreviations

naberezhnaya/nab	*Embankment*
most	*Bridge*
ploshchad/pl	*Square* or *plaza*
prospekt/pr	*Avenue*
sad	*Garden*
ulitsa/ul	*Street*

nore low-key than the
lleries, antiques deal-
ior draw. Highlights
'lery (p. 114), the

Obvodny Canal fountains around Luzhkov
Bridge, and **Pyatnitskaya Street.** The near-
est metro stations are Novokuznetskaya,
Tretyakovskaya, and Polyanka.

T OF MOSCOW IN 1 DAY

uring Moscow in one day means hitting Red Square early and branching out
from there. Bring good walking shoes and as much energy as you can muster. This
itinerary takes you inside the Kremlin walls, gives you a glance at bustling Tverskaya
Street, and leaves you the evening to explore the artsy Arbat neighborhood. ***Note:*** Try
to do this tour on a day when the Kremlin is open (it's closed on Thurs). If that's not
possible, use those extra morning hours for wandering the Kitai-Gorod neighborhood
on the other side of Red Square (see "Neighborhoods in Brief," earlier in this chapter). ***Start:*** *Metro to Ploshchad Revolutsii, Okhotny Ryad, Alexandrovsky Sad, or Teatralnaya—then head to Red Square.*

1 Red Square (Krasnaya Ploshchad) ★★★

The city and country spread out from this sloping plaza, whose "red" ("krasnaya")
label has nothing to do with the Communists, but dates from the Middle Ages,
when the word meant "beautiful." For the full effect, enter the square from the
Resurrection Gates, directly south of Tverskaya Street. Though the gates date
only from the 1990s, they provide a stunning frame for the square. Sunrise over
Red Square is particularly breathtaking. Soviet founder Vladimir Lenin lies
embalmed in the mausoleum on the west side of the square, despite his wish to
be buried.

2 St. Basil's Cathedral (Khram Vasiliya Blazhennogo) ★★★

No trip to Red Square is complete without a peek inside this onion-domed
landmark that has formed the backdrop for "Live from Moscow" international
TV spots for decades. The interior of the 16th-century church has little in common with its famous and festive exterior; dark and narrow passages wind up
steep stairs to mystical, musty chapels and nooks. See p. 103 for details.

3 The Kremlin ★★★

This citadel ringed by red-brick walls and towers has been the seat of Russian
power for most of the past millennium. Some of its grounds and five of its
cathedrals are open to tourists, along with the collections of czarist treasures in
the Armory and the Diamond Fund. The tourist entrance is on the north side of
the Kremlin, at the Borovitsky Gates.
Lines are rarely long. Allow at least 2
hours for the Kremlin experience. The
president's offices are off-limits, but
you may see a motorcade or two pass
through the gates during your visit.
See p. 99 for more information.

> ### A Historic Walking Tour
>
> **For an additional itinerary, mostly in
> The Kremlin, don't miss "Walking Tour:
> Historic Moscow," on p. 125.**

1 Red Square
2 St. Basil's Cathedral
3 The Kremlin
4 Alexander Gardens
5 Bosco Bar and Café
6 GUM and Okhotny Ryad
  Shopping Center
7 Tverskaya Street
  (short version)
8 Theater Square
9 Metropol Café
10 The Arbat

4 Alexander Gardens (Alexandrovsky Sad)

After you emerge from the Kremlin, take some time to rest on a bench or wander through the greenery of Alexander Gardens, which run along the fortress's north wall. This used to be a river that helped protect the fortress from invaders, but in the 19th century it was filled in. Nearer to Red Square is the Tomb of the Unknown Soldier, a solemn spot where veterans and newlyweds often pay tribute. The cities listed around the tomb are those honored for their valiance and suffering during World War II.

5 Bosco Bar ☕ ★

Ignore the pampered and plastified clientele, and sit back and enjoy the view on Red Square instead. The bold design and comfy couches of this cafe inside the GUM department store are key parts of its appeal. Try the exotic salads or rich ice cream. Portions are delicate, so if you've worked up a good appetite, try the less romantic but heartier options in the Okhotny Ryad shopping center (see next stop). GUM, 3 Red Square; ✆ 495/627-3703. See p. 78 for a full review.

6 GUM & Okhotny Ryad Shopping Center

For shoppers and nonshoppers alike, these Russian "trading centers" deserve a look. GUM (p. 135), which stands for State Department Store (even though it's now a capitalist paradise), is the ornate building that runs the full west side of Red Square. The 19th-century gallery boasts footbridges and skylights and a full array of international luxury brands. The Okhotny Ryad shopping center (p. 135) extends three floors underneath the plaza just north of Red Square. Less than a decade old, it houses shops with prices to fit all pocketbooks, as well as several cafes on the bottom floor.

7 Tverskaya Street

Even if you don't have time to explore the length of Tverskaya Street, you can afford a quick stroll up the first block of this crucial Moscow artery, which extends straight north from Red Square. At the top of the first block, turn around and take in the view of the Kremlin and everything else you've seen so far.

8 Theater Square (Teatralnaya Ploshchad)

West of Tverskaya Street, along Okhotny Ryad, you'll first pass the State Duma (the lower house of parliament). Then the unforgettable facade of the Bolshoi Theater comes into view. At this writing, its pale pink portico is once again under renovation. If you can't squeeze in a performance, or if it is still closed for renovations, at least take a look at the miniature version of the theater's interior on display near the ticket office. For a reminder of the not-so-distant Soviet past, look across the fountained plaza in front of the Bolshoi at the statue across the street: It's Karl Marx, etched with the phrase PROLETARIAT OF THE WORLD UNITE.

9 Metropol ☕ ★★

For a quick pick-me-up or leisurely snack, settle into one of the deep armchairs of this cafe in the 19th-century hotel landmark on Revolution Square. Atmosphere is key here, so take a moment to wander the hotel lobby to admire chandeliers and Art Nouveau designs. Desserts are divine and tea is served with a ceremonial touch of the imperial age. Metropol Hotel, 1/4 Teatralny Proyezd; ✆ 499/270-1061.

10 The Arbat

Walk or take the metro from Ploshchad Revolutsii (behind the Engels statue) one stop to the Arbatskaya station. Follow the crowds and the kiosks and you'll end up at the Arbat, a pedestrian street packed with shops, cafes, bars, buskers, and street vendors. The souvenirs inside the shops are of better quality and usually have better prices than those outside. Sure, it's touristy, but locals love it, too. If you're feeling adventurous, explore the lanes that sprout from the Arbat; they once housed Russian literary and artistic giants. The Pushkin House near the other end of the street is a small museum, and the Vakhtangov Theater hosts drama, dance, and other performances. The Arbat is a perfect place to wrap up the day.

THE BEST OF MOSCOW IN 2 DAYS

Use your second day in Moscow to immerse yourself in Russian art at the Tretyakov Gallery, wander the canals of Zamoskvarechye, and explore the cathedrals and historic neighborhood of Kitai-Gorod. Reserve the evening for Pushkin Square and a fuller glimpse of Tverskaya Street, where you'll find more than enough dining and entertainment to keep you busy. *Note:* Make this a day when the Tretyakov is open (it's closed on Mon). *Start:* *Metro to Tretyakovskaya or Novokuznetskaya.*

1 Tretyakov Gallery (Tretyakovskaya Galereya) ★★★

This treasure-trove of Russian art traces the country's 1,200-year history, covering everything from the earliest Orthodox icons to the floating figures of Chagall and jarring images of socialist propaganda. The Vrubel Room is a haven of Art Nouveau whimsy; newcomers to works by this 19th-century artist never fail to be impressed. The guided tour in English is well worth it. See p. 114

2 Lavrushinsky Lane & Canal Fountains

This little pedestrian street heads north from the Tretyakov to a footbridge over the Vodootvodny Canal in a cozy part of town called Zamoskvarechye (see stop 4 on this tour). The Bolotnaya Square on the other side of the canal, with its statue of artist Ilya Repin, was a public execution site in the 16th and 17th centuries; now it's a favorite rest and play spot for local residents, within walking distance of major Moscow sights yet usually devoid of tourists.

3 Uncle Vanya 🍴 ★★

Artsy and accessible, this restaurant has an extensive menu of Russian comfort food throughout the day. Try the hot and cold soups, the meat or fruit dumplings, or just a good pot of tea. It has no real relation to Chekhov's play of the same name, but its alphabet place mats and bookshelves give it a literary feel. 20 Pyatnitskaya Ulitsa (entrance in courtyard); ℂ 495/232-1448.

4 Zamoskvarechye (Land South of the Moscow River)

This awkward name applies to the hump of land across the river from the Kremlin, a neighborhood where Ivan the Terrible sent his best guards to live while

Moscow in 2 Days

1 Tretyakov Gallery
2 Lavrushinsky Lane & Canal Fountains
3 Uncle Vanya
4 Zamoskvarechye
5 Cathedrals of Kitai-Gorod
6 Lubyanka
7 Pushkin Square
8 Café Pushkin
9 Tverskaya Street (long version)

fending off threats from the south. The one- and two-story architecture is uncluttered by office blocks and high-rises, making the area feel intimate and accessible even though it's at the center of modern Moscow. Pyatnitskaya Street boasts the most commerce, with plenty of cafes and some less touristy craft shops.

5 Cathedrals of Kitai-Gorod

Heading back across the Bolshoi Moskvaretsky Bridge toward Red Square, you'll arrive at the neighborhood of Kitai-Gorod. Once a bustling community of traders and nobles, its top sights today are the churches and merchants' houses along Varvarka Street, a showcase of Russian architecture from the 15th to 17th centuries. The adjacent streets house government ministries and agencies. See the walking tour on p. 125; the first five stops of the tour take you through the Kitai-Gorod neighborhood.

6 Lubyanka

No Russian responds indifferently to the dull yellow building overlooking Lubyanka Square—the headquarters of the KGB in Soviet times, and its successor, the FSB, today. Foreigners need not fret the way they used to. The imposing statue of Soviet secret police founder Felix Dzerzhinsky was torn down in 1991, and the KGB museum was even open to tourists for a while. The bald-looking plaza in front of the institution livens up a few times a year, when it hosts New Year's Eve concerts and other events. Take note of the small plaque off to the side of the square honoring those repressed by the Soviet regime (see p. 128).

7 Pushkin Square (Pushkinskaya Ploshchad)

Alexander Pushkin is Russia's favorite poet, and even though he died in 1837, his likeness oversees Muscovites' favorite meeting spot. While Pushkin Square throngs with activity all day, year-round, the statue of Pushkin himself retains an atmosphere of reverence. The McDonald's on the square was the world's largest when it opened in 1989, but it still wasn't big enough to accommodate the endless lines of people curious about the capitalist Big Mac. It's a good source of reliable restrooms. You can get here by taking the metro one stop from the Lubyanka to the Pushkinskaya station.

8 Cafe Pushkin 🍵 ★★

This is a prime way to treat yourself after a long day, while remaining in the mood of bygone Russian aristocracy. A three-story, post-Soviet creation made to look a century older, this Russian restaurant has cuisine as elegant as it is satisfying. Dressed-up versions of Russian staples such as sturgeon and *bliny* share the menu with more innovative items such as shellfish and avocado salad. 26a Tverskoi Bulvar; ✆ 495/739-0033.

9 Tverskaya Street (long version)

Evening is a great time to experience Moscow's main drag in full. Wrought-iron street lamps, monstrous TV screens, and neon signs advertising a planet of international brands illuminate the dark sky. On ground level, shops are open late, and sushi bars, coffee shops, and top-scale eateries—many of them busy 24 hours a day—line Tverskaya. You'll pass the columned red facade of City Hall, the statue of city founder Yuri Dolgoruky (a 12th-c. prince), the former Revolution Museum, and plenty of plaques indicating where Soviet-era dignitaries once lived. See chapters 5 and 8 for restaurant and nightlife options along Tverskaya.

THE BEST OF MOSCOW IN 3 DAYS

The luxury of a third day in Moscow is best enjoyed at a more leisurely pace. Spend the morning at Novodevichy Convent and Cemetery, a secluded spot that feels miles from the downtown rush. Then take a car or the metro to Gorky Park. After lunch, head to the Pushkin Museum of Fine Arts, and spend the evening on a bus tour that hits sights farther afield and wraps up the Moscow experience. ***Start:*** *Metro to Sportivnaya, then a 10-minute walk to the convent.*

1 Novodevichy Convent & Cemetery (Novodevichy Monastyr) ★★

This complex, nestled on a leafy peninsula overlooking the Moscow River, was built in the 16th century and housed many exiled or self-exiled royal wives, daughters, and lovers. Its cathedrals form a stunning window onto Russian architecture. The cemetery below holds the intricate and unusual graves of many of Russia's most famous and talented literary, artistic, musical, and political figures. See p. 107.

2 Gorky Park (Park Kultury i Otdkykha Imeni M. Gorkovo) ★

This is not Moscow's prettiest park or its greenest, but it is the most famous and the most lively. Ice sculptures and iced-over alleys for skating offer pleasure in winter, and concerts and children's festivals keep things lively in summer. The amusement park along the river includes a mock space shuttle that offers riders a chance to feel like they're blasting off. See p. 115.

3 Mama Zoya on the Water 🍽 ★★

This kitschy-looking boat-restaurant boasts some fine Georgian cuisine and a surprisingly homey atmosphere. Mama Zoya's original basement cafe was so popular that she branched out to this dock across from Gorky Park. Try Georgian specialties such as grilled lamb shashlyk or ground-beef kebabs, or the hearty red-bean-and-garlic *loblo* stew. On the docks across from 4/6 Frunzenskaya Naberezhnaya; ✆ 499/242-8550.

4 Pushkin Museum of Fine Arts ★★

This impressive collection of international art from the ancients to the present is often overshadowed by the Hermitage Museum, but the Pushkin is a masterpiece of its own. Don't miss the Impressionists and the controversial "trophy art"—works taken from European Jews by the Nazis, then later seized by victorious Soviet troops. The Museum of Private Collections across the street shows rotating exhibits of top quality and varying tastes. You can walk here from Gorky Park down picturesque Ostozhenka Street, or take the metro one stop from Gorky Park to Kropotkinskaya. See p. 114.

5 Christ the Savior Cathedral ★

This dominant feature of Moscow's skyline has a history as striking as its facade. First built over several decades in the 19th century, the massive cathedral was razed by Stalin in the 1930s and became a public swimming pool. Muscovites were chagrined when the popular pool was gutted in 1994, due to the mayor's decree that a bigger, better Christ the Savior Cathedral be erected in its place.

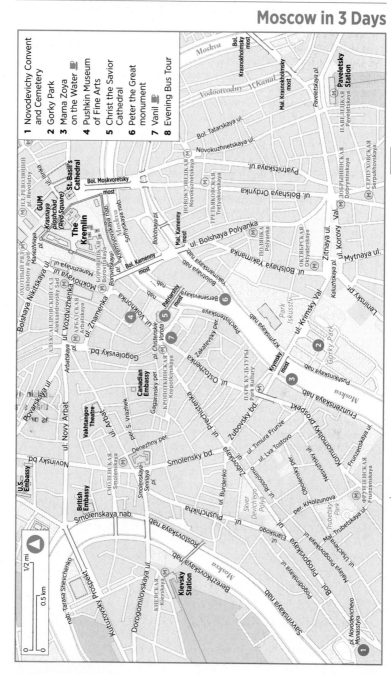

1 Novodevichy Convent
and Cemetery

2 Gorky Park

3 Mama Zoya
on the Water 🍴

4 Pushkin Museum
of Fine Arts

5 Christ the Savior
Cathedral

6 Peter the Great
monument

7 Vanil 🍴

8 Evening Bus Tour

Its newness is palpable, especially after the mystical and musty St. Basil's. See p. 107.

6 Peter the Great Monument

You don't have to cross the river to get a good look at this bronze tribute to Peter the Great; it's so enormous you can study it from the platform of Christ the Savior Cathedral. The oddly proportioned monument, to a czar who detested Moscow and built his own capital on the Baltic Sea, has remained controversial since its 1997 appearance. Sculptor Zurab Tsereteli perched the nautical Peter atop a ship on an island jutting into the Moscow River.

7 Vanil 💻 ★★

Pamper yourself in this sleek European-Asian restaurant that represents some of Moscow's finest and most adventurous cuisine. (It also serves steak and baked fish for the conservative diner.) The soaring ceilings and massive chandeliers seem built to the scale of the staggering Christ the Savior Cathedral across the street. 1 Ostozhenka; 𝄡 495/202-3341. See p. 89.

8 Evening Bus Tour ★★

By now you no longer need to get your bearings, but a bus tour is a great way to take a step back and see the city as a collaboration of remarkable sights. A tour is also a convenient way to reach more distant spots on Moscow's tourist map—those that from the city are little more than parts of a good view. Highlights to look for are Moscow State University in the Sparrow Hills, and Victory Park. If a bus tour isn't available, consider renting a car with a driver. Despite traffic that stays dense until as late as 8pm, evening is an ideal time for a tour because dusk hides the city's imperfections, while street lamps highlight its beauty. See "Organized Tours" in chapter 6.

WHERE TO STAY IN MOSCOW

M oscow has everything the discriminating hotel guest could dream of—for a price. The boom in Moscow hotel space since the end of the Communist era has focused almost entirely on luxury or business-class accommodations. Demand is so high for the scarce midrange hotels that they have little incentive to offer discounts or perks. Nonetheless, the major chains continue to expand into this hungry market, and lower-priced options are not far behind. And an increasing number are combining the historic flavor of particular neighborhoods with modern amenities, for an original and comfortable experience.

WHAT YOU'LL REALLY PAY

The prices quoted here are for hotels' rack rate, the maximum that it charges; it is, however, seriously unlikely that you'll end up paying that rate. You can typically find discounts of up to 20% for rooms when booking through the agencies listed on p. 75, or through websites such as hotels.com or expedia.com (see "Practical Information" at the end of this chapter for more tips, and don't miss the "Currency Confusion at Your Hotel" box on p. 74). During slow times, it's quite possible to obtain a room at an expensive property—say, the **National**—for the same rate as a more moderate one such as one of the Holiday Inns. And if you're the gambling type, you can bid for a room on Priceline.

Price Categories	
Very Expensive	$400 and up
Expensive	$200–$400
Moderate	$100–$200
Inexpensive	Under $100

Note: Quoted discount rates almost never include breakfast or hotel tax.

best MOSCOW HOTEL BETS

o **Best Historic Hotel:** Imperial Moscow, Soviet Moscow and modern Moscow converge in the **Hotel National,** perched at the pivot point between Red Square and the city's main thoroughfare. Vladimir Lenin made history after staying here, and a century of world leaders, writers and others have followed his footsteps. It's also in the avant-garde of discounting, so you don't have to be a president to land a room. See p. 60.

o **Best for Business Travelers:** In a city that tends to care more about luxury than practicality, the **Moscow Marriot Grand Hotel** is one of those rare places that provides all the services business travelers need—from top-grade translators to computer and legal advice—and makes you feel like royalty at the same time. Popular with major U.S. and European corporations for individual and group visits, it also has a formidable Sunday brunch where you're likely to meet someone who's made a fortune in modern Moscow. The other **Marriot hotels** in town are of similar quality. See p. 62.

o **Best for a Romantic Getaway:** Reserve the sauna or a massage for two at the secret hideout of a hotel called **Akvarel.** The top-floor rooms, though a bit pricier, harbor an especially intimate feel, like a luxury attic. Plush drapes help block out the early morning summer sun, and the cozy pastel breakfast room stays open late. Though it feels like a private retreat, it's just a hop from the 24-hour buzz of Tverskaya and clubs and restaurants for a night on the town. See p. 64.

o **Best Splurge:** All the superlatives today's Moscow has to offer are on the menu at the **Ritz-Carlton.** Personal shoppers, room fixtures formed out of precious metals, an exquisite wine list—take your pick. Despite the over-the-top design and amenities, it manages to feel classy and not brash. Guests are certain to spot international celebrities, such as supermodels or Hollywood producers, at the spa or in the penthouse lounge. See p. 60.

o **Most Relaxing Hotel:** For a truly peaceful experience in Moscow you have to leave the city limits to sleep—and you'll find no better bed than those in the **Holiday Inn Vinogradovo.** Try horseback riding or cross-country skiing on a quiet afternoon, before checking into the spa. It's a more upscale Holiday Inn than those found in many American cities, and has unusually large beds and rooms for Moscow standards. See p. 70.

o **Best Service:** Outside the highest-end hotels, the **East-West** is the place to answer your needs around the clock and guide you through the challenges of Russia. Smiles are rare on Moscow's streets so each one here is especially treasured. See p. 61.

o **Best Location:** The **Metropol** is as close as you can get to Red Square without being parked on the middle of its cobblestones. Across the street from the Bolshoi Theater and smack on Revolution Square, it's also at the heart of Moscow's 900-year-old history. The State Duma, or parliament, is a block away as are the Kremlin gates, too. The **National** and **Ritz Carlton** are similarly well-perched with a view on Red Square. See p. 57.

o **Best for Families:** The **Sheraton Palace** set the example for family services in a city in which hotels cater more to superstars and CEOs than toddlers. A children's playroom watched over by cheery, multilingual Russian grad students studying early childhood education is a particular perk. It's not cheap, however, so those on a budget are better off renting a short-term apartment. See p. 63.

o **Best Budget Hotel:** Nothing in Moscow today is truly cheap, but the **Suharevka Hotel** is a bargain for its location and comfortable if quirky rooms. It's homey and bustling with travelers immersing themselves in Moscow, whose advice you can seek for free. **Apartment rentals** are the next-best bargain. See p. 73.

- **Best Views:** To see the Kremlin in its full splendor, you need a bit of distance—so cross the river to the **Baltschug Kempinski** and drink up the panorama. While it's not the highest hotel in town, it's so well-placed that other immense Moscow edifices poke up on the horizon, too. See p. 68.

AROUND THE KREMLIN & RED SQUARE

Staying **around Red Square** puts you at Moscow's heart, and you'll pay for that convenience.

Best For: Travelers with little concern about money, or with limited time or mobility to traverse Moscow's vast scale to get to the Kremlin.

Drawbacks: The lack of hotels on a human scale and budget. It's also a neighborhood that never sleeps, so not one for those seeking a quiet getaway.

Very Expensive

Ararat Park Hyatt ★★★   Ararat is worth a visit just for the view from—and of—its top-floor atrium bar. Named after the mountain where Noah's Ark is believed to have landed, the hotel aims for grandeur and succeeds. Unlike its neighbors, the Metropol and the National, the Ararat inhabits a richly modern building with no claims to historical significance. It has all the services expected of a 21st-century, five-star hotel. There's nothing quiet or subtle about this patch of Moscow, with the Bolshoi Theater, Red Square, and the Kremlin just around the corner, and the haute couture boutiques of Tretyakovsky Proyezd across the street. The top-floor Conservatory lounge and bar offers snacks and cocktails, and its split-level hall is ideal for watching midnight sunsets in July. True to its name, the hotel has an Armenian-themed restaurant as well. (Mt. Ararat was in Armenia until Turkey subsumed it in 1915.)

4 Neglinnaya Ulitsa. www.moscow.park.hyatt.com. © **800/492-8804** or 495/783-1234. Fax 495/783-1235. 220 units. 16,500 rubles standard double; 46,000 executive suite; 75,000 winter garden suite with panoramic views of the Kremlin. AE, DC, MC, V. Metro: Kuznetsky Most or Lubyanka. **Amenities:** 3 restaurants; 2 bars; babysitting; concierge; executive-level rooms; health club; Jacuzzi; room service; sauna; smoke-free rooms; spa. *In room:* A/C, satellite TV, fridge, hair dryer, minibar, Wi-Fi.

Metropol ★   The Art Nouveau mosaic by Mikhail Vrubel that tops the Metropol's facade sets it apart in era and in style from other hotels of its class. Across the street from the Bolshoi Theater and with a view of the Kremlin, the Metropol is a historic and visual treasure. Even the elevators are exquisite: glass-and-wood chambers ringed with mosaics reflecting the building's exterior. The tearoom is a cozy alternative to the almost-too-opulent main dining hall. The rooms are compact, but several offer antique writing tables or armchairs. The Metropol counted author Leo Tolstoy and artist Kasimir Malevich among its guests before the Soviets took it over as offices. Though today's Moscow is a consumerist wonderland, the hotel faces a statue of Karl Marx in Revolution Square, and the Metropol's western wall is still etched with stylized letters reading: THE DICTATORSHIP OF THE PROLETARIAT IS READY TO FREE HUMANITY FROM THE YOKE OF CAPITAL.

1/4 Teatralny Proyezd. www.metropol-mosco.ru/en. © **499/501-7841.** Fax 499/501-7810. 362 units. From 16,500 rubles double; 31,000 rubles executive suite; 77,000 rubles presidential suite. AE, DC, MC, V. Metro: Teatralnaya or Lubyanka. **Amenities:** 3 restaurants; nightclub; concierge; executive-level rooms; health club; Jacuzzi; room service; sauna; smoke-free rooms; spa; Wi-Fi. *In room:* A/C, TV w/ satellite, fridge, hair dryer, minibar.

Where to Stay in Moscow

Akademicheskaya **36**
Akvarel **17**
Ararat Park Hyatt **21**
Arbat **14**
Baltschug Kempinski **32**
Belgrade **12**
Budapest **19**
Cosmos **24**
Domodedovo Airport Hotel **35**
East-West **9**
G&R Hostels **34**
Galina's Flat **29**
Globus **24**
Golden Apple **7**
Golden Ring **13**
Hilton Moscow Leningradskaya **26**
Holiday Inn Lesnaya **2**
Holiday Inn Vinogradovo **3**
Izmailovsky Hotel Complex (Alpha, Vega, Gamma-Delta) **27**
Marco Polo Presnja **8**
Metropol **20**

TVERSKAYA STREET AND ENVIRONS

MOSCOW ZOO (ZOOPARK)

U.S. Embassy

British Embassy

Vakhtangov Theatre

Canadian Embassy

ARBAT DISTRICT

The Kremlin

Bolshoi Theatre

Kievsky Station

Byelorussky Station

0   1/2 mi
0   0.5 km

Common terms and abbreviations
naberezhnaya/nab......Embankment
most.................................Bridge
ploshchad/pl...............Square or plaza
prospekt/pr.....................Avenue
sad.....................................Garden
ulitsa/ul............................Street

Moscow Marriott Grand Hotel **6**	Radisson Slavyanskaya **11**
Moscow Marriott Royal Aurora **18**	Ritz Carlton **16**
National **15**	Savoy **22**
Novotel **1**	Sheraton Palace **4**
Ozerkovskaya **33**	Sovietsky Hotel **1**
Pekin **5**	Sretenskaya **23**
Polesye **31**	Suharevka Hotel **28**
President Hotel **38**	Sverchkov **30**
Radisson Royal Hotel Moscow **10**	Varshava **37**
	Volga Hotel **25**

FAMILY-friendly HOTELS

Because Moscow's hotel scene still caters more to the business visitor than the school-age one, family-friendly details are not yet par for the course. That is changing gradually, led by such chains as **Marriott,** whose three Moscow hotels offer baby-friendly rooms complete with crib, toys, bottles, and sterilizers. **Sheraton Palace** boasts a children's room where clowns entertain kids during mealtimes, and which hosts special holiday events for kids. The **Cosmos** has a bowling alley with croquet-sized balls great for kids' hands, as well as game rooms and a theater that often shows kid-friendly fare. Farther outside town, **Holiday Inn Vinogradovo** offers boat trips, horseback riding, and cross-country skiing in the surrounding countryside. Babysitting services are increasingly available, even if they're not listed on the hotels' official websites and brochures. It's worth a call to check in advance.

Ritz-Carlton ★★★ The city's poshest hotel opened in 2007 in the place of the razed Soviet-era Intourist behemoth, whose drab structure had come in increasingly stark contrast with the vibrant, upscale Tverskaya Street. The Ritz's classicist-style building is topped with a high-tech glass structure that boasts a spacious roof terrace overlooking the Kremlin. Sumptuous interiors include brocaded silk bedspreads and upholstery, rich draperies substantial enough to block out the 4am summer sun, marble countertops, and Murano glass lampshades. All rooms are spacious, with large windows, and suites include such touches as gold-encrusted globes and ebony and ivory chess sets. Bathrooms are roomy and lined with every amenity.

3-5 Tverskaya Ulitsa. www.ritzcarltonmoscow.ru. © **495/225-8888.** Fax 495/225-8400. 334 units. From 17,000 rubles standard double; 150,000 rubles Carlton suite. AE, DC, MC, V. Valet parking and underground parking garage. **Amenities:** 2 restaurants; 2 bars; concierge; health club and spa w/indoor pool, hot tub, sauna, and steam rooms; room service; barrier-free access for travelers w/disabilities. *In room:* A/C, satellite TV, CD/DVD player, hair dryer, minibar, free Wi-Fi.

Expensive

Hotel National ★★ The National is a superbly located and impeccably designed spot from which to discover Moscow. Built in 1903, it housed aristocrats and their arch-enemy Vladimir Lenin, who stayed here (the exact room number is debatable, a victim of Soviet revisionist history) as he imagined a Communist revolution. Perched on the edge of Tverskaya Street, the National looks directly at Red Square and the throbbing heart of the capital. Rooms are decorated in dark lacquered woods and empire armchairs, and even the trouser presses blend with the decor. Hotel marketing materials admit that the single and double rooms are "not large," though they make good use of limited space. A break in the mezzanine cafe will make you feel pampered even if you're not staying here. Clientele includes foreign investors and "new Russian" regulars who never glance at price tags, though the National is increasingly reaching out to tourists through online discounts.

15/1 Mokhovaya Ulitsa. www.national.ru. © **495/258-7000.** Fax 495/258-7100. 201 units. From 8,100 rubles standard double; 47,000 rubles two-room suite with Kremlin view; 70,500 presidential suite. AE, DC, MC, V. Metro: Okhotny Ryad or Teatralnaya. **Amenities:** 2 restaurants; mezzanine cafe; bar/lounge; babysitting; concierge; executive-level rooms; health club; Jacuzzi; small heated indoor pool; room service; sauna; smoke-free rooms; spa. *In room:* A/C, TV w/satellite, fridge, hair dryer, minibar, free Wi-Fi.

Savoy ★★ Tucked on an ever-livening block of cafes and boutiques behind the Bolshoi Theater, the Savoy is irreproachable. Built in 1912, it retains a privileged atmosphere originally designed to serve visiting aristocrats from St. Petersburg and abroad. By the standards of Moscow's over-the-top luxury hotels, this one is relatively small and modest—and that's part of its appeal. It offers top-notch services, a renowned French-Russian restaurant with an unforgettable crème brûlée, and a landmark lobby bar that envelops guests in rococo decor and is favored by Russia's political elite.

3/6 Rozhdestvenka. www.savoy.ru/en. ℃ **495/620-8500.** Fax 495/620-8665. 70 units. From 15,000 rubles standard double; 21,600 business suite; 77,000 rubles Grand Suite. AE, DC, MC, V. Metro: Teatral-naya, Kuznetsky Most, or Lubyanka. **Amenities:** 2 restaurants; bar and lounge; concierge; executive-level rooms; health club; Jacuzzi; indoor heated pool; room service; sauna; smoke-free rooms; spa. *In room:* A/C, TV w/satellite, fridge, hair dryer, minibar.

TVERSKAYA & ENVIRONS

Tverskaya Street is Moscow's main artery and commercial lifeline, so staying around here is guaranteed to be convenient.

Best For: Business travelers and families who can afford high-quality service and amenities, and those who want stores, museums, and restaurants close at hand.

Drawbacks: It's close enough to the main tourist sites to remain out of budget range for many visitors, and the street is clogged with traffic most weekdays.

Expensive

East-West Hotel ★★ More like a well-appointed embassy than a hotel, the East-West is a favorite for its central location on a leafy boulevard and its aristocratic ambience, as well as its personal service. Occupying a small former estate, it's close to the action and to a pleasant playground and paths along Tverskoi Bulvar, but it's set back enough to feel tranquil, even rarefied. Rooms have generous floor space and are decorated with antique or faux-antique bureaus and bathroom fixtures. Mattresses are unusually firm. The hotel is too small for groups, which makes it popular with tourists traveling on their own. Discounts are widely available.

14 Tverskoi Bulvar, building 4. www.eastwesthotel.ru. ℃ **495/232-2857.** Fax 495/956-3027. 25 units. From 7,000 rubles double; from 12,000 rubles suite. Weekends and holidays 7,200 rubles double; from 14,000 rubles suite. AE, MC, V. Metro: Pushkinskaya. **Amenities:** Restaurant; bar; room service; sauna. *In room:* TV w/satellite, fridge, free Wi-Fi.

Holiday Inn Lesnaya ★★ The hotel scene has finally expanded into this up-and-coming district of Moscow, at the upper end of Tverskaya just beyond the Garden Ring Road. Holiday Inn's first Moscow venture was a resort-type facility outside city limits. The Lesnaya, opened in 2005, is a much more convenient, though much less green, option. Its meeting rooms attract business visitors, but its overall range of services makes it a tourist- and family-friendly option as well. Guest rooms are rather large and more luxurious—and expensive—than those in many Holiday Inns in the United States. The Lesnaya is one of the few Moscow hotels offering rooms that are fully wheelchair accessible.

15 Lesnaya Ulitsa. www.holidayinn.com. ℃ **495/783-6500.** 800-80-800-800. Fax 495/225-8281. 301 units. From 7,000 rubles double; 13,400 rubles executive suite. AE, DC, MC, V. Metro: Belorusskaya. **Amenities:** Restaurant; concierge; executive-level rooms; health club; room service; rooms for those w/ limited mobility; smoke-free rooms; free Wi-Fi in lobby. *In room:* Satellite TV, fridge, hair dryer, minibar, Internet 885 rubles per day.

FOREIGNER tax

Price lists are a dizzying affair in Russia. After you've figured out what currency is being quoted (see the box "Currency Confusion at Your Hotel," at the end of this chapter), the most perplexing part for visitors from capitalist economies is that most museums and some older hotels still charge foreigners more than they charge Russians. This is a leftover from Soviet days, when Soviet citizens enjoyed deep subsidies to offset low salaries. The newer hotels, and everything in the "Expensive" range and up, do not employ this practice and charge all clients the same regardless of citizenship. Some hotels, however, still offer lists that include:

- rates for Russian citizens
- rates for citizens of the "near abroad" or the Commonwealth

of Independent States (basically a discount for friendly ex-Soviet states)

- rates for everyone else

It's no use protesting this system. If it's any consolation, Russians staying in such facilities often suffer worse service than international (and higher-paying) guests.

In addition, you'll find different prices depending on how upgraded the room is or how recent the renovations are. These rates are often euphemistically labeled, such as "tourist" rate for the newer rooms and "standard" rate for the older ones. Don't hesitate to ask to clear up any confusion.

Marco Polo Presnja ★   The Marco Polo is one of Moscow's most coveted places to stay. Its regular clients, often from foreign companies, are fiercely loyal and keep many of its rooms occupied year-round, so book early and check for discounts. The leafy neighborhood between the Boulevard Ring and the Garden Ring is ideal for strolling, and nearby Malaya Bronnaya Street offers several unusual shopping and dining finds you won't encounter on the city's main drags. The main attraction nearby is the park at **Patriarch's Ponds** (p. 117). Despite the hotel's relatively modest size, its rooms, bathrooms, closets, and corridors are spacious and airy. Room designs vary, but all are modern and subtly decorated, making good use of natural light. In case of emergency, the private, international-standard European Medical Center is right next door.

9 Spiridonevsky Pereulok. www.presnia.ru/eng. ✆ **499/244-3631.** Fax 495/626-5402. 70 units. From 7,000 rubles double; from 12,000 rubles suite. AE, DC, MC, V. Metro: Pushkinskaya, Tverskaya, or Mayakovskaya. **Amenities:** 2 restaurants; bar and lounge; concierge; executive-level rooms; sauna. *In room:* A/C, TV w/satellite and pay movies, fridge, hair dryer, minibar, free Wi-Fi.

Moscow Marriott Grand Hotel ★★   Conveniently located just a mile away from the Kremlin, Marriott Grand has been popular among business executives and Western officials and frequently held international conferences. Many central attractions are easily walkable, and there are plenty of restaurants and cafes for all tastes. All rooms are spacious and tastefully decorated with some Art Deco canvases and carvings. Another hotel of the chain, Marriott Tverskaya, is located a bit further down the same street, and the third one, Marriott Royal Aurora, is near the Bolshoi Theater.

26/1 Tverskaya Street. www.marriott.com. ✆ **888/236-2427** or 495/937-0000. Fax 495/937-0001. 386 units. From 8,000 rubles double, from 12,500 executive rooms, from 55,000 rubles suite. AE, DC, MC, V. Metro: Pushkinskaya or Mayakovskaya. **Amenities:** 2 restaurants; bar; concierge; executive-level rooms; health club with indoor swimming pool; room service; sauna; smoke-free rooms; spa; Wi-Fi. *In room:* A/C, TV w/satellite, fridge, hair dryer, minibar, safe, free Wi-Fi.

Warning: Some hotels don't include the 18% VAT in their advertised prices, so make sure to check the final price before booking. Many don't include breakfasts, and standards change frequently. Always best to ask on check-in or before.

Sheraton Palace ★ ☺ A sleek modern hotel perched at the top of Tverskaya Street, the Sheraton offers little historic value but plenty of modern convenience. Its child-friendly weekend brunches are a key draw, with multilingual clowns and an activity room that allows parents to indulge in the all-included caviar and champagne and admire the ice sculptures that decorate the dining hall. Despite triple-paned windows, rooms facing Tverskaya still feel its 24-hour hum; those facing the courtyard are more tranquil but have a gloomy view of apartment blocks. The hotel's glass-and-chrome style may lack character, but it offers a refreshing relief from city grime. The Sheraton is still one of the few hotels in town with a real fitness center, including a small jogging track and aerobics classes. Spacious, sumptuous rooms offer various mattress styles upon request. Popular with the investor and luxury tourist classes, the Sheraton's attitude and prices are somewhat more upmarket than those of Sheratons in North America.

19 1st Tverskaya-Yamskaya Ulitsa. www.sheratonplace.ru/eng. ✆ **495/931-9700.** Sheraton 800/325-35353. Fax 495/931-9704. From 6,400 rubles double; 16,000 rubles junior suite. AE, DC, MC, V. Metro: Belorusskaya. **Amenities:** 3 restaurants; cafe; bar; babysitting; children's playroom; concierge; executive-level rooms; health club; Jacuzzi; room service; sauna; smoke-free rooms; free Wi-Fi. *In room:* A/C, TV w/satellite, fridge, hair dryer, minibar, free Wi-Fi.

Moderate

Peking ★ This lemon-colored confection is situated at the crossing of two major arteries: Tverskaya Street and the Garden Ring Road. A plethora of dining and nightlife options, including the Tchaikovsky Concert Hall across the street, are close by. Its windows are reinforced to keep out the traffic din, but courtyard-facing rooms are still preferable to street-facing ones. Named in honor of Sino-Soviet solidarity, the Peking fell into disrepair and Mafia hands in the 1990s. It has been undergoing gradual renovation in recent years. The new rooms cost about 30% more than their older counterparts but boast wider, firmer beds and calmer, sleeker decor; some even have bidets. All rooms are spacious by Russian standards but the older rooms suffer narrow creaky beds, chipped furniture, and flowery wallpaper that seems to have absorbed 3 decades of cigarette smoke and dust. The thugs who made the Peking notorious a decade ago have largely gone straight or elsewhere, and now the lobby is frequented by Russian and foreign businesspeople and tourists attracted by its location and reasonable prices.

5/1 Bolshaya Sadovaya Ulitsa. www.hotelpeking.ru/en. ✆ **495/650-0900.** 8-800-250-0550. Fax 495/650-0902. 90 units. 8,000 rubles double; from 12,000 rubles suite. AE, MC, V. Metro: Mayakovskaya. **Amenities:** 2 restaurants; cafes on each floor; nightclub and casino; concierge; room service; sauna. *In room:* A/C, TV w/satellite, fridge, Wi-Fi

PETROVKA & THE UKRAINIAN QUARTER

Historical buildings and quiet lanes fill **Petrovka and the nearby Ukrainian Quarter,** in contrast to the glare of Tverskaya.

Best For: Travelers looking for something a little different, willing to walk a bit and explore.

Nighttime Companionship

This guide includes no brothels or hotels that charge by the hour, but Russia's lax attitude toward prostitution can be noticeable even in otherwise good-quality hotels. This attitude has fed the demand for prostitutes by traveling businessmen, which in turn means that some hotels, eager to cater to this demographic, double as trysting locales and quietly ignore the sexual commerce in their lobby bars. The ordinary tourist is usually unaffected by this, but foreign men traveling alone may be surprised by a late-night phone call to their rooms offering "female company" for the night. If you make it clear you're not interested—it can't hurt to mention it to the reception desk—the solicitation will stop.

Drawbacks: The high-end hotels here remain too expensive for the locale, and the streets in the Ukrainian Quarter zigzag confusingly; don't forget your map when you're heading home.

Expensive

Akvarel ★★   This modern aquamarine building is so well hidden from the street that it feels remote, yet it's just around the corner from Moscow's top theaters and designer boutiques. The zone surrounding Akvarel was refashioned in the 1990s into a largely pedestrian district with new buildings that vaguely echo the pastel facades of 18th-century Moscow. The hotel, built in 2003, is purely 21st century in style, with a small lobby cafe perfect for perusing Moscow's English-language press over breakfast. It attracts business groups and tourists, and offers deep discounts through online travel agencies. Reflecting the hotel's name (*akvarel* means "pastel" in Russian), rooms are decked in pale blue, green, or peach and feel light and open (though few are truly spacious). Breakfast and VAT are included in the rates quoted below.

12 Stoleshnikov Proyezd, building 3. www.hotelakvarel.ru.© /fax **495/502-9430.** 33 units. From 11,00 rubles double; from 14,350 rubles suite. AE, DC, MC, V. Metro: Teatralnaya, Kuznetsky Most, or Lubyanka. Amenities: Restaurant; concierge; room service; smoke-free rooms. In room: A/C, TV w/satellite, fridge, hair dryer, minibar, free Wi-Fi.

Budapest ★★   A sturdy stone example of the imposing scale and solidity of Stalin-era architecture, the Budapest is slightly farther from the main streets but abuts several intriguing lanes most tourists never see. St. Peter Monastery up the hill is well worth a visit after your morning tea and *bliny*. The building was erected in 1876 as an apartment building, and became a hotel at the turn of the 20th century. It was named after Hungary's capital in the days of Socialist bloc solidarity, and has been under renovation for the past few years. In a neighborhood of federal and city government buildings, the Budapest still attracts official delegations as well as a lively tourist clientele. Rooms are discounted 20% Friday through Monday. The doormen are listless but the rest of the staff are eager to help. Fresh renovations added a pool, health club, and salon.

2/18 Petrovskiye Linii. www.hotel-budapest.ru/en/main. © **495/925-3050.** Fax 495/621-5290. 116 units. From 6,000 rubles double; from 7,500 rubles suite. AE, DC, MC, V. Metro: Teatralnaya or Kuznetsky Most. **Amenities:** Cafe; bar; concierge; room service;, Internet in business center 280 rubles per hr. *In room:* A/C, TV w/satellite, fridge, hair dryer, minibar.

Golden Apple ★   This is the contrast of today's Moscow epitomized: A shamelessly modern boutique hotel designed in bold strokes and shades, tucked inside a

19th century estate that once reportedly housed playwright Anton Chekhov. Despite its almost aggressive style and high official prices, the Golden Apple is fun and accessible. (Online discounts run as much as 80%.) Don't be scared off by the enormous apple in the lobby or the rooms' black curtains, good for blocking out the way-too-early midsummer sunrise. Frequented by well-off Russians and foreigners, it's a good place to start for a night on the town. Try the hookahs in the lounge and then ask the waitstaff where to head next. The surrounding streets have an ever-changing cafe scene (get a courtyard-facing room) and aren't far from Tverskaya's buzz. When you get home, you can vanish into the comfortably firm mattresses or thaw frosty feet on the heated bathroom floors. Angular oak furnishings, Philippe Starck bath fixtures, and apple-themed carpets complete this funky experience.

11 Malaya Dmitrovka. www.goldenapple.ru/en. ⓒ **495/980-7000.** Fax 495/980-7001. 92 units. From 5,300 rubles double. AE, MC, V. Metro: Pushkinskaya. Amenities: Restaurant; bar; concierge; health club; Jacuzzi; sauna; spa; room service. In room: A/C, satellite TV, hair dryer, minibar, Wi-Fi.

Moscow Marriott Royal Aurora ★★   Perched a couple of blocks away behind the Bolshoi Theater, Royal Aurora offers an ideal location for exploring the historic heart of Moscow. Surrounding streets brim with some of the capital's best restaurants and nightclubs mixed with luxury boutiques. It serves an opulent breakfast buffet in an airy, 5-story-high atrium and proudly declares itself the only five-star hotel in Moscow with personalized butler service for each guestroom.

11/20 Petrovka St. www.marriott.com. ⓒ **495/937-1000.** Fax 495/937-1001. 231 units. From 11,500 rubles double, from 18,500 rubles suite, 100,000 rubles Ambassador suite. AE, DC, MC, V. Metro: Teatralnaya. **Amenities:** 3 restaurants; bar; concierge; health club; personalized butler for each room; sauna; smoke-free rooms; spa; Wi-Fi. In room: A/C, TV w/satellite, fridge, hair dryer, minibar, free Wi-Fi.

Sretenskaya ★★   The lush winter garden cafe is reason enough to stay in this hotel, or at least stop in for a drink. New but in the style of the 17th-century mansions that once lined this neighborhood, the two-story hotel is somewhat overpriced for its location, though online discounts are easy to find. The Sretenskaya offers a more intimate Russian experience than the chains, and has all the modern amenities. Adjacent Ulitsa Sretenka has plenty of shops and restaurants less frequented by the tourist crowds, and the neighboring lanes are full of old churches and architectural finds from past centuries—though no major tourist sights. The hotel is located between two metro stations, a good 10-minute walk to either one. Rooms are tastefully arranged with a combination of modern Scandinavian design and a few antiques. Russian and foreign executives are regulars at the Sretenskaya; tour groups are rare because it's so small.

15 Ulitsa Sretenka. www.hotel-sretenskaya.ru. ⓒ **495/933-5544.** Fax 495/933-5545. 38 units. From 7,500 rubles double; from 15,000 rubles suite; weekend discounts available. AE, DC, MC, V. Metro: Sukharevskaya or Turgenevskaya. **Amenities:** Restaurant; bar; concierge; health club; Jacuzzi; small indoor pool; room service; sauna. In room: A/C, TV w/satellite, fridge, hair dryer, minibar, Wi-Fi fees variable.

Moderate

Galina's Flat 🍴   This is among the most modest listings in this book and provides the most intimate way of seeing Russian life. As the name lays out, Galina is a woman renting out rooms in her apartment, with seven beds available in a historic neighborhood around Chistiye Prudy, or Clean Ponds. The downsides: It's cramped, in a fifth-floor walkup, and Galina smokes. Galina's place is a favorite with travelers of all ages looking for personal sightseeing advice, late-night chats over tea, and a decidedly different view of Moscow from the impersonal hotel lobbies found elsewhere. Reserve well in advance for the popular summer season. She's good about responding quickly to e-mail messages.

8 Ulitsa Chaplygina, apt 35. ℃ **495/621-6038.** www.galinasflathostel.com. 6 units. 400 rubles for a bed in a dormitory-style room; 1,000 rubles for a double room. AE, DC, MC, V. Metro: Chistiye Prudy. **Amenities:** Bath, kitchen; TV w/cable.

Polesye (Belarusian Embassy Hotel) An unexpected treasure in this neighborhood of crooked lanes and embassies, this renovated mansion enjoys a convenient yet quiet location and relatively reasonable prices. The building, built in 1780 by architect Matvei Kazakov, pioneer of Moscow Classicism, is among the perks the otherwise impoverished Belarusian government enjoys for its loyalty to Russia as other ex-Soviet republics have distanced themselves from Moscow. The rooms are modest and bear hints of Soviet nostalgia, with their standard-issue wallpaper and heavy dark wardrobes. Though it's connected to the embassy, the hotel is a commercial venture and most of the guests are businesspeople from neighboring countries. Despite the reputation of the Belarusian KGB, past guests insist the staff is more helpful than suspicious and that the ordinary tourist has nothing to fear.

17/6 Maroseika. ℃ **495/777-6622.** Fax 495/628-2827. www.embassybel.ru/embassy/hotel. 88 units. 190 euros double; 248 euros suite (prices pegged to euro). AE, DC, MC, V. Metro: Kitai-Gorod. **Amenities:** Restaurant and bar; cafes on each floor; concierge; sauna. *In room:* A/C, TV w/cable, fridge.

Sverchkov The Sverchkov should serve as an example to would-be Moscow hoteliers: a two-story, 18th-century mansion converted into a small hotel-hostel, tucked in a tranquil courtyard on a historic lane, next to a folk-art museum and within walking distance of Moscow's key sights. Unusually, it has three rooms set up hostel-style with space to accommodate up to 16 people. The downside of such a small place is that it's often full and its services are limited. The prices are rising faster than warranted, in response to demand and the dearth of similar options in the neighborhood. Avoid the run-down basement cafe. The restaurant upstairs is okay, but I recommend dining in the nearby Chistiye Prudy neighborhood. Guest rooms are clean, though some need remodeling—ask when you reserve whether the room has been renovated.

8 Sverchkov Pereulok, building 1. www.sverchkov-8.ru/en. ℃ **495/625-4978.** Fax 495/625-4436. 9 units. From 4,800 rubles standard double; 6,000 rubles suite. AE, DC, MC, V. Metro: Turgenevskaya or Kitai Gorod. **Amenities:** Restaurant; cafe-bar; sauna. *In room:* TV w/cable, fridge.

Volga Hotel ★★ 🔥 Apartment-style hotel accommodation hasn't caught on in Moscow and it's a great shame—and it makes the Volga all the more special. From the studios with eat-in kitchens to the five-room apartments, the prices are fair and options are broad. There are no notable sights nearby, and it's a 7-minute walk to the metro (but conveniently close to the American Medical Center). It's popular among economy-minded business travellers, but the big apartments are a great option if you're travelling in a group without an organized tour. Furniture is new and homey, either Ikea-like Scandinavian or country-style, and mattresses are mediocre but not punishing. The eager staff can point you to markets to fill up the kitchen and help make you feel at home in this often overwhelming city.

4 Bolshaya Spasskaya Ulitsa. Building 1. www.hotel-volga.ru. ℃ **495/783-9100.** 258 units. From 6,800 for studio-style apartment; from 8,400 rubles for 4-room apartment. MC, V. Metro: Sukharevskaya, Krasniye Vorota. Amenities: 2 restaurants; concierge; room service. In room: A/C, satellite TV, kitchen, hair dryer; free Wi-Fi.

ARBAT

The pedestrian **Arbat Street** is a magnet for tourists and Russian shoppers, and a reliable place to eat, pick up souvenirs, and people watch.

Best For: Travelers on a business account or looking for the view from skyscraper hotels that aren't allowed closer to the Kremlin.

Drawbacks: There are no good hotels right on the Arbat itself, and the far end of this neighborhood is a long walk from the stores and restaurants and the metro.

Expensive

Radisson Royal Hotel Moscow ★★ The second-tallest of Stalin's Seven Sisters neo-Gothic buildings dominating Moscow's landscape was built as Hotel Ukraine in 1953. It reopened as part of the Radisson group in 2010 after a three-year renovation. Perched on the bank of the Moscow River facing the Russian government headquarters, the 35-story tower offers top-of-the line amenities mixed with carefully retained Communist-era paintings and sculptures. It has several gourmet restaurants, including the capital's sole Iranian one, and offers its own fleet of yachts for river cruises. Rooms are spacious, tastefully decorated, and spotless.

2/1 Building 1, Kutuzovsky Prospekt. www.radisson.ru/royalhotel-moscow. ℭ **495/221-5555.** Fax: 495/411-0025. 497 units. From 10,000 rubles double; from 18,000 rubles suite. AE, DC, MC, V. Metro: Kievskaya. **Amenities:** 6 restaurants, 3 bars, lounge; concierge; executive-level rooms; health club; Jacuzzi; indoor pool; room service; sauna; smoke-free rooms. *In room:* A/C, TV w/satellite and pay movies, fridge, hair dryer, minibar, free Wi-Fi.

Radisson SAS Slavyanskaya ★ This pioneering U.S.-Russian joint venture set the standard when it opened in 1991 and remains a gleaming oasis in an otherwise dingy neighborhood. Bill Clinton stayed here on a visit when he was president. Its reputation suffered through several management disputes and the murder of its American cofounder in 1996, but the Slavyanskaya's shadiest days appear to have passed. Rooms are large and light and are frequently updated. The hotel's gallery of designer boutiques is still a prime spot for ogling Russia's nouveau riche and the prices they pay for underwear. The hotel has a full-size movie theater that shows American and other films in English, and the stone-paved hotel pool is a blissful escape from city grit. Across the street is a seven-story shopping mall to satisfy any last-minute or luxury need.

2 Europe Sq. www.radisson.ru/slavyanskayahotel-moscow. ℭ **800/333-3333** or 495/941-8020. Fax 495/941-8000. 410 units. From 6,200 rubles double; from 13,300 rubles suite. AE, DC, MC, V. Metro: Kievskaya. **Amenities:** 4 restaurants; bar; lounge; concierge; executive-level rooms; health club; Jacuzzi; indoor pool; room service; sauna; smoke-free rooms. *In room:* A/C, TV w/satellite and pay movies, fridge, hair dryer, minibar, free Wi-Fi.

Zolotoye Koltso (Golden Ring) ★ The entrance alone earns this hotel its "golden" epithet, with its blinding awnings and lobby fixtures (the name really refers to a ring of historic and religious cities north of Moscow). It's one of Moscow's few executive-level hotels that's not part of a chain. The Golden Ring caters more to discriminating Russian clients and their often opulent tastes than to the ordinary tourist. Still, it has a range of room styles and standards, and the decor grows calmer as the prices drop. The hotel towers over the Moscow River and Smolenskaya Square and is nearly adjacent to the Arbat pedestrian zone. The sleepier district of once-prestigious residential blocks behind the hotel is perfect for a quiet tour of "real-life"

Moscow. Guest rooms are spacious and fully equipped; suites include bidets. Look for online discounts or group tours that stay here. Many of the rooms enjoy broad views of the city and/or the river.

5 Smolenskaya Ploshchad. www.hotel-goldenring.ru. ☎ **495/725-0100.** Fax 495/725-0101. 293 units. From 9,000 rubles double; from 11,000 rubles suite. AE, DC, MC, V. Metro: Teatralnaya, Kuznetsky Most, or Lubyanka. **Amenities:** 4 restaurants; 2 bars; concierge; executive-level rooms; health club; Jacuzzi; room service; sauna; smoke-free rooms; spa. *In room:* A/C, TV w/satellite, fridge, hair dryer, minibar, free Internet via Ethernet or Wi-Fi.

Moderate

Arbat ★★   This 1960s hotel is a rare example of good quality, relatively good price, and location concentrated in one place. On a calm street near the commerce of the Arbat and the Garden Ring, the hotel's only downside is the renovation noise as rooms are gradually upgraded. Ask for a room away from the construction. Until the upgrade is finished, the hotel offers a range of room standards and prices, from a spare unrenovated room with a single bed to suites with new leather couches and bidets. Visiting delegations, foreign and Russian, often stay here, taking up many rooms, but it's large enough that it almost always has space available for individual visitors. Rates include breakfast and VAT; it's definitely worth seeking out discounts.

12 Plotnikov Pereulok. www.president-hotel.ru/arbat/index. ☎ **499/271-2801.** Fax 495/271-2996. 104 units. From 7,500 rubles double; from 11,500 rubles suite. AE, DC, MC, V. Parking 330 rubles per day. Metro: Smolenskaya. **Amenities:** Restaurant; bar; concierge; executive-level rooms; room service; smoke-free rooms; free Wi-Fi in lobby. *In room:* A/C, TV w/satellite, fridge.

Belgrade ★   A sister tower facing Zolotoye Koltso across the square offers similar views of the Moscow River and the spires of the Foreign Ministry and has different levels of accommodations and good quality for the money and location. It's around the corner from the Arbat and all the dining and shopping that the pedestrian street has to offer. Gradual renovations mean that modernized rooms (called "tourist" class) are larger, air-conditioned, and have fresher carpeting, brighter lights, and fewer plumbing issues than the older ones (called "standard" class). Don't miss the generous breakfast (1,000 rubles). Service can be stiff, but the hotel is tourist-friendly overall. It's popular enough with business visitors to offer all the essential services that executives demand, but you can get individualized service, too—it doesn't feel like a conference center.

8 Smolenskaya Ulitsa. www.hotel-belgrad.ru. ☎ **499/248-1643.** Fax 499/248-2814. 235 units. From 5,300 rubles double; from 11,000 rubles suite. AE, MC, V. Metro: Smolenskaya. **Amenities:** Restaurant; bar and lounge; room service; free Wi-Fi in lobby. *In room:* A/C, TV w/satellite and pay movies, minibar.

SOUTH OF MOSCOW RIVER

Venturing **south of the Moscow River** and the Kremlin opens a new horizon of galleries, craft stores, and up-and-coming restaurant options.

Best For: Those curious about Russian history or art, and with good walking shoes. Price ranges vary more broadly here than near Red Square.

Drawbacks: Some hotels aren't near enough commerce or transport, and there's less signage in English than you'll find closer to the tourist sites.

Very Expensive

Baltschug Kempinski ★★★   The Baltschug led the post-Soviet transformation of this district across the Moscow River from the Kremlin. Its pristine, buttercup-yellow facade immediately altered the neglected neighborhood of canals and abandoned churches. The Baltschug's top-floor suites have housed presidents and famous visitors, including pop stars such as the late Michael Jackson. It's also a favorite of television crews who use its Kremlin-facing rooms for stand-ups with St. Basil's Cathedral in the background. Commerce in the immediate vicinity is limited but growing. Just over the bridge is Red Square and its attendant activity; the bohemian bustle of Pyatnitskaya Street spreads out in the other direction, to the south. The guest rooms are relatively large, modern, and subtly appointed. Don't miss the sumptuous brunch of pre-revolutionary Russian delicacies and all the caviar you could want.

1 Ulitsa Balchug. www.kempinski.com. © 495/287-2000. Fax 495/287-2002. 232 units. From 9,500 rubles double; from 33,000 rubles executive suite; from 70,000 rubles design suite. AE, DC, MC, V. Metro: Teatralnaya, Kuznetsky Most, or Lubyanka. **Amenities:** 3 restaurants; 2 bars; babysitting; children's center; concierge; executive-level rooms; health club; Jacuzzi; indoor heated pool; room service; 2 saunas; smoke-free rooms; spa; free Wi-Fi for 20 min. In room: A/C, TV w/satellite, fridge, hair dryer, free Internet, minibar.

President Hotel The elegant red-brick complex looks at first like a government building, an impression fueled by the rigorous security screening at the entrance. That's no accident, since the President Hotel was designed at the Communist leadership's request in 1982 for international negotiations and party meetings. Its guests reflect whatever conference is underway: oil executives, political scientists, environmental groups. It can be hard for individual tourists to get "approved" for space, so check well in advance if you're interested. The hotel is rather removed from the top tourist sites, but it is near Gorky Park and the Central House of Artists, Moscow's chief modern art museum. Just behind the hotel, toward the Moscow River, is an unusual collection of deposed statues of Lenin and other fallen Soviet heroes (see the review of Art MUSEON on p. 110). Guest rooms lack color but are well-maintained and spacious. Breakfast and VAT are included in the rate.

24 Bolshaya Yakimanka Ulitsa. www.president-hotel.ru. © 499/271-2800. Fax 499/271-2858. 208 units. From 9,000 rubles double; from 12,000 rubles suite. AE, DC, MC, V. Metro: Polyanka or Oktyabrskaya. **Amenities:** 2 restaurants; bar and lounge; concierge; health club w/personal trainers; room service; presidential rooms; sauna. In room: A/C, TV w/satellite, fridge, hair dryer, Internet 300 rubles per hr.

Moderate

Akademicheskaya ★ 🔖 This hotel lacks grandeur but offers everything else a hotel should: efficient service, clean rooms, and (relatively) reasonable prices. Ask for an upgraded room if they're available; the price isn't that much higher than that of an older room, but the beds are larger and firmer, the bathrooms roomier, and the windows better at keeping out street noise. The older rooms are still a fair value for the money. The corridors are lined with photos of renowned academics, some of whom have stayed at the Akademicheskaya. Scientific conferences still sometimes use the hotel, and an increasing number of tourists are discovering its value. The immediate vicinity has plenty of low-budget commerce. Most major sights require a trip on the metro, which is just across the street. Gorky Park is down the hill, and the stirring statue of Lenin on nearby October Square, one of the few left standing, warrants a viewing.

1 Donskaya Ulitsa. © 495/959-8157. Fax 495/988-8098. 277 units. From 5,400 rubles double; from 7,000 rubles suite. MC, V. Metro: Oktyabrskaya. **Amenities:** Restaurant; bar; concierge; Internet in business center 100 rubles per hr.; sauna. In room: TV w/satellite, fridge.

Ozerkovskaya ★★ 🏊 A welcome addition to the hotel scene south of the Moscow River, the Ozerkovskaya occupies a new brick building set off from the road along one of the canals in the picturesque Zamoskvarechye. Eager staff and cozy yet spacious rooms make the Ozerkovskaya one of Moscow's best hotels in this category. Run by the Central Tourism and Rest Council, whose other facilities are mostly in the countryside, this hotel feels a bit like a country inn. Attic rooms are especially appealing, with skylights in the slanted ceilings and more floor space than below. Firm, queen-size beds and new hardwood floors add to the hotel's appeal. Its location, deep in a residential neighborhood, is not exactly central, but it's certainly quiet. Tretyakov Gallery can be reached on foot; and the Paveletskaya metro station is about a 10-minute walk away. Note the curious neighborhood landscaping, with old tires used as planters and candy-colored bowling balls topping fence posts. Rates include VAT and breakfast.

50 Ozerkovskaya Naberezhnaya, building 2. www.cctr.ru/ozerkovskava.php. ✆ **495/959-2334.** Fax 495/951-9753. 27 units. From 4,750 rubles double; 6,300 rubles suite. AE, DC, MC, V. Metro: Paveletskaya. **Amenities:** Restaurant and bar; executive-level rooms; health club w/very small pool; room service; sauna. *In room:* TV w/satellite, hair dryer, kitchen, minibar, free Wi-Fi.

Varshava (Warsaw) Improved service could make the Varshava a top-value locale. It's still in a decent location, with modern rooms and reasonable rates. The main challenge is the staff's reluctance to speak English, but informational material in several languages is available in the lobby. Though the hotel's name (left over from the days when Poland was part of the Soviet bloc) and service are outdated, the guest rooms offer plain Scandinavian-style furniture in primary colors and none of the patterned wallpaper of Soviet days. Most bathrooms have showers only. International and Russian business travelers often stay here. The hotel is next to the Oktyabrskaya metro station and up the street from Gorky Park. The restaurant on the eighth floor has a rather Mafiosi feel, though the breakfast hall is pleasant. A buffet breakfast is included in the price.

2/1 Leninsky Prospekt. www.hotelwarsaw.ru. ✆ **499/238-8908.** Fax 499/238-9639. 136 units. From 6,100 rubles double; from 8,100 rubles suite. AE, DC, MC, V. Metro: Oktyabrskaya. **Amenities:** Restaurant; bar; health club; sauna. *In room:* TV, fridge, Internet 70 rubles per hr.

OUTSIDE THE GARDEN RING

Most of Moscow's hotels—and all of the truly affordable ones—lie outside the Garden Ring Road.

Best For: Anyone without a hefty expense account and ready to take the Metro to get downtown.

Drawbacks: The distance from the Kremlin and other sites is limiting if you take a taxi or car and get stuck in traffic.

Expensive

Holiday Inn Vinogradovo ★ ☺ This resort-type facility is unlike anything else Moscow has to offer. Well-removed from the city, it's tucked in a forest 4km (2½ miles) beyond the bypass marking the city limits, not too far from Sheremetevo International Airport. The free shuttle to and from town takes a while but makes the hotel feel less remote. The plus side of such a distant locale is the availability of outdoor amenities unheard-of at other Moscow hotels: horseback riding, sledding, and cross-country skiing in winter; watersports on a nearby lake in summer. This makes it a big draw for families traveling with children. The rooms are situated around a central courtyard, but better to ask for a lake- or church-facing room. Guest rooms and bathrooms are generous, and some doubles offer two double beds instead of two singles— a rare luxury in Russia. Kids eat free. Pets are allowed.

Dmitrovskoye Shosse. www.himv.ru. 📞 **495/937-0670.** Fax 495/937-0672. 154 units. From 3,800 rubles double; from 9,000 rubles suite. AE, DC, MC, V. 4km (2½ miles) north of Moscow Ring Rd. along Dmitrovskoye Shosse (visible from the hwy.). **Amenities:** 2 restaurants; 2 bars; executive-level rooms; health club; indoor pool; room service; sauna; smoke-free rooms. *In room:* TV w/satellite, fridge, free Wi-Fi.

Hilton Moscow Leningradskaya ★★

The stone-layer-cake building itself is reason enough to stay in the Leningradskaya, renovated in 2008 by Hilton from the cellars to the soaring spire. It's one of the strange and stunning "Seven Sisters" of Stalin-era Gothic architecture (see p. 24 for historical background), and while it's not central, it's around the corner from the train station that takes you to or from St. Petersburg—and that gives the hotel its nostalgic name. The taupe-and-beige rooms are big enough to dance in, thanks to generous Soviet designers, and beds are queen- or even king-size, a rarity in Russia and a draw for American business and leisure travellers. Most have a separate shower and bath, and the hotel's height allows broad views from pretty much anywhere. Be sure to check out the ballroom, its inlaid ceilings and gilded gates teetering between opulence and kitsch. Deep discounts are common, and suites are not worth the sharply higher price. The Leningradskaya is well-equipped for kids but lacks any family-friendly food options on the premises.

21/40 Kalanchevskaya Ulitsa. www.hilton.com. 📞 **495/627-5550.** Fax 495/627-5551. 220 units. From 8,500 rubles double; from 16,500 rubles suite. AE, DC, MC, V. Metro: Leningradskaya. Amenities: Restaurant; cafe-bar; babysitting; concierge; health club; room service; sauna; spa. *In room:* A/C, satellite TV, fridge, hair dryer; Wi-Fi.

Sovietsky Hotel ★

Everything about the hotel is big: The 12-foot-plus ceilings, the malachite columns, the Art Nouveau chandeliers, the regal corridors built on a space-is-no-object scale. The guest rooms have relatively generous floor space and seem even bigger because of the high ceilings. The Sovietsky was built in the 1950s on the site of a legendary restaurant, **Yar** (p. 93), there for more than a century. It fell into disrepair as the country that it was named after collapsed, then launched massive renovations. It's now increasingly popular with business and pleasure travelers, Russian and international. The room decor remains largely stuck in the Soviet era, with clashing flowery prints on wallpaper, curtains, bedspreads, and carpets. The restaurant is worth a tour to glimpse the wall-to-wall-to-ceiling frescoes. The summer terrace in the courtyard is a calmer place to dine. Pets are accepted, and all rooms now have air-conditioning, still rare in Russia.

32/2 Leningradsky Prospekt. www.sovietsky.ru. 📞 **495/960-2000.** Fax 495/250-8003. 100 units. From 6,080 rubles double; from 9,600 rubles suite. AE, DC, MC, V. Free guarded parking. Metro: Dinamo. **Amenities:** Restaurant (plus summer terrace dining); 2 bars; nightclub; lounge; children's center; concierge; health club; room service; sauna; free Wi-Fi in lobby. *In room:* A/C, TV w/satellite, fridge, hair dryer.

Moderate

Alpha This is one of the hotels in the **Izmailovsky Hotel Complex,** a collection of adjacent, nearly identical hotel towers that were originally under single ownership as Moscow's biggest hotel, with more than 8,000 rooms. Now they are four separate entities named after letters of the Greek alphabet. I've included three of the hotels in this section; the fourth hotel, the Beta, is in such disrepair that I don't recommend it. The complex is far from the city center but right next to a metro station—and to the biggest outdoor crafts and souvenir bazaar in town, the renowned Izmailovsky Market (see chapter 7 for shopping hints). The drab 28-story towers are linked by terraced concrete plazas with fountains in the summer, a design that seemed futuristic when they were built in the 1980s but now seems rather bleak. The Alpha is closest to the metro and the most garish of the complex's four hotels. Its labyrinthine lobby clearly posts its rates on a huge board and harbors a sushi bar.

71 Izmailovskoye Shosse. www.alfa-hotel.ru. (C) **499/166-4602.** Fax 499/166-4601. 945 units. From 2,700 rubles double; from 6,200 rubles suite. AE, MC, V. Metro: Izmailovsky Park. **Amenities:** 3 restaurants; cafe; 2 bars; concierge; health club; room service; sauna. *In room:* TV w/satellite, fridge, free Wi-Fi.

Best Western Vega Hotel   The Vega became the world's largest Best Western when the international chain added it to its network in 2011. Originally designed as the best part of the Izmailovsky Hotel Complex (see also listings for the Alpha and Gamma-Delta hotels), it has more amenities and snootier staff than its neighbors, though externally they appear similar. Rooms are compact but recently renovated and decorated in taupe and other soft neutral tones. The nightclub attracts some dubious figures after midnight. While well out of town, it's quite close to the metro, and has all the mainstream services Best Western provides.

71 Izmailovskoye Shosse, building 3. www.bestwestern.com. (C) **800/780-7234** or 495/956-0506. 966 units. From 3,300 rubles double; from 4,950 rubles suite. AE, DC, MC, V. Metro: Izmailovsky Park. **Amenities:** 5 restaurants; 2 bars; concierge; Jacuzzi; room service; sauna. *In room:* Cable TV in all rooms, hair dryer in some rooms, minibar, free Wi-Fi.

Cosmos ★★ ☺   This sweeping, semicircular structure looks down over the showcase **All-Russian Exhibition Center** (p. 117) that, like the hotel, was built to shameless Soviet scale. Size does matter at the Cosmos: 25 floors, more than 1,700 rooms, 9 restaurants. Built for the 1980 Olympics, it is back in demand among foreigners of all nationalities. The style is late Soviet, where practicality trumps aesthetics. Endless corridors lead to basic rooms, most of which have views of large swaths of Moscow—though not its most picturesque. Guest rooms and bathrooms are surprisingly compact. Location is the major drawback. Though the metro is nearby, it takes a good 5 minutes just to walk up the Cosmos's long driveway, and the metro ride to the center of town takes 20 minutes. Bonuses include water aerobics, a children's pool with water slides, and a bowling alley. Breakfast and VAT are included in the room rate.

150 Prospekt Mira. www.hotelcosmos.ru. (C) **495/234-1206.** Fax 495/234-2463. 1,700 units. From 3,750 rubles double; from 6,150 rubles suite. AE, DC, MC, V. Metro: VDNKh. **Amenities:** 5 restaurants; 2 cafes; 2 bars; nightclub; lounge; casino; babysitting; children's center; concierge; health club; Jacuzzi; 2 indoor pools; room service; sauna; spa; concert hall. *In room:* A/C, TV w/satellite, fridge, minibar, free Wi-Fi.

Gamma-Delta ★ 🗡   The sleekest, friendliest, and fairest-priced hotel in the Izmailovsky Hotel Complex (see also listings for the Alpha and the Vega), this is the closest to a Western-standard facility in this price range. Lobby computer screens tastefully and helpfully display prices and services in Russian and English. The 2002 renovation couldn't rid the hotel of its clumsy gray structure, but the soft tones of the room decor distract you from the outer ugliness. The hotel is actually two buildings, the Gamma and the Delta, connected on their lower floors. Staff is friendly and accustomed to international travelers (non-Russian speakers).

71 Izmailovskoye Shosse. www.izmailovo.ru. (C) **495/737-7070.** Fax 495/166-8173. More than 1,000 units. From 2,700 rubles double; from 4,050 rubles suite. AE, DC, MC, V. Metro: Izmailovsky Park. **Amenities:** 9

restaurants and bars; concierge; room service; sauna; free Wi-Fi in lobby. *In room:* TV w/cable, fridge, hair dryer, free Wi-Fi.

Inexpensive

G&R Hostels Though Moscow lacks hostels of the traditional sort, several independent entrepreneurs have taken over a floor or more of existing buildings and converted them into low-budget accommodations. G&R is one of the more reliable in this category, occupying three floors of the drab and unremarkable Hotel Asia in southeast Moscow. The hostel offers family-style units with private bathrooms and telephones, in addition to singles and doubles with shared bathrooms. Run by an Indian-Russian team, staff is English-speaking and accommodating. The hostel can arrange for visas and reasonably priced airport transfers, a big plus in this price category. The main drawback of G&R—like most Moscow hostels—is its distance from the center of town. G&R is almost on top of a metro station (Ryazansky Prospekt), however, and the ride to the center takes about 15 minutes. The surrounding neighborhood has markets, shops, and a few cheap cafes. Prices include VAT and breakfast, and discounts are available.

3/2 Zelenodolskaya St. www.hostels.ru. (C) **495/378-0001**. Fax 495/378-2866. 30 units. 70 euros double w/shared bathroom; 95 euros double w/bathroom; 105 euros family suite (prices pegged to euro). MC, V. Metro: Ryazansky Prospekt. **Amenities:** Visa support; common kitchen; Internet in business center. *In room:* Some rooms w/cable TV, fridge.

Globus Hidden behind the enormous Cosmos Hotel is the Globus, a modest hotel within an anonymous-looking apartment block. Its rooms include kitchenettes; in fact, many are renovated studio apartments. The price is reasonable, with three categories of rooms: those with Russian TV; those with satellite TV, hair dryer, and air-conditioning; and those with two rooms, Jacuzzi, bidet, and coffeemaker. The big drawback is the limited English-language service, though the staff is eager to help with taxis and theater tickets. The Globus is a 5- to 10-minute walk to the metro and the All-Russian Exhibition Center.

17 Yaroslavskaya Ulitsa. www.hotelglobus.ru. (C) **495/686-4189**. Fax 495/647-2115. 50 units. From 2,000 rubles double; from 5,000 rubles suite. Pets 1,000 rubles per day. AE, MC, V. Metro: VDNKh. **Amenities:** Restaurant; bar; sauna; free Wi-Fi in lobby. *In room:* See description of categories above.

Suharevka Hotel More Russian than any of the chain hotels and better located than any of Moscow's hostels, the Suharevka draws Russia enthusiasts and return visitors from scholars to artists. It's one of a small but growing number of "mini-hotels" in Moscow, basically a few rooms or floors of an apartment building converted into a hotel/hostel. It draws a fair number of Russians with a more international outlook than many you'll meet. Its decor is funky, with each of its 12 rooms bearing slightly different bed linens and drapes, but all are comfortable. A shared kitchen is available for those wanting to cook; it's a good way to meet other visitors, too.

16/18 Bolshaya Sukharevskaya Ploshchad. www.suharevkahotel.ru. (C) **910/420-3446**. 12 units. 2,000 rubles double; 400 rubles for bed in hostel room. MC, V. Metro: Sukharevskaya. **Amenities:** Restaurant; visa support; common kitchen; free Wi-Fi in lobby. *In room:* Some rooms w/cable TV.

NEAR THE AIRPORT

Domodedovo Aerohotel As shiny and serviceable as the nearby Domodedovo Airport, this hotel is in a forested industrial zone far away from the center of town. The staff and a few customers in the brightly lit restaurant are the only things Russian

currency CONFUSION AT YOUR HOTEL

Many hotels, restaurants, and chic shops list their prices in "monetary units" (abbreviated Y.E. in Russian). The unit was essentially another way of saying "dollars" while adhering to the Russian law that forbids businesses from trading in any currency other than the ruble. This practice doesn't make much sense now that the ruble has been as stable as the dollar in recent years, but it persists nonetheless. Today the monetary unit is pegged to the dollar, the euro, or somewhere in between. Restaurants and hotels will have a note at the front desk and on the menus or price lists indicating the current "monetary unit exchange rate" (for example: 28 rubles = 1 Y.E.). It's a good idea to have a small calculator handy for times such as this. Even if the price is listed in dollar-pegged "units," however, you have to pay your bill in rubles. Whew!

about the place. The newest of Moscow's slim airport hotel selection, it favors beige-toned upholstery and chrome fixtures of good but not designer quality. Try for a room with a tree view, not one facing the highway clogged with traffic during the long rush hours. There's a convenient direct train into town, a 45-minute ride. One advantage of the distance is that real estate is cheaper so rooms are more ample than downtown. Prices, however, are still high.

Domodedovo Airport. www.airhotel.ru. ☏ **495/795-3572.** Fax 495/795-3569. 215 units. From 6,900 rubles double; from 10,100 rubles suite. AE, DC, MC, V. Free secure parking. **Amenities:** 2 restaurants; bar; nightclub; concierge; executive-level rooms health club; indoor pool; room service; sauna; smoke-free rooms. *In room:* A/C, TV w/satellite, minibar, Wi-Fi.

Novotel This French-Russian venture is the only decent hotel at Sheremetevo-2 Airport, and is the first landmark you see as you approach the airport by car. The drab gray building matches the drab gray airport. However, the hotel's interior is much cleaner and friendlier than the terminal nearby. There's little French about its style except for its restaurant, which serves by far the best food within a several-mile radius. The hotel offers free shuttle service downtown, but be prepared for long traffic jams anytime close to rush hour. VAT is included in room rate.

Sheremetevo-2 Airport. www.novotel.com. ☏ **495/626-5900.** Fax 495/626-5901. 492 units. From 5,100 rubles; from 12,300 rubles suite. AE, DC, MC, V. Free secure parking. **Amenities:** 2 restaurants; bar; nightclub; concierge; executive-level rooms; health club; indoor pool; room service; sauna; smoke-free rooms. *In room:* A/C, TV w/satellite, minibar, Wi-Fi.

PRACTICAL INFORMATION

The Big Picture

Most of the better deals on hotels are found beyond the Garden Ring Road, well away from the main sights. This can be a major factor in your Moscow experience, since traffic to and from the center can eat up a chunk of the day. However, if your hotel is near a metro station and you're comfortable on public transport, this can reduce travel time considerably and make faraway accommodations more bearable. See "Moscow Neighborhoods" in chapter 3, and neighborhood descriptions earlier in this chapter, for a review of the districts referred to above.

Suites are quite common even in older Soviet hotels, and always mean an extra room with sofa, unless noted. A double quite often means two single beds, pushed together or across the room from each other. Make it clear when you reserve if you want a double bed. Single rooms and single rates for double rooms are widely available, so if you're traveling alone, be sure to ask.

Only major chain hotels offer car rentals in the standard sense, but most can arrange a car with a driver for a few hours or the duration of your stay, generally at a reasonable or negotiable price. The listings refer to this service as a "transport desk." See "Getting There & Getting Around" in chapter 17 for a rundown on car rentals.

Getting the Best Deal

The prices may look shockingly exorbitant, and they're rising every year—yet almost no tourist pays these "rack rates," or the highest official rate a hotel offers. You can almost always get a discount at these hotels—even 50% or more—by reserving through an online travel agency or even the hotel's online service. Unless noted, rack rates do not include breakfast or the 18% VAT. When you reserve online or through a travel agent, VAT is usually included. Many hotels charge for Wi-Fi in-room but offer it free in the lobby.

Deep discounts are available on www.waytorussia.net and www.hotelsinrussia. com. Even knowing Russian isn't enough to avoid the extra fees some hotels charge for non-Russian taxpayers (see "Foreigner Tax," earlier in this chapter.)

You can also look for deals on online travel booking sites like **Travelocity, Expedia, Orbitz, Priceline,** and **Hotwire,** or you can book hotels through **Hotels.com, Quikbook** (www.quikbook.com), and **Travelaxe** (www.travelaxe.com).

Prices especially soar during June and July. During big sporting events, trade fairs and festivals, rooms in all standards of hotel can fill up quickly. Book ahead. Arriving in Moscow without a reservation is highly risky, especially late at night or on holidays, when tourist agencies are closed.

Reservations

In Moscow, you need to pay at least a day's deposit to reserve a room. This almost invariably means paying by credit card by phone, Internet, or a travel agent. You can usually cancel a room reservation 1 week ahead of time and get a full refund. A few hotel keepers will return your money up to 3 days before the reservation date, but some will take your deposit and never return it, even if you cancel far in advance.

Among booking services, **Way to Russia** (www.waytorussia.net) is among the most upfront and reasonable, and rooms are almost always discounted. Its website and staff are responsive and seem to "get" what Western visitors are looking for—and don't automatically assume you're flush with cash or looking for a Russian wife, like some Russian agencies. **Hotels in Russia** (www.hotelsinrussia.com) also offers reservation services for a range of budgets, though with a somewhat more Russian mindset.

Also see "Tips on Accommodations," p. 294, for more booking guidelines.

Alternative Accommodations

If you're planning more than a week in Moscow, or if you are with a family, investigate apartment rentals. If you're on your own and eager to learn Russian or see the warmer side of this cold country, try out a homestay, where you're likely to be welcomed into the home of a Russian babushka (grandmother). You'll save money on both housing

Keep a hotel business card or brochure with you at all times, with the hotel's name and address written **in Russian.** You can show this to cab drivers or emergency workers to ensure you get home safely.

and dining, too. Serviced apartments come with basic kitchen facilities and varying levels of maid service. Some have minimum stays of a week, and monthly or even longer stays are available.

One good option is **Moscow Apartments** (Moscow; 📞 **495/662-2224;** www.moscowapartments.net), which offers apartments of one to three rooms with furnished kitchens, in secure buildings. Look for those closer to the center of town; while they are more costly than those on the edge of town, you are more likely to find convenient stores and public services, and neighbors who speak English or are accustomed to foreign boarders. Be sure to find out the exact address, since apartment agencies can underestimate walking time to the nearest metro. **Host Families Association** (www.hofa.ru) and **Russian Travel Service** (www.123travel.ru) can help with homestays.

Also see "Homestays & Apartment Rentals" on p. 295.

WHERE TO EAT IN MOSCOW

Russia's culinary traditions run from the daylong, table-crushing feasts of the 19th-century aristocracy to the cabbage soup and potatoes on which generations of ordinary Russians were raised. In today's Moscow you can find food to satisfy any palate, in marked contrast to the decades of Soviet shortages. The city's dining scene has evolved much faster than its hotel scene, fortunately, and there are now restaurants to suit any pocketbook or craving—and at any time of day or night. Moscow seems to have more 24-hour restaurants than anywhere in Europe.

best MOSCOW DINING BETS

5

- **Best Traditional Russian Cuisine**: If money is no object, the best Russian immersion for your palate is at **Kitezh,** where caviar-filled tarts whet your appetite for more. More budget-minded diners should aim for **Uncle Vanya** instead. See p. 92.
- **Best Romantic Dinner**: Escaping the over-the-top decor in high-end Moscow restaurants is no easy task, making **Carre Blanc** all the more welcome for its understated luxury and intimacy. Order some oysters and a corner table in the piano bar and forget anyone else exists. See p. 92.
- **Best Quick Lunch**: After a morning of hiking the hills of the Kremlin, dive into **Drova** for a fast, filling meal. It's got branches in a few neighborhoods, and won't dent the wallet. Or look for a "business lunch" in any good restaurant, bound to be speedier and cheaper than the multi-course version. See p. 89.
- **Best Caucasian Cuisine**: No visitor to Russia can avoid food from the Caucasus Mountains region, which has bled into nearly everyone's kitchen. **Genatsvale,** with a few locales in Moscow, offers accessible and herb and spice-rich Georgian cuisine. See p. 90.
- **Best Place to Take Tea**: You don't have to stay in the historical **Metropol Hotel** to savor its tea service—and it's a lot more affordable than a hotel suite. **Café Pushkin's** tea selection is even better though the setting is less authentic. See p. 83.
- **Best for Families**: The buffet-style **Yolki-Palki** restaurants solve the picky-eater problem and have play areas, with a more Russian, or Central Asian feel than the American fast food chains. If you need universal kid food, **TGI Friday's** multiple Moscow locations are always a safe bet. See p. 86.

Price Categories	
Very Expensive	$70 and up per person without alcohol
Expensive	$50 and up
Moderate	$20 and up
Inexpensive	Under $20

- **Best Dinner on a Budget**: For Russian fare, try **Traktir Kupechesky** and dig into crayfish and beefy soups for as close as you'll get to a peasant's budget as any in downtown Moscow. **Gogol** and **Propaganda** are funkier and livelier options, though get there early before the music starts. See p. 89.
- **Best Splurge**: If money is no object, take a huge appetite and park yourself at **Varvary.** It will take hours to try the 12-course tasting menu, but you will have a journey's worth of memories in a single meal. See p. 83.
- **Best Views**: Nothing beats **1 Red Square** for its locale. Winter or summer, day or night, the square takes your breath away between every bite. See below.

AROUND THE KREMLIN & RED SQUARE

Very Expensive

1 Red Square (Krasnaya Ploshchad, 1) ★★ RUSSIAN   The name says it all. Even if the food were dismal—which it's not—this would be a worthwhile visit just for the view on Moscow's main plaza. From the top floor of the National History Museum on the north side of Red Square, you gaze directly across the cobblestone expanse leading to St. Basil's Cathedral. The menu is appropriately Russian and traditional, including a re-creation of the "czar's menu" of a century ago. The emphasis is on fish and appetizers, and most dishes have a lighter touch than standard Russian restaurant fare. The delicate *koulebiaka* is a culinary feat of sturgeon blended with rice, cream, and spices, carefully baked inside a flaky pastry. The appetizer (*zakuski*) menu has several versions of fish or meat in aspic, and vegetarian options such as mushrooms on toast. Sample one of the home-brewed liqueurs such as *kedrach,* made with pine nuts—strange but satisfying. Musicians play traditional Russian stringed instruments some evenings.

1 Red Square (enter through Historical Museum). ⓒ **495/692-1196.** www.redsquare.ru/english. Reservations recommended. Main courses 600 rubles and up; business lunch 500 rubles. AE, MC, V. Daily noon–midnight. Metro: Ploshchad Revolutsii or Okhotny Ryad.

Expensive

Bosco Bar ★★ INTERNATIONAL   In any other European city, a plaza like Red Square would be ringed with sidewalk cafes and other commerce. Not so in Moscow—until Bosco Bar emerged at the turn of the millennium, at last cracking open the long facade of the GUM department store that runs nearly the length of Red Square. The cafe remains the only access to GUM from the square, which enhances its exclusivity. The cafe is a decadent but oh-so-satisfying way to absorb the atmosphere of Moscow's epicenter, elbow-to-elbow with the people who make modern

Moscow tick. Food is flawlessly prepared but often flimsy and overpriced; this is a better stop for coffee or a sample of one of the cafe's 20 flavors of ice cream. If you're hungry, try the shrimp and arugula salad or one of the reasonably priced pastas. The entrance from within GUM is concealed behind the Bosco Sport store.

3 Red Square. ℂ **495/627-3703.** www.bosco.ru/restoration/bar. Main courses 700–1,500 rubles. AE, DC, MC, V. Daily 10am–10pm. Metro: Ploshchad Revolutsii.

Sushi Vyosla ★ JAPANESE   One of the few places to last several years on Moscow's fierce and fickle sushi bar scene, this restaurant is as hip and fresh as ever. Some of its pretension has faded with time, fortunately. Plates of ever-fresh and ever-changing sushi, sashimi, and rolls float around the bar on a continuous river. (*Vyosla* means "oars" in Russian.) The compact hall is usually full of wealthy Russians talking business or stopping in for a quick bite between shopping sprees. It's not a place for leisurely dining, but that means you never have to wait long for a seat. Choices change daily, though you can request standard rolls and sushi combinations from the chefs on the island in the middle of the "river." Anything with Baltic Sea eel or scallops is worth sampling.

25 Nikolskaya Ulitsa (entrance from Tretyakovsky Proyezd shopping center). ℂ **495/937-0521.** www. sushi-vesla.ru. Rolls 150 rubles and up. MC, V. Daily noon–midnight. Metro: Lubyanka or Teatralnaya.

Moderate

FAQCafe ★ INTERNATIONAL   This cafe/club/art gallery/performance space seems to have found the right combination of creative energy, efficient service, and good food in an excellent location, yet few tourists have discovered it. It's frequented more by designers, writers, and photographers here to bat about new ideas. Paper and pencils at each table inspire customers to create while they wait, and the often-amusing results are posted on the walls. The real action starts after 11pm, with movies, music, and performances, but during the day this is an arty, comfortable, and convenient spot for lunch or a snack. Try the grilled pork with basil, or the curried chicken. They also offer a decent Caesar salad, pastas, and club sandwiches—and an extensive list of coffees and teas.

9 Gazetny Pereulok, building 2. ℂ **495/951-5227.** http://faqcafe.ru. Main courses 300–400 rubles. AE, MC, V. Daily noon–6am. Metro: Okhotny Ryad.

Krem ★ ITALIAN   A good lunch option just a short walk east of the Red Square, Krem attracts young Russian businesspeople with discriminating palates. The quick,

---

Finding Vegetarian Food

Although vegetarianism remains marginal in Russia, vegetarian restaurant-goers are getting a boost from a surprising source: the revived observance of Russian Orthodox traditions. The Orthodox calendar requires believers to abstain from meat and dairy products during several periods throughout the year, most notably during the 40 days of Lent preceding Orthodox Easter and the 40 days preceding Orthodox Christmas (Jan 7). Many Russian restaurants offer "Lenten menus" (*post*-no-ye men-*yoo*) during these periods, with carefully conceived variations on their house specialties sans the meat broth and lard. During non-Lenten periods, feel free to ask the cooks for meatless suggestions.

Moscow Restaurants

Baba Marta **47**
Bosco Bar **32**
Café Pushkin **18**
Carre Blanc **3**
Donna Clara **21**
Drova **35**
Durdin **1**
Dzhondzholi **10**
Expeditsiya **37**
FAQ Cafe **27**
Farsi **25**
Genatvale **45**
Gogol **17**
Grilyazh **42**
Il Patio **5**
Kitezh **14**
Korrea's **7**
Krem **28**
Kremlyovsky
  Café **30**
Mayak **26**
Metropol **33**

Common terms and abbreviations

naberezhnaya/nab	*Embankment*
most	*Bridge*
ploshchad/pl	*Square* or *plaza*
prospekt/pr	*Avenue*
sad	*Garden*
ulitsa/ul	*Street*

Na Melnitse **20**
Noah's Ark **38**
Okhotny Ryad
  Food Court **29**
One Red Square **31**
Parizhsk **44**
Pavilion at
  Patriarshy **22**
Poslednaya
  Kaplya **11**
Prisoner of the
  Caucasus **4**
Ragout **2**
Rakhat Lukum **16**
Rostik's **6**
Shesh-Besh **41**
Shinok **23**

Starlite Diner **8**
Sudar **24**
Sushi Vyosla **34**
Taras Bulba **13**
Tchaikovsky
  Concert Hall **9**
The Sad **43**
Traktir
  Kupechesky **36**
Turandot **19**
Uncle Vanya **40**
Vanil **46**
Varvary **12**
White Sun in
  the Desert **15**
Yar **1**
Yugos **39**

Making Restaurant Reservations

All high-end restaurants listed here have English-speaking staff, and most tour guides or concierges can help you reserve a restaurant table. But if you find yourself needing to make a reservation without help or Russian skills, here are a few useful phrases:

Zdras-tvoo-tye. (Hello)

Mozh-na re-zer-*vee*-ro-vat stol na ... ? (May I reserve a table for ...?)

-se-*vohd*-nya *ve*-che-rom (tonight)
-*zav*-tra *ve*-che-rom (tomorrow night)
-v syem cha-sov (at 7pm)
-v voh-syem cha-sov (at 8pm)
-na ... che-loh-vek (for ... people)

For help with numerals and days of the week, see p. 315.

---

unobtrusive, and stylish waitstaff blend in with the neat lines of the silver and black decor, accommodating the rushed lives of Russia's business class. The lunch buffet offers salads and meats with an Italian bent, plus a few Russian touches like beet-and-herring salad and rich rye bread (not to be missed). Dinner is largely Northern Italian, with specialties such as delicately prepared Venetian calves' liver and fresh pastas.

3 Solyanskiy Proyezd. ☏ **495/623-4902.** Main courses 800 rubles and up. MC, V. Mon–Sat 11am–midnight. Metro: Biblioteka Imeni Lenina.

Inexpensive

Kremlyovsky Cafe RUSSIAN   The only public food available inside the Kremlin walls is found in this bright but bland cafe in one of the gray Soviet-era buildings in the complex. Its shelter from competition has given it no incentive to lure tourists, but the management has surprisingly refrained from jacking up the prices. It's good for small, open-faced salmon or cheese sandwiches, cabbage pies, and mayonnaise-heavy salads. While not worth paying the Kremlin entrance fee just to eat here, the cafe is a welcome spot for a cool or hot drink after a tiring tour. The basement hall serves a fuller lunch from noon to 2pm, with mediocre Russian soups and thin steaks.

Kremlin, btw. Patriarch's Palace and Palace of Congresses. No phone. Lunch 1,300–2,000 rubles. Fri–Wed 11am–5pm. Metro: Okhotny Ryad.

Okhotny Ryad Shopping Center ☺ FOOD COURT/INTERNATIONAL   It may not be fine dining, but the kid-friendly food court on the bottom floor of this shopping center just off Red Square offers familiar and unfamiliar fare, all at budget-pleasing prices. For a treat you won't find at home, try the apricot-stuffed or cabbage-filled pies at Russkoye Bistro. If you're looking for pizza, however, stick with Sbarro's and skip the inferior Russian imitation. The hall gets busy and ear-splitting in the evening; lunchtime on a school day is a much mellower time to visit. On the upper floors are a TGI Friday's and a few pub-cafes that offer pleasant outdoor dining in the summer months, with views of the fountains and playful statues from Russian fairy tales that ring the mall, and the Kremlin as the ultimate backdrop. Try the Phlegmatic Dog Internet Café for a quick and original bite.

Manezh Sq. Food court prices 50–250 rubles main course. Credit cards not accepted in food court but MC, V accepted at cafes on top floor. Daily 10am–10pm. Metro: Okhotny Ryad.

TVERSKAYA & ENVIRONS
Very Expensive

Varvary ★★ RUSSIAN/INTERNATIONAL   Moscow's top haute cuisine restaurant of the nation's arguably most renowned chef Anatoly Komm is a gourmet paradise with tasting menus that take hours to savor. Its name means Barbarians, a sardonic reference to what some Russians see as a Western perception of them. Komm's "molecular" cuisine creates striking twists of some traditional Russian and European recipes. Interiors are an artful mix of lace, velvet, opulent carpets, and crystal chandeliers.

8A Strastnoi Blvd. ℂ **495/229-2800.** www.anatolykomm.ru. Reservations obligatory. 12-course degustation menu 8,500 rubles; a 3-course menu 5,950 rubles. AE, MC, V. Noon until everyone is finished eating. Metro: Pushkinskaya.

Expensive

Cafe Pushkin ★★★ RUSSIAN   Perhaps Moscow's most sophisticated 24-hour restaurant, the three-story Cafe Pushkin has the feel of a 19th-century mansion but dates from the late 1990s. Each of the floors has a different thrust, with a cherrywood bar and well-lit cafe on the first floor, a more formal dining room on the second, and a decadent and breezy summer cafe on the top. The menu weighs a ton—both the Russian and English versions—and the script is so flowery as to be unreadable at times. Pretty much anything listed is bound to be successful, though standouts are *ukha,* a creamy, spiced fish soup that manages to be both light and filling; and grilled sterlet with forest mushrooms. Prices are high—you're paying for the faux-pre-revolutionary atmosphere and top-quality service as well as the food. The vodka selection is impressive and impressively priced, and the hot chocolate and dessert selections offer good, low-budget options. Nonsmoking floor available.

26a Tverskoi Bulvar. ℂ **495/739-0033.** www.cafe-pushkin.ru. Reservations required for restaurant and summer terrace. Main courses 1,000–2,800 rubles. AE, DC, MC, V. 1st floor daily 24 hr.; top floors daily noon–midnight. Metro: Pushkinskaya.

Pavilion at Patriarshy ★ RUSSIAN/INTERNATIONAL   This picturesque pavilion overlooking Patriarch's Ponds has gone through several lives in recent years, but the latest incarnation looks to be its most successful. Its spacious, beige-themed main hall is ringed by a balcony hung with pop-art portraits and filled with greenery to make it feel summery and outdoorsy year-round. The restaurant has made it on the circuit of Moscow's young, hip professionals, who seem to expect sushi on any menu. The pavilion complies, but the rest of its repertoire is more intriguing. Try the white mushroom soup served with a quarter-loaf of rich, brown caraway-flavored bread; the cottage cheese tartlets (*syrniki*); or the borscht with duck breast. Skip the sushi.

7 Bolshoi Patriarshy Pereulok, building 1 (on the grounds of Patriarch's Ponds park). ℂ **495/697-5110.** www.restsindikat.com/restaurants/pavilion. Main courses 400–1,000 rubles. AE, DC, MC, V. Daily 24 hr. Metro: Mayakovskaya.

Turandot ★★ INTERNATIONAL   Come here if you need a break from the crush of crowded public transport and want to feel like a pampered, refined aristocrat. While the food is top-notch, the experience is the main draw. Considered by many as Moscow's most intricately decorated restaurant, Turandot is next door to Café Pushkin; both are owned by Andrei Dellos. While the Pushkin aims at restoring the feel of a 19th-century Russian noble mansion, Turandot tries to imitate the atmosphere of an 18th-century French rococo palace, complete with carved ceilings, painted wall panels, opulent chandeliers, and museum china. All the decor was meticulously created by hand to create what feels like a unique dining experience. The cuisine is an equally intricate fusion of Chinese and Japanese traditions with modern Russian and international trends. Greens, fish, and meat are always fresh and delectable, and the menu is always changing.

26/5 Tverskoi Bulvar. (©) **495/739-0011.** www.turandotpalace.ru/en. Reservations recommended. Main courses 1,200–2,000 rubles. AE, DC, MC, V. Daily noon–midnight. Metro: Pushkinskaya.

Moderate

Donna Clara ★ ITALIAN/RUSSIAN   Chic and cozy, this cafe is a great place to stop during a stroll through the similarly chic and cozy Patriarch's Ponds neighborhood. The cafe is on Malaya Bronnaya, a street that figures in literary masterpieces such as Bulgakov's *Master and Margarita,* and that's now lined with original boutiques. Donna Clara is good for a quick coffee or a long, drawn-out one, and for lunch as well. Highlights include their pasta, veal in cream sauce, and green salads (as opposed to the marinated ones). A three-course prix-fixe lunch runs less than 250 rubles. They serve a breakfast for late risers (they don't open until 10am). The desserts are the cafe's strong point; try the cherry strudel or the yogurt cheesecake. There's even a nonsmoking section, a welcome option in the evenings when the main hall fills up with the cigarette-loving, after-work crowd.

21/13 Malaya Bronnaya Ulitsa. (©) **495/690-6974.** www.donnaklara.ru. Main courses 400–700 rubles; business lunch 310 rubles. No credit cards. Mon–Sat 10am–midnight; Sun noon–midnight. Metro: Push-kinskaya.

Dzhondzholi ★ GEORGIAN   A hidden treasure on a small street off Tverskaya, Dzhondzholi offers filling Georgian cuisine in a warm and simple decor. Its big summer terrace makes the place especially appealing in the warm season. Their *khachapui*—three-cheese layered pies—are so rich you may not have room for the generous lamb and beef and ground chicken kebabs. Populated more by locals in the know than big tourist groups, the restaurant is named after a Georgian plant whose flower buds are used to make pickles. Ask to try some.

20/1 Tverskaya St., entrance from Nastasyinski Pereulok. (©) **495/650-5567.** Main courses 300–550 rubles. Daily 11am–midnight. Metro: Tverskaya.

Il Patio ☺ ITALIAN/RUSSIAN   This small chain's management was the first in Moscow to recognize the city's need for reasonably priced restaurants with edible food and decent service, a concept that didn't exist 15 years ago. It now has 22 restaurants around town. Thin-crust pizzas, generously spiced pastas, a salad bar, and a children's menu may be standard fare in your hometown, but in Moscow they remain scarce. Il Patio is a safe choice for kids or the unadventurous, or if you're sick of Russian fare. It opens early for breakfast, too. The salad bar includes Russian mayonnaise-based salads and garlic-marinated vegetables, in addition to fresh raw greens. The selection of vegetarian pizzas is broader than those at most other Russia pizza joints.

> ### Impressions
>
> *Already Olga's hand was gripping the urn of perfumed tea, and tipping Into the cups its darkling stream; Meanwhile a hallboy handed cream.*
> —Alexander Pushkin describing a delicate romantic moment in his epic poem *Eugene Onegin*

Sushi

Just because a restaurant brags about its sushi menu doesn't mean Japanese food is exclusively served. An inordinate number of not-at-all Japanese restaurants now include some sushi and sashimi on the menu, just to keep up with the Moscow obsession with raw fish on rice. My advice is to skip the sushi page and order whatever the restaurant does best. If you're a sushi fan, go to a real Japanese restaurant instead.

2 Pervaya Tverskaya-Yamskaya Ulitsa.© **495/651-0884.** http://il-patio.rosinter.ru. Main courses 400–700 rubles. AE, MC, V. Weekdays 8am–midnight; weekends noon–6am. Metro: Mayakovskaya.

Ragout ★ RUSSIAN/FRENCH   Created by a top food columnist and his friends, Ragout offers inventive cuisine based on French culinary traditions at affordable prices. They pride themselves on using only the best natural ingredients and describe their concept as a cross between a French bistro and a British gastropub. It's always packed, but reservations aren't hard to land and aren't necessary if you're willing to wait a bit. Try the rich filet mignon with stuffed tomato and a selection of sauces, or salmon in beet marinade. A fine selection of vegetarian dishes is also available—a rarity. The surrounding neighborhood sees few tourists but is increasingly hip among Muscovites.

69 Bolshaya Gruzinskaya St.© **495/662-6458.** http://caferagout.ru/en. Main courses 450–900 rubles. AE, DC, MC, V. Reservations recommended. Mon–Wed 8am–midnight; Thurs–Fri 8am–2am; Sat–Sun noon–midnight. Metro: Belorusskaya.

Starlite Diner ☺ AMERICAN   If you're desperate for a 4am burger, you'll be forgiven for heading to this silver trailer parked incongruously in a Moscow square. This all-night diner has become an institution in its decade on the Moscow dining scene, thanks largely to expats who flock here with their families on weekend mornings, or with their Russian clubbing partners after a night of partying. It inhabits a leafy square convenient but well-hidden from the Garden Ring Road, and offers one of the city's few summer terraces free of exhaust fumes. Check out the informal lending library in the back near the restrooms. Burgers are generous and juicy, and fries are crisp. Most of the fare is authentic American, though the bagels are frozen. Prices are higher than at any diner you'll find back home, but they may be worth it to say you ate a banana split in Moscow. Starlite has several other locales elsewhere in town, including 16/5 Bolotnaya Ploshchad (© 495/951-5838; metro: Tretyakovskaya), and 9a Korovy Val (© 495/959-8919; metro: Oktyabrskaya).

16 Bolshaya Sadovaya Ulitsa.© **495/650-0246.** www.starlite.ru. Main courses 300–650 rubles. AE, DC, MC, V. Daily 24 hr. Metro: Mayakovskaya.

Inexpensive

Poslednaya Kaplya RUSSIAN   A democratic and lively place to recharge, this cafe is convenient but not on most tourists' radar, and a bargain for this neighborhood. The name means "Last Drop"—and the drinks are worth a sample, from the nourishing mulled wine to draft beers and vast selection of teas from across China, black, green, red, and white. The food's worth it, too. The wide selection of appetizers can combine for a full meal, from Spanish omelets to skewered pork. It offers an unusually large selection of vegetarian dishes including a passable risotto, as well as grilled

family-friendly RESTAURANTS

Russians rarely take their children to restaurants, largely because for decades dining out was an occurrence too rare and costly to be wasted on finicky little ones who pose a threat to crystal glassware. The international chains are starting to change that, and a few homegrown restaurants are adopting highchairs and children's menus, too; they're still relatively rare, so don't expect them everywhere you go. Among top-end establishments, the best family venues are the Sunday brunches at the big hotels. **Sheraton Palace** is especially child-centered, with a well-equipped playroom, clown performances, and free balloons. The all-you-can-eat buffet has enough options for the pickiest of eaters. Mid-range suggestions include **Il Patio,** whose restaurants offer children's seats and menus, as well as servers who are patient with scampering little ones (a rarity here). It serves plenty of familiar pizzas and pastas. The budget chain **Yolki-Palki** (which translates into something like "Good grief!") offers simple, all-you-can-eat Russian cuisine and is one of the few places where you'll see Russian kids eating out. The mini-pancakes (olady) and jam-filled dumplings (vareniki) are good finger foods. The American-style **Starlite Diner** has

milkshakes and cereal and attracts expat families on weekend mornings. The fried-chicken chain, **Rostik's KFC,** has familiar fare and a play area in most of its restaurants, but the equipment is often crowded and shabby. The most child-friendly places in town are still the U.S. chain **TGI Friday's** (main branches at the Okhotny Ryad shopping center and at 18/2 Tverskaya St.) and, of course, the ubiquitous **McDonald's.** (Check out their flagship restaurant on Pushkin Sq., the world's biggest when it opened in 1989.)

Some **Yolki-Palki** branches follow. All are open daily 11am to 11pm. None takes credit cards.

- 14 Klimentovsky Pereulok, building 1. ☎ **495/953-9130.** Metro: Tretyakovskaya.
- 1 Bolshaya Gruzinskaya Ulitša. ☎ **495/605-3445.** Metro: Krasnopresnenskaya.
- 12 Bolshaya Dorogomilovskaya Ulitsa. ☎ **499/243-2019.** Metro: Kievskaya.
- 8/10 Neglinnaya Ulitsa. ☎ **495/628-5525.** Metro: Kuznetsky Most or Teatralnaya.
- 11 Novy Arbat. ☎ **495/691-7654.** Metro: Arbatskaya.

beef and fish. Tucked behind the bustling Pushkin Square, it fills up on weekend nights with young clubbers, and is a calmer, friendlier scene during the day.

4/3 Strastnoy Blvd. ☎ **495/692-7549.** http://lastdrop.ru. Main courses 200–600 rubles. Daily noon–6am. Metro: Pushkinskaya.

Rostik's KFC ☺ RUSSIAN/AMERICAN   This is, as you might guess, an American-Russian fried-chicken collaboration (now solely owned by KFC parent Yum! Brands). Cheap, fast, and kid-friendly, Rostik's KFC offers standard chicken combos plus nuggets and chicken wraps. The slightly more Russian options include lamb shish kebab and smoked salmon wrapped in Armenian lavash bread. There's not much in terms of light dining. The urban setting means the kids' play area is indoors. The Mayakovskaya branch is the most convenient, but keep an eye out for other branches around town.

2/1 Pervaya Tverskaya-Yamskaya Ulitsa. ☎ **499/251-4950.** www.rostikskfc.ru. Meal packs 80–150 rubles. No credit cards. Weekdays 9am–midnight; weekends 10am–midnight. Metro: Mayakovskaya.

Tchaikovsky Concert Hall INTERNATIONAL   The lobby of the concert hall has turned into a more elegant version of a shopping mall food court, with a cluster of inexpensive restaurants. It's a good place to fuel up and freshen up before a concert or at any time of day. **Delifrance** has croissants and French patisserie and boulangerie treats; **Tandoor** has good, predictable Indian fare; the coffee bar boasts multiple blends including decaf (unusual here); and there's even a **Pizza Hut.**

4/31 Triumfalnaya Sq. ☎ **495/699-3957.** Snacks from 30 rubles; meals from 160 rubles. No credit cards. Daily noon–8pm. Metro: Mayakovskaya.

Yolki-Palki RUSSIAN   This chain has over 40 restaurants around Moscow, offering a salad bar and some simple and filling Russian fare, like borscht, *bliny* (pancakes) pelmeny (dumplings) and various meat courses. The decor is simple; a branch near the Bolshoi Theater feels better than others.

8/10 Neglinnaya ☎ **495/628-5525.** Main courses 200–450 rubles. No credit cards. Daily 11am–5am. Metro: Kuznetsky Most or Teatralnaya.

PETROVKA & THE UKRAINIAN QUARTER

Very Expensive

Expeditsiya ★★★ ARCTIC   One of Moscow's stranger culinary experiences, this restaurant offers recipes collected from Arctic tribes during expeditions to Russia's Far North. The food is hit-or-miss, but the decor and inventiveness of the restaurant's creators make it an unforgettable stop on any Moscow tour. A helicopter used in Arctic expeditions stands in the central hall, and a river runs under the glass floor. Clientele and staff are a bit too haughty for a place with such a rugged theme. Reindeer and trout feature prominently on the menu. And if you really want to experience extremes, there's a steam bath (banya) downstairs.

6 Pevchevsky Pereulok. ☎ **495/775-6075.** www.expedicia.ru. Main courses from 1,500 rubles; business lunch 500 rubles. MC, V. Daily noon until the last guest leaves. Metro: Kitai-Gorod.

Expensive

Kitezh ★★★ RUSSIAN   From the pre-revolutionary Russian alphabet used on the menu to the restaurant's name (a mythical city that would disappear when enemies approached), Kitezh sees its purpose as upholding tradition and legend. If you have just one real Russian meal in Moscow, make it here. The restaurant is poised in a stone basement that re-creates a 17th-century farmhouse atmosphere, across from a 14th-century monastery on a quiet stretch of historic Petrovka Street, a great district for a post-meal stroll. Allow a couple of hours to savor the large portions and to digest the various courses. Sauces are rich, divine, and heavy. This is one of the few Russian restaurants that does justice to beef stroganoff, which despite its Russian roots is more common outside Russia. The pikeperch is expertly seasoned and sauced. Desserts include thick, jello-like *kisel,* and light and buttery *bliny* with homemade jam.

23/10 Ulitsa Petrovka. ☎ **495/650-6685.** www.kitezh-town.ru. Reservations recommended. Main courses 600–1,400 rubles. AE, MC, V. Daily noon–midnight. Metro: Kuznetsky Most.

Noah's Ark (Noyev Kovcheg) ★ ARMENIAN   The staff at Noah's Ark take responsibility for your pleasure during the several hours required for a meal here. Each course is discussed with the waiter before the order is made; and each must be accompanied by the appropriate spirit—preferably Armenian brandy (which they call *konyak*). Nestled in one of the steep, zigzag lanes of the Ukrainian Quarter, the restaurant can be hard to find; however, it's worth the exploration of this quiet and oft-ignored neighborhood in Moscow's historic center. The atmosphere gets pretentious on weekend nights, as rich Armenian and Russian executives try to outdo each other by ordering the most expensive items on the menu. The *meza*, or appetizers, incorporate the spices and fruits of the Caucasus Mountain region, with an emphasis on cilantro, apricots, and pomegranates. The *dolma*, grape leaves stuffed with lamb and rice, are succulent. The plain roast lamb is better than the cubed version.

9 Maly Ivanovsky Pereulok. ✆ **495/917-0717.** www.noevkovcheg.ru/en. Reservations recommended for dinner. Main courses 400–900 rubles; business lunch 600 rubles. AE, DC, MC, V. Daily noon until the last customer leaves. Metro: Kitai-Gorod.

Moderate

Na Melnitse (On the Windmill) ★ RUSSIAN   Na Melnitse transports you from the clogged traffic of the Boulevard Ring outdoors to a bucolic farmyard centered around a windmill. Its three dining halls are decked out as a farmyard with a stream and live pheasants, a country attic, and a blacksmith's workshop. From a culinary standpoint, the best thing about the restaurant is the half portions offered for many of its dishes, allowing you to eat lightly or sample several of its traditional Russian specialties. Fish features prominently, but the veal dishes are just as successful. Try one of the homemade liqueurs—a small 50-gram glass is enough to sample the flavor without losing your lucidity.

24 Sadovaya-Spasskaya. ✆ **495/625-8890.** www.namelnitse.ru. Main courses 500–1,500 rubles. AE, MC, V. Daily noon–midnight. Metro: Krasniye Vorota.

Taras Bulba-Korchma ★ UKRAINIAN   The decorators went a bit overboard on the Ukrainian country kitsch, but the food is hearty, reliable, and free of pretense, and the atmosphere is cheery in this fast-growing chain that includes 15 restaurants around town. You can recognize the restaurants by the doormen, who are extravagantly decked out as Cossacks all seasons of the year. The name comes from a story by Nikolai Gogol, a tragic and epic tale of an aging 18th-century warrior (Bulba) who sets off with his sons to join a Cossack band fighting for Ukrainian independence. The menu has plenty of meat and potatoes, but also several soups based on beets, cabbage, or forest greens. Ukrainian cooking makes heavy use of garlic, so if you're not a fan, let your server know. If you do like garlic, try the *pampushki,* garlic-infused buttery rolls. This restaurant is popular among busy, middle-class Russians looking for a taste of the countryside.

The most central location at 30/7 Petrovka✆ **495/694-6082.** www.tarasbulba.ru/en/index.php. Main courses 400–600 rubles. MC, V. Sun–Thurs noon–11pm; Fri–Sat noon–2am. Metro: Pushkinskaya.

White Sun of the Desert (Beloye Solntse Pustyni)★ CENTRAL ASIAN   White Sun of the Desert, named after a cult Soviet film about central Asia, features cuisine from Uzbekistan and its neighbors, including a few dishes with an Arabian or Chinese flavor. The lunch buffet is a staggering smorgasbord of fresh, marinated, and dried fruits and vegetables; grilled lamb; delicately spiced ground-meat kebabs; and flaky pies. The menu offers several versions of the central Asian favorite *plov*, a lamb-based rice pilaf. The staff is costumed in technicolored turbans and wide-legged pants, a theatricalized version of traditional Uzbek desert garb. Hookahs and belly dancing are offered after 8pm. It's one of a series of kitschy yet elite themed restaurants around town.

29/14 Neglinnaya St. ℂ **495/625-2596.** www.bsp-rest.ru. Reservations recommended for dinner. Main courses 800–1,600 rubles. AE, DC, MC, V. Mon–Sat 11am–midnight. Metro: Chekhovskaya or Tsvetnoi Bulvar.

Inexpensive

Drova 🍴 RUSSIAN   This chain of low-price, all-you-can-eat Russian restaurants has helped bury the 2-hour lunch tradition. Moscow's workers dive into Drova at 1pm; load up on Russian coleslaw *(kvashennaya kapusta)*, spicy red bean stew *(lobio)*, and ground-beef kebabs; gulp down some tea; and are out the door by 1:30pm. With a new location just off the Red Square and plenty of other convenient addresses around town, Drova is a good place for tourists to sample several Russian dishes risk-free. If you don't like something, go back and get something else. It's all included in the 630-ruble price. The wood (fake and real) decor reflects its name, which means "logs" in Russian.

5 Nikolskaya. ℂ **495/698-2696.** www.drova.ru. All-you-can-eat 630 rubles. AE, DC, MC, V at both locations. Daily 24 hr. Metro: Lubyanka or Chistiye Prudy. Several other locations around town.

Gogol RUSSIAN/INTERNATIONAL   Lurking behind an arch on a posh pedestrian street, this restaurant/bar/concert space is anything but chic. Grungy performers slump against the arch, and students inside grab post-party bites, making the atmosphere laid-back and cutting-edge simultaneously. The outdoor courtyard is a great summer breathing space and party spot. Food is basic and cheap. I recommend the *pelmeni* (small meat dumplings)—lightly spiced, juicy, and filling. There are plenty of vegetarian options, primarily on the appetizer menu. Gogol is rarely crowded in the daytime, and if the terrace is open, there's plenty of space to relax. Films on Thursdays, concerts Tuesdays through Sundays.

11 Stoleshnikov Pereulok, building 1. ℂ **495/514-0944.** www.gogolclubs.ru. Main courses 250–430 rubles. No credit cards. Daily 24 hr. Metro: Chekhovskaya or Kuznetsky Most.

Traktir Kupechesky (Merchants' Inn) ★ RUSSIAN   To a Russian, the crayfish is a summertime staple as crucial to the national cuisine as caviar, and much more accessible. If you're a fan, make it a point to visit this restaurant, since it's a glimpse of what for many Russian men is the ultimate dining experience. The bright red crustaceans are the main draw, whether boiled in beer, spiced, or doused in cream sauce. Grilled fish is also on offer, as well as seafood-based appetizers and salads. The only appropriate beverage for a crayfish lunch is Russian beer. The constant crunch of the shells provides a surreal soundtrack for the sight of young and middle-aged Russian businessmen on their lunch break, trying not to drip sauce on their suits.

11/4 Maroseika, building 1. ℂ **495/621-8545.** Main courses 300–800 rubles. No credit cards. Daily 11am–11pm. Metro: Kitai-Gorod.

ARBAT

Expensive

Vanil ★ RUSSIAN   This may be Moscow restaurateur Arkady Novikov's most successful creation, a masterful blend of Russian ingredients, European cooking techniques, and a smattering of Asian cuisine aimed at the increasingly demanding Muscovite nouveau riche palate. The sparkling chandeliers face little other decorative competition in the airy interior, leaving diners to concentrate on the restaurant's subtleties—especially its food. Hits include the barabulka fish filet with asparagus and orange sauce, and the rich and ever-changing soups. A Szechuan duck-liver soup might unexpectedly include oysters when they're in season. The restaurant is not as imposing as the massive Christ the Savior Cathedral across the street, but it's not a casual experience, either. Save this for a special night.

1 Ostozhenka. © **495/637-1082.** http://eng.novikovgroup.ru. Reservations required on weekends, recommended on weekdays. Main courses 1,000–2,650 rubles. AE, DC, MC, V. Daily noon–midnight. Metro: Kropotkinskaya.

Moderate

Baba Marta ★ BULGARIAN   This friendly restaurant may be your only chance to try Bulgarian cuisine, so why not? It's similar to Russian cooking, but with copious feta cheese, olives, and a few other southern European touches. Folk musicians dance through the hall and waitstaff sometimes join in, keeping things festive even on the gloomiest of winter nights. Embroidered wall hangings and traditional pottery enhance the Slavic atmosphere. Any dish with Bulgarian cheese is worth sampling, as are the hearty soups. Salads are rather heavy, as are the wines—make sure you clarify whether you want dry or sweet, since the house wine is somewhat sugary.

8 Gogolevsky Bulvar. © **495/232-9209.** www.babamarta.ru. Main courses 400–1,300 rubles. Business lunch 380 rubles. MC, V. Sun–Thurs noon–11pm; Fri–Sat noon–2am. Metro: Kropotkinskaya.

Genatsvale ★★ GEORGIAN   This family-run restaurant—whose name means "comrade" in Georgian—is Moscow's best introduction to the colorful and flavorful cuisine of Georgia. The country-style dining hall is a welcome dose of earthiness on this street of chic restaurants and posh residences. The only drawback is the cabaret show, a performance of overly loud Georgian love songs accompanied by tinny synthesizers. Come here for lunch or early dinner to avoid it. Try the three-cheese *khachapuri*, a kind of sauceless pizza; the finely ground lamb kebab; or the garlic-walnut paste rolled in thinly sliced eggplant. It's a good choice for vegetarians, who can easily fill up on a selection of appetizers (which is what most Georgians seem to do). The restaurant has another location on the Arbat, which is more convenient but is gaudier and less pleasant and cozy.

12/1 Ostozhenka. © **495/695-0401.** http://restoran-genatsvale.ru. 300–850 rubles. MC, V. Daily noon–midnight. Metro: Kropotkinskaya.

Parizhsk ★ 📖 RUSSIAN/FRENCH   Its name is a Russified version of the word "Paris," and its cuisine is a Russified version of familiar and nourishing French fare. The dark woods of the furniture contrast with the playful light fixtures, and the atmosphere is laid-back. It attracts local journalists and graduate students, as well as anyone looking for a good meal around the clock, though tourists rarely venture in. The *confit de canard* in cherry sauce is a good choice, and the crème brûlée is divine. Russian beer competes with French wines on the menu, both reasonably priced. Parizhsk is open around the clock, which attracts some of the post-party crowd in the wee hours, and makes it a safe and friendly place to head if jet lag has you discombobulated.

13 Zubovsky Bulvar, building 2. © **499/255-2912.** www.parizhsk.ru. Main courses 400–830 rubles. AE, MC, V. Daily 24 hr. Metro: Park Kultury.

Inexpensive

Mayak ★ FRENCH/ITALIAN   A cafe located on the premises of Mayakovsky Theater and frequented by artists and rowdy bohemians. Food is simple and filling, with a range of pastas, grilled meats, and salads. The interiors are built around massive old cupboards. Nonsmokers beware, it's a smokers' haven.

19 Bolshaya Nikitskaya. © **495/691-7449.** www.clubmayak.ru. Main courses 250–500 rubles. Daily noon–midnight. Metro Arbatskaya.

SOUTH OF MOSCOW RIVER

Expensive

Grilyazh ★★ RUSSIAN/EUROPEAN   The stylized grillwork at the entrance and the discriminating maitre d' tell you right away to expect the best from this restaurant. Specializing in Italian- and French-inspired Russian cuisine, the food is sometimes as pretentious as the service, but overall it's a pleasing experience in fine dining. At the top of the otherwise bohemian Pyatnitskaya Street, it occupies a two-story mansion full of Art Nouveau light fixtures and antique furniture. Russian executives like to hold banquets here, but it's also a good spot for a romantic interlude, with its soft lighting and exclusive atmosphere. The wine list is impressive. The tuna and salmon carpaccio with ginger and greens is a winning appetizer, and the duck breast with "poacher's" sauce makes a hearty main course. The borscht with garlic rolls is surprisingly better than the lobster bisque.

1/2 Pyatnitskaya Ulitsa, building 1. © **495/953-9323.** www.grillage.ru. Reservations recommended. Main courses 800–1,800 rubles. AE, MC, V. Daily noon–midnight. Metro: Novokuznetskaya.

The Sad ★★ INTERNATIONAL   Part of an up-and-coming neighborhood around the Red October chocolate factory, this seafood-leaning venue beckons diners with a sprawling tropical garden—complete with birds—in this wintry city. *Sad* means garden in Russian, but the owners added the English article 'the' so that English speakers wouldn't think it's a sorrowful place and stay away. The menu by a highly acclaimed chef is rooted in Spanish tradition. Raviolis filled with dorado and cod are delectable, as well as seabass in herbs. Leave room for dessert.

4/1 Yakimanskaya Naberezhnaya. © **495/783-8108.** Main courses 600–2,600. AE, DC, MC, V. Daily 10am–10pm. Metro:Kropotkinskaya, Polyanka.

Moderate

Shesh-Besh ★ AZERBAIJANI   This chain is a cheerful and tasty introduction to Azerbaijani cuisine, a combination of Turkish, Greek, and Russian flavors with a distinctly Caucasian (as in the Caucasus Mountains) accent. It goes overboard with its multicolored decor and faux-traditional costumery, but the pillows are comfy and the service is friendly. The *souffra,* or salad bar, is heaped with fresh and marinated vegetables, along with stalks of cilantro, parsley, and dill that you're supposed to munch raw to cleanse the palate. Grilled meats are the pride of the Caucasus, but also worth trying is the *cutaby,* a thin, crepelike dough stuffed with fresh greens, sheep's cheese, or ground lamb. Their chief gimmick is a game called *shesh-besh* (it means "six-five"), in which you toss two dice, and if you get a six and a five you get a free pitcher of (barely drinkable) wine or other beverage. Shesh-Besh's two most convenient locations are listed below.

24 Pyatnitskaya, building 1. ☏ **495/959-5862.** www.rmcom.ru/page-shesh-besh-about. Main courses 200–560 rubles. MC, V. Daily noon–midnight. Metro: Novokuznetskaya. Also at 6a Smolenskaya Ploshchad. ☏ **495/241-6542.** Metro: Smolenskaya.

Uncle Vanya ★★ RUSSIAN   This cozy, artsy treasure left its original location in a theater basement to relocate to another basement in this even more cozy, artsy section of town. The restaurant takes its name from one of Anton Chekhov's plays. It has no real link to the playwright, but maintains a literary atmosphere and decor reminiscent of early-20th-century Russia, when Chekhov reached his zenith. The menu of Russian favorites is accessible and safe, with highlights including cold sorrel soup (*zelyoniye shchi*), wild mushrooms, and buckwheat kasha. The restaurant serves a hearty breakfast, too. The whimsical place mats are a good way to learn the Russian alphabet. A talented, understated jazz trio plays most evenings.

20 Pyatnitskaya, building 2 (entrance in courtyard). ☏ **495/951-0586.** www.dvrest.com. Main courses 400–800 rubles. MC, V. Daily 8:30am–midnight. Metro: Novokuznetskaya.

Inexpensive

Shokoladnitsa ★ RUSSIAN   Cafes of this chain are full of young Russian women discussing their jobs and boyfriends over tea or chocolate *bliny* (crepes). A good rest stop any time of day, it offers cheap soups and mediocre salads. Its name translates as "a pot of hot chocolate." The chocolate items on the menu are probably your best bet here.

10 Bolshoi Klimentovsky pereulok. ☏ **495/951-3703.** http://shoko.ru/moskva. Desserts and snacks from 180 rubles. No credit cards. Daily 24 hr. Metro: Tretyakovskaya. Other cafes of the chain around town.

OUTSIDE THE GARDEN RING

Expensive

Carre Blanc ★★ FRENCH   Chic and delicious, this restaurant is a perfect marriage of French cuisine and a Russian setting. Rather off the beaten track, it's an excellent choice for an evening splurge or a languorous summer brunch. The main dining hall of this 18th-century mansion is sparsely elegant, the adjoining piano/jazz bar has a sleek design, and the brasserie in back is an upscale version of laid-back, offering a menu similar to the one in the main hall but at discounted prices. Opt for the summer terrace when the weather is fine. The oysters and other seafood, flown in daily, are a house specialty, though if you come from a seaside hometown it might seem silly to order seafood in landlocked Moscow. Instead, try the foie gras with fennel or the traditional but excellent veal. The wine list is predictably good, as is the sommelier.

19/2 Seleznyovskaya. ☏ **495/258-4403.** www.carreblanc.ru. Reservations recommended. Main courses 900–1,500 rubles. Business lunch 500 rubles. AE, DC, MC, V. Daily 11am–11pm. Metro: Novoslobodskaya.

Farsi ★★ IRANIAN   The only Iranian restaurant in town, located in one of Stalin's landmark neo-Gothic towers, offers opulent dishes cooked by an Iranian chef based on millennia-old Persian recipes. Its decor is worthy of a shah's palace, and big windows offer unbeatable views of the Moscow River. Inside the newly renovated Radisson Royal Hotel, the restaurant isn't soft on the pocketbook but is an elegant setting for a special night out.

2/2 Kutuzovsky Prospect, building 1. ☏ **499/243-2020.** www.farsi-moscow.ru. Main courses 500–1,200 rubles. AE, DC, MC, V. Daily noon–midnight. Metro: Kievskaya.

Prisoner of the Caucasus ★ CAUCASIAN   Named after a popular Soviet film (like White Sun of the Desert, reviewed earlier in this chapter), this restaurant plumbs the cuisines and stereotypes of the ex-Soviet lands of the Caucasus Mountains: Georgia, Armenia, and Azerbaijan. People don't come here just for the food but for the wild mountain ambience, which includes caged livestock and waiters decked in capes and daggers. It can be over the top but is fun for large groups or a weekend night out. The extensive appetizer bar is the best way to sample the unfamiliar fare; choose from piles of marinated and fresh vegetables, smoked meats, and spicy salads. The grilled meats (especially lamb) are recommended. Georgian wine is off the menu for political reasons, but its recipes survive.

36 Prospekt Mira. ☏ **495/680-5177.** Main courses 540–1,430 rubles. AE, MC, V. Daily noon–midnight. Metro: Prospekt Mira.

Shinok ★ UKRAINIAN   Among the most exclusive of Moscow's restaurants, Shinok is a tangle of juxtapositions. Its genre is Ukrainian farmhouse, with a multilayered dining hall decorated with haystacks, chicken cages, and the occasional goat, and waitstaff adorned as milkmaids and cowhands. Yet its prices are purely urban, and its clientele is decked out in Armani and Dior. Service is efficient, if somewhat haughty. The chefs present elegant, satisfying versions of countryside standards such as borscht with garlic rolls, potato-stuffed dumplings (*vareniki*), and suckling pig. The cold sorrel soup (*zelyoniye shchi*) is tangy and filling, and the egg-and-spice–stuffed carp is mouthwatering. The wines are overpriced; stick to beer or alcohol-free. This is a good splurge option, though count on taking a taxi home since it's a long way from the metro—or even better, order a taxi in advance to avoid the overcharging cabbies lying in wait outside.

2 Ulitsa 1905 Goda. ☏ **495/651-8101.** www.shinok.ru. Reservations recommended. Main courses 600–2,200 rubles. AE, MC, V. Daily 24 hr. Metro: Ulitsa 1905 Goda.

Sudar ★★ RUSSIAN   Expansive and proudly Russian, this restaurant is best appreciated over a long dinner after you've had some time to explore the rest of Moscow. It's located in a district full of reminders of Russia's military victories: the Triumphal Arch, designed to mimic Napoleon's Arc de Triomphe; Victory Park, marking the defeat of the Nazis; and the Battle of Borodino Museum, depicting the brutal battle with Napoleon's Grande Armée. Inside, the restaurant's fireplace is inviting on a cool night, and its bookshelves are lined with Russian tomes. The cuisine is Russian tinged by the French influences so popular in 18th- and 19th-century court circles. Top choices include braised rabbit with forest mushrooms, crab salad, and the dessert of baked apple with honey, cranberries, and almonds.

36A Kutuzovsky Prospekt. ☏ **499/249-6965.** www.sudar.ru. Main courses 600–1,800 rubles. AE, DC, MC, V. Daily noon–midnight. Metro: Kutuzovskaya.

Yar ★ RUSSIAN   This 19th-century landmark on the ground floor of the Sovietskaya Hotel earned popularity for its festive Gypsy music and decadent menus. After recovering from the stale Soviet years, it's again as opulent as ever, if a bit overpriced. The stunning and spacious Red Hall is named not for the Communists, but for the favored color of the partying nobility. Russia's new rich and visiting executives make business deals here, and though there's no dress code you'll feel uncomfortable in jeans. Neither staff nor diners are in much of a hurry, which gives you plenty of time to savor the *Dobry Molodets* ("Good Fellow") meat stew. Russians consider soups like this a first course, though it's hearty enough for a meal. The dishes are frivolously named, so don't be afraid to ask what the "Lady's Caprice" dessert contains. The baked grouse with figs and chestnuts is excellent.

32/2 Leningradsky Prospekt. ✆ **495/960-2004.** www.sovietsky.ru. Reservations recommended weekends. Main courses 1,200–1,700 rubles. AE, MC, V. Mon–Sat 11am until the last guest leaves. Metro: Dinamo.

Moderate

Correa's ★ INTERNATIONAL   If you need fresh fruits and vegetables or familiar flavors after one too many Russian marinated salads, try Correa's. Named after the New York chef who runs it, the restaurant caters to expats and adventurous Russians. The food is generally grilled or braised instead of fried or boiled as in much of Russian cuisine, but heavier dishes also make an appearance (for example, the house-made foie gras). Highlights include Caesar salad, eggplant-and-mushroom pizza, and carrot cake. The simple stone-and-wood hall is small and the kitchen is partly visible, giving the place an intimacy and casualness most Russian restaurants lack. Since reservations are not taken, avoid rush hours (noon–2pm and 7–9pm) if you don't want to wait. Correa's opens for breakfast, too—a rarity here. There's not much to see nearby, but Tverskaya Street and the zoo are not too far away. The owners also opened five other locations across town and two more in posh neighborhoods on the city's outskirts.

32/34 Bolshaya Gruzinskaya. ✆ **495/933-4684.** www.correas.ru/en. Main courses 400–600 rubles. AE, DC, MC, V. Mon–Fri 8am–10pm; Sat–Sun 9am–10pm. Metro: Belorusskaya or Mayakovskaya.

Inexpensive

Durdin RUSSIAN   This cozy spot brews flavorful, satisfying beers to go with its hearty stews and grilled meats. Sepia images of dirigibles and other retro images decorate the spacious, stylish, and comfortable restaurant. It's one of the few places in town with a good beef stroganoff, with choice pieces of meat. The potatoes sautéed with wild mushrooms are a hearty meal. German-style sausages are popular here and of course its beers, from the wheat beer to the smooth pilsners. You can also try five different beers for 160 rubles in small glasses. Or you can try beer cocktails, such as dark beer with black currant juice (not as bad as it sounds, but filling enough for a meal). The owners have opened three other restaurants across town.

56 Bolshaya Polyanka. ✆ **495/953-5200.** www.durdin.ru. Main courses 400–1,200 rubles. MC, V. Daily noon–midnight. Metro: Dobryninskaya.

PRACTICAL INFORMATION

Priyatnovo appetita! That's how you say "Bon appetit" in Russian, and you're bound to hear it while in Moscow. And you're bound to have some good food here, regardless of what warnings you may have heard before leaving home. The farther out of the city center you venture, the more limited your overall choices, though that, too, is changing fast. All restaurants listed here offer menus in English unless noted.

Restaurants generally serve continuously from lunch through dinner, and few are open before noon. Though reliable American and European restaurants proliferate, try some that specialize in Russian or fusion Russian-European cuisine. An even better idea is to sample the cuisines from other countries in the neighborhood that you're less likely to find at home: the Caucasus Mountains herbs and spices of Georgia, Azerbaijan, and Armenia; or the central Asian *plov* (a rice pilaf dish, usually with raisins,

Go along quickly and set all you have on the table for us. We don't want dough-nuts, honey buns, poppy cakes and other dainties, bring us a whole sheep, serve a goat and forty-year-old mead! And plenty of vodka, not vodka with all sorts of fancies, not with raisins and fla-vorings, but pure foaming vodka, that hisses and bubbles like mad.

–Nikolai Gogol, in his novel *Taras Bulba*

spices, and beef or lamb) of Uzbeki-stan and Tajikistan. These cuisines have worked their way into Russian cooking over the centuries, and they boast a much richer selection of fruits, vegetables, and spices than Russia's cold climate can produce.

Russians themselves, who can get traditional *pelmeni* (meat ravioli) and buttery rye *bliny* (crepelike pancakes) at home, seem to prefer French or Japanese food when they eat out. Sushi in particular has experienced a boom in recent years that is rather disconcert-ing for such a landlocked city.

Top-end hotels such as the **Metropol** and **Marriott** offer elaborate, all-you-can-eat Sunday brunches, replete with caviar and Russian delicacies as well as an abun-dance of standard breakfast foods, salads, meats, and mouthwatering desserts. While not cheap, they're a worthwhile splurge on a bad-weather day for the atmosphere, satisfying food and broad selection. These hotels often offer pleasant afternoon tea service, good for an elegant pick-me-up that won't cost nearly as much as a meal.

International chain restaurants, hotel restaurants, and those in the top price cate-gories all have nonsmoking sections; elsewhere it's hit-or-miss. The trend for non-smoking sections is catching on fast, so call in advance to check on this if smoke is a major issue for you.

Menu prices can be confusing, since they're often pegged to either the dollar or the euro. Prices listed here are in rubles, since when the check comes you'll have to pay in rubles at the current exchange rate. See the "Currency Confusion at Your Hotel" box on p. 74 for a fuller explanation. Credit cards are catching on quickly but are rarely accepted in small or inexpensive cafes.

Restaurants are spread out around town, but a few streets have a high concentra-tion of options for various wallet sizes any time of day: **Arbat Street, Nikolskaya Ulitsa,** and the upper end of **Tverskaya** are sure bets for hungry travelers.

For a history of Russian dining traditions and descriptions of typical dishes, see "Eating & Drinking" in chapter 2; for a glossary of menu terms, see chapter 18.

RESTAURANTS BY CUISINE

AMERICAN

Starlite Diner (Tverskaya & Environs, $$, p. 85)

ARCTIC

Expeditsiya ★ (Petrovka & Ukrainian Quarter, $$$$, p. 87)

BULGARIAN

Baba Marta ★ (Arbat district, $$, p. 90)

CAUCASIAN (GEORGIAN, ARMENIAN, AZERBAIJANI)

Dzhondzholi ★ (Tverskaya & Environs, $$, p. 84)

KEY TO ABBREVIATIONS:
$$$$** = Very Expensive   **$$$** = Expensive   **$$** = Moderate   **$ = Inexpensive

Genatsvale ★★ (Arbat district, $$, p. 90)

Noah's Ark ★ (Petrovka & Ukrainian Quarter, $$$, p. 88)

Prisoner of the Caucasus ★ (Outside the Garden Ring, $$$, p. 93)

Shesh-Besh ★ (South of Moscow River, $$, p. 91)

CENTRAL ASIAN

Farsi (Outside the Garden Ring, $$$, p. 92)

White Sun of the Desert ★ (Petrovka & the Ukrainian Quarter, $$, p. 88)

Yolki-Palki ★ (Tverskaya & Environs, $, p. 87)

FOOD COURT

Okhotny Ryad Shopping Center (Around Red Square, $, p. 82)

FRENCH

Carre Blanc ★★ (Outside the Garden Ring, $$$, p. 92)

Mayak (Arbat district, $, p. 91)

INTERNATIONAL

Bosco Bar ★★ (Around Red Square, $$$, p. 78)

Correa's ★ (Outside the Garden Ring, $$, p. 94)

FAQCafe ★ (Around Red Square, $$, p. 79)

Okhotny Ryad Shopping Center (Around Red Square, $, p. 82)

Tchaikovsky Concert Hall (Tverskaya & Environs, $, p. 87)

The Sad (South of Moscow River, $$$, p. 91)

Turandot ★★ (Tverskaya & Environs, $$$, p. 83)

ITALIAN

Donna Clara ★ (Tverskaya & Environs, $$, p. 84)

Il Patio (Tverskaya & Environs, $$, p. 84)

Krem ★ (Around Red Square, $$, p. 79)

Mayak (Arbat district, $, p. 91)

JAPANESE

Sushi Vyosla ★ (Around Red Square, $$$, p. 79)

RUSSIAN

Cafe Pushkin ★★★ (Tverskaya & Environs, $$$, p. 83)

Donna Clara ★ (Tverskaya & Environs, $$, p. 84)

Drova (Petrovka & Ukrainian Quarter, $, p. 89)

Durdin (Outside the Garden Ring, $, p. 94)

Il Patio (Tverskaya & Environs, $$, p. 84)

Kitezh ★★★ (Petrovka & Ukrainian Quarter, $$$, p. 87)

Kremlyovsky Cafe (Around Red Square, $, p. 82)

Na Melnitse ★ (Petrovka & Ukrainian Quarter, $$, p. 88)

1 Red Square ★★★ (Around Red Square, $$$$, p. 78)

Poslednaya Kaplya (Tverskaya & Environs, $, p. 85)

Shokoladnitsa ★ (South of Moscow River, $, p. 92)

Sudar ★★ (Outside the Garden Ring, $$$, p. 93)

Traktir Kupechesky ★ (Petrovka & the Ukrainian Quarter, $, p. 89)

Uncle Vanya ★★ (South of Moscow River, $$, p. 92)

Vanil ★ (Arbat district, $$$, p. 89)

Yar ★ (Outside the Garden Ring, $$$, p. 93)

RUSSIAN/AMERICAN

Rostik's (Tverskaya & Environs, $, p. 86)

RUSSIAN/EUROPEAN

Grilyazh ★★ (South of Moscow River, $$$, p. 91)

RUSSIAN/FRENCH

Parizhsk ★ (Arbat district, $$, p. 90)

Ragout ★ (Tverskaya & Environs, $$, p. 85)

WHERE TO EAT IN MOSCOW | Restaurants by Cuisine

RUSSIAN/INTERNATIONAL

Gogol (Petrovka & the Ukrainian Quarter, $, p. 89)

Pavilion at Patriarshy ★ (Tverskaya & Environs, $$$, p. 83)

Varvary ★ (Tverskaya & Environs, $$$$, p. 83)

UKRAINIAN

Shinok ★ (Outside the Garden Ring, $$$, p. 93)

Taras Bulba-Korchma ★ (Petrovka & the Ukrainian Quarter, $$, p. 88)

6

EXPLORING MOSCOW

M oscow is less a beautiful city than a collection of beautiful sights, many of them hidden beyond the expansive modern boulevards that successive Soviet governments bulldozed through town. The key to delighting in Moscow is to not let it overwhelm you. Keep your eye out for twisted gold cupolas peeking from residential courtyards, turn your gaze upward to admire the caryatids and atlantes supporting the balconies of otherwise unremarkable apartment buildings, and stay cool when challenges come your way. You'll be rewarded by the discovery of a new world, one that daily news reports from Red Square can't possibly convey. Taking in even a few main sights can give you an idea of the hardships that made Ivan the Terrible so terrible, introduce you to the nuances of icon painting, and help you appreciate the motivations and misjudgments of the Soviet regime. All this is essential to understanding why Russia and the Russians are the way they are today.

The things to see in Moscow fall roughly into four categories: church-related, art-related, Soviet-related, and everything else. Try to get a taste of each, regardless of your interests. The Kremlin is a category unto itself, representing every era of Russian history for the past 700 years and continuing to emanate an aura of mystery and authority as the seat of modern Russian politics. It is the most logical starting point for any glimpse of Moscow, providing a historical and contextual frame for viewing the rest of the city.

Moscow's art museums are often unfairly overlooked and overshadowed by the magnificent Hermitage Museum in St. Petersburg; try to squeeze in at least one of them. Closing days for museums vary, and many close 1 day a month for maintenance in addition to their weekly days off. Many museums adhere to the Soviet policy of charging foreigners significantly more for admission than Russians (see the box "Foreigner Tax" on p. 62). The foreigner's fee is usually equivalent to what you would pay at a similar site in western Europe. In addition, admission fees, though posted and paid for in rubles, are usually pegged to the U.S. dollar and therefore change frequently. Children 7 and under are always admitted free, unless noted.

Roughly half of Moscow's buildings date from the Soviet era, which spawned a range of architectural styles and governing attitudes despite its overall authoritarian bent. Much of the Soviet legacy has been (rightly) discredited in recent years, but ignoring Russia's Soviet history gives you a half-picture of what the country is about. Brilliant artists, writers, and architects managed to produce masterpieces in the Soviet era despite the pressure and whims of the state.

Moscow may not boast the literary traditions that St. Petersburg does, but many of Russia's most famous writers lived and worked here, and Muscovites are proud enough of the country's literary heritage to erect museums in their honor. Most of these museums label their exhibits in Russian only, though I've listed some below that offer printouts in English describing room contents. Among other Moscow highlights are the aristocratic estates around the city's edges, which often host festivals in the summer.

Many of the cathedrals listed here are functioning churches as well as museums, and services can be held almost any time of day. That doesn't bar visitors; however, you should follow local custom during your visit (see the box "Visiting Churches," later in this chapter).

THE KREMLIN ★★★

This 28-hectare (69-acre) fortress, called *kreml* in Russian, emerged in the 12th century as a wooden encampment, and survived many an invader to become synonymous with modern totalitarianism in the 20th century. Physically it's still a citadel, surrounded by unscalable red-brick walls and tightly guarded gates, though the river and moat that once protected its north and east sides were filled in nearly 200 years ago. These defenses make it all the more magical once you get inside, a world away from the din and modernity beyond. Its oak and birch walls were replaced with white stone ones in the 1360s, which were replaced again by 2.2km (1⅓ miles) of red-brick ramparts in the 1490s. Much of that brick remains standing today. Most of the buildings inside were wooden, however, and suffered several devastating fires. Despite its forbidding location and reputation, Mongol Tatars sacked the fortress in 1382, and revolt and bloodshed were familiar plagues throughout the centuries. Ivan the Terrible, Ivan the Great, Boris Godunov, and the first century of Romanov czars ruled from the Kremlin palaces. The Kremlin suffered some neglect after Peter the Great moved his capital to the swampland of what would become St. Petersburg, but it flourished again in a very different way when the Soviets made it the seat of Communist power.

Architecturally, the complex centers around its churches, as did Russian life and politics until the 20th century. The administrative and residential buildings and the tranquil, car-free plazas complement the cathedrals and reflect centuries of development and design. The Russian president no longer lives here, but his motorcade whisks him to work here every morning. Several buildings used for state functions are off-limits to tourists, with violators strictly reprimanded.

The ticket desk is a confusing affair, with different fees for different buildings and lower fees for Russians. The ideal itinerary would include everything: entrance to the Kremlin itself, Cathedral Square, the Armory, and the Diamond Fund. However, the latter two are open at limited times, not

Impressions

Fortress, sanctuary, seraglio, harem, necropolis, and prison . . . this violent contrast of the crudest materialism and the most lofty spirituality—are they not the whole history of Russia, the whole epic of the Russian nation, the whole inward drama of the Russian soul?
　　　　　　—Maurice Paléologue, *An Ambassador's Memoirs*, 1925

always on the same day. You can purchase tickets separately for each attraction. At the very least, choose the entrance–plus–Cathedral Square ticket, which allows you access to the chief buildings and will fill up a good hour or two. Visiting the cathedrals plus the Armory Museum will take you an entire afternoon.

Cathedral Square (Sobornaya Ploshchad) ★★★ forms a monument to Russian architecture of the 15th and 16th centuries, and its cathedrals deserve a thorough tour inside and out. It's easiest to start at **Ivan the Great Bell Tower,** which shows selected pieces from the Armory Museum. The tower was built in three stages over 3 centuries, starting in 1505, giving it a rather inconsistent appearance. Its heaviest and lowest bell is a staggering 64 tons (compared to Big Ben's 13.5 tons), but it is still dwarfed by the Czar Bell (see below). Continue to the **Cathedral of the Archangel Michael,** also built in 1505. Italian architect Alevisio Novi introduced the Corinthian capitals and Venetian shell scallops in the gables. The cathedral holds the tombs of Russia's rulers from Ivan I (1328–41) to Tsar Ivan V (1682–96), Peter the Great's predecessor. The interior of the church is fittingly somber, its hall of coffins surrounded by small shrines. The **Cathedral of the Annunciation** was built in 1482, and was where the czars were christened and married. Its tiers of tented gables and *kokoshniki* (pointed arches) are reflective of early Moscow architecture. Faded frescoes line the stone walls and columns from marbled floor to painted ceiling, their enormous faces and curved figures gazing over the central chamber. Renowned icon painter Andrei Rublev is buried here. Next door is the reconstructed **Red Staircase** mounted by centuries of czars after coronation. Also from these stairs, a young Peter the Great watched relatives impaled during an uprising that prompted him to flee Moscow to found his own capital. Tucked in the corner is the small **Church of the Deposition of the Robe,** built in a more traditional style of the late 15th century, with narrow windows and stained glass, the latter a rarity in Russian churches. It's

crown of monomakh (SHAPKA MONOMAKHA)

A key reason to visit the Kremlin early in your trip is to view the Crown of Monomakh *(Shapka Monomakha)*. Once you've seen this unusual crown, you'll recognize its likeness on many of your other stops: in the shape of church cupolas, in paintings of medieval Russia in Tretyakov Gallery, in frescoes in any Orthodox cathedral, even in modern fur hats on display at Russian designer boutiques. The crown was made of eight triangles of gold joined to form a cone; studded with red, blue, and green gems; topped with a cross; and trimmed with a brim of sable. The shape recalls the hats worn by central Asian khans, and reflects Russia's cross-continental geography. According to legend, the crown was presented to Prince Vladimir Monomakh of Kiev (1053–1125) by his grandfather, Byzantine Emperor Constantine IX. Though most historians say the existing crown wasn't made until much later (around the 14th c.), it still came to symbolize Russia's claim to the heritage of Byzantium. It was used in coronations at least as far back as the 1400s, until Peter the Great introduced more Western-style crowns in the 1700s. The Crown of Monomakh remained a key Kremlin treasure, and Peter and his successors continued to use the orb and scepter symbolizing the czar's dominion over the earth. All three are on display at the Armory Museum in the Kremlin.

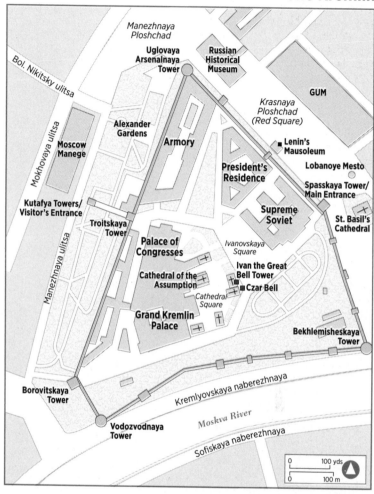

now a museum of wooden figures and church relics. Behind it you see the layered cluster of 11 domes that top **Terem Palace,** the oldest structure in today's Kremlin and the quarters of Russia's rulers until Peter the Great.

The most prominent building on the square is the **Cathedral of the Assumption ★★**, a white limestone building with scalloped arches topped by almost chunky golden domes. Started in 1475 by Italian architect Aristotle Fiorovanti, this church is the most tourist-friendly of the cathedrals on the square, with detailed English labels on icons and architectural details, and plenty of room for groups. The church is light and spacious, unlike any of the other churches on the square—or indeed of this period. Czars were crowned here, and patriarchs of the Russian Orthodox Church were inaugurated and buried here—the Patriarch's Seat is built into one of the pillars.

Napoleon's cavalry stabled horses here during their brief occupation of Moscow in 1812. Most of the frescoes date from a later restoration, in the 1660s. The **Patriarch's Palace** and the **Cathedral of the Twelve Apostles** are next door, both part of one structure that is now a museum of 17th-century Russian life and art. The exhibit includes a goblet with no base, requiring drinkers to toss back a full cup of wine in one gulp. The huge stove was used for making holy oil (involving more than 50 ingredients) once every 2 or 3 years. Other personal effects include a 17th-century chess set with knights mounted on elephants.

The Armory Museum ★★ (© 495/695-3776), despite its name, holds much more than guns. The Russo-Byzantine building, dating from the 19th century, occupies the spot where royal treasures were housed since the 14th century and offers a sweeping introduction to Russian history. Exhibits include the Fabergé eggs exchanged by Russia's last royal couple, Czar Nicholas II and Empress Alexandra, on Orthodox Easter for 3 decades; the silver goblet used by the man considered Moscow's founder, 12th-century Prince Yuri Dolgoruky; the velvet caftan Peter the Great wore while training in Holland's shipyards; and the gold brocade robes he wore at his coronation. The throne display, a Goldilocks-style delight, includes a compact throne for the diminutive Czar Paul and a double throne for Peter the Great and his co-ruler, his feeble half-brother Ivan. The imperial carriages will simultaneously satisfy fashion fans and car buffs. The weaponry through the ages is also impressive. Admission is limited to four sessions per day of 1 hour and 45 minutes each, at 10am, noon, 2:30, and 4:30pm. Audioguides in English are available and worth the 150 ruble price tag if you're not with a group.

The Diamond Fund holds the crown jewels, including Catherine the Great's coronation crown, the 89-carat Shah diamond presented to Nicholas I by the Shah of Persia in the early 1800s, and the 190-carat Orlov diamond that one of Catherine the Great's lovers gave her in an (unsuccessful) effort to keep her attentions. The fund can be visited only with a 30- to 40-minute tour, held every 2 hours and reserved ahead; it costs 500 rubles on top of the ticket to the Kremlin grounds. If you're short on time or money, skip it. The entrance is through the Borovitsky Gate of the Kremlin (© 495/629-2036; www.gokhran.ru/ru/exhibition). Open Friday to Wednesday from 10am to 5pm.

The Grand Kremlin Palace, not open to tourists, is used to receive foreign dignitaries. Watch television footage of a Kremlin reception and you may glimpse luxurious St. George's Hall, encircled with statues representing Russia's military victories throughout the centuries. The building, originally erected in the 1840s, underwent a costly renovation in the 1990s that uncovered a massive corruption scandal involving the Kremlin property department and questionable Swiss construction companies.

The staggeringly huge **Czar Cannon** and **Czar Bell** are two striking and bizarre features of the Kremlin and indeed of Russian history. The cannon, with a 40-ton barrel, was designed in 1586 to defend the Kremlin's Savior Gate, but it has never been fired. The chassis and the cannonballs alongside were built 3 centuries later and give a sense of the enormity of the weapon (though it was designed to fire stones and not cannonballs). The bell is by far the largest in the world, at 200 tons, 6.1m (20 ft.) high, and nearly 6.6m (22 ft.) in diameter. It was built in the 1730s but was abandoned and cracked before it could be rung. Both remain monuments to Russian ambition and royal excess.

Kremlin entrepreneurs recently reintroduced the centuries-old changing of the guard on Cathedral Square—but for a fee. The elaborate and carefully choreographed ceremony, which involves 12 horses, 45 soldiers in czarist-era uniforms, and the presidential orchestra, is held every Saturday at noon for visitors who pay 700 rubles for a special ticket. In addition to the guard-changing ceremony, the ticket includes tours of the churches on Cathedral Square (but not the Armory or Diamond Fund).

Note: The Kremlin is sometimes closed to the public during state visits, and other important ceremonies. Check with your hotel concierge or tour guide before you go.

You can buy Kremlin tickets at Kutafya Tower in Alexander Gardens (📞 **495/695-3776;** www.kreml.ru/en). Access to the grounds costs 350 rubles for adults, 100 rubles for students with ID and for children 7 and up. Admission to the Armory costs 700 rubles for adults, 200 rubles for students and for children 7 and up. An audioguide costs 200 rubles. Taking photos is forbidden inside the Armory and Cathedrals. Bag check (downstairs beneath the ticket offices) costs 50 rubles if you leave a backpack, double if you leave a camera or video camera. **Tip:** If you plan to visit Lenin's Mausoleum (see below), do so before reclaiming your bags. The Kremlin is open to visitors Friday through Wednesday from 10am to 5pm unless there's a special event, as noted above. Armory admission times are limited; see above for details. The closest metro stops are Okhotny Ryad and Biblioteka Imeni Lenina.

Guided tours can be booked between 10am and 5pm at 📞 **495/697-0349.**

AROUND RED SQUARE

Red Square (Krasnaya Ploshchad) ★★★   One of the world's most recognizable public spaces, Red Square is as impressive in reality as it is on-screen. Its uneven surface leads to a rounded peak at the center, from which Moscow unfurls on all sides. The square was already famous by 1434, when it was dubbed "Trading Square." Its current name appeared in the 1660s, when the word *krasnaya* meant "beautiful" or "important" as well as "red." The name took on different connotations in the 20th century, when the red flag–bearing Communists staged massive parades and demonstrations on the aptly titled square. Tanks no longer roll over its cobblestones on Soviet holidays, but the square still hosts big parades and the occasional rock concert. The best way to enter is through Resurrection Gates, next to the History Museum. Before heading to St. Basil's Cathedral, note the other two churches on the square: Kazan Cathedral in the northeast corner (a 1990s reproduction of a 17th-c. church), and the new and rather kitschy Gate Church of the Iberian Virgin beneath Resurrection Gates. On the last Saturday of every month, you can see the changing of the guard. Watching the sun rise or set over the landmark square is unforgettable, especially during the long days of summer.

Red Square (Krasnaya Ploshchad). No phone. Free admission. Metro: Ploshchad Revolutsii or Okhotny Ryad.

St. Basil's Cathedral (Khram Vasiliya Blazhennogo or Pokrovsky Sobor) ★★   The geometric domes and vivid tones of this 16th-century cathedral are almost garish up close, but they perfectly complement the solid red brick of the Kremlin wall and the gray cobblestones of Red Square. The church was built to honor the victory over Mongol Tatars in 1555, and legend has it that Ivan the Terrible had its architect's eyes poked out to keep him from making anything to rival Moscow's "stone flower." Inside, the cathedral is more reminiscent of the Middle Ages. The church lacks one large

Common terms and abbreviations

naberezhnaya/nab	*Embankment*
most	*Bridge*
ploshchad/pl	*Square* or *plaza*
prospekt/pr	*Avenue*
sad	*Garden*
ulitsa/ul	*Street*

Novodevichy Convent & Cemetery **17**

Obraztsov Puppet Theater **4**

Olimpiisky Sports Complex **19**

Pushkin Apartment Museum **13**

Pushkin Museum of Fine Arts & Museum of Private Collections **11**

Red Square **26**

Revolution Museum **6**

Russian Air Force Museum **30**

Sandunovskiye Banyi **23**

Spaso-Andronikov Monastery **29**

St. Basil's Cathedral **27**

Tolstoy House Museum **16**

Tretyakov Gallery **28**

Impressions

The streets teemed with spectators, some coming out of their houses to watch the extraordinary spectacle, others moved to indignation or even pity.
    –Jacob Reitenfelts, nephew of the czar's doctor, describing the execution of revolutionary Stepan Razin in front of St. Basil's in 1671

chapel, instead housing several dim and chilly sanctuaries reached by climbing deep and treacherously worn stairs and wandering through narrow, winding passages. Literature about the different chapels and niches is surprisingly limited, though vendors offer icons and souvenirs. St. Basil's is essentially a union of nine different churches and styles, and nine different chapels, beneath nine domes, each unique in size, form, and color. From the upper-floor windows you get a close-up view of the pilasters and a broad view of the Moscow River. You should be able to see everything in an hour or less.

Red Square. ✆ **495/698-3304.** www.saintbasil.ru. Admission 250 rubles adults, 50 rubles students and children over 7. Daily 11am–5pm. Metro: Ploshchad Revolutsii.

Lenin's Mausoleum (Mavzolei Lenina)   Yes, the embalmed body of the founder of the Soviet state is still on display in a mausoleum on Red Square. The stark Constructivist pyramid of red granite and gray and black labradorite was built in 1930, 6 years after Vladimir Lenin's death. The lines of pilgrims and solemn changing of the guard are long gone, and threats to bury him—as he wished for himself—have surfaced every few years since his USSR collapsed in 1991. In the meantime, the curious and a few faithful are shepherded through the cool, dim chamber by guards who make sure no one stands still long enough to ask any questions. The whole visit takes barely a few minutes. Equally fascinating are the gravestones of other Soviet icons along the Kremlin wall, which can be accessed only by visiting the mausoleum. Admirers still heap flowers on Stalin's grave daily. Because Nikita Khrushchev left office in disgrace, he is the only dead Soviet leader not buried here. Other remains here include those of Yuri Gagarin, the first man in space; and American journalist John Reed. Cameras and bulky backpacks are forbidden; they must be left at the bag check by the Borovitsky gate to the Kremlin, a good 5-minute walk away. It's easiest to visit here right after seeing the Kremlin, and then go get your bags.

Red Square. No phone. Free admission. Tues–Thurs, Sat, and Sun 10am–1pm. Metro: Ploshchad Revolutsii, Teatralnaya, or Okhotny Ryad.

National Historical Museum (Nationalny Istorichesky Muzei)   The intricately paneled and turreted crimson building on Red Square is the official repository of Russian historic artifacts, though Tretyakov Gallery (reviewed in the "Major Museums" section later in this chapter) and the Kremlin provide richer pictures of the country's 1,200-year-old history. The Historical Museum reopened in the 1990s after renovation, and hawkers lure tourists in from the throngs on Red Square. The exhibits are labeled in Russian only, and maps and tours in other languages are scarce. An audioguide in English is promised to arrive soon. Several exhibit halls remain closed to the public. The whole museum takes about an hour to tour. It's an impressive collection of garments, manuscripts, and weaponry from centuries past. The restaurant **1 Red Square** (p. 78), on the second floor, is a deluxe dining choice in a prime location.

1 Red Square. ✆ **495/692-3731.** www.shm.ru. Admission 250 rubles, 60 rubles students and children. Photo, video permission 130 rubles. Wed and Fri–Sun 10am–7pm, Thurs 11am–9pm. Closed Tues. Metro: Okhotny Ryad, Ploshchad Revolutsii, or Teatralnaya.

Alexander Gardens (Alexandrovsky Sad)   This green strip beneath the Kremlin's north wall was once a river that further isolated the fortress from its enemies. Now it's perfect for a peaceful stroll and perhaps a taste of ice cream or the savory pies sold along the path (avoid the hot dogs). At the gardens' entrance is an elegant marble monument of a helmet abandoned next to a flame. This **Tomb of the Unknown Soldier** was erected to honor those killed in World War II, and is surrounded by plaques to Soviet cities honored for their valiance and suffering at Nazi hands. The tomb, and the surrounding gardens, are often graced by newlyweds making a tour of Moscow sights after exchanging rings. The gardens run parallel to Mokhovaya Ulitsa, between the street and the Kremlin wall.

Metro: Ploshchad Revolutsii, Teatralnaya, or Okhotny Ryad.

CATHEDRALS, MONASTERIES & CONVENTS

Christ the Savior Cathedral (Khram Khrista Spasitelya) ★   This is not the oldest church in town, nor is it historically revered. It is the largest and the most expensive, though, and an unmistakable part of the skyline. It occupies such a key geographical and political spot in today's Moscow that it warrants a visit. Every stage of its existence has invited controversy. Originally built over 5 decades in the 19th century, the cathedral was a monument to Russia's victory over Napoleon, and to the gilded yet modernizing architecture of the day. Stalin ordered it razed in the 1930s and made plans for an immense Palace of Soviets in its place. Those plans never materialized, and the site became a large and popular indoor/outdoor swimming pool. In 1994, Moscow Mayor Yury Luzhkov drained the pool and ordered a speedy reconstruction of the cathedral. The finished product boasts staggering domes plated with gold alloy and clifflike white walls rising above the Moscow River, and it houses huge Orthodox church conferences and many official ceremonies. Lighter and airier than most Orthodox churches, it attracts some believers but turns away more traditional ones. A chronicle of Russian military victories is engraved on the marble panels leading to the main hall. Set aside about an hour to see the cathedral.

15 Volkhonka. ✆ **495/637-1276.** http://xxc.ru/english/index.htm. Tues-Sun 10am-5pm, Mon 1-5pm. Metro: Kropotkinskaya. Free admission. Individual tours 300-900 rubles depending on length and whether you need English translation, at ticket booth on Soimonovsky Proyezd.

Novodevichy Convent & Cemetery (Novodevichy Monastyr i Kladbishche) ★★ If you visit only one holy site in Moscow, make it this one. The convent, founded in 1524, became, over ensuing eras, a carefully arranged complex of churches in a variety of architectural styles. The stark white walls and gold-trimmed green domes of the **Cathedral of Our Lady of Smolensk** complement the deep red of the **Gate Church of the Intercession,** the two main churches in the complex. The fortress-like walls surrounding the convent reflect one of its key early purposes: to sequester daughters, sisters, and wayward wives of the nobility. Ivan the Terrible and Peter the Great sent their female foes here, which meant the convent enjoyed generous funding from the Kremlin. Today that disturbing page in the convent's history is largely forgotten. It is a haven of tranquillity, its adjoining pond and shaded paths a world away from the crowded rush of the rest of town. Don't miss the **cemetery** down the hill behind the convent. Considered Moscow's most prestigious burial site since the 18th century, it bears the unique and artful gravestones of many of Russia's literary,

Russian Orthodoxy is among the world's most ritual-oriented religions, yet almost since its birth more than 1,000 years ago, believers have differed over which rituals are more spiritually "correct." In the 1600s, a century after the Protestant Reformation began sweeping western Europe, the powerful and popular leader of the Russian Orthodox Church, Patriarch Nikon, introduced major reforms to church ritual. Ironically, many of the changes were intended to bring the church back to its earlier traditions, but he set off a furor among many believers who accused him of tampering with their faith. The period of reforms later became known as the Schism. Even today, pockets of Old Believers who refuse to accept the "new" rules can be found in remote Russian forests and even in a few big-city congregations.

Nikon's reforms eventually gained sway, so that believers now cross themselves with two fingers instead of three, and church architecture abandoned the tent-roofed tower (or *shatyor*) used in St. Basil's Cathedral and other pre-Nikonian cathedrals. A few decades later, Peter the Great further modernized and westernized the church by ordering Orthodox men to shave their beards—previously considered a sin. Peter also introduced the Julian calendar, which dated from the birth of Christ instead of from creation as the earlier Russian calendar had. Implementation of the new rules was unforgiving, and thousands of Old Believers fled into the forests to escape forced conversions. Those who were caught often burned themselves to death, singing hymns as they went up in flames. The Old Believers eventually won the freedom to worship under Catherine the Great in 1771, and some families returned to the big cities, though they were often marginalized.

The Old Believers (*staroobryadtsy* in Russian), also known as the Dissenters (*raskolniki*), eventually split into subsects, including the relatively liberal *popovtsy*, who were willing to deal with Orthodox priests; the *bezpopovtsy*, who totally rejected the official church and the state; the *skoptsy*, who castrated themselves to demonstrate their faith; and the *khlisty*, who believed in salvation through sin. Grigory Rasputin, controversial advisor to Czar Nicholas II and his wife, Alexandra, was rumored to belong to this last group.

For a glimpse at the Old Believers' world, visit **Nikolsky Old Believers' Commune (Nikolskoye Staroobryadtsoye Kladbishche)** in eastern Moscow. The striking Gothic-style church was commissioned in 1790, and its aristocratic sponsors included the respected Ryabushkinsky and Morozov families. They spent fortunes acquiring the religious art—dating from before the Schism—displayed in the church. Its unusual architectural features include sunburst windows, obelisks, and elaborate reliefs. The commune, at 29 Ulitsa Rogozhskiy Posyolok, holds services at 8am and 6pm Monday through Saturday, and at 7am and 10am Sunday (© **495/361-5198;** Metro: Ploshchad Ilyicha, Taganskaya).

musical, and scientific heroes—and more recently, modern Russia's first president, Boris Yeltsin. Pick up a map at the entrance to locate the graves of writers Anton Chekhov, Nikolai Gogol, and Mikhail Bulgakov; composer Dmitry Shostakovich; filmmaker Sergei Eisenstein; and Nikita Khrushchev, the only Soviet leader not buried at the Kremlin wall (because he died in disgrace instead of in office). Mikhail Gorbachev will likely choose Novodevichy as his resting place; his wife Raisa is

Moscow and its environs boast hundreds of beautiful Orthodox churches, many reopened in the 1990s after decades as storehouses, offices, or abandoned lots. Don't hesitate to wander into any church that appeals to you, as long as you do so respectfully. Dress codes are rarely enforced, but men are expected to remove their hats, and women should keep their heads covered (a hood or small scarf is enough to deflect critical glances). Both genders should wear clothing covering legs and shoulders. You will be rewarded by a hushed hall covered in frescoes and illuminated largely by candles. If you enter during a service, you're likely to hear the pure, hypnotic melodies of the priest or a choir, always a cappella. Services are held frequently throughout the day but attendance is generally low; believers often prefer to come and pray individually.

already here. Note also the curious grave-top monuments, such as a tank (for a World War II commander), a telephone (for a communications minister), and the tragicomic statue of circus clown Yuri Nikulin. The cemetery is a bit of a walk from the nearest metro station through an otherwise unremarkable neighborhood. Reserve this trip for a good-weather day, and allow 2 or 3 hours.

1 Novodevichy Proyezd. ✆ **499/246-8526.** Admission to the grounds free; a combined ticket including churches and exhibits 150 rubles. Cemetery admission 50 rubles. Cathedrals may be closed to tourists on Easter and feast days. Mon and Wed–Sun 10am–5:30pm, closed Tues and the first Mon of each month. Metro: Sportivnaya.

Spaso-Andronnikov Monastery ★   Founded in 1360, this monastery on the east bank of the Yauza River was slated for demolition in the Soviet era. Instead, it became a museum of early Russian art. Today the museum shares the site with monks who are again using the monastery for its original purpose. While simpler and less well-preserved than the Kremlin's cathedrals or Novodevichy, this monastery feels more authentic. Tour groups usually ignore it, making it calmer and less souvenir-heavy. Andrei Rublev, perhaps Russia's greatest icon painter, spent his last years in this monastery and died here in 1430. You can see many of his works here—if you have any interest in Orthodox icons, this is *the* place to visit. Andrei Tarkovsky's film *Andrei Rublev* is a chilling and gripping journey through medieval Russia that took years to make it past Soviet censors, and provides a great context for visiting this monastery. It's rather out-of-the-way, so give yourself at least an hour once you get here.

10 Andronyevskaya Ploshchad. ✆ **495/678-1467.** www.rublev-museum.ru. Admission to grounds free, icon exhibit 150 rubles, applied art museum 120 rubles. Thurs–Tues 11am–6pm; closed last Fri of the month. Metro: Ploshchad Ilicha, then a 10-min. walk toward the Yauza River.

SOVIET SIGHTS

Although many monuments of Socialist realism around town have been deposed, a few remaining examples are worth viewing if you're in the neighborhood. **The Gagarin Monument** is a sweep of steel rocketing toward the cosmos, topped with a sculpture of the first man in space, Yuri Gagarin. Gagarin remains a cult figure in Russia, seen as the man who made the world finally take Russians seriously (Gagarinskaya Ploshchad; Metro: Leninsky Prospekt). **The Lenin monument** on

Oktyabrskaya Square shows the Soviet founder with a crowd of enthusiastic followers at his feet preparing to build a nation (Oktyabrskaya Ploshchad; Metro: Oktyabrskaya). **The Worker and Collective Farmer** is the best and biggest of the collection, but was under renovation at press time. It's an oversized statue of a man and woman reaching boldly toward the sky; he's holding a hammer and she, a sickle (at the entrance to the All-Russian Exhibition Center; Metro: VDNKh).

Most cities' public transit systems are necessary eyesores. Moscow's is a masterpiece and worth a mention here. Central planning meant that Stalin was free to pour funds and artistic energy into creating the metro. Today it's the world's busiest subway system, yet even trains that run every 90 seconds aren't enough to diffuse crowding. The system is still cleaner than most other big-city subways. Its oldest stations, dating from the 1930s and 1940s, are its grandest, particularly those on the Circle Line. The newer stations at the edges of town are corridors of bland but well-polished white tile. Even if you don't use the metro to get around, take a peek at one of the following stations: **Ploshchad Revolutsii,** with its bronze sculptures of Soviet swimmers, mothers, and sailors holding up the marble columns; **Kievskaya** (Circle Line stop), with its cheerful mosaics portraying Ukrainian-Russian friendship; **Novokuznetskaya,** with its cast-iron streetlights; and **Novoslobodskaya,** with its Art Nouveau stained glass.

For an even closer view of the metro, with models and an avalanche of statistics, visit the tiny **Metro Museum** atop the Sportivnaya station (© **495/622-7309**); free admission; Monday 10am to 4:30pm, Tuesday to Thursday 9am to 4:30pm, Friday 9am to 3pm; closed Saturday and Sunday and last Monday of every month. The friendly director is a former metro driver who has a lifetime of stories to share (though in Russian only). Most stations are quite deep, and all have head-spinningly long escalators; some of the stations such as the mosaic-ceilinged **Mayakovskaya** were even built as bomb shelters during World War II. See "Getting Around Moscow" on p. 286 for metro ticket prices.

Revolution Museum (State Museum of Contemporary Russian History) This museum officially changed its name in the 1990s but is still commonly referred to as the Revolution Museum. The thrust of the exhibits is the same, though the moral weight has been lifted and now much of it appears more kitschy than political. Beyond the excess of red (banners, carpets, lighting), the museum is a piece of Russian history saved from the hands of those who would have erased the Soviet era from memory the way the Soviets tried to erase czarist-era memories. Newer exhibits include labor camp grave posts and *glasnost*-era efforts at a more honest look at history. The museum is housed in an elegant building on Tverskaya Street that once hosted Masonic meetings. Allow an hour or so.

21 Tverskaya St. © **495/699-6724.** http://eng.sovr.ru. Admission 100 rubles. Tues–Wed and Fri 10am–6pm; Thurs, Sat, and Sun 11am–7pm; closed Mon and last Fri of each month. Metro: Pushkinskaya, Tverskaya, or Chekhovskaya.

Art MUSEON ★ Another example of Russia's confused allegiances in the post-Communist era, this park gathers together scores of busts and full-size statues of Lenin and other now-disgraced Soviet icons. The pieces were torn down in the democratic fervor of the early 1990s, but not destroyed. Many ended up in a graceless heap in an alley in nearby Gorky Park before a group of independent artists righted them and gave them a new home behind the modern art museum. Despite its political overtones, the park is a peaceful and pleasant place, with wooden bench swings,

3 Mitino
Volokolamskaya
Myakinino
Strogino
Krylatskoye
Molodyozhnaya
Kuntsevskaya
4
Pionerskaya
Filyovsky Park
Bagrationovskaya
Fili
Kutuzovskaya
Studencheskaya
Slavyansky Bulvar
Park Pobedy
Kievskaya
Smolenskaya
Smolenskaya
Aleksandrovsky Sad
Borovitskaya
Arbatskaya
Biblioteka Im. Lenina
Park Kultury
Oktyabrskaya
Frunzenskaya
Sportivnaya
Vorobyovy Gory
Universitet
Prospekt Vernadskovo
Yugo-Zapadnaya **1**

7 Planernaya
Skhodnenskaya
Tushinskaya
Shchukinskaya
Oktyabrskoe Pole
Polezhaevskaya
Begovaya
Ulitsa 1905 Goda
Mezhdunarodnaya
Vystavochnaya
Barrikadnaya
Krasnopresnenskaya
5
Pushkinskaya
Chekhovskaya
Tverskaya
Arbatskaya
4

2 Rechnoy Vozkal
Vozny Stadion
Voykovskaya
Sokol
Aeroport
Dinamo
Timiryazevskaya
Dmitrovskaya
Savyolovskaya
Mendeleyevskaya
Novoslobodskaya
Tsevetnoi bd.
Mayakovskaya
Pushkinskaya
Tverskaya
Okhotny Ryad
Teatralnaya
Ploshchad Revolutsy
Kropotkinskaya
Polyanka
Dobryninskaya
Serpukhovskaya
Tulskaya
Shabolovskaya
Nagatinskaya
Leninsky Prospekt
Nagornaya
Akademicheskaya
Nakhimovsky Prospekt
Profsoyuznaya
Sevastopolskaya
Novye Cheryomushky
Kaluzhskaya
Chertanovskaya
Belaevo
Yuzhnaya
Konkovo
Prazhskaya
Tyoply Stan
Ulitsa Akademika Yangelya
Yasenevo
Annino
Novoyasenevskaya
(Bitsevky Park) **6**
Bulvar Dmitriya Donskogo **9**

9 Altufievo
Bibirevo
Otradnoye
Vladikino
Petrovsko-Razumovskaya
10 Mariyna Roshcha
Dostoevskaya
Ploshchad Suvorova
Sukharevskaya
Trubnaya
Turgenevskaya
Chistiye Prudy
Kuznetsky Most
Lubyanka
Kitai-Gorod
Tretyakovskaya
Novokuznetskaya
Paveletskaya
Avtozavodskaya
Kolomenskaya
11 Kashirskaya
Varshavskaya
11 Kakhovskaya
Kantemirovskaya
Tsarytsino
Orekhovo
Domodedovskaya
Krasnogvardeyskaya
Brateyevo

6 Medvedkovo
Babushkinskaya
Sviblovo
Botanichesky Sad
VDNKh
Alekseevskaya
Rizhskaya
Prospekt Mira
Komsomolskaya
Krasnive Vorota
Sretensky Bulvar
Kurskaya

1 Ulitsa Podbelskovo
Cherkizovskaya
Preobrazhenskaya pl.
Sokolniki
Krasnoselskaya
3 Shcholkovskaya
Pervomayskaya
Izmailovskaya
Izmailovsky Park
Semyonovskaya
Elektrozavodskaya
Baumanskaya
8 Novo Gireevo
Perovo
Shosse Entuziastov
Aviamotornaya
Kurskaya
Chkalovskaya
Ploshchad Ilicha
Rimskaya
Marksistskaya
Taganskaya
5
Proletarskaya
Krestyanskaya Zastava
Volgogradsky Prospekt
Tekstilshiki
Kuzminki
Ryazansky Prospekt
Vykhino **7**
Dubrovka
Kozhukhovskaya
Pechatniki
Volzhskaya
Lublino
Bratislavskaya
Maryino
10
Borisovo
Shipilovskaya
Zyablikovo **2**

1	Sokolnicheskaya
2	Zamoskvoretskaya
3	Artbatsko-Pokrovskaya
4	Filevskaya
5	Koltsevaya
6	Kaluzhko-Rizhskaya
7	Tagansko-Krasnopresnenskaya
8	Kalininskaya
9	Serpukhovsko-Timiryazevskaya
10	Lyublinskaya
11	Kakhovskaya
	Under Construction
⊙⊙	Transfer station

bird feeders, and a garden of exotic and Russian pines. The statues of Soviet leaders are interspersed with other icons such as pianist Van Cliburn, and surrounded by lanes of Avant-Garde sculptures. It's easy to combine this with a visit to the Museum of Modern Art (see review below). Allow a half-hour or so for exploring and resting in the park.

10 Krymsky Val (behind the Central House of Artists). © **499/238-3396.** www.muzeon.ru. Admission 100 rubles. Daily 9am–9pm. Metro: Oktyabrskaya or Park Kultury.

Museum of Cosmonautics (Muzei Kosmonavtiki) ★ ☺ 🔋   Housed beneath a giant aluminum monument of a rocket soaring into space, this museum is a tribute to the minds and might that put the Soviet Union head-to-head with the United States in the Space Race. This is the team that sent the first man and woman into space, among the Soviet space machine's other accomplishments. The museum itself enjoyed a recent renovation, though still can feel heavy with nostalgia for former grandeur. Overall, its message and appeal are still universal. Exhibits include space-suits, moon rocks, pieces of rockets and satellites, and film of early space flights. Though most items are labeled in Russian only, a good English-language audioguide is now available and worth the additional fee. Although space travel and a career as an astronaut have lost their appeal for many children, travel-obsessed kids and sci-fi fans will have a great time here. Allow an hour, plus travel time to get here since it's far from the center (but right on top of a metro station).

Prospekt Mira 111. © **495/683-7968.** www.space-museum.ru. Admission 200 rubles adults. Audiogu-ide in English 300 rubles. Tues–Sun 11am–7pm; closed Mon and last Fri of each month. Metro: VDNKh.

Museum of GULAG History (Muzei Istorii GULAG)   This stop is not for the faint of heart. Tucked on a street of posh boutiques, a gloomy archway leads into a courtyard strung with barbed wire and hung with huge portraits of victims of the GULAG, or Soviet labor camp. The sign beneath the portraits reads: THESE ARE 12 OF MANY MILLION . . . , referring to the millions of Soviet citizens who passed through labor camps. Most were punished for political crimes, often only imagined by a para-noid Communist leadership. Many were killed or tortured. Those who survived usu-ally faced repression and discrimination for the rest of their lives, as did their families. The Moscow city government runs this museum, one of the city's newest. The federal government has a more complex attitude toward its Soviet predecessors; while many of the "repressed" were rehabilitated under Boris Yeltsin in the 1990s, the current administration has little interest in reviewing that period of Russia's history.

16 Petrovka. © **495/621-7310.** www.gmig.ru. Admission 100 rubles, tours for up to four people 800 rubles. Tues–Sat 11am–4pm. Metro: Kuznetsky Most.

Museum of Armed Forces   Military history buffs and those who like weapons will appreciate this collection of Czarist and Soviet uniforms, medals, arms, and other military memorabilia spanning the period from the 18th century to the Cold War times. The museum's courtyard houses a sizable arsenal of Soviet tanks, cannons, jets, and helicopters.

2 Ulitsa Sovetskoy Armii. © **495/681-6303.** http://cmaf.ru. Admission 75 rubles; English-language tours for up to five people, 2,000 rubles. Wed–Sun 10am–5pm. Metro: Novoslobodskaya, Tsvetnoi Blvd.

Russian Air Force Museum   A former Soviet military air base outside Moscow houses dozens of combat planes starting from World War I designs to the latest jets Russia has produced. The museum was off-limits to outsiders during Soviet times and is still administered by the air force. Visits by foreigners are by appointment only,

CONQUERING THE COSMOS

The big, bad Soviet Union, America's rival in the race to space and nuclear superiority, was as surprised at its superpower status as the outside world. An unwieldy mass of illiterate peasants before Lenin came along, Russia took just a few decades to reach the scientific heights needed to conquer the cosmos.

The Soviet government poured funding and pressure on its rocket scientists, who stunned the world when they beat the Americans in sending the first satellite into space in 1957. **Sputnik,** the name of the vessel and the Russian word for "satellite," instantly entered the international vocabulary. A month later a Soviet mutt named **Laika** orbited the earth. She was merely setting the stage, however, for the Soviets' next breakthrough: **Yuri Gagarin's first manned flight** in April 1961—a month before U.S. astronaut Alan Shepard made the journey. Gagarin came to represent Russia's victory over its own backward and repressive past, with a literal and figurative blast into the future. The anniversary of his flight, April 12, is informally celebrated as a national holiday, and his smiling image is one of the few Soviet-era faces that evokes universal pride. Just 2 years later, textile worker–turned-cosmonaut Valentina Tereshkhova became the **first woman in space,** a full 20 years before the United States sent Sally Ride into orbit in 1983.

The Soviet space program suffered plenty of defeats, including the deaths of four cosmonauts in accidents on the Soyuz-1 in 1967 and the Soyuz-11 in 1971, but propagandists largely concealed them from the public. Pilots from dozens of countries flew to space on Soviet rockets, and it wasn't until the late 1980s that the bankruptcy of the Soviet Union started crippling its once-mighty space machine. **Mir space station** became a remarkable symbol and victim of Russia's post-Soviet plight. Launched in 1986, just weeks after the U.S. shuttle *Challenger* exploded in tragedy, the Mir orbiting lab was built to last 3 or 4 years. But when the country that launched it crumbled in 1991, the Mir's crew was told to stay aloft for another 6 months while the government found money to bring them home. The station and Russia's space program scraped by, helped out by a once-unthinkable partnership with NASA, which had no space station of its own. After a string of accidents in the late 1990s, the Mir was finally sent to a choreographed demise in the Pacific Ocean in 2000.

Russia's space program has since dedicated most of its energies to the International Space Station—and to sending the world's first **"space tourists"** into orbit. The once-secretive compounds at Star City and Korolev outside Moscow now occasionally open their doors for well-paying tourists, who can test their stamina on centrifugal machines even if they don't plan any space journeys.

For a cheaper and less stomach-churning way to learn more about the Russian space program, visit the **Museum of Cosmonautics** (reviewed above) or climb aboard a real **Buran space shuttle** in Gorky Park (reviewed below). Three, two, one, blastoff . . . .

and it will take up most of a full day because of the travel time, but it's a truly only-in-Russia experience that is well worth the effort if aviation interests you.

Posyolok Monino, 38km (24 miles) southeast of Moscow on Gorkovskoye Hwy. Fees vary. © **495/526-3327** or 495/747-3928. www.monino.ru. Commuter trains from Yaroslavsky Railway Station to Station Monino. Mon–Tues and Thurs–Fri 9:30am–5pm; Sat 9am–2pm.

6 MAJOR MUSEUMS

Tretyakov Gallery (Tretyakovskaya Galereya) ★★★ This collection of master-pieces awes both newcomers to Russian art and connoisseurs. Started by the Tretya-kov brothers, merchant philanthropists in the 1800s, the gallery was Russia's first public art museum. The brothers' collections are a big part of it, but many works were nationalized from private collections by the Soviets. The museum is the premier repository of Russian art, starting with the earliest Orthodox icons, which date from Russia's conversion in the 9th century. It then traces the country's history through the naturalism of the 19th century, the Art Nouveau works of Mikhail Vrubel, and the 20th-century Avant-Garde works of Malevich and Kandinsky. Seek out Ilya Repin's heart-wrenching portrait of Ivan the Terrible ripped by remorse after slaying his son in a rage, and underrated talents such as the eerie Impressionist Arkhip Kuindzhi. Several artists represented had only a casual relation to Russia, but that doesn't diminish their artistic value. Much improved by a lengthy renovation, the Tretyakov reopened in 1995 with a visitor-friendly layout and increased services for non–Russian speakers. Viewing the museum chronologically makes the most sense, though it requires one clumsy detour to view the earliest icons on the second floor. The English audioguide is good if you're on your own. Allow a full morning or afternoon for this one. The pedestrian street in front is ideal for strolling, and the adjacent restaurant is a treasure of Russian cuisine, though it's often full.

10 Lavrushinsky Pereulok. ☏ **499/230-7788.** www.tretyakovgallery.ru. Admission 360 rubles, 220 rubles students and children over 7. Audioguide 250 rubles. No credit cards, but there's an ATM. Small group tours in English, price negotiable depending on size of group. Tues–Sun 10am–7:30pm. Metro: Tretyakovskaya or Novokuznetskaya.

Pushkin Museum of Fine Arts (Muzei Izobratitelnykh Isskustv imeni Pushkina) ★★ This rich and worthwhile museum is often overlooked in favor of St. Petersburg's Hermitage Museum. In fact, the two complement each other, and both deserve a look. Most visitors head straight for the impressive collection of French Impressionist works, though the museum also boasts ancient Greek sculp-tures and Egyptian bronzes, as well as works by Rembrandt, Rubens, and the Italian masters of the Renaissance. There is also a small but worthwhile collection of post-Impressionist and modernist art. Be sure to view the ever-expanding exhibition of controversial paintings stolen from European Jews by the Nazis and later seized by looting Soviet troops (Russians call them "rescued" artworks), including pieces by Renoir, Daumier, and van Gogh. Note that this Pushkin Museum is merely named after Russians' favorite author Alexander Pushkin; if you want to see a museum about him, skip ahead to the "Literary Moscow" section below.

12 Volkhonka. ☏ **495/609-9520.** www.arts-museum.ru. Admission 300 rubles, 150 rubles students and children 7 and up. Audioguides 250 rubles; available at the coat check downstairs. Tues–Sun 10am–7pm. Metro: Kropotkinskaya.

Museum of Private Collections A section of the Pushkin Museum in an adja-cent three-story mansion hosts rotating exhibits from private Russian collections, often of very high caliber. Recent shows have included a collection of antique glass, engravings from the collection of the Norwegian ambassador, and still lifes by Russian "Wanderer" artists (*peredvizhniki*).

10 Volkhonka. ☏ **495/697-1610.** www.arts-museum.ru/museum/buildings/mlk/index.php. Admission 100 rubles, 60 rubles students and children 7 and up. Wed–Sun noon–7pm.

Cult of the Coat Check

Regardless of what time of year you travel, you are sure to face this peculiarly Russian form of hospitality. All museums and theaters (and even many restaurants) will not let you past the foyer unless you take off your outer layers and leave them at the coat check. In the depth of winter this is a welcome way to shed heavy and soggy coats and hats, and it's a service usually free of cha[...] mer day, however, [...] fight if you want [...] with you as you [...] spaces. When yo[...] are not expected but are greatly [...] ciated, even small amounts. You may find that the woman who so sternly disrobed you upon arrival has mended your dangling button.

New Tretyakov Gallery/Museum of Modern Art (Novaya Tretyakovka) ★ A gargantuan concrete slab of a building across from Gorky Park houses Moscow's main modern art museum (the New Tretyakov) and the Central House of Artists, a cluster of galleries, concert spaces, and art shops (see next review). The New Tretyakov follows Tretyakov Gallery's trajectory into the modern era, starting with Russian art from the 1920s and heading to the present. The building's scale and style are well-suited for the Constructivist canvases of Vasily Kandinsky and Kasimir Malevich, and for its impressive collection of Soviet Avant-Garde art. The museum has suffered in recent years from competition by more cutting-edge galleries, but it still mounts big-name exhibits. Entrance to the museum is on the south side of the building, not the side facing the street.

10 Krymsky Val. ✆ **499/230-7788.** www.tretyakovgallery.ru. Admission 360 rubles adults, 220 rubles students and children over 7. Tues–Sun 10am–7:30pm. Metro: Oktyabrskaya or Park Kultury.

Central House of Artists (Tsentralny Dom Khudozhnika) ✆ These four floors of galleries and art shops are great for getting a look at what Russia's artists are currently up to, but most people come to buy gifts. The unusual and creative souvenirs include art books in Russian and English, embroidered felt boots, Art Nouveau tea sets, Constructivist vases, tongue-in-cheek T-shirts, and Soviet postcards. Inexpensive evening concerts and other experimental performances draw Moscow's creative crowd. Many visitors come for the informal art market that wends along the adjacent embankment, though beware of rules for exporting works of art (see "Visas & Customs" on p. 297).

10 Krymsky Val. ✆ **499/230-1782.** http://cha.ru. Admission 200 rubles adults, 100 rubles students. Tues–Sun 11am–8pm. Metro: Oktyabrskaya or Park Kultury.

PARKS & GARDENS

Gorky Park ★ The official name of this famed, sprawling green space is Central Park of Culture and Rest, named after Maxim Gorky, but Russians refer to it as Park Gorkovo (Gorky Park) or Park Kultury (the name of the nearby metro station). The most visited—and least restful—part of the park is near the entrance, where an amusement park, ponds, and a dizzying array of game booths, trinket stands, and street performers compete for attention. The park extends several acres beyond that, tracing a swath of green between the southwest loop of the Moscow River and the

t Sparrow Hills. The park amusements are standard fare for most West-
s (especially savvy young ones), with a couple of notable exceptions: In
ne paths are specially coated with ice for skaters, and ice sculptures pop up
d the park for children to climb on. Also, a real Buran space shuttle, designed
. space flight but scrapped for lack of funding, is now parked along the river and
open to visitors. It doesn't emulate weightlessness, though it will shake you up a bit
in a blastoff simulation. Some of the other rides are in dodgy condition. Note the
Lenin carving over the park's columned entrance.

Krymsky Val. Admission free. Metro: Oktyabrskaya or Park Kultury.

Victory Park (Park Pobedy)   The Great Patriotic War, as Russians refer to World
War II, is a crucial part of Russia's collective memory, and this park seeks to pay
tribute to those who brought the Soviet Union victory over the Nazis. The crushing
cost of the war—27 million Soviet lives, more than was suffered by any other country—remains a painful and defining memory even today. Children frolic on tanks
parked along the park's lush lanes, and newlyweds pose in front of its various monuments. In a post-Soviet gesture of religious tolerance, the park now houses a synagogue, a mosque, and an Orthodox chapel. The stirring images of the Victory
Museum are worth viewing, though be prepared for a jolt when you exit into crowds
of carefree in-line skaters. Don't miss the collection of World War II aircraft, armor,
and artillery along the back road.

Kutuzovsky Prospekt. Daily sunrise–sundown. Metro: Park Pobedy. Victory Museum © **499/148-5550.**
www.poklonnayagora.ru. War museum 120 rubles adults. Tues–Sun 10am–7pm.

Izmailovsky Park ★   Most tourists only make it as far as the enormous souvenir market in the park's corner (p. 134), but the park itself is well worth deeper investiga-
tion. Take the metro to the next stop (simply called Izmailovskaya) past the market,
and stumble off the train into a maze of trails that wind among dense forest, hidden
ponds, and gurgling streams. Wooden pavilions scattered through the park house
picnickers or clusters of chess players in heated play. It's a superb spot for cross-

---

The Silvery Islet (Serebryanny Bor)

This unusual island in northwest Moscow is a surprising refuge of oak-lined
paths, silky dunes, and even beaches.
It's well upstream from the factories
and other pollutants that make the
Moscow River so murky in the center of
town. The island's relatively clean air
and parkland, and its proximity to the
Kremlin, made it a prime spot for
dachas (country cottages and gardens)
for the Soviet elite, and its well-pro-
tected cottages are still prized real
estate. Several small beaches line the
two shores, some more secluded than
others, including sections preferred by
nudists and gays. Water equipment

such as pedal boats and canoes are
available for rent, beach volleyball
games are common, and a few rides
have been set up for children. On hot
summer weekends the island gets
crowded, but summer weekdays, or
pleasant weekends in spring or autumn,
are great times to enjoy a break from
traffic-clogged streets and watch Muscovites unwind.

To get to the island, take the metro
to Polezhayevskaya; then take trolley
bus no. 20, 21, or 65 to the last stop, on
the island. A taxi ride from downtown
Moscow takes about 15 minutes, except
during rush hour.

country skiing half the year if you have your own equipment, or for biking or hiking in summer.

Izmailovskoye Shosse. Daily until sundown. Metro: Izmailovskaya.

Patriarch's Ponds (Patriarshiye Prudy) ★★ ☺ This patch of green in central Moscow is a great getaway from the buzz of nearby Tverskaya Street and the Garden Ring, and an unmatchable spot for lazy people-watching. Mikhail Bulgakov made the neighborhood famous and gave it a permanently bohemian reputation with his novel *Master and Margarita*, in which the devil meets the protagonists next to the ponds. There's actually just one pond now, which serves as an ice rink in winter and shelters a few swans in summer. Kids appreciate the playground, surrounded by bronze screens depicting the fables of another favorite Russian author, Ivan Krylov. The benches fill up in late afternoon, as young people congregate with guitars and beer. Nearby Café Margarita carries on the Bulgakov tradition, and offers funky fare along with Gypsy or jazz music.

Malaya Bronnaya Ulitsa. 24 hr. Metro: Mayakovskaya or Tverskaya.

Botanical Gardens (Botanichesky Sad) This vast, overgrown park is quite far from the center of town, and is fairly lifeless for much of the year given Moscow's climate. In season, however, the flowers are often unusual and breathtaking. Outside the chief displays, the park is rather overgrown and labyrinthine, but it's still a lovely place for a stroll, bike ride, or picnic. Since they're so far off the main track, the gardens are worth visiting only if the weather's clear, or if you're visiting the adjacent All-Russian Exhibition Center (see next review). Wear good shoes.

Daily until sundown. Metro: Botanichesky Sad.

All-Russian Exhibition Center (formerly VDNKh) ☺ It used to be called the Exhibit of the Achievements of the People's Economy, and the park's design certainly has a propagandistic feel, with its "friendship of peoples" fountains and pavilions once used to show off the fruits of Soviet factories, the nuclear energy industry, and collective farms. The stunning centerpiece is a fountain with gilded statues of women representing each of the 15 former Soviet republics. Its current contents reflect the hard-core capitalism of today's Moscow. Some halls are packed with vendors selling the latest DVD players, cellphones, and PDAs; others hawk in-line skates and high-speed bikes; still others have stalls packed with stuffed animals and Chinese-made plastic toys. Some pavilions still house international expos, from high-tech fairs to sugar refinery trade shows. Amusement park rides are scattered throughout the grounds, with the fast and enormous Ferris wheel a major draw. There's even a fishing pond, where you can catch, cook, and eat real fish for a 2,000-ruble fee. The park is far from the center of town, but if you're staying nearby or have kids, it can make for a fun afternoon. Muscovites call it by its Soviet acronym, VDNKh, pronounced "veh-deh-en-KHA."

Free admission; exhibits sometimes charge entrance fee. Daily 9am–9pm. Metro: VDNKh.

ARISTOCRATIC ESTATES

Several former private estates seized by the Soviets have been turned into museums or concert spaces, with their extensive grounds now used for picnics, jogging, and cross-country skiing. The **Kuskovo** estate boasts a porcelain exhibit and a luxurious orangerie. On the Fourth of July it's taken over by the American Chamber of

Commerce for a bash that Muscovites have come to love (✆ **495/375-3131;** http://kuskovo.ru; Metro: Ryazansky Prospekt). The Palace is open Wednesday to Sunday, 10am to 6 pm April to October, 10am to 4pm October to April. The neoclassical **Ostankino** mansion, like Kuskovo, belonged to the prominent noble family the Sheremetevs. It has a small exhibit of 18th-century art and artifacts, and hosts chamber music concerts throughout the summer. Bikes, scooters, and in-line skates available for rent. (Ostankino Park; ✆ **495/683-4645;** www.ostankino-museum.ru; May–Sept only, Wed–Sun 11am–7pm; Metro: VDNKh).

The **Tsaritsino** estate is Catherine the Great's never-finished masterpiece, meant to be her residence on Moscow's outskirts before she lost interest in and money for the project. The lush grounds, now within city limits, are easy to lose yourself in on a lazy summer day (1 Dolskaya Ulitsa; ✆ **495/325-4844;** www.tsaritsyno-museum.ru, museum Wed–Fri 11am–6pm, Sat 11am–8pm, Sun 11am–7pm; Metro: Tsaritsino).

Kolomenskoye ★★★ ☺ This park, museum, festival site, and religious history tour is the jewel of Moscow's estate museums. Extending several acres along the Moscow River well south of the city center, Kolomenskoye gathers churches and historic buildings from the 15th to the 20th century in a huge green space perfect for picnicking, sledding, or lounging in the grass. It holds several festivals throughout the year themed around Russian holidays (including Butter Week, described in the "Calendar of Events" on p. 35), with different period dress and performances (in Russian only). The breathtaking white facade of the 16th-century Church of the Ascension is closed to the public due to disrepair, but it's a perfect backdrop for a roll down the grassy slope. Apple orchards, a honey farm, and tea huts provide fun and nourishment for kids. A boat dock launches leisurely trips up and down this section of the river, though the view opposite Kolomenskoye is industrial and colorless. The site is a good 10-minute walk from the metro, its only drawback.

1 Letnyaya Ulitsa. ✆ **499/615-2768.** www.mgomz.ru. Admission to the park 175 rubles. 7am–midnight Apr–Nov, 8am–9pm Nov–Apr; museums Tues–Sun 10am–5:30pm. Metro: Kolomenskaya.

LITERARY MOSCOW

Tolstoy House Museum ★★ This is the most authentic and atmospheric of Moscow's "house museums," laden with original belongings and details that help you reenact the long winters that Leo Tolstoy, his wife, and their 13 kids spent here from 1882 to 1901. The museum includes the stable yard, Tolstoy's treasured garden, and a souvenir shop in the room where he stored his printing press. The dining table is laid out with the family's English china, and the walls are still covered with some of the original oilcloth wallpaper. The children's toys and etchings give the whole house an intimate feel. For literature buffs, the most powerful room is Tolstoy's study, where he penned *The Death of Ivan Ilyich,* among other works.

21 Ulitsa Lva Tolstogo. ✆ **499/246-9444.** http://tolstoymuseum.ru. Admission 200 rubles, English-language group tour 1,500

> ## Impressions
>
> *You, greedy mob standing by the throne,*
> *Executioners of Freedom, Genius and Glory!*
> *Hidden under the protection of laws*
> *Before you justice and truth are silent*
> –Mikhail Lermontov, blaming the frivolity of court circles for fellow 19th-century literary giant Alexander Pushkin's death in a duel

Funny Feet

Don't be alarmed if a Russian museum employee stops you at the entrance and makes you put on plastic or felt slippers. Many Russian museums, especially "house museums" or those installed in former palaces, require visitors to cover their shoes to protect wood floors from soggy street shoes. The free slippers (called *bakhili*) are stored in bins near the coat check.

rubles. Tues, Wed, Fri 10am–6pm, Thurs 1–9pm, Sat and Sun 11am–6pm. Closed last Fri of the month. Metro: Park Kultury.

Chekhov House Museum ★   This is the house where the doctor-turned-playwright Anton Chekhov first found literary success, as an author of short stories and one-act plays. He lived in the pink two-story house with his family between the autumn of 1886 and the spring of 1890.

6 Sadovaya Kudrinskaya. ✆ **495/691-6345.** Admission 100 rubles. Tues, Thurs, Sat 11am–6pm; Wed and Fri 2–8pm. Closed last day of the month. Metro: Barrikadnaya.

Pushkin Apartment Museum   Russia's favorite poet, Pushkin, lived here right after his marriage. The building was made into communal apartments in the Soviet era. Tchaikovsky also lived in the building.

53 Arbat St. ✆ **499/241-9295.** http://pushkinmuseum.ru. Admission 100 rubles, group English-language tours 1,000 rubles. Wed noon–9pm; Thurs–Sun 10am–6pm. Metro: Arbatskaya or Smolenskaya.

Mikhail Lermontov House Museum   Chronicler of Russia's Caucasus campaigns, poet and painter Lermontov lived in this cheerful yet studious pink house during his formative student years.

2 Malaya Molchanovka. ✆ **495/691-5298.** Admission 50 rubles. Thurs and Sat–Sun 11am–4pm; Wed and Fri 2–5pm. Metro: Arbatskaya.

ESPECIALLY FOR KIDS

Moscow doesn't appear at all child-friendly on the surface, and Russia's plunging birth rates only exacerbate Moscow's image as a city for grown-ups. That said, Russians revere their kids, and Moscow has plenty for children to do if you're a bit creative. The **circus** is a world-famous draw, the **zoo** is impressive, and several **puppet theaters** around town offer top-quality performances. The shows are in Russian only, but younger children are often content to enjoy the visuals. Be aware that animal rights activism remains totally alien to Russia, so sensitive parents would be advised to stay away from the circus and zoo if this is an issue. Seasonal festivals, such as those at **Kolomenskoye** (see review earlier in this chapter), are a sure winner for kids, as are the attractions at **Gorky Park** (see review earlier in this chapter). Another kid pleaser is the **Police Relay Race** that whips around the Garden Ring the first Sunday after Police Day on October 24. The highlights are the motorcycle and patrol car races; see local newspapers for details of the best vantage spots.

Moscow Circus Named after Y. Nikulin (Tsentralny Tsirk) ★★   The breathtaking, ballet-like acrobatics are what set this circus apart from its counterparts outside Russia, though many come to see the musical cats, gymnastic elephants, and clowns that know tragedy as only a Russian can. On weekends there are three shows a day. The performances are long: 2 hours, with an intermission.

13 Tsvetnoi Bulvar. (C) **495/625-8970.** http://circusnikulin.ru. Tickets 350–2,300 rubles, depending on seats, time of day, and who's performing. Free for kids 6 and under accompanied by an adult. Metro: Tsvetnoi Bulvar.

New Moscow Circus (Novy Tsirk) ★ The quality here is just as good as at the central circus, it's just farther out of town in a less picturesque setting. This venue offers more varied performances and a bigger hall, meaning it's cheaper and easier to get tickets if the central circus is full. It's right across from a metro station, meaning little legs don't have to walk far to get from the circus tent to convenient transport.

7 Prospekt Vernadskogo. (C) **495/930-4073.** http://bigcirc.ru. Tickets 200–1,500 rubles adults and children 7 and up. Metro: Universitet.

Moscow Zoo (Zoopark) This zoo in the center of town is divided into two parts connected by a whimsical footbridge. The dolphinarium is packed in summer, and the petting zoo is a scramble of groping hands on weekends. Try a Tuesday or Wednesday morning for leaner crowds.

1 Bolshaya Gruzinskaya. (C) **499/252-3580.** http://moscowzoo.ru. Admission adults 200 rubles, children 17 and under accompanied by adult are free. Tues–Sun 10am–8pm May–Oct; 10am–5pm Nov–Apr. Metro: Barrikadnaya or Krasnopresnenskaya.

Obrazstov Puppet Theater (Kukolny Teatr) Half the fun of this performance space is the enormous cuckoo clock on the facade that puts on a show of its own every hour. The performances are in Russian but the repertoire includes well-known tales such as "Puss in Boots," "Pinocchio," and "Jack and the Beanstalk." The quality of the puppets and the actors is superb. The performances run from 1 to 2 hours, which may be long for the youngest guests.

3 Sadovaya-Samotechnaya St. (C) **495/699-5373.** http://puppet.ru/?lang=en. Tickets 250–1,500 rubles. Metro: Tsvetnoi Bulvar.

ORGANIZED TOURS

Most organized Moscow tours in English are unadventurous and overpriced, an unfortunate remnant of Soviet days when only certain sites were open to tourists and only the state tourist agency Intourist was authorized to escort them. One welcome exception is **Patriarshy Dom Tours** ((C) 495/795-0927; in the U.S. 650/678-7076; www.russiatravel-pdtours.netfirms.com), which offers informative and unusual tours of Moscow that most tourists don't see. Selections include metro tours, tours of Jewish Moscow, antiques tours, Easter tours in medieval Orthodox towns, and tours of Bulgakov in Moscow. The tours run from an hour to a weekend in length.

For general city tours and Kremlin tours, **Capital Tours** (4 Ilinka Ulitsa, inside Gostiny Dvor, Entrance 6, downstairs; (C) 495/232-2442; http://capitaltours.ru) is the best-equipped and most friendly. Its Kremlin tours include the Armory and run 6 days a week at 2pm for 1,550 rubles including admission. City bus tours run daily between 10am and 6pm for 1,000 rubles.

Intourist is still around and improving its service slowly to keep up with competition. It offers Kremlin and city tours, cruises along the Moscow River, and weekend trips to Sergiev Posad and Vladimir and Suzdal (all described in chapter 9). Most tours must be booked 2 days in advance. Offices are across town, including 11

Stoleshnikov Pereulok; © 495/234-9509 and 2 Novy Arbat © 495/234-4480. www.intourist.ru.

Intourist also has offices in the **Cosmos** hotel (p. 72).

OUTDOOR PURSUITS

Moscow's climate means its chief outdoor pursuits involve snow and ice. Most Russians aren't particularly into casual sports; rarely will you see anyone out for a jog. City streets are unwelcoming to bikers and in-line skaters, though the vastness of Moscow's parks makes them great places for just about any physical activity. Check out the "Parks & Gardens" section earlier in this chapter for specific suggestions.

Boating

There are very few places where you can row your own boat in Moscow, other than the small ponds at Chistiye Prudy (see the "Walking Tour" at the end of this chapter) and **Patriarch's Ponds** (p. 117). Several companies offer trips up and down the Moscow River on small ferries from May to September. Most leave across from the Kremlin or across from Kievsky Station. **The Capital Shipping Company** (© 495/ 225-6070; www.cck-ship.ru/) is the chief operator, with a boat that takes a 90-minute trip from Kievsky Station to the Novospassky Monastery and makes several stops along the way. It costs 400 rubles one-way (150 rubles for children 6–11, younger children free).

Fishing

In deepest winter, you'll often glimpse men in fur hats perched on the frozen-over Moscow River waiting for something to bite. This is not recommended because of the risk of the ice cracking and the questionable quality of the catch.

You can however cast your own line at the **All-Russian Exhibition Center** (p. 117), and cook and eat your catch for 2,000 rubles.

Gyms

Gym culture has only recently hit Moscow, and is still limited to a few chains. If your hotel doesn't have a health club, try **Planeta Fitness**'s several branches for a day pass (© 495/933-7100; www.fitness.ru), or World Class (© 495/788-0000; www. worldclass.ru).

Hiking

The city's bigger parks are good for a few hours of hiking, as are several forested areas outside town. **Bitsevsky Park** is a long rectangle of green space south of the center, crisscrossed with streams and ravines, hilly enough to hold one of the city's two downhill ski slopes, and dense enough to muffle the sounds and smells of this enormous city. **Losiny Ostrov** occupies a huge swath of evergreen forest in the northeast corner of the city, and is a few minutes by taxi from metro Shcholkovskaya, or a good 15-minute walk. Beyond the Moscow city limits, organized trails are rare, but forests and streams are ubiquitous. To avoid getting lost, you should go with a group or a reliable Russian guide. The most popular and pristine spots are along the Moscow River upstream (northwest) of the city, such as around Usovo, Tryokhgorka, and Zvenigorod. All three can be reached by commuter train (*elektrichka*) from Belorussky Station. Patriarshy Dom tours (see listing under "Organized Tours," above) occasionally offers English-language weekend hikes in the warmer months. The **Central Moscow Tourist Club** also arranges hikes, usually in Russian, but the club will arrange English guides for a fee (20 Bolshoi Karetny Pereulok, bld. 2; ℭ **495/699-7502;** www.gctk.narod.ru/kontakt.html).

Ice Skating

Gorky Park (p. 115) floods its main lanes in the winter, turning them into a rough but exhilarating open-air skating zone. You can rent skates here for 150 rubles. The ponds at Patriarch's Ponds (p. 117) and Chistiye Prudy (see the "Walking Tour" at the end of this chapter) also are transformed into free skating rinks in winter, though you need your own skates; if the winter has been mild, be sure the ice is thick before you try.

Red Square now has a skating rink open from end of November to mid-March, though the ice is artificial (ℭ **495/788-4343;** 250–500 rubles entry, 250 rubles rental).

Note: At most Moscow rinks, you must leave a deposit of about 1,000 rubles to rent skates.

In-Line Skating

Victory Park (p. 116) has the smoothest paths for in-line skating and several good slopes for an afternoon workout. The lanes around Moscow State University and its lookout point are great for the view. Skating on city sidewalks is not advised, as they're usually too crowded and Muscovites have little experience with dodging skaters.

Jogging

Moscow's air quality and sidewalk disrepair is such that jogging through your hotel neighborhood would be crueler to your body than it would be kind. Any parks mentioned in this book can offer good running routes. There's also a great path along the river beneath Sparrow Hills (Vorobyoviye Gory), which run along the south side of the Moscow River where it forms a loop beneath Moscow State University; and another along the Moscow River behind the Radisson Royal Hotel (former Hotel **Ukraina**) (p. 67). Running during daylight hours is recommended. Casual joggers may get a few stares, since the only Russians who run for fun are generally current or former athletes.

Skiing

Moscow has several downhill ski slopes, believe it or not. They are small and crowded and not cheap, but a fun way to take advantage of wintry weather. Most accessible are those at Krylatskoye (Metro: Krylatskaya) and Bitsevsky Park (Metro: Bitsevo). All offer basic equipment rental, including snowboards. Cross-country skiing options are endless. **Izmailovsky Park** (p. 116), Bitsevsky Park (directly south of the city center, accessible by metro station Bitsevo), Losiny Ostrov (a tranquil, wooded mass that covers the northeast corner of the city map; best reached by taxi), and Sokolniki (near the metro station Sokolniki) are just some of the spots within city limits where you can get in a few hours of skiing without spotting a vehicle. Basic ski rentals are available at Sokolniki and Bitsevsky. A package of cross-country skis, boots, and poles rents for 400 to 500 rubles. The website www.mski.ru is in Russian only but has a good readable map of skiing sites to get you oriented.

banya BLISS

It's not on most tourist itineraries, but if you can squeeze it in, there's no better way to shed city grime and immerse yourself in Russian culture than to visit a banya. Something between a steam bath and a sauna, the banya has been an important cleansing and resting ritual for centuries. Traditional banyas are huts built alongside rural houses, where families take turns steaming themselves clean, then plunge into a tub of cool water or a nearby stream, or roll in the snow to cool off. In Moscow, banya culture ranges from elite spa-type facilities with expensive body masks and luxurious pedicures (for both sexes) to more proletarian facilities used by residents of communal apartments tired of waiting in line for the shower at home. Thought to cure many ills, the banya is a great rainy-day activity for tourists, too, if you pick one with a bit of history. In the women's halls, bathers treat the steam water with eucalyptus oil and coat their skin with honey, coffee grounds, or whatever other remedy they learned from grandma. In the men's halls, business deals are often made over copious beer and snacks. In both halls you're likely to see bathers beating each other (gently) with birch branches; the practice is believed to accelerate and enhance the cleansing process. The steam is great for warming up in winter; the icy pools cool you off in summer.

Sandunovskiye Banyi, an ornate and cheerful 19th-century bathhouse, is a favorite with "new Russians" and Moscow-based expatriates. They have two levels of service for each gender. A 2-hour deluxe-level session costs 1,800 rubles; a 2-hour standard-level session costs 1,200 rubles. The differences between the deluxe and standard sessions are minimal; a "deluxe" session basically translates into more elegant furnishings and a larger steam room. Sheets, towels, and slippers can be rented for 50 to 150 rubles, or you can bring your own. The deluxe level is offered Tuesday through Sunday from 8am to 10pm; the standard level is offered Wednesday through Monday from 8am to 10pm. You'll find the baths at 14 Neglinnaya St., buildings 3 to 7; the entrance is on Zvonarsky Pereulok (✆ **495/625-4631;** www.sanduny.ru). Metro: Kuznetsky Most or Trubnaya.

Seleznyovskiye Banyi is a more modest and out-of-the-way option. This bathhouse has been serving customers since 1854 and is the one Russian connoisseurs prefer, especially the men's hall with its "professional steamers" running the show. A standard 2-hour session costs 850 rubles for men and women; entrance to the deluxe halls (men only) costs 1,100 rubles. The baths are open Tuesday through Sunday from 8am to 10pm, and are located at 15 Seleznyovskaya Ulitsa, building 2 (✆ **499/978-8491;** Metro: Novoslobodskaya).

S lyokhim parom, as the Russians say, or "Good steam to you."

SPECTATOR SPORTS

Figure Skating

Russia is still a breeding ground for world-class skaters, though the top Russian names now train in North America or Europe. The local, regional, and international championships held here showcase some stars-in-waiting, and you might even glimpse a future Olympic medalist. Most tournaments are in January or February in the **Olimpiisky Stadium** (see below for complete address and contact information); check the Russian Figure Skating Federation website (http://fsrussia.ru) or the International Skating Union (www.isu.com) for schedules.

Hockey

Russians are among the world's best practitioners of hockey, which is no surprise given their nation's icy latitude. Many NHL stars have come back to play with their home teams—or coach them—which has boosted the level of play after the rough and cash-poor 1990s. Sponsorship from Russia's flush oil corporations has also helped. Check *The Moscow Times* (www.themoscowtimes.com) or the Russian Hockey Federation (www.russianhockey.net) for Russian or European championship matches, or for season matches involving CSKA (Red Army) or Dinamo, Moscow's premier clubs. Crowds at the **CSKA Sports Complex** can be rowdy, especially for evening matches or highly sensitive standoffs, such as Russia and Ukraine. Join in the fun and keep a low profile, and you should have no trouble. Tickets are sold at theater kiosks around town. Chances of getting tickets for a big championship match at the stadium are slim, unless you resort to scalpers. For smaller matches it's easy to show up and purchase tickets; prices can be as low as 75 rubles. Advance tickets are also available at theater kiosks around town. See below for complete address and contact information for the CSKA arena.

Soccer

Soccer actually beats out hockey as Russians' favorite sport. Any Muscovite you meet can fill you in on the standings of their home teams, CSKA, Dinamo, Spartak, and of course the national team. Hotel employees can often help you get tickets. The season for local matches runs March to November. Tickets for major international matches are bought up by speculators and not available at the stadium the day of the game, but any other match is easy to get into on the spur of the moment for just a few dollars. Theater kiosks around town also sell advance tickets to the bigger events. The main stadium is are **Luzhniki Sports Complex** (avoid sections B and D, where the roughest fans gather). Dinamo Stadium is closed for renovations. See below for complete address and contact information for the stadiums. See www.uefa.com for upcoming European League matches in Moscow.

Tennis Tournaments

Russian names have packed the rosters of the world's top tennis tournaments in recent years, with the women especially dominating the sport. Moscow's Kremlin Cup, held every October at Olimpiisky Stadium, has become a big international tournament, and Moscow frequently hosts the Davis Cup as well. Tickets for these events are available online at www.kremlincup.ru or www.daviscup.com. Theater kiosks around town also sell tickets, though you must purchase them well in advance. Matches are held at the following venues:

o **Luzhniki Sports Complex,** 24 Luzhniki Ulitsa. ℰ **495/785-9717.** www.luzhniki.ru. Metro: Sportivnaya.

o **CSKA (Red Army) Sports Complex,** 39a Leningradsky Prospekt. ℰ **495/613-2288.** Metro: Aeroport.

o **Olimpiisky Sports Complex,** 16 Olimpiisky Prospekt. ℰ **495/688-1533.** www.olimpik.ru. Metro: Prospekt Mira.

WALKING TOUR: **HISTORIC MOSCOW**

START: **Red Square.**

FINISH: **Chistiye Prudy (Clean Ponds).**

TIME: **2½ to 3 hours.**

BEST TIMES: **Wednesday through Sunday mornings, when exhibits a~ ~, crowds are thinner than in the afternoon.**

This tour covers several centuries of Moscow's history, taking in some major sights and some lesser-known ones. It starts with the obvious, becomes more subtle, and ends with a peek into the Ukrainian Quarter, a neighborhood few tourists explore. The city's design has been too haphazard for the tour to be chronological, but it provides a sense of how the eras blend to make modern Moscow. The walk turns sharply uphill about halfway through, so save some energy and wear comfortable shoes. The first five stops along the tour take you through the neighborhood of **Kitai-Gorod**, with its showcase of Russian architecture from the 15th to 17th century.

Start at Red Square, taking a moment to get your bearings from the peak of this sloped plaza. Then head down toward the beckoning cupolas of:

1 St. Basil's Cathedral

The oldest building on this tour, this 16th-century cathedral has come to symbolize Russia to the rest of the world, but it was almost torn down by Stalin as an anachronistic eyesore. Legend has it that a favorite architect rescued the cathedral by threatening to take his own life on its stairs. Climbing its labyrinthine stairwells and corridors, note how cramped and cool it feels inside, compared to its vivid, abundantly designed exterior.

When leaving the cathedral, turn away from the Kremlin, down Varvarka Street. Ignore, if you can, the street's most prominent feature, stadium-size Hotel Rossiya (if it hasn't yet been razed, as the mayor threatens). Take the stairs on the right-hand side of the street down to the path that runs alongside a string of churches and mansions. This is one of the few sections of Moscow preserved as it was in centuries past, a sort of accidental architectural museum. The first building, the pink-and-white Church of St. Barbara, is closed. Continue to:

2 English Courtyard (Angliisky Podvorye)

This wooden-roofed building is one of the oldest civilian structures in Moscow, a 16th-century merchant's center granted to English traders by Ivan the Terrible to boost trade between the countries. It's now dwarfed by the hotel next door. The small exhibit inside is worth a visit in order to see the building's interior and artifacts (and everything is labeled in English as well as in Russian). The building also hosts concerts of medieval music. Open Wednesday 11am to 9pm, Friday 11am to 7pm; Tuesday and Thursday 10am to 6pm, Saturday and Sunday 11am to 6pm. (© **495/698-3952;** www.mosmuseum.ru).

Continue up the path, noting the yellow-and-white (and no longer functioning) Church of St. Maxim the Blessed. The next few buildings were once part of the Znamensky Monastery. The strange four-story building at no. 10 houses:

The Museum of the Romanov Boyars

The Romanov Boyars (nobles) lived here before Mikhail Romanov was crowned czar in 1613, launching the Romanov imperial dynasty. The only original part of this building is the basement; the rest was added later to re-create conditions of 16th-century Moscow. The building was once part of a vast mini-city that stretched down to the Moscow River. The thick walls, small windows, and rugged conditions were typical of the day, even for aristocratic families such as this one. The museum is open Wednesday from 11am to 7pm, Monday and Thursday through Sunday from 10am to 6pm (☎ **495/698-1256,** www.shm.ru/romanovy.html). It's closed on Tuesdays and the first Monday of each month.

Head to the building next door, the last one along the row, just beneath the hotel driveway:

4 St. George's Church

This church was built in two different eras, the 16th and 18th centuries, and its two parts remain different colors as if to draw attention to the church's split personality. It's the only one of Varvarka Street's churches to hold regular services; you may see an Orthodox wedding if you're here on a weekend.

Head up the stairs to Varvarka proper, and continue down the hill. The street opens onto a busy intersection that can be crossed only by underground walkway. The sole remaining part of the 16th-century Varvarka gate tower is the white stone base, still visible in the underground passage. Once you're underground, continue straight along your trajectory from Varvarka. Take the first stairwell on your left above ground. You should emerge in front of:

5 Cyril and Methodius Monument

Perched in the middle of Slavic Square, this monument portrays the two 9th-century monks credited with inventing the Cyrillic alphabet, used in Russia and many Slavic countries to this day.

Up the hill behind the monument stretch the leafy slopes of Novaya Ploshchad (New Square), crisscrossed by shaded paths lined with benches.

6 Cafes along Novaya Ploshchad 💭

There are several midrange cafes along the east side of Novaya Ploshchad, but if the weather's fine, a better alternative is an ice cream or snack from the street vendors nearby. You can perch on a bench or flat stone in the square for a rest and a mini-picnic.

At the top of Novaya Ploshchad, the square opens onto a neo-Gothic, mustard-colored building:

7 The Polytechnical Museum

Built in the 1870s to promote science and technology during Russia's industrial boom, the museum now houses (rather outdated) collections of clocks, rockets, early movie cameras, typewriters, and other technological innovations over the past century. It's open Tuesday through Sunday from 10am to 6pm. Closed last Friday of each month. Model robots and electronic instruments are switched on briefly every 2 hours starting at 11am (☎ **495/625-0614,** http://eng.polymus.ru).

1 St. Basil's Cathedral
2 English Courtyard
3 Museum of the
  Romanov Boyars
4 St. George's Church
5 Cyril and Methodius
  Monument
6 Polytechnical Museum
7 Lubyanka
8 Monument to Victims
  of Soviet Repressions
9 Church of Archangel Gabriel
  & Church of St. Theodore
10 Chistiye Prudy
11 Pavilion Café ☕

Head to the plaza on the opposite side of the museum from Novaya Ploshchad, and look across it at the building that no Russian feels indifferent toward:

8 Lubyanka

The Bolshevik secret police seized this granite-and-sandstone building from an insurance company in 1918, and its residents have spied on Russians ever since. Its six-story stone facade takes on a sinister feel when you imagine the persecutions and interrogations that have gone on here. Now it's the headquarters of the Federal Security Service, once led by Prime Minister Putin.

The bare patch in the grass across from Lubyanka is the site where a monument to Soviet secret police founder Felix Dzerzhinsky stood for decades before pro-democracy protesters tore it down in 1991.

In the little green space between Lubyanka and the Polytechnical Museum, note the small stone and plaque:

9 Monument to Victims of Soviet Repressions

A lonely slab of stone from the Solovetsky Islands, an Arctic prison camp for enemies of the Soviet regime, honors the millions of people repressed by the Soviet government. The stone was brought here and placed across from Lubyanka during the soul-searching days after the Soviet collapse, but gatherings here have dwindled in recent years as new concerns occupy Russian minds. A nearby plaque written in English and Russian tells visitors to contact Memorial, Russia's leading human rights organization and the group responsible for the monument, for more information.

Head back into the capitalist rush of modern Moscow by crossing over to Myasnits-kaya Ulitsa, to the right of Lubyanka. Follow the street past a string of bookshops and cafes until you see Krivokolyonny Pereulok off to the right. Take this street (which translates as "Crooked Knee Lane") past the 18th- and 19th-century mansions now housing offices and apartments, until you reach two churches clustered together:

10 Church of the Archangel Gabriel & Church of St. Theodore Stratilites

The twisting gold dome of the Church of the Archangel Gabriel is the most noticeable of its nontraditional architectural features. Commissioned in 1705 by Peter the Great's advisor, Alexander Menshikov, the church is a clear example of the period when European classicism overrode Russian architecture, with grand buttresses and cornices not seen on most Orthodox churches. The 19th-century, quasi-Gothic Church of St. Theodore Stratilites is next door.

Continue a few dozen yards to the end of Krivokolyonny Pereulok. You'll emerge onto Chistoprudny Bulvar, a boulevard with a stretch of green space running down its center. Enter the park and head right, until you reach:

11 Chistiye Prudy

This area was referred to as "Dirty Ponds" in the days when it housed a meat market, whose refuse ran into the murky pools. The 19th-century city government cleaned it up and rechristened it "Clean Ponds," or Chistiye Prudy. Only one pond remains; it's a mecca for skaters and toddlers on sleds in winter, and for rental boats in summer.

12 Pavilion ☕

Pavilion (✆ 495/697-5110), perched on the ponds, is packed most evenings with a haughty, hipper-than-thou crowd, but it's a lovely spot for a midday bite. The wooden deck makes it feel homey. The food is a mélange of Russian, European, and central Asian cuisines.

SHOPPING IN MOSCOW

Most visitors limit their Moscow shopping to a few nesting dolls and some Soviet memorabilia, but a bit of perseverance can uncover unusual crafts and striking gifts. Hand-embroidered table linens from the textile-producing towns along the Volga are a good buy, as are scarlet-and-gold Khokhloma wooden spoons, intricate wooden Easter eggs, or jewelry cut from richly colored Siberian stones you won't find at home, such as lilac-colored charoite and deep pink rhodonite.

Moscow has also become one of the world's fastest-growing luxury shopping destinations, with a bigger Prada store than Milan, and Russian designers' top-of-the-line creations that sell for jaw-dropping prices. There are also plenty of midmarket clothing chains such as Benetton and Mexx, but overall, Moscow remains less touched by this kind of globalization than other European capitals.

Moscow's vendors are quite market-savvy after more than a decade of capitalism. That means the shocking bargains of black market days are long gone, but it also means that quality is more reliable and competition has livened up the selection of products available. Beware, as in any big city, of con artists on the street trying to sell a "real" silver fox hat or czarist medal for a suspiciously low price. Several typical Russian souvenirs are described below. For advice on buying lacquer boxes or the lacy silver designs of Russian filigree, see the sidebars "Box That Up" on p. 250 and "Fine Russian Filigree" on p. 256.

THE SHOPPING SCENE

When you buy anything in Russia, keep in mind that you'll want to take it home—and Customs officers can bar the export of anything antique, any book printed before 1960, or any painting or other work of art considered of cultural value to Russia. You'll have no problem with the majority of souvenirs, and even the antique or valuable ones can usually be cleared for export by the Ministry of Culture. This process takes a few days, involves getting the item appraised and then approved, and can cost anywhere from 10% to 100% of the item's value. If you're in doubt about a purchase, check with the vendor about its exportability, and also with a tour guide or other third party, if possible. Many hotel concierges can help you get Culture Ministry clearance. Otherwise, you can try contacting the ministry's Moscow appraisal and certification agency (8 Neglinnaya

russian ORTHODOX ICONS

The haunting, gold-flaked biblical images on Orthodox icons hold a magnetic appeal for many visitors to Russia, regardless of their faith. The angular, distorted faces and figures may seem jarring if compared to western Renaissance art, but that's because Russian icon painters were not aiming at three-dimensional realism. Russian Orthodox icons are rich in symbolism but lacking in light or shadow; they do not aim to render beauty but to honor and inspire spirituality. Modern icons strictly follow the traditions and images established centuries ago, and all must be blessed by an Orthodox priest. The design is carved into a wood panel, then hand-painted. Gold leaf and silver crowns can make the icon more valuable, but they don't make it any more authentic. The vendor should be able to explain what era of icon-painting is represented or what artist is being emulated. Most of the icons for sale today are safe for export, but any made before the Soviet era require permission. Be sure to get a receipt even for the new ones, preferably with the date of production (*data izgotovleniya*) printed on it. The larger icons are more likely to arouse the suspicion of Customs officers.

Icons are best purchased at Orthodox monasteries or cathedrals, though they are also available in kiosks around town. Novodevichy Convent (p. 107) is known for an extensive collection.

Ulitsa, 3rd floor, room 29; ☎ **495/921-3258** or 692-1532). The rules change frequently, but items like samovars and old icons are always on the iffy list (see the box "Russian Orthodox Icons," below).

Hotel gift shops are the most expensive places in town for souvenirs, and heavily touristed areas such as Red Square are a close second. Better bets are the small crafts shops or outdoor markets farther from the center of town. For Orthodox icons and other church-related paraphernalia, the monasteries have the most authentic and attractive selection.

Moscow has no traditional sales tax, so the price printed on an item is the price you'll pay, as long as you know what currency is being cited (see the "Currency Confusion at Your Hotel" box on p. 74). Prices include VAT (value-added tax), which adds from 5% to 18% to the item's original price. The Russian VAT is not refundable at the border as it is in some European countries.

Shops and shopping centers are generally open daily from around 10am to 8pm. Food stores open earlier, and kiosks around town are often open round-the-clock. Most stores are closed on Russian holidays, and smaller stores are closed Sunday or Monday. A very few shops still close for an hour at lunch, usually from 1 to 2pm.

Companies such as **DHL** (11 Pervaya Tverskaya-Yamskaya; ☎ **495/956-1000**) and **UPS** (7 Derbenevskaya Naberezhnaya, building 4; ☎ **495/961-2211**) can ship paintings, rugs, or other large items to your home and take care of any clearances you need.

GREAT SHOPPING AREAS

Just about any souvenir, bauble, or item of clothing can be found just off Red Square, at the two major shopping centers: **GUM** and **Okhotny Ryad.** Heading up

Moscow Shopping

Aktsia **12**
Antikvariat na Bronnoi **13**
Arbatskaya Lavitsa **5**
Aromatny Mir **24**
Art Bureau **30**
Atrium **26**
Biblio Globus **23**
Bulgari **21**
Cartier **15**
Central House of Artists **31**
Detsky Mir **11**
Dom Knigi **10**

Common terms and abbreviations

naberezhnaya/nab	*Embankment*
most	*Bridge*
ploshchad/pl	*Square* or *plaza*
prospekt/pr	*Avenue*
sad	*Garden*
ulitsa/ul	*Street*

Eliseyevsky
  Gastronom **17**
Gorbushka Market **1**
GUM **19**
Izmailovsky Market **25**
Kupina **8**
Mekha **16**
Moscow Cultural
  Fund **28**
Moskva **14**
Okhotny Ryad **18**

Russkaya Vyshyvka **7**
Samotsvety **4**
Sedmoi Kontinent **3**
Shakespeare & Co. **29**
Skazki Starovo Arbata **6**
Stockmann **2**
Tretyakov Gallery **27**
Tretyakovsky Proyezd **21**
Tsentr Yuvelir **9**
TsUM **22**
Vologodsky Len **20**

Tverskaya Street, you'll find more variety, and you can enjoy the long stroll and historic plaques interspersed with shoe stores and specialty food shops. One to look out for is **Eliseyevsky Gastronom,** a refurbished version of an elite 19th-century food emporium that now offers Russia's most expensive chocolates, premium vodkas, and smaller and more affordable treats such as tasty Russian tea cookies and salted herring. For a dazzling glimpse at the Russian new rich, wander through the boutiques of the world's top fashion and jewelry designers in gleaming **Tretyakovsky Proyezd,** designed to replicate a 19th-century gallery. It's not far from Red Square, between Teatralny Proyezd and Nikolskaya Ulitsa.

Russian Clothing Sizes

For help selecting the right sizes when you're shopping for clothes or shoes, see the "Clothing Size Conversions" on p. 287, which compares American, European, British, and Russian sizes.

The Arbat has fashioned itself as Moscow's premier shopping district, though most of the souvenir booths lining the center of the pedestrian street are overpriced and seem to offer the same merchandise as their neighbors. The Arbat's better shopping deals can be found in its few remaining crafts shops, which sell boxes made of carved birch wood in traditional Russian patterns, hand-embroidered bed and table linens, and traditional Russian caftans and gowns. Look for children's sizes, too—some make good choices for holiday or Halloween outfits. Prices drop as you move west along the street. The New Russian Store is worth a peek inside; the tongue-in-cheek boutique of traditional Russian handiwork caters to—and makes fun of—Russia's extravagant nouveau riche. On a recent visit I saw a delicate ceramic cellphone and a lacquer box painted with a scene of thuglike businessmen being fed grapes by scantily clad nymphs.

A less abundant but more original shopping area is **Pyatnitskaya Street** in Zamoskvarechye, south of the Kremlin. Several independent artists sell their paintings and sculptures in galleries and small shops here, along with traditional Russian crafts. This is also where Moscow's few vintage clothing stores reside, plus a few shops offering secondhand designer wear.

Moscow's shopping mecca for foreign and Russian visitors alike is the huge openair bazaar at **Izmailovsky Park,** in eastern Moscow outside the Garden Ring. The rough-and-tumble stalls and garage-sale feel of a few years back have been replaced by organized rows of vendors behind a cheerful, towering facade of carved wood. On weekends an entrance fee of 50 rubles is charged. Inside, you'll find 10 times the selection of *matryoshka* nesting dolls than the Arbat displays, plus Russian spaceprogram memorabilia, malachite chess sets, intricate and original jewelry, blue-hued Uzbek plates, surprisingly-patterned quilts, Soviet propaganda posters, booths and booths of lacquer boxes, wooden toys, and much more. Most prices are negotiable, and all vendors speak some English. Get off at the Partizanskaya metro stop and follow the crowd.

Muscovites often spend their weekends at the open-air food and clothing markets scattered around town, where they buy produce, meat, diapers, winter boots, cleaning supplies, and any number of things at prices much lower than those in department stores or supermarkets. The quality ranges from cheap Chinese toy trucks to fine Russian-made shearling coats. If you're curious, check out the food and clothing markets at Izmailovsky (to the left of the souvenir bazaar) or Fili (btw. the Bagrationovskaya metro station and the Gorbushka electronics market).

THE SHOPPING CENTER

The concept of the shopping mall as North America knows it remains [...] sian shoppers, though they have their own version of shopping centers th[...] same purpose. Moscow's premier shopping gallery is **GUM** (pronounce[...] which stands for State Department Store. This magnificent, oblong building ex[...] nearly the full eastern side of Red Square, and is organized into three open arcade[...] of three floors connected by curved bridges and anchored by a fountain at the center. The shops bear little resemblance to the 19th-century stalls of GUM's early days or to the rows of drab, identical stores that inhabited it in Soviet times. Today, designers such as Christian Dior, Max Mara, and their Russian counterparts fill the most prestigious Red Square–facing storefronts, and shoe and clothing stores fill the upper floors. The food selection is disappointing; the several bland cafes seem designed for people-watching rather than for culinary enjoyment. (The exception is **Bosco Bar,** reviewed on p. 78.)

Ordinary shoppers prefer the partially underground **Okhotny Ryad** mall, a grandiose project by Moscow Mayor Yuri Luzhkov that attracted the ire of conservationists for digging into treasured archaeological sites just outside the Kremlin walls. It's now a thriving, three-story shopping haven densely packed with stores for nearly all pocketbooks. Souvenirs here are pricey, but the food court on the bottom floor is a cheap and reliable bet for children, with international standards and their Russian fast-food rivals. The mall's design is eclectic, with a shallow dome on top shaped like the Northern Hemisphere, and terraces below overlooking fountains decorated with sculptures from Russian fairy tales.

A more upscale choice nearby is **TsUM** (pronounced "tsoom"), or **Central Department Store,** which has some prestigious international brands among its broad and democratic selection, and whose stores offer frequent, deep discounts.

SHOPPING IN MOSCOW | The Shopping Centers

Nesting Dolls

Matryoshka nesting dolls are so ubiquitous in today's Russia that they're almost banal, but a quality doll can be a symbol of Russian art and history. The first dolls, believed to be based on a Japanese tradition, were created in the 19th century in the Orthodox Church center of Sergiev Posad. The richest versions depict scenes from Russian fairy tales opening up to reveal the next stage in the story. The most common version is a rosy-cheeked woman in a vibrant headscarf, holding a series of sisters or daughters inside. The dolls are usually made from birch wood, and a proper set of dolls will be made from the same tree so that the wood responds uniformly to temperature and humidity changes.

Matryoshka dolls are a great, inexpensive gift. The basic versions can sell for as little as 50 rubles at open-air markets. Older kids and adults may appreciate those with more intricate designs—or those with a theme such as all of Russia's leaders over the past century stacked inside each other (or U.S. presidents, or international pop stars . . .). Most vendors will claim the dolls are hand-painted, but a better gauge of quality is your own eye. If the colors are delicate and distinct, it's worth more than a *matryoshka* with crude and over-bright pictures. Sergiev Posad's Toy Museum has a small display on the history of the dolls (see the side trip to Sergiev Posad in chapter 9).

are architecturally bland and largely aimed at the new
you've forgotten your umbrella or your purse strap
Center in front of Kievsky Train Station (2 Kievsky
clothes, accessories, groceries and a top-floor disco.
nt of Kursky Train Station (10 Zemlyanoi Val; metro:
nd midrange clothing shops, a well-stocked supermar-

A TO Z

This is a sho...... al recommendations, though a little exploring can uncover much more.

Antiques & Collectibles

See the discussion of export rules at the beginning of this chapter before you purchase any antique.

Aktsia   A specialist in antique books and unusual inventions, this store also sells paintings and sculptures. 21/18 Bolshaya Nikitskaya St. ✆ **495/691-7509.** www.akcia-antique.ru. Metro: Arbatskaya.

Antikvariat na Bronnoi   Atmospheric and packed with stuff, this store is getting more upscale as rich Russian clients discover it. 7/14/5 Sytinsky Pereulok, bld. 1. (in courtyard). ✆ **495/211-9340.** www.antikvario.ru. Metro: Pushkinskaya.

Art

Arts Bureau (Khudozhestvennoye Buro)   This renowned gallery inside the New Tretyakov Modern Art Museum holds regular auctions for its most valuable works as well as regular sales of its icons, paintings, and other items. They will take care of any export issues for you. 10/14 Krymsky Val. Office 49A. ✆ **499/230-0091.** www.artsbur.ru. Metro: Oktyabrskaya or Park Kultury.

Central House of Artists (New Tretyakov Gallery)   The ground floor of Moscow's Modern Art Museum is a must-see for anyone interested in Russia's current art scene—either in viewing or in buying a sample. The large hall serves as a showcase

---

 An Outdoor Art Market

For a less official selection of modern art, visit the outdoor market along the embankment of the Moscow River next to the Central House of Artists. Year-round, regardless of weather, vendors display works ranging from naturalist landscapes to charming images of modern and not-so-modern Russia. Prices are negotiable, and you'll get a better deal if you speak Russian or have a Russian-speaking helper. There's even a stall run by a framer who can mount the work for you. Though these works are all new and shouldn't pose a problem at Customs, be sure to get a receipt with the artist's name and the year the work was created. The underground walkway between the Central House of Artists and Gorky Park is also packed with art vendors, but prices here are higher and the choices less inspiring.

for new painters, sculptors, and craftspeople, whose works are for sale at the dozens of stalls that crowd the space. You can also find unusual gifts and souvenirs here such as birch-wood candlesticks or irreverent Constructivist tea sets. 10 Krymsky Val. ✆ **499/238-9634.** Closed on Mondays. www.cha.ru. Metro: Oktyabrskaya or Park Kultury.

Books

Biblio-Globus You'll find this rich and varied Russian book emporium just beneath the computer center of the successor to the KGB. Its multilevel, packed selection includes books in English, children's picture books, and antique books, and can suck you in for hours if you're not careful. Ask the information desk for help to save time. 6/3 Myasnitskaya St. bld. 1. ✆ **495/781-1900.** www.biblio-globus.ru. Metro: Lubyanka or Kuznetsky Most.

Dom Knigi (House of Books) This landmark store is a great source of art books in Russian and English, travel guidebooks, maps, and old lithographs. Books in English are on the second floor facing the back. 8 Novy Arbat. ✆ **495/789-3591.** www.mdk-arbat.ru. Metro: Arbatskaya.

Moskva This big store a short walk up Tverskaya from the Kremlin offers a good selection of art and photography books in several languages, travel books in English, a nice history section, a decent choice of antique books, and much more. 8 Tverskaya. ✆ **495/629-6483.** http://moscowbooks.ru. Metro: Okhotny Ryad or Pushkinskaya.

Shakespeare and Co. Way off the beaten track in the basement of a residential building, this laid-back shop has an eclectic selection of English-language novels and guidebooks. Call in advance to ensure they are open, as hours vary. 5/7 Pervy Novokuznetsky Pereulok. ✆ **495/951-9360.** Metro: Paveletskaya.

China & Porcelain

The blue-and-white ceramic style known as Gzhel (pronounced "Guh-zel") carries hints of the Dutch Delft Blue, but with an outcome that's more homey and distinctly Russian. Named after the town southeast of Moscow where the style originated, Gzhel appears most often in thick ceramic teacups, figurines, or furniture tiles (especially on old palace fireplaces). Each piece is hand-painted and individually molded, finished, glazed, and fired. The more valuable ones have subtle hints of gold woven into the patterns.

You'll find Gzhel pieces and china from St. Petersburg's **Lomonosov Porcelain Factory** (see chapter 14) at most large souvenir stores around Moscow.

Crafts

Two top spots for uniquely Russian crafts are Izmailovsky Market, described in "Great Shopping Areas," and Central House of Artists, listed under "Art," above. Several stores on the Arbat are also good sources, as is:

Moscow Cultural Fund Hand-painted ceramics in Russian folk themes, original painted dolls, wind chimes—gifts for every budget can be had here. The fund has two cramped but highly satisfying shops. 41 Prospekt Mira. ✆ **495/680-5366.** Metro: Prospekt Mira. Also at 16 Pyatnitskaya Ulitsa. ✆ **495/951-3302.** Metro: Novokuznetskaya.

Discount Shopping

Izmailovsky Market (Vernisazh) The souvenir and gift bazaar is the main draw, but trinkets and some quality discount clothing can be found at the adjacent open-air market. See the description under "Great Shopping Areas" above. The market is open daily from around 8am to 5pm. Metro: Partizanskaya.

Fashion & Shoes

CHILDREN'S

Detsky Mir This was the primary children's department store in the Soviet era. Its flagship store is closed for renovations, but two branches have a solid selection of toys and children's clothing. 24 Krasnaya Presnya. ℰ **495/739-4622.** Metro: Krasnopresnenskaya. A branch focusing on children under 1: 11 Novy Arbat. ℰ **495/691-2221.** www.detmir.ru. Metro: Arbatskaya.

WOMEN'S & MEN'S

GUM This arcade features mostly international couture brands, but in a distinctly Russian atmosphere. You won't save money shopping here, but you are certain to be pampered if you want to try something on. See description under "The Shopping Centers" above. 3 Red Square. ℰ **495/788-4343.** www.gum.ru. Metro: Ploshchad Revolutsii or Okhotny Ryad.

Okhotny Ryad The shops in this mall get cheaper as you descend farther underground, so that the bottom floor offers the best buys. It's a huge hit with young Muscovites and is a dependable clothing source for tourists and expat shoppers, with an enormous selection of styles and prices. Mostly international brands are offered. 1 Manezhnaya Sq. ℰ **495/737-8449.** www.ox-r.ru. Okhotny Ryad, Ploshchad Revolutsii, or Teatralnaya.

TsUM The historic Art Nouveau building flanking the Bolshoi Theater sells a broad range of international luxury brands including Christian Dior, Gucci, and Prada, as well as many more midrange brands. Search for good deals during massive summer and winter sales. 2 Petrovka. ℰ **495/933-7300.** www.tsum.ru. Metro: Okhotny Ryad, Ploshchad Revolutsii.

Food

Azbuka Vkusa A gourmet paradise, this Russian chain sells French foie gras, Italian prosciutto and other international delicacies, and a broad selection of wine at high prices (though that doesn't matter to the glitzy Russian clientele). Some unusual Russian spirits are available here for gifts. 19 Petrovka, 8 Kutuzovsky Prospekt, numerous other stores across the city. ℰ **495/504-3478.** www.azbukavkusa.ru.

Eliseyevsky Gastronom An abundant collection of teas, sweets, and other Russian goods is on display beneath the soaring ceilings of this flowery, ornate shop, which has a 100-year history of serving Russia's discriminating palates. A good source of sweet gifts, unusual Russian tea tins, or just a stylish afternoon snack. 14 Tverskaya St. ℰ **495/650-4643.** www.eliseevskiy.ru. Metro: Teatralnaya or Chekhovskaya.

Sedmoi Kontinent This Russian supermarket chain is a good source of unusual tea cookies and meringues, pickled herring and eel, and herbal liqueurs—as well as the full range of grocery-store staples. Two prominent locations, both open 24 hours, are listed here. 1 Manezhnaya Ploshchad, Okhotny Ryad Shopping Center. http://7cont.ru. Metro: Okhotny Ryad. Second location: 63 Bolshaya Gruzinskaya, in shopping center basement. Metro: Belorusskaya. Third central location: 12/1 Bolshaya Lubyanka. Metro: Lubyanka.

Fur

Russia's climate and centuries-old traditions mean fur coats and hats are winter staples. If you're comfortable with the idea, browse the unique collections at Mekha na

couture A LA RUSSE

For most of the 1980s and 1990s, Russian fashion was best characterized by a TV ad for the Wendy's fast-food chain. At a Soviet fashion show, an emcee shouted "Eveningwear!" and a stern, shapeless woman stomped down a runway in a burlap sack, carrying a flashlight. "Beachwear!" the emcee cried, and the same woman in the same sack appeared, holding a beach ball. Wendy's, the ad claimed, offered the dizzying choices so unavailable behind the Iron Curtain. Indeed, for decades Russians wore variations on the same gray suits and uncomfortable shoes made in Soviet-bloc textile factories, and the brave ones offered visiting tourists money for their Levi's jeans and leather jackets.

All that changed after 1991. The birth of Russia's nouveau riche, a class of people dripping with money made in privatizations and hungry for once-inaccessible luxuries, affected marketing departments at fashion houses around the world. Boutiques along the tony Rue de Faubourg St-Honore in Paris now keep Russian-speaking staff to handle the steady stream of Russian customers ready to drop several thousand dollars in cash at one go. Miami's Versace boutique counts Russians as its most reliable customers. Sales at the Prada boutique in Moscow rival those at its flagship store in Milan. Russian models, too, are a hot commodity on runways in Paris and Milan.

Meanwhile, Russian designers have matured fast, and are increasingly collaborating with American, Italian, and French colleagues. Perhaps as a backlash against years of dull uniformity, Russian fashion tends to be brightly colored, sparkly, sexy, and daring, something you're sure to notice on the streets of Moscow or St. Petersburg. Russians' love for showing off labels is starting to fade, but you still may see people dressed head to toe in gear covered in the names CHANEL and DIOR. To see work by Russian designers, try the Tretyakovsky Proyezd shopping zone, where many are concentrated in one place (1 Tretyakovsky Proyezd; metro: Lubyanka) or the following boutiques:

Valentin Yudashkin Trading House (Moscow). 19 Kutuzovsky Prospekt. © 499/240-1189. www.yudashkin.com. Metro: Kievskaya or Kutuzovskaya.

Igor Chapurin Boutique (Moscow). 12 Bolshoi Savvinsky Pereulok, bld. 6. © 499/246-0553. Metro Frunzenskaya or Sportivnaya. *Another location:* In GUM. © 495/620-3365. http://chapurin.com. Metro: Ploshchad Revolucii.

Pyatnitskoi, 13 Pyatnitskaya (© **495/951-9880,** metro: Lubyanka or Kuznetsky Most). You can also try Mekhovoy Salon (Fur salon) at 36/9 Novy Arbat, where several times a year they hold trading fairs that offer a larger selection and more price range (© **926/910-8214;** www.1fursalon.ru; metro: Arbatskaya). Better deals can be found at many outdoor markets, such as Izmailovsky (see "Great Shopping Areas" above).

Gifts/Souvenirs

The Moscow Cultural Fund (under the "Crafts" section above) and Izmailovsky Market (under "Great Shopping Areas," earlier in this chapter) are the best places to shop for souvenirs and gifts for family and friends back home, in addition to the following.

vitsa This longtime staple on the Arbat still has one of the best
...tional Russian souvenirs. The range of *matryoshka* dolls is impres-
...ate boxes of carved birch wood make for original and relatively
... do the wooden toys featuring Russian fairy tale mainstays such
... mushrooms. Prices are not exorbitant as they are in some of the
... street. You can always head outside and bargain with the street
...for a better deal, though quality is always uncertain. 27 Arbat St. ☎ **495/690-5689**. Metro: Arbatskaya, Smolenskaya.

Jewelry

Izmailovsky Market, described under "Great Shopping Areas" earlier in this chapter, is a good place to look for jewelry bargains, especially on semiprecious stones from Siberia. Samotsvety, listed below, is a strongly recommended spot, and I've included two high-end options as well.

Bvlgari The sleekest of Moscow's jewelry boutiques, on the city's sleekest street. Where Russia's nouveau riche seek the latest in jewelry design. 1/1 Tretyakovsky Proyezd. ☎ **495/933-3390**. www.bulgari.com. Metro: Lubyanka.

Cartier The Moscow boutique of the renowned jeweler has an extensive selection of both fresh and classic pieces. 19 Kuznetsky Most. ☎ **495/937-9040**. 7 Stoleshnikov Pereulok. ☎ **495/510-5060**. www.cartier.com. Metro: Pushkinskaya, Tverskaya.

Samotsvety A conveniently located store with a broad selection of jewelry for any taste, including some unusual Russian stones and filigree items hard to find at home. Prices are definitely higher than what you'll get from street vendors on the Arbat Street outside, but at least in the store there's no question you're purchasing valuable goods. A large selection of silver, gold, and amber. 35 Arbat St. ☎ **499/241-0765**. Metro: Smolenskaya or Arbatskaya.

Tsentr Yuvelir em]This chain's reliable quality and lower prices draw in Muscovites but few visitors. It focuses on standard gold and silver items but harbors a few unusual finds as well. 6 Novy Arbat. ☎ **495/691-2272**. www.c-j.ru. Metro: Arbatskaya.

Linens

Linen tablecloths, curtains, bed coverings, and clothing from the textile towns along the Volga River bear distinctly Russian patterns. Because few people have heard of Russian linen, these items make for great and unexpected gifts. Even the handmade items are much cheaper than goods of pure linen you find in the West. Some crafts stores, as well as the Izmailovsky Market (see "Great Shopping Areas," earlier in this chapter), are good sources in addition to these stores.

Russkaya Vyshyvka A treasure-trove ideally located in the middle of Arbat Street, with some well-priced, winning gift finds and new ideas for your own home. Linen table designs run the range from hand-sewn napkins for as little as 50 rubles to embroidered runners costing 1,250 rubles. Slavic-themed tea cozies and potholders, layettes for newborns, traditional Russian caftans for children and adults, and bed linens complete this strongly recommended collection. 31 Arbat St. ☎ **499/241-2841**. Metro: Arbatskaya, Smolenskaya.

Vologodsky Len This small shop near Red Square features linen from the Volga-area producers. Included are clothing for children and adults, at reasonable prices and with striking red-and-gold or blue-and-gold patterns. 4 Ilinka St. ☎ **495/232-9463**. www.linens.ru. Metro: Ploshchad Revolutsii or Kitai-Gorod.

GORBUSHKA ELECTRONICS market

For a mind-boggling selection of software, music, DVDs, videos, and computer games, head to Gorbushka, Moscow's biggest "underground" market for legal and illegal electronic goods. In the 1990s, it was upgraded from a chaotic outdoor venue at Gorbunov Park to a spacious, clean warehouse up the street, on Ulitsa Barklaya (it's visible from the Bagrationovskaya metro station). Despite years of industry pressure, Russia remains a major producer of pirated software, music, and movies. The good news is that efforts to fight piracy have brought the prices of licensed goods down to levels well below what you'll pay at home—for example, the latest *Die Hard* DVD was available in an official Russian version the same time it was available in the United States, but at half the price. At Gorbushka, the selection includes more and more licensed products, and a fair share of obscure Russian recordings from decades past. The enormous hall for vendors of CDs, DVDs, MP3s, videos, cassettes, and software is surrounded by a larger network of minishops selling electronics of every kind, often quality brand names at prices below the department stores'. It's a good place to pick up camera accessories or cheap batteries. If you want to buy movies, keep in mind that not all DVDs can be viewed on your player at home, and that not all offer English versions, so check with the vendor just in case. Russian videos are in PAL format (not compatible with most North American VCRs), and even American films are voiced over in Russian unless indicated. Be prepared for crowds, especially on weekends.

Gorbushka offers a mix of legal products and pirated goods, but beware of the stands you'll see in metro stations and at street corners around town: Their only trade is the illegal stuff, from the latest Hollywood blockbuster to CD-ROMs packed with Microsoft programs. Taking pirated goods out of Russia is illegal, and Customs officers can (though rarely do) seize them when you leave and levy a small fine.

Museum Stores

In addition to Tretyakov Gallery, Central House of Artists (listed under "Art" above) is a highly recommended stop for any museum or art-related shopping.

Tretyakov Gallery The gallery has no single store, but several stands in its lobby sell reproductions from postcard to poster size, along with a large selection of books, many in English. 10 Lavrushinsky Pereulok. ☏ **499/230-7788.** Metro: Tretyakovskaya or Novokuznetskaya.

Music

Moscow's biggest bookstore, Dom Knigi (listed under "Books" earlier in this chapter), has an extensive selection of Russian and international sheet music, and a decent selection of CDs as well.

Gorbushka This vast and bustling market offers the broadest selection of Russian and foreign artists, though you'll have to ask around if you're looking for anything obscure. See the "Gorbushka Electronics Market" sidebar below for more information. 8 Ulitsa Barklaya. www.gorbushka.ru. Metro: Bagrationovskaya.

Toys

See Detsky Mir under "Fashion & Shoes" above for the biggest source of toys in Moscow, from baby rattles to high-tech video games. For more original Russian toys, check out the Izmailovsky Market (described under "Great Shopping Areas," earlier in this chapter) for carved wooden musical toys and chess sets, among other finds, at reasonable and negotiable prices. All the stores on the Arbat have good toy selections, including remarkable dolls in traditional Russian garments. See "Gifts/Souvenirs" above for more suggestions.

Vodka & Wine

See also Sedmoi Kontinent and other food stores, listed under "Food," above, which have a large and reasonably priced selection of vodkas for all tastes as well as wines from places like Moldova and Bulgaria.

Aromatny Mir   You'll find a broad selection of vodkas you won't find at home, including several flavored with Russian wildflowers and herbs, as well as the rich Armenian brandies. Numerous stores across town; some of the most central locations are listed here. 22 Malaya Bronnaya, bld. 1. ℰ **495/690-6493**. Metro: Pushkinskaya. 33/1 Gogolevsky Boulevard. ℰ 495/691-1487. Metro: Arbatskaya. 29 Ulitsa Pokrovka. ℰ **495/917-1160.** Metro: Kitai-Gorod.

MOSCOW AFTER DARK

A large proportion of Moscow's tourists come primarily for its performing arts or, increasingly, its nightlife. Its reputation in both departments is well-deserved. The Bolshoi Theater is merely the most famous of the city's top-quality ballet and opera houses, which survived the cash and identity crisis of the 1990s to emerge livelier and just as talent-packed as before. Prices are no longer rock-bottom bargains, but most performances will still cost less than in the West, especially classical music concerts.

The club scene, meanwhile, raced out of the restrictive Soviet era to make Moscow one of the most cutting-edge party spots in Europe, complete with sex, drugs, and enough over-the-top behavior to impress even the most jaded clubbers. Not so long ago, Russia's bar scene was limited to hotel lobbies and seedy, standing-only beer halls frequented largely by construction workers. Today's gamut of bars is as broad as that of any European capital, with cool cocktail bars, kitschy Soviet theme bars, billiards bars, cigar bars, sports bars, and more. The booming Russian beer industry has helped, with several brewery-run bars around town.

Less obvious but no less impressive is Moscow's jazz scene, the legacy of devoted musicians who coveted banned LPs in the Soviet era and have taken Russian jazz to a nuanced, world-weary level.

The most thorough English-language listings for theater, music, and movies are found in the Friday edition of *The Moscow Times* (www.themoscowtimes.com), the *Russia Journal* (www.russiajournal.com), and the monthly magazine *Passport* (www.passportmagazine.ru). The intentionally offensive weekly *eXile* newspaper (www.exiledonline.com) is a guide to hedonistic Moscow as well as the premier English-language source of bar and club advice.

THE PERFORMING ARTS

Russians take their arts very seriously, and even the smallest of dance companies and music schools demands perfection from performers to a degree that no other nation seems to match. This leaves less room for amateur and experimental performance, but means that any show you see in Russia will feature rigorously trained artists. Despite this rigidity, Russian dancers, singers, and musicians manage to infuse their art with a powerful, often tragic, passion. Even if it sounds trite, you'll never forget watching a Russian ballerina interpret the dying swan in *Swan Lake* in her

Buying Tickets

Russian theaters rarely run one show at a time. Instead, they have a constantly rotating repertoire; for example, the Bolshoi Theater runs *Giselle* once or twice a month all season long. Tickets for top venues are available through most hotels, though they often include a hefty service charge, and the choice is limited. If you're looking for something cheaper or more unusual, you can try the independent theater kiosks throughout the city and in several metro stations. These can offer same-day tickets for conservatory concerts or daring new operas. Lists of available performances are often written out on index cards in Russian, making for chaotic reading. If you're looking for something specific, just ask—there's a good chance either the vendor or another customer will speak English. These sources are generally reliable, but be sure to check your ticket (sometimes just a flimsy paper with the theater's name and the show's name stamped on it) for the proper date and time. Dates are written European-style, with the day before the month, and times are usually written using the 24-hour clock. Punctuation varies too. So "19.00; 01.07.10" means 7pm on July 1, 2010.

(and Tchaikovsky's) homeland, or hearing a Russian pianist resurrect Rachmaninoff in the conservatory where the great composer played. For a historical overview of Russian ballet, theater, classical music, and opera, see "The Performing Arts" in chapter 2.

Performances generally start at 7pm. Moscow's major theaters close down in July and August. Some, such as the Bolshoi Theater, stay open but send their regular troupes on vacation (or on tour) in the summer and host visiting companies instead.

Festivals to watch for include the **Cherry Orchard Arts Festival** in early May, with symphony concerts, plays, and dance parties; the **Easter Arts Festival** in spring, with classical music concerts, church concerts, and dance performances; and the **Russian Winter Festival** around Christmas and New Year's, featuring top Russian dancers and musicians. The **Tchaikovsky Competition,** one of the world's premier classical music contests, is held every 4 years at the Moscow Conservatory. For more information on these and other festivals, refer to the newspapers and magazines discussed in the chapter introduction, above.

Dance

Bolshoi Theater   Moscow's top dance venue remains the Bolshoi, the showcase for several generations of internationally adored ballet stars. The company has at last begun loosening up its long-stale repertoire, though the results are mixed so far, and Tchaikovsky's classics still form its backbone. Besides the impeccable dancing, another major reason to visit the Bolshoi is the sumptuous setting. The 18th-century theater is fronted by a triumphant sculpture of Apollo's chariot topping the eight-columned portico. A blinding abundance of red and gold decorates the interior, inspiring viewers even before the curtain (still embossed with the Soviet hammer and sickle) opens. Its four balconies rise steeply over the orchestra seats and above the velvet-lined czar's box (long referred to as "Stalin's box"). The seats are separate, movable chairs, and the balconies are divided into separate cabins of a few seats each. Most hotels can arrange tickets, but at a hefty markup. The official ticket office is in an adjacent building, with computer screens listing available seats and their prices—but in Russian only. Lines are not long. Tickets must be purchased at least a week in advance. For the main stage, prices range from 750 to 5,000 rubles, with big draws such as the ever-popular *Swan Lake* more expensive than others. A smaller, newer stage hosts performances of the same caliber as those on the main stage, but at about half the price. Tickets can also be purchased online before your trip.

Note: The Bolshoi is currently undergoing extensive, much-needed renovations that will expand it two-fold, adding a 26-meter deep second stage underground. The main stage shut down in 2005, and is to reopen in late 2011 after a massive renovation. The second stage has remained open, hosting the main company and all the same performances. 1 Teatralnaya Sq. *(C)* **499/250-7317.** www.bolshoi.ru. Metro: Teatralnaya.

Moiseyev Ballet   Founded in 1937 by Bolshoi Theater choreographer Igor Moiseyev, this company sought to break free from the restraints of classical dance and has been putting on brilliant performances of their mixture of ballet and folk dance ever since. Folk dances emphasize rhythms from Russia and other former Soviet republics. The company performs at different theaters around town (and around the world), so keep an eye out for their posters at theater kiosks (called *teatralniye kassy*) or for ads in the English-language press. 31 Tverskaya St. *(C)* **495/699-5372.** www.moiseyev.ru. Metro: Pushkinskaya.

Moscow Operetta Theater   This charming theater staged ideologically correct musicals, mocking the aristocracy and the consumer class, for decades after its founding in 1927, but over the years it gradually shed most of them from its repertoire. Today, the theater mostly sticks to classics and accessible musicals, such as *The Merry Widow* and *My Fair Lady*, but also features new Russian operettas. Performances are in Russian, but if the fare is familiar it's well worth a visit—the performers are quite strong. 6 Bolshaya Dmitrovka Ulitsa. *(C)* **495/925-5050.** www.mosoperetta.ru. Metro: Teatralnaya.

Stanislavsky Nemirovich-Danchenko Theater   This opera and ballet theater is a more modest but well-respected younger sister of the Bolshoi, with an impressive interior and talented company. The repertoire is unadventurous, though a current renovation of the building may result in upgraded shows too. Reliable choices include *Le Corsaire, Don Quixote,* and of course anything Tchaikovsky. It's a good option if the Bolshoi is sold out or beyond your budget. 17 Bolshaya Dmitrovka. *(C)* **495/629-2835.** www.stanmus.com. Metro: Pushkinskaya.

State Kremlin Palace   The spectacular performances by the Kremlin Ballet Company suffer from this unfortunate venue, an enormous hall built to house Communist

---

   Up All Night

Moscow is a city that doesn't sleep, so if you can't sleep because of a switch in time zones, don't despair. Whether it's a midnight burger, a 3am tanning session, 5am sushi, or home electronics at 6am that you crave, Moscow's many all-day, all-night establishments are ready to accommodate you. Venturing out alone in the dark is unwise, but if you have a traveling companion you should be fine. If there's nothing near your hotel, call a cab—all major taxi companies work 24 hours. (See "Getting Around" in chapter 17 for phone numbers of reputable taxi companies.) Look for signs on establishments saying 24 or круглосуточно (round-the-clock).

Moscow Nightlife

Apshu **51**
Art Garbage **45**
B-2 **16**
Baza **36**
BB King **29**
Bi-Ba-Bo **11**
Billiard Café-Club **6**
Boar House **46**
Bolshoi Theater **27**
Chaliapin House
  Museum **14**
Che **33**
Chinese Pilot
  Jao Da **44**
Central Station **34**
Columned Hall **22**
Conservatory **47**
Cosmic **10**
Dome Bar **9**
English Court **48**
Fabrique **50**
Fasol **37**
Gazgolder **41**
Golden Palace **1**
Gorbunov House
  of Culture **7**
Helikon Opera **23**
Help **3**
Ikra Club **40**
International House
  of Music **54**
JVL **2**
Karma Bar **31**
Le Club **52**
Maly Theater **32**
Modest Charm of the
  Bourgeoisie **35**
Moiseyev Ballet **30**

Common terms and abbreviations
naberezhnaya/nab.......*Embankment*
most...........................*Bridge*
ploshchad/pl..............*Square* or *plaza*
prospekt/pr................*Avenue*
sad............................*Garden*
ulitsa/ul.....................*Street*

Rosie O'Grady's **25**
Russkaya Piramida **5**
Samalyot **4**
Shtolnya **53**
Soho Rooms **8**
Sport Line Club **56**
Stanislavsky Nemirovich-
 Danchenko Theater **19**
State Kremlin Palace **26**
Strelka **13**
Tabakov Theater
 Studio **39**
Tchaikovsky
 Concert Hall **17**
Tinkoff **12**
Uncle Sam's Billiard Bar
 and Café **55**
Vermel **49**
Vysotka **15**
Woodstock **21**

Moscow Art Theater **20**
Moscow Conservatory **24**
Moscow Operetta
 Theater **28**
New Opera **18**
Petrovich **38**
Project OGI **42**
Propaganda **43**
The Real McCoy **15**

Party congresses. The sleek but bleak 1970s-era design kills most of the beauty and wonder projected by the performers. Still, the performances are strong and this is a fine place to come if you can't afford tickets anywhere else. Many organized tours include shows here. If you're on your own, tickets cost as little as 65 rubles, but it's worth paying a bit more to get centrally located seats instead of seats on the very-far-away balcony or at the fringes. Concentrate on the dancing, not the surroundings, which include 6,000 seats equipped with electronic voting buttons and earphones for simultaneous interpretation of political congresses. State Kremlin Palace (aka the Kremlin Palace of Congresses), on the Kremlin grounds; entrance through Borovitsky Gates. ℃ **495/620-7831**. www.kremlin-gkd.ru. Metro: Borovitskaya or Biblioteka Imeni Lenina.

Classical Music

Classical music performances in Russia are perhaps the country's most underrated pleasure. The performers are rigorously trained, the concert halls are rich with history and architecturally inspiring, and you can enjoy it all for just a few dollars. For the full experience, select a performance of a Russian composer in a hall where he once played, even if the music is unfamiliar. In addition to the listings below, several estate museums around town host chamber music concerts in the warm-weather months. Combine the performance with a walk around aristocratic gardens and a tour of the museum exhibit for an idyllic summer evening. See "Aristocratic Estates" on p. 117 for addresses.

Chaliapin House Museum You'll really feel transported to pre-revolutionary Russia during a concert in this house, where opera singer Fyodor Chaliapin lived and performed for friends and family. A cluster of chairs around the piano ensures intimacy with the soloists and small ensembles that perform here a few nights a week. Take a few minutes to explore the museum before the show, including the display of some of Chaliapin's costumes. It's hard to imagine that during Soviet times, the Chaliapin home held communal apartments for up to 60 people. 25 Novinsky Bulvar (next to the U.S. Embassy). ℃ **495/605-6236.** www.shalyapin-museum.org. Metro: Barrikadnaya.

Columned Hall (Kolonny Zal) This early-18th-century mansion became the "House of Unions" under the Soviets, who made its magnificent gold-and-white ballroom (the Columned Hall) into the elite concert space it remains today. Lenin and Stalin both lay in state here, as millions of Russians filed past to pay their respects. English author George Bernard Shaw celebrated his 75th birthday here. Now its repertoire includes visiting international symphony orchestras and choirs, children's performances, and even fashion shows. 1 Bolshaya Dmitrovka. ℃ **495/692-0736.** www. domsojuzov.ru. Metro: Teatralnaya.

English Court (Angliiskoye Podvorye) This 16th-century boardinghouse for English merchants has been turned into a museum that hosts chamber music concerts 1 or 2 evenings a week. See the "Walking Tour" on p. 125 for more on the history of this building and neighborhood. 4a Varvarka Ulitsa. ℃ **495/698-3952.** Metro: Kitay Gorod or Ploshchad Revolucii.

International House of Music (Mezhdunarodny Dom Muzyki) This vast, ultra-modern venue is now the primary one for international music stars. It's reserved for major events, which are priced like similar venues in Europe. The acoustics are excellent, and nearly any seat provides great sound. Take a walk around the island before the concert, among futuristic office towers and picturesque bridges. 52 Kosmodamianskaya Naberezhnaya, building 8. ℃ **495/730-1011.** www.mmdm.ru. Metro: Paveletskaya.

Moscow Conservatory (Konservatoria)   This is the most popular and most historic place to hear Russian and international compositions performed by some of the country's top orchestras and soloists. The conservatory, housed in an 18th-century mansion now fronted by a statue of Tchaikovsky, who taught here for 12 years, is still the premier training ground for Russian musicians. The bigger shows with visiting symphony orchestras are in the Grand Hall (Bolshoi Zal). The smaller Rachmaninoff Hall and the Small Hall (Maly Zal) offer more intimate atmospheres, often featuring performances by rising student stars. Tickets for the Grand Hall can be as low as 100 rubles. 13/6 Bolshaya Nikitskaya St. ✆ **495/629-0225.** www.mosconsv.ru/english.phtml. Metro: Arbatskaya.

Tchaikovsky Concert Hall (Kontsertny Zal Im. Tchaikovskogo)   This 19th-century concert space has an impressive columned facade and a more modern outlook than the conservatory. It presents a range of musical styles, from the classics to performances for children, folk music, piano jazz, and Avant-Garde shows. 4/31 Triumfalnaya Sq. ✆ **495/232-0400.** www.classicalmusic.ru. Tickets 60–1,000 rubles. Metro: Mayakovskaya.

Opera

Russian opera is less renowned abroad than its ballet, but opera fans will appreciate hearing gems by Rimsky-Korsakov, Mussorgsky, and Tchaikovsky in their home country, performed by top-notch singers. Opera tickets at the **Bolshoi Theater** cost less than ballet tickets and sell out less often, but that's more a reflection of ballet's popularity than the opera's quality.

Bolshoi Theater   Operas at the Bolshoi stick to the classics, such as *The Marriage of Figaro, The Barber of Seville,* and *Carmen,* but they may include pleasant Russian works such as Tchaikovsky's *Iolanta.* Mussorgsky's *Boris Godunov* is a major draw for Russian audiences, delving into the 16th and 17th centuries, when Russian history was fraught with battles for succession and much shifting of alliances—but the opera reflects more of the romantic nationalism of the 19th century when Mussorgsky wrote it than the murky turmoil of Godunov's era. Hearing opera at the Bolshoi is just part of the experience; viewing the grandiose theater is the other half, once it reopens after renovations. See the listing under "Dance" above for details on the theater and how to get tickets. Tickets must be purchased at least a week in advance unless you get them through your hotel. Operas are staged at least once or twice a week. 1 Teatralnaya Sq. ✆ **499/250-7317.** www.bolshoi.ru. Metro: Teatralnaya.

Helikon Opera   This theater, a rounded space of graduated platforms that feels almost intimate, presents more innovative and controversial performances than the Bolshoi, such as updated renditions of Wagner's *Ring* Cycle. The theater's popularity among Russians means tickets are often scarce. The main building at 19 Bolshaya Nikitskaya St. closed for renovation and the company performs at its second stage. 11 Novy Arbat bld. 2 ✆ **495/695-6584.** www.helikon.ru/eng_default.php. Metro: Arbatskaya.

New Opera (Novaya Opera)   Stylistically somewhere between the Bolshoi and the Helikon, the New Opera has a strong repertoire of standards and a few more anthology-style shows. Highlights include *La Traviata* and other Verdi works, Tchaikovsky's *Eugene Onegin,* and Rimsky-Korsakov's *Snow Maiden.* 3 Karetny Ryad, bld. 2. ✆ **495/694-0868.** www.novayaopera.ru. Metro: Pushkinskaya.

Stanislavsky Nemirovich-Danchenko Theater   As with its ballet company, the Stanislavsky's opera company is strong and respected, though it is often overshadowed by colleagues at the Bolshoi. The theater itself is similarly shaped and decorated, and a current renovation is expected to renew the shine on the banisters and refresh the repertoire. Operas are staged about once a week, and tickets are cheaper and easier to obtain here than those for the Bolshoi or the other opera houses. 17 Bolshaya Dmitrovka. ✆ **495/629-2835.** www.stanmus.com. Metro: Pushkinskaya.

Theater

English-language theater troupes sometimes visit Moscow and perform Russian classics, and occasionally Russian theater companies stage a few performances in English. See the English-language newspaper *The Moscow Times* for listings of English-language theater (www.themoscowtimes.com).

Maly Theater   The theater is called "Maly" (small) only because it's across from the Bolshoi (which means "big" or "grand"), but the Maly's hall is full-sized and its performances are top-quality. Most shows are in Russian, with an emphasis on classics from Chekhov, Ostrovsky, and Griboyedov, but international companies occasionally perform both Russian and foreign works in English. 1 Teatralnyi Proyezd, bld. 1. (across from the Bolshoi). ✆ **495/624-4083.** www.maly.ru. Metro: Teatralnaya.

Moscow Art Theater (MKhAT imeni Chekhova)   This was where playwright Anton Chekhov and the Stanislavsky method of acting made it big, and actors and writers from around the world have been making pilgrimages here for a century. It's worth stopping by even if you don't attend a performance; you can view the strange and scrawny statue of Chekhov in front and wander the pleasant pedestrian street while you're at it. Inaugurated in 1898, the theater and the company that bore its name brought together Stanislavsky's innovative acting school, Nemirovich-Danchenko's more established name and theater studio, and Chekhov's new brand of psychological drama. Today the theater puts on some of Moscow's most popular plays, from revivals of Russian classics to premiers of plays dealing with Chechnya and other up-to-date themes. The second stage hosts more experimental works for a slightly lower ticket price (though ticket prices for both stages are well below those in London or New York). English-language performances are rare. Don't confuse this theater with the Moscow Art Theater named after Maxim Gorky, a more modern venue with a less lofty reputation. 3 Kamergersky Pereulok. ✆ **495/629-8760.** http://mxat.ru/english. Metro: Teatralnaya.

> **Theater Dining**
>
> Because Moscow's theaters are spread out throughout town, there's no real theater district dining. Many Russian restaurants don't start dinner service until 7pm, which is when most performances begin, so you may have to wait until after the show to eat. If you're in the area of the Bolshoi Theater in summer, treat yourself to an after-theater confection at the Metropol tearoom followed by a stroll through Red Square to watch the midnight sunset.

Tabakov Theater Studio   Oleg Tabakov is perhaps Moscow's most famous and energetic theater director, with several studios around town and fresh performances constantly enlivening his repertoire. His chief performance space is a stuffy basement hall in the picturesque Chistiye Prudy neighborhood, always full of enthusiastic, friendly theatergoers. If you're learning Russian, attending a show here is a great way to get some practice—the hall is so small you can watch the actors enunciate, and the visuals aid comprehension. 1A Ulitsa Chaplygina, bld. 1. (through the arch and to the right). ✆ **495/623-6125.** http://tabakov.ru/en/. Metro: Chistiye Prudy.

THE CLUB & MUSIC SCENE
Dance Clubs & Discos

Moscow's club scene has been called the hottest, wildest, most expensive, and most offensive in Europe. It attracts top DJs from London and New York, top models, and plenty of uncontrolled substances. Although the industry has been driven by the excesses of Russia's new rich, it offers plenty of options for less affluent onlookers as well. Even if you're not a clubber, you'll find it worthwhile to get a glimpse into the world where modern Moscow absorbs and expends its energy. Be prepared for strict "face control" at the most popular spots, with jeans and athletic shoes inadmissible and men's attire appraised as carefully—or more so—as women's. The earlier you go, the shorter the lines and the more relaxed the door policy, but you're in for a long and possibly dull wait before the real partying starts, well after midnight.

The hippest places rarely remain so for more than a few months, so listings get stale fast. Check *eXile* newspaper (www.exile.ru) or *The Moscow Times* (www.the moscowtimes.com) for the latest hot spots. Here are a few places that have stood the test of time.

Che As in Guevara, of course. This self-proclaimed egalitarian nightspot has a relaxed door policy and cheap drinks flowing all night to the beat of fairly mainstream club music. Open daily 24 hours. 10/2 Nikolskaya Ulitsa. ℂ **495/621-7477.** www.clubche.ru. Metro: Lubyanka.

Fabrique This former workshop of Design University hosts fashion shows of Russian designers and plenty of fashion-oriented parties. It's set up like an enormous loft with concrete walls and good acoustics. 2 Kosmodamianskaya Naberezhnaya. ℂ **495/953-6576.** http://fabrique.ru/. Metro: Novokuznetskaya.

Fasol Thursday night is the only worthwhile time to visit, when a 1980s theme brings an enthusiastic crowd of college students and plenty of professionals. The music is international hits from the era, most remixed for modern sound. 28 Prospekt Mira. ℂ **495/680-2833.** No cover weekdays, 300 rubles Fri–Sat. http://fasol-club.ru. Metro: Prospekt Mira.

Gazgolder Moscow's latest club hot spot is a former factory, now converted into several separate club spaces—and with military-level door control. Gazgolder and Gazgallery are the most exclusive (no sneakers allowed) and specialize in electro music. 5/1 Nizhny Susalny Pereulok. ℂ **985/226-3346.** http://gazgolder.com.

Karma Bar The basement attracts just about everyone, but its ever-fresh rotation of DJs keeps it from being too mass-market. Salsa dancing takes place on Sunday nights. Open Thursday through Sunday from 7pm to 6am. 3 Pushechnaya Ulitsa. ℂ **926/688-8939.** http://karmabar.ru. No cover for women; cover 300 rubles for men Fri–Sat. Metro: Kuznetsky Most.

Modest Charm of the Bourgeoisie (Skromnoye Oboyaniye Burzhuazi) This compact hall is the favored "pre-party" spot of Moscow clubbers. It features lounge music in a mellow atmosphere to get you in the mood before the real party-hopping begins. It's open daily 24 hours. 24 Bolshaya Lubyanka. ℂ **495/623-0848.** www.bourjousia.ru. Metro: Lubyanka.

Propaganda The cafe tables quietly vanish around 11pm and the dance floor starts throbbing within minutes to the beats of house, trance, and techno. The lines

If you'd rather not stay up late or stand in line, try having a midday "business lunch" in one of the top clubs, which often have their own restaurants. It's a chance to glimpse the sleek interiors and a few of the glitzy regulars while you eat lunch, usually for a quite reasonable price.

get long on weekend nights, and the doormen seem fierce, but they don't care about how you're dressed—they're just trying to control crowds. The place is popular with students, expats, straights, gays, artists, and young capitalists. Try to get a table upstairs for a little more space and a perfect people-watching angle. Open daily from noon to 6am. 7 Bolshoi Zlatoustinsky Pereulok. ℂ **495/624-5732.** www.propagandamoscow.com. Metro: Lubyanka or Kitai-Gorod.

Sohorooms   Dress up and go early here to get in before glamour controls get too tight. Then you can watch the Russian showbiz royalty and visiting Hollywood stars dance the night away. 12 Savvinskaya Naberezhnaya, building 8. ℂ **495/988-7474.** www. sohorooms.com. Metro: Sportivnaya, Kievskaya.

Rock & Pop

Russian rock sprang from a semidissident scene of trading bootleg Beatles and Rolling Stones LPs, and has had a rough time evolving with today's freer-than-free Russian youth culture. A blend of ironic pop and Russian hip-hop has largely eclipsed rock as the soundtrack for the post-Soviet generation. The biggest Russian stars today masterfully blend the traditions of their pioneering rock predecessors—lyrics tinged with Russian fatalism and melodies in minor keys—with the latest mixing technology and a dose of humor. Beneath all this usually lies a musician with classical training.

Art Garbage   This is a reliable venue for up-and-coming Russian and European rock and some mainstream bands. Open Friday to Sunday from 11am to 6am. 5 Starosadsky Pereulok, building 6 (deep in the courtyard; follow the graffiti). ℂ **495/628-8745.** Cover for concerts 200–350 rubles. www.art-garbage.ru. Metro: Kitai-Gorod.

B-2   The city's chief music venue, this multilevel club showcases popular and more obscure bands and is always hopping. Open daily 24 hours. 8 Bolshaya Sadovaya Ulitsa. ℂ **495/650-9909.** Cover 100–700 rubles, depending on band. www.b2club.ru. Metro: Mayakovskaya.

Gorbunov House of Culture (Dom Kultury im. Gorbunova)   This theater-style venue is a required stop for Russian rock giants, as well as international stars and local and European alternative bands. The balcony offers a calmer alternative to the sweaty main floor. This is the club that helped spawn Moscow's thriving bootleg music market, which has since moved down the street into a former TV factory and has grown to respect copyright laws. (see listing for Gorbushka on p. 141). 27 Novozavodskaya Ulitsa (just south of Filyovsky Park). ℂ **499/148-0795.** Metro: Bagrationovskaya.

Ikra Club   Hopping music from local and visiting guitar bands and full dinners are on tap in this three-story estate-turned clubhouse. Its name means Caviar Club, and you can get a caviar snack but the appetizers are better. 8a Ulitsa Kazakova (inside the Gogol Theater) ℂ **495/778-5651.** Cover 200–400 rubles. http://ikraclub.ru/!english. Metro: Kurskaya.

Jazz & Blues

It sounds strange to look for jazz and blues in a land of Arctic frost and Slavs, but the search is worthwhile. Russia's version of jazz and blues is certainly its own, with its melancholy coming from a different kind of slavery and isolation. See the website www.jazz.ru/eng for a more detailed rundown.

BB King Moscow's only real blues bar showcases the legendary Russian band Crossroads and top blues artists, as well as several crossover and mediocre musicians. Their seafood okra gumbo is out of this world. Open daily from noon to 2am. 4/2 Sadovaya-Samotechnaya Ulitsa. ✆ **495/699-8206.** www.bbkingclub.ru Cover for concerts 350–400 rubles. Metro: Tsvetnoi Bulvar.

JVL One of the most inventive jazz clubs in town, JVL has its own recording studio and equipment. It's open Monday through Saturday from noon until the last guest leaves. Enter from 21 Sushyovskaya Ulitsa, then go through the arch. 14/19 Novoslobodskaya. ✆ **495/978-1030.** Cover 1,000 rubles, includes concerts, drinks and food. http://jvl.night.ru/. Metro: Novoslobodskaya.

Le Club This laid-back, friendly venue was one of the first music clubs in Moscow. Open daily noon to 2am. 16 Ulanskiy Pereulok, bld. 1. Hotel Ulansky. ✆ **495/632-9264.** Cover 500–1,000 rubles. http://le-club.ru. Metro: Chistye Prudy.

Folk & Alternative

Traditional Russian folk music is best heard at seasonal festivals or at the Tchaikovsky Concert Hall. Less formal, more rock-tinged versions can be heard at the following clubs around town.

Apshu This is a good choice for seeing the exploration of new genres by Russia's nonmainstream musicians and some well-known international visitors. Check out the bathtub in the middle of the hall lined with a mattress and blanket for anyone who wants to climb in. 10 Klimentovsky Lane, building 1. ✆ **495/953-9944.** www.apshu.ru. Metro: Tretyakovskaya.

Chinese Pilot Jao Da The two halls here often offer starkly contrasting music to keep you sharp, from Tuvan throat singers to British folk artists to techno salsa played by a DJ. Open daily 24 hours. 25/12 Lubyansky Proyezd, bld. 1. ✆ **495/624-5611.** Cover for some shows 200–400 rubles. Metro: Kitai-Gorod.

Project OGI You could visit here just to read the concert listings or flyers on the wall. More fun is to come on a night featuring Finnish percussionists or other music you might not find at home. Open daily 24 hours. 8/12 Potapovsky Lane, building 2. ✆ **495/627-5366.** www.proektogi.ru. Metro: Chistye Prudy.

Vermel No longer as cutting-edge as it once was, Vermel is still a cozy spot for Celtic duets, Russian bards, and other non-pop offerings. Open Monday to Friday from noon to 5am, Saturday and Sunday from 6pm to 6am. 4/5 Raushkaya Naberezhnya. ✆ **499/238-3303.** Cover Fri–Sat 350 rubles. www.vermel.ru. Metro: Novokuznetskaya.

Nightclubs & Cabaret

Several hotels have their own nightclubs, though quality varies widely. Cabaret-style shows offered by the international chains such as the Marriott hotels are certain to be elegant, pricey, and relatively sterile. Older Soviet hotels offer cabaret shows of stale pop music, a few *chansons,* and inevitably a topless or near-topless kick-line finale. A night at the theater followed by a colorful local bar will offer greater cultural value and more fun than such cabarets. Nightclubs (as distinct from dance clubs) are plentiful but often double as bordellos, and even the places that look chic or elite generally include a strip show. A favorite spot among many male expats is Night Flight, which you'll see vigorously advertised.

THE BAR SCENE

Moscow is full of places that call themselves bars but that can be anything from a fine dining establishment or repository of rare Armenian brandy to a funky book-lined cafe or a grungy pub where the neighborhood gathers to watch soccer matches. The only thing they have in common is their willingness to serve you alcohol.

Boar House   The wee hours get rather raunchy, but the rest of the time this is a reliable, relaxed spot for decent beer, international sports matches, and multilingual conversation. 26 Zemlyanoi Val. © **495/917-0150.** www.hotdogsbar.ru. Metro: Kurskaya.

Conservatory   This atrium bar on the top floor of the Ararat Park Hyatt Hotel is one of the few elegant and accessible places to watch Red Square at night. The ergonomic design and gorgeous customers are as eye-catching as the view from the wraparound windows. Cocktails and expensive French wines are the specialties, but the beer is fine, too. 4 Neglinnaya Ulitsa. © **495/783-1234.** Metro: Teatralnaya or Kuznetsky Most.

Dome Bar   Another trendy place in the up-and-coming Red October district, Dome is a lounge bar complete with a cozy movie theater showing latest releases. It has concerts and dances over the weekends and also offers enjoyable food. 3/10 Bersenevsky Pereulok, bld. 7. © **499/788-6524.** http://domebar.blogspot.com. Metro: Kropotkinskaya.

Help   This cocktail bar has about 200 selections undergoing constant revision. Reasonably priced and chic but unpretentious. 27 Pervaya Tverskaya-Yamskaya, building 1. © **495/995-5395.** http://helpbar.ru. Metro: Belorusskaya.

Petrovich   The schtick here is Soviet nostalgia, aimed at Moscow's worldly, post-Soviet creative set. Much of the humor on the menu and in the decor will be lost on anyone who didn't grow up under Brezhnev, but don't let that worry you. Its creative drinks menu is well worth a visit, as is its lunch buffet. Unfortunately, Petrovich is ostensibly a private club at night, so unless you tell the guards you're meeting someone or otherwise finesse your way in, it may be hard to get in after 6pm. The entrance in the courtyard is on the left through an unmarked gray door. 24 Myasnitskaya St. bld. 3. © **495/623-0082.** http://club-petrovich.ru/eng/. Metro: Chistiye Prudy.

The Real McCoy   Its atmosphere aims for American hillbilly bar, but it turns into a raucous urban dance club after midnight. In early evening the popular after-work drink spot offers jazz, swing, and occasional bluegrass bands. It's located in the basement of an enormous apartment tower. 1 Kudrinskaya Sq. © **499/255-4144.** http://mccoy.ru. Metro: Barrikadnaya.

Rosie O'Grady's   Irish bars are a standard in any city around the world by now; Moscow's Rosie O'Grady's went from being the only place in town with imported beer on tap to becoming an institution that's always friendly and a good source of Guinness for students and seniors alike. And then it moved across town. Live music and concerts. 5 Prospekt Mira, bld. 1. © **495/545-1728.** http://rosie.ru/?lang=en. Metro: Sukharevskaya or Prospekt Mira.

Strelka Strelka is one of the most enjoyable and popular bars in town, one of a string of bars and clubs that has opened in refurbished red brick buildings of a former chocolate factory called Krasny Oktyabr (Red October). Live music, rooftop terrace with views of the Moscow River. 14 Bersenevskaya Naberezhnaya. ✆ **495/771-7416.** www. strelkainstitute.com/#url=/bar Metro: Kropotkinskaya.

GAY & LESBIAN NIGHTLIFE

Whatever stigmas surround homosexuality in Russia, they fade as soon as night falls. Russia's clubs are among its most gay-friendly venues, and many hold special gay nights once a week. In addition, the gay club scene is thriving and evolving, though the hottest spots tend to be accessible only by word-of-mouth—not out of fear of persecution, a likely and terrifying possibility in the Soviet era, but out of fear that the masses will find out about them and dilute their chic. Clubs change orientation and open and close frequently. The website Gay.ru has an English-language page (www.gay.ru/english) with up-to-date listings. See chapter 17 for more gay-friendly resources in Russia.

Baza A mixed club with a friendly and feisty atmosphere, Baza is tucked in a seedy courtyard. 6 Milyutinsky Pereulok, bld. 1. ✆ **495/627-3193.** Metro: Lubyanka.

Central Station No cover for men. Excellent dance music, open to anyone. 4 Yuzhny Proyezd. ✆ **495/988-3585.** www.centralclub.ru. Metro: Komsomolskaya ot Krasnye Vorota.

Propaganda This eternally popular club has a mixed crowd throughout the week but throws the city's best-known gay parties Sunday night. Open daily noon to 6am. 7 Bolshoi Zlatoustinsky Pereulok. ✆ **495/624-5732.** www.propagandamoscow.com. Metro: Lubyanka or Kitai-Gorod.

Sharm This club replaced well-known Dusha i Telo (Body and Soul) in another location. Open daily 11pm to 6am. Dubininskaya 69, korpus 74. ✆ **495/645-0766.** www.club chance.net. Metro: Paveletskaya or Tulskaya.

MORE ENTERTAINMENT
Billiards

If you have any interest at all in billiards or pool, it's worth discovering the Russian version while you're here. Called *russky billiard* or *russkaya piramida*, the game is played on a table much larger and thicker than a pool table, and with enormous cues. The balls, all one color, are nearly twice as big as pool balls, but the pockets are quite small, making it much harder to score the requisite 71 points. Up to four people can play at once. The game dates back to Peter the Great's time, when he brought back the billiard-table concept after his voyages to the West, and Russians adapted the game to their tastes. Long a game reserved for the elite, today it enjoys a much wider following, and the billiards bars around Moscow cater to all pocketbooks. Tables run between 250 and 750 rubles an hour depending on the establishment, and few but the most elite spots take reservations for tables. In addition to Russian billiards, most places offer tables and equipment for "American pool," English snooker, and French carambole.

Billiard Cafe-Club Island of Crimea Housed on the ground floor of the Expo-center, a sprawling complex for international conferences and events, this club offers tables for all tastes and a multilingual clientele. Open noon to 4am. 12 Krasnopresnenskaya

Naberezhnaya. Expocenter. Entrance 2. ✆ **495/258-1925.** www.ostrov-krim.ru. Tables 1,000 rubles per hr. Metro: Ulitsa 1905 Goda (take a taxi from the metro).

Russkaya Piramida   Tables for Russian billiards, snooker, pool, and carambole are available in two adjacent halls on the grounds of the renowned CSKA (Red Army) sports complex. Open daily 24 hours. 39a Leningradsky Prospekt (in the sports complex set back from the main rd.). ✆ **495/157-8040.** Tables 120–240 rubles per hr. Metro: Aeroport, Dinamo.

Uncle Sam's Billiard Bar and Cafe   This is a popular and laid-back spot among expats and tourists, with 15 tables for American pool and Russian billiards. Daily noon to 6am. 5 Zatsepsky Val. ✆ **499/235-6530.** http://unclesamscafe.ru. Tables 110–600 rubles per hr., depending on time of day. Metro: Paveletskaya.

Bowling

Russians discovered bowling over the past decade, partly in thanks to the Coen brothers' film *The Big Lebowski,* a cult hit among Russian audiences. The country's first bowling alleys aimed at a decidedly different clientele from the pot-bellied, working-class crowd in the film. Bowling started in Moscow as a sort of polo for the new rich, with the impeccably buffed lanes costing upward of 3,050 rubles an hour, and bowlers decked out in Prada and Versace. Today bowling has trickled down to a broader player base, with some serious bowlers mixed in with the after-work crowd and family parties. All alleys provide "disco bowling" at night, switching to black light and cranking up the music after 10pm or so. The following alleys are good choices:

o **Bi-Ba-Bo**: 9 Karmanitsky Pereulok (in courtyard across from John Bull Pub); ✆ **495/937-4337;** 700 to 1,600 rubles per hour per lane depending on time of day; http://bibabo.ru. Metro: Smolenskaya.

o **Cosmic**: 2 Presnenskaya Naberezhnaya, inside Afimoll shopping mall; ✆ **495/915-8765.** 360 to 1,320 rubles per hour depending on time of day; Metro: Vystavochny Tsentr. Also 6, Prospect Vernadskogo, Capitoly shopping mall. ✆ **495/644-4232.** Metro Universitet. http://cosmik.ru.

o **Samolyot** (Airplane): 14/1 Presnensky Val; ✆ **495/234-1818;** http://moscow. samolet-bowling.ru. 360 to 1,200 rubles per hour per lane depending on time of day; Metro: Ulitsa 1905 Goda.

o **Sport Line Club**: 15 Kozhevnicheskaya Ulitsa, bld. 1; ✆ **495/959-6935;** 300 to 1,290 rubles per hour per lane depending on time of day; www.sportline-club. ru. Metro: Paveletskaya.

o **Vysotka**: In the Stalin tower at 1 Kudrinskaya Ploshchad; ✆ **499/252-2309;** 900 rubles per hour; www.visotka-club.ru. Metro: Barrikadnaya.

Movies

The language barrier makes moviegoing a challenge for most visitors, though the **Moscow International Film Festival,** which takes place every even-numbered year in June and July, offers an often surprising repertoire of international films in their original languages. Also, the **International Film Center** (15 Druzhinnikovs-kaya Ulitsa; ✆ **495/255-9692;** www.kinocenter.ru; Metro: Barrikadnaya or Krasno-presnenskaya) has a rich and varied schedule of movies from across borders and eras; you might luck into a silent film treasure from Sergei Eisenstein or a big-screen showing of *West Side Story* in English. Make sure that any English-language film you're interested in is subtitled, not voiced-over, which is common in Russia. If you're itching for a new Hollywood blockbuster in English, try **Dome Cinema** at Penta Olympic Renaissance Hotel (18/1 Olimpiisky Prospekt; ✆ **495/931-9873;** www. domecinema.ru; metro: Prospekt Mira). Many other big movie theaters also run English-language films in original sound once or several times a day. See *The Moscow Times* weekend edition or other English-language publications for weekly listings.

SIDE TRIPS FROM MOSCOW

Venturing outside Moscow demonstrates how deeply the capital differs from the rest of the sprawling country it represents. Beyond the clogged beltway that marks the city limits, the casinos, chain stores, and English signage quickly vanish, revealing an ungroomed landscape of rivers, oak groves, and clusters of wooden houses. Moscow's outskirts look nothing like the suburban sprawl so familiar to North Americans and Europeans. Here, the "inner city" is the most elite place to live, the urban fringes are depressed districts of dreary apartment blocks for those not rich enough to afford a Moscow address, and beyond that is endless countryside—and the occasional enclave of multi-million-dollar estates for Russia's expanding new rich.

The most-visited and most historically revealing destinations around Moscow are along the Golden Ring (Zolotoye Koltso), a circle of eight cities, dating back to the 11th century, that served as a nucleus of Russian culture and politics. Their splendid Orthodox cathedrals and monasteries and their medieval fortresses form their key attractions. I've included three of them here: Sergiev Posad, considered Russia's holiest Orthodox site, plus Vladimir and Suzdal, two towns usually visited together. Sergiev Posad is a feasible day trip and can be reached relatively easily on your own. Vladimir and Suzdal are farther afield, so I recommend an overnight trip. The other stops are closer to Moscow and focus on the secular: the landscaping marvels of the estate at Arkhangelskoye, and the simple charms of the writers' village at Peredelkino.

To get the most out of these trips, go with a tour group or get an individual tour guide. Unless you've done extensive background reading, you'll miss much of the context and significance of these towns if you tackle them alone.

Be warned that roads outside the big cities (and sometimes within them) are rough and potholed, so if you take a bus, be prepared for some bouncing. Watch how quickly traffic thins as you leave town, as urban turns to rural and high-rises abruptly give way to rickety outhouses.

SERGIEV POSAD

75km (47 miles) NE of Moscow

This town's magnificent 14th-century monastery and its history as the holiest of Russia's Orthodox shrines draws pilgrims from around the country, and plenty of non-Russian tourists. The trip serves as a course in Russian architecture and sociology, as well as an immersion into Orthodox traditions. Music enthusiasts can delight in informal choral concerts—even a small midday church service produces hypnotizing harmonies. The town also claims to be the birthplace of the *matryoshka*, the ubiquitous nesting doll. Visiting the monastery, *matryoshka* shopping, and wandering the run-down but charming streets are enough to make this Moscow's most satisfying out-of-town day trip. It's also the only city on the historic Golden Ring that's a comfortable 1-day trip from the capital.

Essentials

Sergiev Posad, called Zagorsk in the Soviet era, can be reached by bus, commuter train, or taxi. Many hotels and tour companies arrange bus trips here. **Patriarshy Dom** tours has an informative and intimate English-language tour (℘ **495/795-0927;** in the U.S. ℘ 650/678-7076). **Intourist** offers a more standard trip, which includes more religious history and less propaganda than in Soviet times. (Several locations across town include 11 Stoleshnikov Pereulok, ℘ **495/234-9509;** and 2 Novy Arbat, ℘ **495/234-4480,** www.intourist.ru.)

The character of Podmoskovye ("the region surrounding Moscow") is evolving as the city's ever-expanding upper classes set up camp—in other words, build multimillion-dollar homes—in the exclusive villages once reserved for *dachas* (country cottages) of the Communist Party elite. Meant to complement their luxurious Moscow apartments, these nouveau riche homes often reach absurd levels of extravagance and incongruity. Keep your eyes peeled as you take your side trips and you're sure to spot some of them. Look for castle-like modern constructions surrounded by massive security gates or fences, often fronted by armed guards. Turrets, buttresses, and Japanese gardens are common architectural features. These new homes are the only places in Russia you're likely to see a closely mowed lawn.

If you're traveling on your own, consider taking a bus from the main Shcholkovsky Bus Terminal. The cheap, direct trip takes about 2 hours (though tour buses manage to make the trip a bit quicker). The bus you need is labeled MOSCOW–SERGIEV POSAD–YAROSLAVL, meaning you get off midjourney. The driver may know only a few words of English. You'll be dropped off at the bus station near the monastery.

The commuter train, called *elektrichka*, leaves from Yaroslavsky Train Station (go to the suburban ticket desk, called *prigorodniye kassy*). The ride is cheaper and smoother than the bus, but it's slightly less convenient. It makes a few stops on the 1½-hour journey, and you have to be able to read SERGIEV POSAD in Russian to make sure you don't miss your stop (see chapter 18 to study up on the Russian alphabet). When you get off, it's a 10-minute walk through town to the cathedrals. Train cars are fitted with hard wooden benches that can be crowded on weekend days, especially in summer. Weekdays during off season they're calm and pleasant, as long as you don't get stuck with a curious or alcoholic seatmate. Tickets on the bus or train cost less than 330 rubles.

An excellent but pricier option is hiring a car and driver for the day. That way you can depart and return at your leisure, and perhaps take some side roads to better view the countryside. The price of the trip is negotiable, and costs more if you get an English-speaking driver or guide. Try your hotel tour desk, or contact My Moscow Taxi (www.mymoscowtaxi.com).

What to See & Do

Trinity Monastery of St. Sergius (Troitse-Sergiyevo Lavra) is the place to start. Sergius of Radonezh founded the monastery in 1345, and it gained a reputation as the source of Russian military and spiritual strength after his blessing was believed to have inspired victory in one of Russian history's most crucial battles, against the Mongol Tatars at Kulikovo Pole in 1380. For centuries, Russian czars and commoners trekked here in pilgrimage, traveling in gilded carriages or on foot for days or weeks, many fasting throughout the journey. The site was so charged with history that even Stalin couldn't bring himself to raze it, though its monks were sent to labor camps after the Bolshevik Revolution. Stalin even allowed the monastery to reopen after World War II as the spiritual center of the emasculated, state-monitored Orthodox Church of the Soviet era.

Sergius was canonized after his death, and his remains lie in the monastery's **Cathedral of the Trinity.** This cathedral boasts several works by Andrei Rublev, Russia's most famous icon painter. Many pilgrims come to Sergiev Posad just to see his iconostasis masterpiece, *Old Testament Trinity.* The monastery's version is a copy; the original now hangs in Moscow's Tretyakov Gallery. The cathedral started a trend with its use of *kokoshniki,* the pointed arches that became a defining feature of Moscow church architecture in ensuing centuries.

The monastery's current walls were built in the mid–16th century, as was the **Cathedral of the Assumption** that rises in the center of the complex. Its four blue onion domes around a larger gold one may look familiar—they were inspired by the Cathedral of the Assumption in the Kremlin. The Chapel Over the Well is a dizzying structure carved with flowers and vines and blue arabesques, built over a spring discovered in 1644. Pilgrims still come with empty bottles, jugs, and buckets to fill with its holy water.

Among the prominent people buried at the monastery is **Boris Godunov,** Russia's ruler from 1598 to 1605, the only czar not buried in Moscow or St. Petersburg. He ascended to the throne in controversy and his death plunged Russia into the Time of

Troubles, a decade of war and jockeying for power. Godunov's court enemies are also here, in more elegant tombs inside the Cathedral of the Assumption.

A century later, Peter the Great took refuge here from the *streltsy* royal guards and later from the Regent Sofia, who was conspiring to keep him from power. He later showered funding on the monastery, and his daughter Elizabeth, who became empress, bestowed it with the title of *lavra,* the highest religious rank for an Orthodox monastery.

The monastery's **Museum of History and Art** (✆ **495/786-2708;** www. musobl.divo.ru/novosti.html) houses an impressive collection of jewel-encrusted robes, gems, and icons from centuries past. The more unusual garments and exhibits are on the second floor. Entrance to the monastery is free, but the museum charges a fee of 130 rubles. Permission to take photos also costs a fee. Anyone wearing shorts will not be let on the grounds. The monastery, the main resident of Ulitsa Krasnaya Armii, is open daily from 8am to 6pm. The churches are open to the public Monday through Friday, and the museum is open Tuesday through Sunday from 10am to 6pm.

The monastery produced wooden toys as far back as Sergius's time, for children of local residents and visiting royalty. In the 19th century the town became a center of *matryoshka* workmanship, and now many rare nesting dolls and other wooden toys and dolls are on display and for sale at the town's **Toy Museum** (✆ **49654/-02581;** www.museumot.com; 123 Ulitsa Krasnoi Armii; Wed–Sun 10am–5pm). For tips on *matryoshka* purchasing, see chapter 7. If you have time and energy, wander south of the monastery around Kelarsky Pond, a popular spot for amateur artists in summer.

Where to Eat

For such a touristed town, Sergiev Posad has minimal dining options. Russians outside the big cities don't generally eat out, and residents here are no exception. The coziest option is **Russky Dvorik,** a wooden cottage between the train station and the monastery at 134 Prospekt Krasnoi Armii, with traditional Russian fare for about 500 rubles per person per meal. **Café Posadskoye** is a cheaper, simpler version, opposite the monastery at 22 Prospekt Krasnoi Armii. Large groups prefer the neighboring **Russkaya Skazka,** with overpriced but passable Russian standards and a spacious dining hall. **Kovcheg Hotel** has a comfortable dining hall offering fairly flavorless food. There's even a McDonald's if nothing else suits you.

SUZDAL & VLADIMIR

Suzdal is 215km (134 miles) NE of Moscow; Vladimir is 175km (109 miles) NE of Moscow

Suzdal's conservative, tranquil beauty complements Vladimir's grand heritage, and together they form an ideal weekend trip away from Moscow's madness. Vladimir was a major political, religious, and cultural center when Moscow was still an unremarkable provincial capital. Suzdal houses a fortress and a collection of riverside convents and monasteries that date back to the town's heyday in the 11th to 13th centuries. Its populace and architecture stay loyal to tradition despite the steady flow of tourists. Vladimir, once a provincial capital more prosperous and holy than Moscow, centers around its incomparable **Cathedral of the Assumption**, whose architectural features caused a sensation when it was completed in 1158 and inspired cathedral designers for centuries to come. The town has grown and modernized more than Suzdal; it has more tourist services, but less charm. Both towns are lush and breezy in summer. They are inviting in winter, when snowflakes glisten off the cathedral

Suzdal

9

SIDE TRIPS FROM MOSCOW | Suzdal & Vladimir

Vladimir

spires and bilberry bushes along the road, and when the thick walls of the cathedrals lure you in from the cold.

Essentials

PLANNING YOUR TRIP

The distance, Moscow traffic, and lack of direct train routes make it nearly impossible to visit both these towns in 1 day. If you're short on time, you could take a day trip to Vladimir alone. Visiting Suzdal as a day trip from Moscow is worthwhile only if you have a car, preferably with a driver or guide who knows the roads and the town. I strongly recommend spending the night to savor both these towns. Vladimir's city website has a comprehensive English-language link, including hotel advice (www. vladimir-city.ru/welcome).

Tours that arrange transportation and accommodations will save you time and energy and are probably your best bet. The main drawback is that they favor the drab hotels of Vladimir over the romantic overnight offerings in Suzdal. Of the English-language tour companies, **Patriarshy Dom** (✆ **495/795-0927;** http://russiatravel-pdtours.netfirms.com) offers occasional trips here, but check before you leave home since the dates might not be convenient. **Intourist** offers more frequent but very standard trips. (Locations across town include 11 Stoleshnikov Pereulok; ✆ **495/234-9509** and 2 Novy Arbat ✆ **495/234-4480;** www.intourist.ru.)

GETTING THERE

Tour buses are the most convenient way to see both towns. Otherwise, intercity buses run direct to Vladimir from Moscow's main Shcholkovsky bus station (p. 160) a few times a day on weekends, and just once or twice a day during the week. To get to Suzdal, you need to transfer at Vladimir's run-down bus station and find the bus labeled SUZDAL in Russian. The trip to Vladimir takes 2 hours, with another 40 minutes to get to Suzdal. The train to Vladimir leaves from Moscow's Kursky Train Station and takes 2½ hours, for about 400 rubles for a standard seat or 1,100 for a seat in a private, four-person cabin. You can also arrange for a car and driver from Moscow, either at your hotel or by calling a taxi company (see "Getting Around" in chapter 17 for taxi listings).

GETTING AROUND

There are no official tourist offices for either town, so if you can't read the Russian alphabet, you'll have a hard time getting around on your own. Taking a walk along the Kamenka River in Suzdal gives you a great perspective of the city, and it's hard to get lost since the domes of the monastery cathedrals are visible from almost anywhere in town.

Vladimir, on the other hand, is too large and spread out to be able to enjoy fully on foot, though Bolshaya Sadovaya and Bolshaya Moskovskaya streets have some concentrated dining and shopping. If you stay at a Vladimir hotel, you can hire a taxi for an hour to show you the city sights. Prices are negotiable and should be much lower than in Moscow—no more than 400 rubles or so an hour.

What to See & Do

VLADIMIR

The **Golden Gates** mark what was once the western entrance to Vladimir when they were built in 1164, and are a logical place to start viewing the town. The massive arch supports a church and is flanked by two castle-like structures added later. The enormous wooden doors that once kept outsiders away are long gone, and the city has grown up all around the gates. You'll find the gates at the intersection of Dvoryyanskaya Ulitsa and Bolshaya Moskovskaya streets.

Next, head to the **Cathedral of the Assumption** (on Sobornaya Ploshchad, or Cathedral Sq.; ✆ **4922/32-4263;** www.museum.vladimir.ru) overlooking the Klyazma River. The key Russian building of its era, it was founded in 1158 by Vladimir Prince Andrei Bogolubsky (whose name means "god-loving"). The cathedral suffered massive looting and violence during Tatar invasions, but was restored in the 18th century. The heavy tiered bell tower and unadorned white walls dominate the adjacent square. English-language brochures are available for a small fee. It's open all days except Monday from 1pm to 4:45pm Admission is 70 rubles (100 rubles with a guide).

The **Cathedral of Dmitry** (✆ 4922/32-4263), across the square from the Cathedral of the Assumption, is unlike any other Russian church in the region, and its exterior is more fascinating than its interior. Detailed carvings climb the cathedral's steep stone walls on all sides. The images are surprisingly secular, depicting princes of the period at their various activities. The carvings at the base are more precise and two-dimensional, while farther up the facade the carvings are cruder but set in deeper relief so as to be visible from street level. The interior is almost austere in comparison, light and free of excess. The cathedral is open Monday and Thursday 10am to 4pm, Wednesday and Friday to Sunday 10am to 5pm, closed on Tuesday.

SUZDAL

Suzdal thrived between its founding in A.D. 1024 and its sacking by Mongols in A.D. 1238, and has remained peripheral ever since. Its residents have retained a quiet dignity and sometimes the town feels untouched by Russia's past century of upheaval. The town centers around Trading Square (Torgovaya Ploshchad) and nearby Red Square (Krasnaya Ploshchad), which hosts the town hall and post office. The 11th-century **Kremlin**—the word means "fortress" in Russian—retains some of its original walls and houses a museum and restaurant. The Kremlin's rather run-down state reminds you how old it really is.

Suzdal's highlights are its convents and monasteries. The oldest and the first on most tours is **Rizopolozhensky Monastery** (20 Kremlyovskaya Ulitsa; ✆ 492/312-1624), founded in 1207. Most structures inside date from 300 years later, including the three-domed Rizopolozhensky Cathedral at the center of the complex. Monks again wander the grounds, seemingly unperturbed by tourists. It's open Wednesday through Monday from 10am to 4pm (closed the last Fri of every month).

Your next priority should be **Pokrovsky Convent** (Ulitsa Lenina; ✆ 492/312-0908), which came to be used as a storehouse for the first wives of Russian czars seeking younger companionship, including Peter the Great's wife Evdokia Lopukhina. The solemn grounds are again a functioning convent, and include an unusual inn of wooden cottages open for tourists. In summer, the nuns graze cows at dawn in the surrounding fields. The convent is open Thursday through Monday from 9:30am to 4:45pm.

Across from the convent is **Euthimiev Monastery-Fortress** (Ulitsa Lenina; ✆ 492/312-0746), which earned political popularity in the 16th and 17th centuries and substantial donations from czars and nobility. Its high, thick stone walls reveal its dual purpose as a fortress as well as a monastic refuge, and served it well when Catherine the Great founded a prison here for political opponents. The central Spaso-Preobrazhensky Cathedral combines several styles of Vladimir-Suzdal architecture from the 11th to the 16th centuries. It's open Tuesday through Sunday from 10am to 5pm.

One of the few Soviet contributions to Suzdal was the **Museum of Wooden Architecture and Peasant Life** (Pushkarskaya Ulitsa; ✆ 492/312-0937), across the Kamenka River from the Kremlin. It includes *izbas* (small wooden homes), mills, and wooden churches brought here from surrounding Vladimir Province. The museum costs 100 rubles and is open May through October, Wednesday to Monday from 9:30am to 4:30pm. In June the town hosts a lively **crafts festival.**

A newer addition is the **Wax Museum,** with some traditional Russian figures as well as internationally known faces (10B Ulitsa Kremlovskaya; ✆ 985/763-8451; www.wax-museum.ru; 300 rubles).

A wander around Suzdal gives you good glimpses of the decorative wooden frames of typical Russian houses, and a peek at the compact but rich vegetable gardens that feed many rural families.

Where to Stay

VLADIMIR

Accommodations here are much cheaper and generally more intimate than in Moscow, but the selection and services are limited. Because Suzdal lacks any large hotels, most organized tours put groups in Vladimir, often at the **Golden Ring Hotel** (27 Chaikovsky St.; ☏ **4922/40-0800**). It's a bland, Soviet-style tower 4km (2½ miles) from the center of town, meaning you rely on buses or taxis to get around. The advantage is that it has plenty of space (170 units) and that a basic double costs only 2,400 rubles (http://vladimir.amaks-hotels.ru). A more creative and environmentally friendly option is the **Russian Village** (**Russkaya Derevnya;** 5A Moskovskoye Shosse; ☏ **4922/38-3690;** www.rusderevnya.ru) complex, on the edge of town abutting a forest. Recently built of local pine and with energy self-sufficiency and respect for nature in mind, it has three motel-like buildings all with a view on the woods. The hotel can help arrange transport to the key sites. It runs about 2,300 to 4,500 rubles a night.

SUZDAL

Small groups and individuals prefer to stay in Suzdal's more romantic inns and lodges. A top choice is **Likhoninsky House** (34 Slobodskaya Ulitsa; ☏ **4923/12-1901;** aksenova-museum@mt.vladimir.ru), a wooden home with a small museum of local history and seven cozy guest rooms, located just behind Rizopolozhensky Monastery. One single has a fireplace with a mattress over it, so you can sleep on top as Russian families did for centuries. (There's also a regular bed.) Most rooms have traditional country furniture. The house is a 5-minute walk from the center and costs just 500 to 1,400 rubles per night. Reserve a few weeks in advance.

If you've ever fancied monastic life, try a night at **Pokrovskaya Hotel** (76 Ulitsa Pokrovskaya; ☏ **4923/12-3385**) on the grounds of Pokrovsky Convent. The wooden cottages are basic but quite roomy and comfortable. It used to be run by Intourist so the service is less than effusive but doesn't spoil the experience. Rates are about 2,800 rubles per night for two people.

A higher-end option is the bright and inviting **Hotel Sokol** (2a Torgovaya Ploshchad; ☏ **4923/12-0987**), a sunny yellow building next to the Kremlin with recently renovated rooms for 3,200 rubles per night (www.hotel-sokol.ru).

Where to Eat

VLADIMIR

Restaurant options are expanding more quickly than hotels, though they remain limited. The best restaurants are along Bolshaya Moskovskaya Street. Most bars (several of them quite seedy) are on Bolshaya Sadovaya Street. **Stary Gorod,** opposite the Cathedral of Dmitry, is a pleasant restaurant with European-influenced Russian cuisine at reasonable prices, and unusually competent service for a provincial town. Main courses run around 400 to 600 rubles. **Sobornaya Ploshchad,** the restaurant next door, is almost as good and costs a bit less, with main courses about 250 rubles.

SUZDAL

Though its name means "monastic dining hall," the **Trapeznaya** in the Kremlin is one of the most cheery, colorful restaurants in Suzdal. It's housed inside the fortress, up a set of steep stone stairs. Try their *zhulien,* wild mushrooms baked in sour cream and cheese; or the juicy meats cooked in clay ovens. Main courses run 250 to 500 rubles. (Kremlin; © **4923/12-1763**).

A dining hall at **Pokrovsky Convent,** also called **Trapeznaya** (Ulitsa Pokrovskaya; © **4923/12-0889**), serves hearty food in a more austere setting, with hard wooden benches and narrow windows in the stone walls. Try the fresh cranberry juice or home-brewed mead. Local residents prefer the raucous atmosphere of the **Kharchevnya** (73 Ulitsa Lenina; © **4923/12-0722**) restaurant and bar. The pancakes with honey and cream are divine and the rich soups nourishing. They serve very reasonably priced main courses from about 150 rubles.

ARKHANGELSKOYE

20km (12 miles) W of Moscow

This accessible estate offers an excellent opportunity to appreciate aristocratic architecture and breathe pine-scented air at the same time, without traveling too far from your hotel. Owned by a series of wealthy princes from the 17th to the 20th centuries, the estate once housed one of Russia's richest private art collections. Its design still bears testimony to the whims of its owners, with its frivolous pavilions, a Grecian-style mausoleum, and a Gothic bridge. Plenty of Russians come here just to wander the grounds, hide amid the tunnels of rose-covered trellises, look over granite balconies at children frolicking in the Moscow River on a summer day, or picnic on a bench in the oak groves.

Essentials

Surprisingly few organized tour groups visit here, preferring to take visitors to the more famous towns along the Garden Ring. That's part of Arkhangelskoye's appeal, making it feel more like a discovery. Most Moscow tour guides and many Moscow hotels can arrange an individual trip, with or without an English-speaking guide. You should be able to negotiate such a tour for around 2,000 rubles per car for the day, plus the cost of the guide (1,300 rubles). In the calmer days of July and August, the ride from central Moscow shouldn't take more than 40 minutes one-way, meaning you can make the whole trip in an afternoon. The rest of the year, Moscow traffic can make the one-way trip take an hour or even two.

If you go on your own, ride the metro to Tushinskaya, then bus no. 549 to Arkhangelskoye; the bus ride takes about half an hour, runs three times an hour, and costs about 60 rubles. Drivers are unlikely to speak much English, but the estate is the last stop so you can't miss it. Patriarshy Dom occasionally offers a summer English-language tour (© **495/795-0927**).

What to See & Do

The architectural epicenter of the estate is **Yusupov Palace,** which is set back from the Moscow River in an overgrown grove. Many visitors don't notice the palace at first, instead heading for the long facade of the more exposed, Stalin-era Military Convalescent Home overlooking the river. The palace originally dated from the 1670s, when it belonged to the family of Prince Cherkassky. Little remains from that era, however, since in the 1730s it became the pet project of Nikolai Golitsyn, who later became a favorite of Catherine the Great. The building's classical form and Ionic pillars date from Golitsyn's time, but much of the interior—including the art collection—was designed under the direction of Prince Nikolai Yusupov, who bought the estate in 1810 and whose name the palace retains.

Yusupov was a devoted art patron, amateur scientist, and philosopher, as well as one of Russia's richest property owners. A renowned bon vivant, he called Arkhangelskoye "a corner of paradise." He brought many of his treasures to Arkhangelskoye when he moved in, and in 1825 he turned the palace into one of Russia's first public art museums. More than 500 paintings by European masters, including Tiepolo, van Dyck, and Boucher, graced its walls. The library held 16,000 volumes and was often visited by famous writers of Yusupov's day, including Alexander Pushkin. Sculptures, antique furniture, tapestries, and rare china completed the collection. The palace itself has been undergoing renovations for years, and only parts of it are open to visitors. The estate stayed in Yusupov's family for more than 100 years, until the revolution saw it fall to Bolshevik hands. Its last owner, Felix Yusupov, went down in history as the prince who shot Grigory Rasputin, the controversial spiritual adviser to Czar Nicholas II and his family. The Soviets turned the estate into a museum in 1919.

Leading down from the palace toward the river are the geometrical, Italian-style **gardens,** which were long neglected but are again being planted with roses and grape vines. The surrounding pavilions are in various states of disrepair, making them seem older than they are—almost like the ancient Greek temples they emulate. The **military convalescent home** was built in the 1940s for the Red Army elite. Still in operation today, it is closed to visitors. Its terraces overlooking the river are accessible, and its staircases are the best way to reach the riverbank.

Before or after visiting the river, head left to see the rest of the grounds. Highlights include the **Gothic bridge** over the ravine and the rose-colored granite-and-limestone temple built as a **mausoleum** for the Yusupov family in the late 19th century. The Corinthian columned **Holy Gates** lead up to the **Church of the Archangel Michael,** which dates from 1667 and is the oldest building on the grounds. It's also the source of the estate's name. Note the remains of the theater across the main road from the palace, which Yusupov had built for his troupe of serf actors and musicians.

The estate is open Wednesday through Sunday from 10:30am to 5pm (© **495/363-1375**). Entrance to the grounds is 100 rubles.

Where to Eat

There's nothing to eat on the grounds of the estate itself except ice cream and cold drinks from stands in the warmer months. Just outside the grounds, across the main road, is the charming wooden **Arkhangelskoye Restaurant** (Ilyinskoye Shosse; © **495/797-5455**). It's rather touristy since it's the only place to eat here, but the satisfying Russian food and drinks are served in a more relaxed setting than you'll find in Moscow. The walls are decorated with panels made to resemble lacquer boxes from the town of Palekh, and the long windows look out on the surrounding woods. Anything with wild mushrooms is worth trying, including the mushroom soups or veal with mushrooms. Salads are heavy on mayonnaise or sour cream in the traditional Russian style. Main courses 200 to 500 rubles. The restaurant is open daily from 11am to 11pm.

PEREDELKINO

15km (9⅓ miles) SE of Moscow

This tranquil "writers' colony" contrasts with the religious ornamentation of the Golden Ring towns and the romantic pomp of the aristocratic estates in and around

Peredelkino

Moscow. Peredelkino appeals to a different state of mind. It is the place to go for a glimpse at more human-sized architecture in a picturesque wood, and for a lesson in 20th-century Russian literature and a reminder of what it meant to be a dissident in a totalitarian state. Before the Revolution, the village was part of the Kolychev family estate, but it was taken over by the Soviet government in the 1930s to house members of the influential Writers' Union. Its residents—including Alexander Solzhenitsyn and Boris Pasternak—often fell victim to shifts in Communist Party policy and ideology. The village still feels artsy despite its official beginnings and its carefully planned layout (and the bankers who have since moved into several of the homes). In Soviet times, officially sanctioned writers got the best *dachas,* but censors were such fickle beasts that the fear of arrest or exile hung over many who wrote here. Peredelkino has lost some of its intellectual verve but is still a sacred spot for many Russian and visiting foreign writers.

Essentials

Some tour packages offer trips here, but they're not all that common. **Patriarshy Dom Tours** arranges a worthwhile trip (© **495/795-0927**). Many Moscow hotels can arrange an individual car with driver and/or English-speaking guide. A guide is highly recommended, since unless you've done extensive background reading, you'll miss much of the village's history. The cost of an individual tour will vary depending on how upscale your hotel is. You'll find it worthwhile to shop around at other hotels to see if they can arrange something cheaper. Expect to spend at least 1,200 rubles per car for the day plus 250 rubles per hour for a guide. The trip should take about an hour one-way from central Moscow if you avoid rush hours (8–10am and 5–8pm).

Otherwise, the trip is a fairly easy 30 minutes on the *elektrichka,* or commuter train, from Kievsky Station in Moscow. After you exit, you either must walk 15 to 20 minutes along a wooded path by the train tracks until you reach the *dachas* of Peredelkino, or take bus no. 47 and go three stops to the end of Ulitsa Pavlenko. This street is the best place to begin.

What to See & Do

The best place to start is at the **Pasternak House Museum** (Ulitsa Pavlenko; © 495/934-5175; www.pasternakmuseum.ru), a tribute to Boris Pasternak's life and work and the saga surrounding *Doctor Zhivago.* Museum employees (there are only a few) are a good source of tips on what else to see in town. Pasternak's life reflected those of many Russian writers struggling to publish and stay in their homeland without offending the Soviet censors. The fate of his novel *Doctor Zhivago* was almost as tumultuous as the story itself. Pasternak wrote the novel (which is about the Russian Revolution and ensuing civil war) during Stalin's rule but kept it under wraps. Encouraged by signs of thaw under Nikita Khrushchev, Pasternak brought the novel out into the open—only to be expelled from the Writers' Union and to see the book banned by Soviet authorities. The book was eventually published abroad and earned a Nobel Prize, but Pasternak was forced by Soviet leaders to turn down the honor. The writer died of lung cancer in this house in 1960. The book wasn't published in Russia until a generation later, in 1986. The modest *dacha* includes some paintings by Pasternak's father and fragments from the writer's other works. Pasternak is best known to most Russians as a prolific poet, and many of his poems are on display here, though in Russian only, as are his translations of Shakespeare (translations were a safer path for writers of Stalin's era than original works). Note also the painting of Leo Tolstoy, a longtime Pasternak family friend. The museum is open Thursday through Sunday from 12am to 4pm (closed the last day of the month); admission is 250 rubles.

The **Church of the Transfiguration** and the **cemetery** behind it are also worth visiting, if only to see Pasternak's grave. Once a sacred site of pilgrimage for members of Moscow's intelligentsia and dissident community, it is still often heaped with fresh flowers. The church itself, located near the train station, originally dated from the 15th century, and was closed for much of the Soviet era. Today it's worth a visit to see how much more modest and intimate rural Russian churches are when compared with the magnificent cathedrals of Moscow and the Golden Ring.

The best way to appreciate Peredelkino is to wander the streets of wooden homes and imagine the intellectual activity and often surreptitious creativity the village engendered. If you're lucky, one of the residents tending a garden may point out a particular writer's house or unusual sight. Solzhenitsyn, who won a Nobel Prize for his brutal account of Soviet labor camps in the *Gulag Archipelago,* stayed in Peredelkino before his exile in 1974, diligently continuing to chronicle Soviet abuses in tiny,

DAY excursions: THREE SURE BETS

Stalin's World War II bunker—hidden beneath a football stadium but big enough to accommodate and entire tank battalion—has been open to the public since 1996. When it was built in 1934 to 1936, in response to increasing German militarism, newspapers announced the construction of a 120,000-seat stadium, academy, and art institute—none of which was ever completed. Whether tasteless Soviet kitsch or a unique insight into the cult of personality, Stalin's bunker is simply surreal. At $160 each for a group of two (dropping to $55 for groups of three-plus), it's easier and cheaper to visit with an organized tour. Russkie Prostori tours (✆ **495/983-0334**; http://russkie-prostori.com) make regular visits.

Retreat of the Tsars since the 14th century (and childhood home of Peter the Great), **Kolomenskoye** is host to numerous free festivals throughout the year. These include Maslenitsa (the orthodox answer to Mardi Gras) and an Easter Sunday procession to the white-steepled Church of the Ascension. Entrance to Kolomenskoye's grounds is free. Purchase tickets for the museums to the right of the Front Gate—prices vary but start from 200 rubles (✆ **499/615-2768;** www.mgomz.ru).

Much of Star City is still accessible only to its employees—or to "space tourists" willing to pay. But ordinary earthlings can get access to the world's largest centrifuge, a full-size model of the *Mir* space station, and a well-stocked museum chronicling the glory years. Those old enough to remember Gagarin's flight will feel a pang at the sight of the model Vostok capsule: and anyone under the age of 10 will be fascinated to learn, once and for all, how astronauts cope with no toilets in space. Best seen as part of an organized tour. Patriarsky Dom Tours visits every 2 months or so (2,100 rubles). Visitors to the museum will need to contact its administration department separately, in advance (✆ **495/526-3842;** www.gctc.ru/eng).

easy-to-hide notebooks. In a sign of changing times, the head of the Russian Orthodox Church, Patriarch Alexy II, had a *dacha* here where he lived until his death in 2008.

Where to Stay & Eat

There's only one official place in town to eat or sleep, unless you have friends in Peredelkino. **Villa Peredelkino** (2a Pervaya Chobotovskaya Alleya; ✆ **495/435-8345;** call for current rates), near the train station, was the official resort of the Young Communists' League (Komsomol) in its younger days. It has since been taken over by an Italian family, who renovated the pleasant rooms, added a sauna, and rent cross-country skis in winter. The English-speaking staff is usually quite helpful. The restaurant offers good Italian cooking, including melon with prosciutto and excellent veal, but at prices closer to Moscow standards than rural ones.

Another pleasant option is to rent a room or house for the weekend from one of the residents, who often post ads on the website www.expat.ru. These accommodations are reasonably priced and can offer such bonuses as a steam in a wooden bathhouse, a home-cooked meal, or the inside scoop on Peredelkino history from a longtime resident.

For day visitors, try lunch in the Writers' House, at Children of the Sun (Deti Solntsa; 4 Pogodina Ulitsa; © **495/731-2216;** www.detisolntsa.ru), with a lovely summer veranda overlooking the pine forest. Prices are high, with a full meal at least 1,500 rubles, and service slow, but the surroundings are exceptional. And anyone hankering for 24-hour sushi can try nearby Tanuki (31 Borovskoye Shosse; © **495/ 733-0100;** www.tanuki.ru).

ST. PETERSBURG NEIGHBORHOODS & SUGGESTED ITINERARIES

St. Petersburg, for all its size and grandeur, is best viewed in small glimpses, by first studying the columns and crannies of each square at a time, and only then looking at the genius of the city plan. You could spend a full day walking up and down Nevsky Prospekt, its main thoroughfare, or tracing the banks of the Neva River. Either itinerary would exhaust and overwhelm you, and probably do little to enhance your understanding of the city's brilliance and beauty. The tours below are designed to help you appreciate both the minutiae and the scale that St. Petersburg comprises. Though they are as compact as possible, the tours still include long quayside walks, so bring good shoes.

The Neighborhoods in Brief

THE PRIMARY DISTRICTS

The city's historical and royal heart beats around **Palace Square (Dvortsovaya Ploshchad)**, presided over by the resplendent, sea-green Winter Palace, home of the Hermitage Art Museum. This small district houses few hotels and restaurants, but it's a crucial starting point for experiencing St. Petersburg. The curved facade of the General Staff headquarters faces the Winter Palace from across the square, its three-layered arch leading to Nevsky Prospekt while shielding the square from the street noise and bustle. The square opens westward toward the Admiralty Building, whose ever-glistening spire acts as a compass point for the city, the nexus of three main avenues. Farther west lies the Decembrists' Square, anchored on one end by the enormous single-domed St. Isaac's Cathedral, and on the other by the fearsome Bronze Horseman statue rearing up over the stone banks of the Neva River.

Nevsky Prospekt is St. Petersburg's geographical anchor, an elegant avenue named after medieval Russian warrior Prince Alexander Nevsky. When you're touring the city, it helps to bear in mind where you are in relation to Nevsky at any given time. The hotels on upper Nevsky, near Palace Square, are mostly top-notch and top-price. Lower Nevsky has a few mid-range Soviet-era options and an increasing number of inexpensive bed-and-breakfasts. Restaurants on the avenue range from Russian fast food for a few rubles to members-only nouveau riche hide-outs. More creative dining options can be found on the side streets just off Nevsky.

North of central Nevsky are the Square of the Arts and the Summer Gardens, an area that includes the often underrated Russian Museum, the St. Petersburg Philharmonic, several theaters and galleries, and the dizzying domes of the Church on the Spilled Blood. Hotels here are scarce, but bars and cafes dot the neighborhood.

Heading east toward the bend in the Neva River takes you to the **Taurida Gardens** and **Smolny Cathedral and Convent.** This quiet neighborhood, generally termed **North of Nevsky,** is ideal for casual strolling and admiring the city's lesser-known architectural wonders. It has a strong selection of private hotels, with reasonable prices and eager service, though some are rather far from the metro and Nevsky. Continuing south brings you to the Alexander Nevsky Monastery and Nevsky Prospekt's eastern end.

South of Nevsky, the neighborhoods become defined by a series of canals, the chief ones being the Moika Canal, Griboyedov Canal, and Fontanka River. The area includes such landmarks as the Mariinsky (formerly Kirov) Theater, the St. Petersburg Conservatory, Dostoyevsky's House Museum, and several picturesque bridges and embankments perfect for a romantic or introspective evening. Less chic and touristy than the area north of Nevsky, this area is more innovative in dining and entertainment, with several restaurants and bars competing for largely local business. The hotel industry is starting to catch up, with "mini-hotels" popping up along the lanes and quays.

On the north side of the Neva, the Peter and Paul Fortress forms a beacon overlooking the rest of the city. This often overlooked part of town, including **Vasilevsky Island** and the **Petrograd Side,** is spiffing up more slowly than the area around Nevsky but has produced several chic and inviting restaurants and a few small, inexpensive hotels. Several ship-restaurants line the shore on this side of the Neva, playing up the city's marine traditions. You must take the metro or a taxi to get here from Nevsky and the main museums and shopping.

NEW HOLLAND (ISLAND)

It's covered in cobwebs and is not on most tourists' itineraries, but this island is unlike anything you'll find elsewhere, and provides a fascinating way to immerse yourself in St. Petersburg's history. Peter the Great named it after his sojourn in Holland, where he learned shipbuilding and was inspired to found Russia's navy. Formed by the creation of two canals on the city's western edge, the island became a key naval training and testing ground, and has housed a submarine testing pool, a prison, an arsenal, timber storehouses, and a printing press.

New Holland (Novaya Gollandiya in Russian) was closed to the public for most of its history, until the military abandoned it in 2003 and ceded its real estate to the city. Its banks are long overgrown, and its stately brick warehouses stand largely empty amid a network of artificial pools and canals, giving it a mystical, "lost city" feel. Many of the buildings are protected architectural monuments, but the city has done little to renovate or maintain them amid heated debate about what to do with the island. Some want to make it a tourist complex, with hotels, restaurants, and entertainment spaces; others want to make a cultural center with theaters and galleries; others propose a commercial center, or conference center, or elite residential zone. So far, only a few businesses have moved in, and it has staged exhibits by Russian and foreign artists intrigued by the space and its history. The easiest way to enter now is via Konnogvardeisky Bulvar. Guards may ask where you're headed, so just explain that you're a tourist (tu-*reest* in Russian). Even if you don't go in, walk or drive around the island and take a moment to look through the strikingly elegant New Holland Arch, designed by French architect Vallin de la Mothe in 1779.

The triangular island is between the Moika Canal, Kryukov Canal, and Admiral Canal. The nearest metro stations are Nevsky Prospekt and Sadovaya Ploshchad.

St. Petersburg Neighborhoods

Common terms and abbreviations

naberezhnaya/nab	*Embankment*
most	*Bridge*
ploshchad/pl	*Square* or *plaza*
prospekt/pr	*Avenue*
sad	*Garden*
ulitsa/ul	*Street*

It's been called St. Petersburg's Bloomsbury or Peter the Great's precursor to Manhattan, yet Vasilevsky Island (Vasilevsky Ostrov) is something all its own. It's just across the Neva River from the Hermitage, but far enough from the bustle of Nevsky Prospekt that many visitors never make it here. A growing cluster of mini-hotels, restaurants, and shops is starting to change the island's rather remote, removed reputation.

Peter the Great considered basing his capital on Vasilevsky Island, but its location made it too vulnerable to storms and flooding. Its western shore is buffeted by winds from the Gulf of Finland year-round, and the spit (called the Strelka) at its eastern tip bears the brunt of the Neva as it splits off into two branches right before reaching the sea. The first bridge built from the island to the "mainland" across the Neva had to be taken down every autumn until the spring thaw because of the rough winters. Despite these challenges, the island quickly became the city's learning center, housing St. Petersburg's first museum, observatory, and university.

St. Petersburg State University still dominates the eastern side of the island, with several of its buildings dating from the 18th century. In the 19th century, factories grew up on the western reaches of the island, and its mix of students and workers made it a hotbed of revolutionary activity. Today, the west side of the island remains a rather bleak landscape of neglected harbors and warehouses, while the east side boasts vibrant student life and commerce, with a few pedestrian streets and restored churches. Finding addresses on Vasilevsky is highly logical, yet confusing at first. The island is laid out on a numbered orthogonal grid, but the north–south streets have different names for each side of the street, so that the first street is called "1st Line" (1-aya Liniya) on the east side and "2nd Line" (2-aya Liniya) on the west side. Highlights of the island include **Menshikov Palace, Kunstkamera** and the **university complex,** and **Leytenanta Shmidta Embankment,** good for a walk. The nearest metro station is Vasileostrovskaya.

10

St. Petersburg in 1 Day

NEIGHBORHOODS & ITINERARIES

THE BEST OF ST. PETERSBURG IN 1 DAY

This blitz tour begins at Palace Square and the Hermitage, for an intense morning of history and art that provides context for the rest of the St. Petersburg experience. The semicircle of sights surrounding this nucleus provides a sense of the careful vision of the city's designers infused into their masterpiece. A walk along the embankment and across the Neva to the Peter and Paul Fortress rounds out the day. An optional stroll along Nevsky Prospekt is reserved for evening, when the avenue lacks its midday intensity. **Note:** Don't do this tour on Monday, when the Hermitage is closed. **Start:** *Metro Nevsky Prospekt. Then follow Nevsky west to Bolshaya Morskaya Ulitsa and turn right, entering Palace Square through the arch.*

1 Palace Square (Dvortsovaya Ploshchad) ★★★

Site of czarist processions, raucous imperial revelry, revolutionary riots, Soviet displays of worker unity, and anti-Communist demonstrations, Palace Square encapsulates St. Petersburg's rich and troubled 300-year history. The best way to enter it is through the Triumphal Arch from Nevsky Prospekt. If you get here before 10am, you'll have it mostly to yourself and have plenty of time to explore its facets before the Hermitage opens at 10:30am. See "Around Palace Square" in chapter 13 for more information.

1 Palace Square

2 State Hermitage Museum

3 Literaturoye Café ☕

4 Moika

5 St. Isaac's Cathedral

6 Bronze Horseman

7 Admiralty

8 Strelka ☕

9 Peter and Paul Fortress

10 Nevsky Prospekt

2 State Hermitage Museum ★★★

With a collection second in size only to that of the Louvre, the Hermitage would be an international treasure even if it were housed in a concrete warehouse. But its packaging, the resplendent Winter Palace, enhances the experience of viewing world art from the ancient Egyptians to the French Impressionists. Entering through the tranquil courtyard, you forget that the mighty Neva River splashes against the palace's other face. Get a map at the entrance—or even better, print one out from the museum website before you leave home—and plan your visit in order to avoid exhaustion. See p. 223 for a complete review.

3 Literaturnoye Café 🖵 ★

A city landmark perched on the corner of Moika Canal and Nevsky Prospekt, this cafe plays up its past as a haunt of Alexander Pushkin and other 19th- and 20th-century poets and writers. The first floor has been taken over by a KFC, but the second floor is great for a cup of tea or a midday meal overlooking the city in a cozy setting. The terrace is nice on a summer day, but awfully tiny. The cafe is located at 18 Nevsky Prospekt (✆ 812/312-6057). See p. 210 for a full review.

4 Moika

For a reminder of the city's swampy past, wander the embankment of Moika Canal as it heads south from Nevsky Prospekt. You'll pass little commerce and few tourists, but you'll see quaint arched bridges closer in scale and style to those of western Europe than to Moscow. An exception is the Blue Bridge between St. Isaac's Cathedral and City Hall, a cast-iron bridge so wide that you don't notice the water under it. Note the Stroganov Palace on the opposite bank. The Moika's more remote banks inspired philosophical and suicidal strolls by Dostoyevsky's heroes. Many of the historic buildings you pass are rather dilapidated and look better from a distance or at dusk.

St. Isaac's Cathedral (Isaakevsky Sobor) ★★★

The Moika opens onto Isaac's Square just south of the staggering gold dome of St. Isaac's Cathedral. Unadorned by the peripheral cupolas that characterize other Russian churches, St. Isaac's is a monolith inside and out. To 20th-century Russians it stood less as a religious symbol than a wartime bastion, having survived shelling by Nazi forces during the 900-day blockade of the city then known as Leningrad. The balcony surrounding the dome, sometimes open to visitors, offers a stunning vista. See p. 231 for more information.

6 Bronze Horseman (Medny Vsadnik) ★★

St. Petersburg's most famous rider, the Bronze Horseman, rears fearlessly over the Neva River at the opposite end of Decembrists' Square from St. Isaac's. It depicts Peter the Great commanding his city in a rather fierce and autocratic interpretation favored in the era of Catherine the Great, who commissioned the monument. Alexander Pushkin made the statue come alive to generations of Russians with his brooding, stormy poem of the same name. See "Monuments, Memorials & Squares" in chapter 13 for more information.

7 Admiralty ★★

Following the shore of the Neva eastward from the Bronze Horseman, you come to the carefully classical Admiralty building. Its spire is the building's raison d'être, providing a compass point visible from the city's chief avenues. Once used as a fortified shipyard, the Admiralty is now a naval academy, and though it's closed to the public, its grounds are worth a wander. Its 400m-long (¼-mile) facade blends in with the Senate building next door, and both provide a counterweight to the Winter Palace up ahead, framing the Palace Bridge (Dvortsovy Most) across to Vasilevsky Island. See "Around Palace Square" in chapter 13.

8 Sit on Strelka 🍺 ★★

There's not much in terms of snacks along this walk, but if you have a bottled drink or something to munch on in your bag, this spit of land pointing into the Neva is a great place to stop and enjoy it. It's adorned by the two Rostral Columns representing four great rivers, which were all Russian at the time the columns were built: Neva, Volga, Dnieper, and Don. It gets windy here, but the view can't be beat. The spit is on Vasilevsky Island, at the north end of Palace Bridge (Dvortsovy Most).

9 Peter and Paul Fortress (Petropavlovskaya Krepost) ★★★

This next stop demands either a good 15-minute walk or a taxi ride. Rabbit Island, the sandbar upon which Peter chose to base himself while his city arose from the marsh, later became the Peter and Paul Fortress. You can wander the grounds for free but must pay to visit the cathedrals and galleries. It's worth the fee to see the Peter and Paul Cathedral, which holds the tombs of Russia's royal families from Peter's until that of the last Romanov czar, Nicholas II. See the "Peter & Paul Fortress" sidebar on p. 229.

10 Nevsky Prospekt

Evening is the ideal time to discover St. Petersburg's main thoroughfare, as the daytime traffic thins (a bit) and dusk, or the long summer sunset, softens its harsher edges. The street's architectural precision can still be appreciated by streetlight. Passersby are less rushed, and the dining and bar scenes buzz with Russian and just about every other language. See chapters 12 and 15 for restaurant and nightlife suggestions.

THE BEST OF ST. PETERSBURG IN 2 DAYS

A second day in St. Petersburg is best spent discovering why the city still considers itself Russia's cultural capital. Starting at the Square of the Arts, this tour takes in the masterpieces of the Russian Museum and the ensemble of theaters joining it on the square. The eye-catching Church on the Spilled Blood, the sculpted Summer Gardens, the prestigious banks of the Fontanka River, and the architectural nuances of Ostrovsky Square follow. Rest up and shop in Gostiny Dvor, then use this evening for a visit to the renowned Mariinsky Theater. **Start:** *Metro to Gostiny Dvor, then take Mikhailovskaya Ulitsa north of Nevsky to the Square of the Arts.*

1 Square of the Arts (Ploshchad Isskustv) ★★

A masterpiece of classical symmetry, this square includes the Mikhailovsky Palace, which now houses the Russian Museum, the St. Petersburg Philharmonic, the Mussorgsky Opera and Ballet Theater, and a statue of Pushkin that pulls it all together (even though it wasn't added until 1957). Take your time to circle it and note the vistas from every side street. See "Monuments, Memorials & Squares" in chapter 13.

2 Russian Museum ★★★

Even if you can't name a single Russian artist, this museum is a superb introduction to Russian art through the ages. Its display of Orthodox icons shows more clearly than any book the evolution of their styles. The Constructivist and post-Impressionist images by Kandinsky, Chagall, and Malevich take on different meaning in their original, Russian setting. Though exhibits are labeled in English, the audioguide is very worthwhile. See p. 234 for a full review.

3 Stray Dog Cellar (Podval Brodyachy Sobaki) ♉ ★

Ensconced in a basement just off the Square of the Arts, this friendly cafe flourished in the early 1900s as an artists' den. Poet Anna Akhmatova and her contemporaries once held readings and staged raucous and daring performances here. The cafe is again enjoying a revival, hosting musical shows and one-act plays. Grab a coffee, lunch, or some jam-filled pancakes. The cafe is at 5/4 Square of the Arts (Ploshchad Isskustv; ✆ 812/312-8047). See p. 213 for a full review.

4 Church of the Savior on the Spilled Blood (Tserkov Spasitelya Na Krovi) ★

The festive facade of this church is almost gaudy and frivolous, despite its morbid name. The real name is the Church of the Resurrection, but it earned its common moniker because it was erected on the site where Czar Alexander II was assassinated in 1881. Brilliantly restored, the church's interior is almost as vivid as its exterior. Look for the tiles marking the exact spot of the murder. The adjacent embankment is full of souvenir vendors; the better deals and quality are on the opposite side of the canal. See p. 230 for a full listing.

5 Mikhailovsky Castle & Gardens (Mikhailovsky Zamok)

The castle itself was built by the paranoid Czar Paul I, who felt too exposed in the Winter Palace. The interior, now an Engineering Museum, reflects his more austere tastes. It is worth visiting if the weather is lousy or if you're interested in latter-day mechanical developments. Otherwise, use this time to wander the lush grounds, which make the bustle of Nevsky seem worlds away. See the walking tour on p. 243 for more information.

6 Summer Palace & Gardens (Letny Dvorets, Letny Sad) ★★

Farther on is the compact Summer Palace that Peter built, a cheery (though unheated) contrast to the somber citadel of Mikhailovsky Palace. The surrounding gardens hosted decadent imperial balls, and include Renaissance-era statues Peter had imported from Italy to perfect his meticulously planned parks. See p. 235 for more information.

0 | 1/2 mi
0 | 0.5 km

ZAYACHY OSTROV

Petropavlovskaya (Peter and Paul) Fortress

Troitsky most

Neva

PETROGRADSKY OSTROV

Malaya Neva

Birzhevoy most

nab. Makarova

Neva

Suvorovskaya pl.

6

Letny sad

Marsovo Pole

nab. Kutuzova

Gagarinskaya ul.

Birzhevaya ploshchad

pl. Akademika Sakharova

VASILEVSKY OSTROV

Dvortsovy most

Winter Palace (Hermitage Museum)

Millionaya ul.

nab. reki Moika

Church of the Savior on the Spilled Blood

Moika

nab. reki Fontanki

Dvortsovaya Ploshchad

4

Universitetskaya nab.

Bolshaya Neva

Admiralty

Alexander's Column

Konyushennaya ul.

2 Russian State Museum

5

1

7

most Belinkovo

Narodny most

pl. Iskusstov

ploshchad Dekabristov

Griboedov

Italyanskaya ul.

most Leytenanta Shmidta

Galernaya ul.

St. Isaac's Cathedral

Mai. Morskaya ul.

3

Kazanskaya pl.

Nevsky prospekt

10

Anichkov most

Konnogvardeysky bl.

Isaakievskaya ploshchad

Bol. Morskaya ul.

Gorokhovaya

Kanal

ulitsa

9

НЕВСКИЙ ПРОСПЕКТ– ГОСТИНИЙ ДВОР
Nevsky Prospekt– Gostiny Dvor

M **8**

Pochtamtskaya ul.

nab. reki Moika

Moika

Voznesensky prospekt

Kazanskaya ul.

Sadovaya ulitsa

Lomonosova

pl. Truda

pl. Lomonosova

Dekabristov

ulitsa

11

Korsakova

Sadovaya ul.

САДОВАЯ– СЕННАЯ ПЛ.– СПАССКАЯ
M Sadovaya– Sennaya pl.– Spasskaya

Sennaya pl.

nab. reki Fontanki

prospekt

ulitsa Pravdy

Rimskovo-

prospekt

Nikolskaya ploshchad

Obukhovsky most

Pionerskaya pl.

M

Sadovaya ul.

Zagorodny

ПУШКИНСКАЯ– ЗВЕНИГОРОДСКАЯ
Pushkinskaya– Zvenigorodskaya

pl. Turgeneva

Kanal Fontanka

Izmaylovsky prospekt

Vitebsky Station

nab. reki Fontanki

Troitsky prosp.

13-ya

1-ya Kras.

2-ya

Tekhnologicheskaya pl.

ТЕХНОЛОГИЧЕСКИЙ ИНСТИТУТ
M Tekhnologichesky Institut

nab. Obvodnovo Kanala

1 Square of the Arts	**5** Mikhailovsky Castle and Gardens	**9** Gostiny Dvor Shopping Arcade
2 Russian Museum	**6** Summer Palace and Gardens	**10** ...lli... 🍺
3 Stray Dog Cellar 🍺	**7** Fontanka River	**11** Mariinsky Theater
4 Church of the Savior on the Spilled Blood	**8** Ostrovsky Square	

10

NEIGHBORHOODS & ITINERARIES | St. Petersburg in 2 Days

7 Fontanka River

The river was so named because it once fed the luxurious fountains of the Summer Gardens. Today its embankments house some of the city's architectural masterpieces; note Sheremetev Palace on the east side, where Anna Akhmatova once lived. It now houses a musical instrument museum (p. 234). The circular building on the west bank houses the well-known city circus (see "Especially for Kids" on p. 240). Study the horse sculptures anchoring the four posts of Anichkov Bridge, which carries Nevsky Prospekt across the Fontanka.

8 Ostrovsky Square ★

Head back west on Nevsky Prospekt to Ostrovsky Square, recognizable by its monument to Catherine the Great (see "Monuments, Memorials & Squares" in chapter 13). The statue incorporates images of the empress's favorites in various moods and poses, and usually gets giggles out of kids. Behind her is the Alexandrinsky (or Pushkin) Theater (p. 258), which puts on ballets, operas, and plays, and is a superb alternative to the Mariinsky Theater if tickets aren't available. In summer you can enjoy intermission on the columned balcony and feel like royalty.

9 Gostiny Dvor Shopping Arcade

This spot has been a raucous outdoor market, an upmarket arcade supplying delicacies to the aristocracy, and a Soviet department store with rows of identical shops. Today it's a tightly packed modern shopping mall. You can get fresh apricot or cabbage pies for a few cents in its cafes, or a fur coat for a few thousand dollars. Both a landmark and a convenience, it also has public toilets and 1-hour film developing.

10 ...ili... ☕

This busy corner cafe across from Gostiny Dvor attracts young Russians and tourists alike. Its name means "either . . . or" and is good for the indecisive: It has a bistro, a restaurant, and Internet tables, and is open around the clock. There's nothing elite about it, but it's nicer than any of the cafes inside Gostiny Dvor. Ice cream, salads, and soups are safe and satisfying choices. The cafe is at 54 Nevsky Prospekt (ⓒ 812/331-9090).

11 Mariinsky Theater (formerly Kirov Theater) ★★★

The aquamarine walls hint at the city's naval ambitions, but everything else about the Mariinsky celebrates St. Petersburg's cultural heritage. Its exterior symmetry and interior opulence alone are worth the price of a ballet ticket. If orchestra seats are sold out or beyond your price range, don't be afraid of the upper balconies. They offer a better view of the magnificent ceiling fresco and a more relaxed viewing experience. See p. 259 for a full listing.

THE BEST OF ST. PETERSBURG IN 3 DAYS

Although St. Petersburg itself has plenty more to explore, a third day offers an ideal opportunity to whiz up the Baltic Coast to Peterhof, the palace Peter modeled partly on Versailles. The ride itself—on hydrofoil, ferry, or the private boats roaming the shore—is part of the adventure, offering a seafarers' view of the city and surrounding forest. In the winter, you can take a bus or commuter train and enjoy the countryside

that way. You can easily return in time for a dinnertime cruise through the city's canals in the months when they're not frozen over (May–Oct). ***Start:*** *The piers on Dvortso-vaya Naberezhnaya in front of the Winter Palace, or the bus stop outside Nevsky Prospekt metro station. Nearest metro: Nevsky Prospekt.*

---

1 Peterhof (Petrodvorets) ★★★

Gliding up to the pier of this opulent "country house" is the most impressive way to greet it. The dense forest is suddenly cleaved by a hill of fountains cascading from the palace toward the sea. The palace holds so much gold it's almost headache-inducing. The long and rather narrow structure gives every room a view of the sea, but this means that visitors are herded in one direction with little room to maneuver. Explore the caves beneath the fountains for an inside view of this 18th-century engineering feat. See chapter 16 for more on visiting Peterhof.

2 Imperatorsky Stol 🍵 ★

Dining options on the palace grounds are mediocre, but Imperatorsky Stol (✆ 812/427-9106) is the most pleasant. Housed in the orangerie close to the river, it's a good spot for a hot drink or a full, Russo-European meal. See "Peterhof" in chapter 16 for more information.

3 Evening Canal Cruise

Once you're back in town, continue the waterway theme with a canal tour. Boats holding up to 15 people start from Griboyedov Canal just north of Nevsky Prospekt. They offer English-speaking tours or tour guides. Private boats also roam the area offering rides for up to five people for an always-negotiable price, which is often less than the group-tour price. During the White Nights of summer, the private boats run much of the night. However, they often lack security features, so they're not a good option if you're traveling with kids.

WHERE TO STAY IN ST. PETERSBURG

V ariation and innovation characterize St. Petersburg's hotel scene, and after years of slow maturation, there's something to suit everyone, with more of a democratic selection than in Moscow. The mid-range market, with the arrival of international chains and some excellent small independents, has finally come of age. From historic Nevsky Prospekt to progressive ecological hotels tucked in quiet neighborhoods, you're sure to find a suitable nest while you explore Peter the Great's city.

WHAT YOU'LL REALLY PAY

The prices quoted here are for hotels' rack rates (maximums); it is, however, seriously unlikely that you'll end up paying those rates. You can typically find discounts of 20% to 50% for rooms when booking through the agencies listed on p. 294, or through websites such as hotels.com or expedia.com (see "Getting the Best Deal" later in this chapter for more tips). During slow times, it's not impossible to obtain a room at an expensive property for the same rate as a more moderate one. If you're the gambling type, you can bid for a room on Priceline. *Note:* Quoted discount rates do not always include breakfast or hotel taxes.

Price Categories	
Very Expensive	$300 and up
Expensive	$200–$300
Moderate	$100–$200
Inexpensive	Under $100

See "Practical Information" at the end of this chapter for more on booking deals.

best ST. PETERSBURG HOTEL BETS

○ **Best Historic Hotel:** To feel like a tsar or tsarina, or anyone in the imperial family, choose the **Astoria** or attached **Angleterre**—it's as close as you'll get in 21st century St. Petersburg. The emperors' real homes are now museums, but these hotels have tapped into the opulence and

A CITY OF mini-hotels

The city's tri-centennial in 2003 saw the opening of more than 500 so-called mini-hotels, which makes this a bargain location for tourists. The White Nights, however, can see the best-known venues (and many apartments) double their off-season rates. Don't stand for it. A bit of research can uncover low-cost rooms even in high summer. Start with the St. Petersburg Small Hotels Association (www.inn.spb.ru). The majority of the mini-hotels used to be **kommunalki,** Soviet communal apartments with several families sharing a kitchen and bathroom. The mini-hotels now feature individual bathrooms, Western refurbishment, scrupulous cleanliness, basic breakfasts, and even Wi-Fi. But you do need to be prepared for scruffy entrance halls to the apartment buildings (often with well-concealed intercoms) and no elevators. Take care when booking: Some mini-hotels may charge, in some cases quite steeply, for registering your visa, or for issuing a visa support letter. Unless you're here for less than 3 days (in which case you are not required to register at all), there's little you can do about this, particularly once you've arrived. You can avoid unexpected high visa costs by securing a booking and free invitation letter through a tour agency. See p. 297 for more information on visas.

refinement of eras past. Layers of Russian history converge in the hotels and surrounding streets for a dizzying view of the city's 300-year life. See p. 189.

○ **Best for Business Travelers:** The **Corinthia Hotel St. Petersburg** accommodates executives from multinationals and successful startups, group conferences, and individual negotiators, catering to the needs of each with quiet ease. Various sizes and styles of conference room are on offer, as are translators, drivers, and legal assistance. See p. 193.

○ **Best for a Romantic Getaway:** Tucked on a little-visited canal, **Alexander House** exudes calm and intimacy a universe apart from the touristed rush of Nevsky Prospekt. The couple who run it cater to individual needs and guests of all kinds. Their respect for the environment produces a sensually pleasing hotel experience hard to find elsewhere. Reserve tickets at the nearby Mariinsky Theater and dine nearby on caviar and champagne for two before wandering back here in the languor of the White Nights. The **Sokos Hotel Palace Bridge,** with its full-service spa, is a strong runner-up. See p. 198.

○ **Best Splurge:** If the sky's the limit, go for the **Grand Hotel Europe.** The harpist in the otherworldly atrium accompanies your immersion into luxury, and the staff anticipates your needs from the moment you check in. Presidents favor this spot over larger locales, presumably for the exceptional attention on offer. Even if you can't afford a night here, be sure stop in for tea. See p. 194.

○ **Most Relaxing Hotel:** At the **Sokos Hotel Palace Bridge,** you can choose from eight—yes, eight—different kinds of saunas and steam rooms to melt your troubles away. Massage and other bodywork are next on the menu at this hotel on the up-and-coming but still off-the-tourist-track Vasilevsky Island. See p. 200.

○ **Best Service:** If you can't afford five stars but need any kind of help, the staff at the **Nevsky Hotels Group** is ready and waiting. They'll find the right room for you among their selection of eight varied locations around town, adjust services as needed, and help land ballet tickets any season. See p. 195.

- **Best for Families:** Travelers with kids but limited finances should look to the **Northern Lights,** walking distance from key sights and friendly to the under-18 crowd. Those on a bigger budget are sure to be satisfied at the **Corinthia Hotel St. Petersburg** or the **Ambassador Hotel,** each with a wide range of childcare and other services. See p. 194.
- **Best Budget Hotel:** Any **mini-hotel** (see description earlier in this chapter) is bound to please your wallet anytime of year. See p. 188.
- **Best Views:** The low-lying cityscape of central St. Petersburg means it offers few sky-high views. The top floors of the **Astoria** and **Angleterre** hotels afford vistas of the city's imperial and revolutionary nucleus, as well as St. Isaac's Cathedral. For views of the Winter Palace, the best vantage point is across the river at the **Courtyard St. Petersburg Vasilievsky.** See p. 201.

AROUND THE HERMITAGE

All visits to the city revolve around the Hermitage Museum and Palace Square and its attendant history, and staying here envelops you in their magic.

Best For: Those with a passion for St. Petersburg's imperial past, or limited time to see the city's key sights. Unlimited finances make it much easier to find a nice place to stay here.

Drawbacks: For such a central neighborhood, not all hotels in the area are close to a metro station, meaning a fair amount of walking if you're not in a tour bus or chauffeured car.

Very Expensive

Astoria ★★★ An example of Art Nouveau at its apex, the five-star Astoria offers 21st-century decadence in a pre-revolutionary setting, overlooking St. Isaac's Cathedral with the Neva River in the background. It's a personal favorite for multiple reasons. It's preserved its historic design and ambience, though furnishings have been modernized to create spacious, sleek rooms and generous bathrooms. The Astoria and adjacent **Angleterre** (see below) opened in 1912 on the site of a 19th-century English/Russian hotel venture. They were appropriated by the Soviets, and the Astoria was later used as a field hospital during the Nazi blockade of Leningrad in World War II. A favorite of well-to-do tourists and executives alike, the Astoria underwent its latest renovation in 2002. Designers retained the crystal chandeliers and tapestries but relegated the antique chairs to the corridors. Unfortunately, the mirrored, Art Nouveau Winter Garden is open only for special events—peek inside and imagine the balls held here a century ago.

39 Ulitsa Bolshaya Morskaya. www.thehotelastoria.com. © **812/494-5757.** Fax 812/494-5059. 211 units. From 25,000 rubles double; from 51,000 suite. AE, DC, MC, V. Metro: Nevsky Prospekt. **Amenities:** 2 restaurants; bar and lounge; concierge; executive-level rooms; health club; Jacuzzi; pool; room service; sauna; smoke-free rooms; spa; free Wi-Fi in lobby. *In room:* A/C, TV w/satellite, fridge, hair dryer, Internet, minibar.

Angleterre ★★ Initially a wing of the Astoria, the four-star Angleterre shares a designer and a kitchen with its "sister hotel," though they're now under separate management. See the above review for details on the building's history. Today the Angleterre is a slightly less expensive, less well-preserved neighbor of the Astoria, but it is still a luxurious place to stay in an ideal location. Corridors are plainer, and the

Where to Stay in St. Petersburg

Alexander House **10**
Ambassador Hotel **11**
Angleterre **7**
Arbat Nord **14**
Astoria **8**
Corinthia Nevsky
  Palace **23**
Courtyard St. Petersburg
  Vasilievsky **2**
Dostoyevsky Hotel **21**
Fifth Corner **20**
Grand Hotel Europe **18**
Herzen House **6**
Ibis St. Petersburg
  Centre **26**
NasHotel **3**
Nevsky Hotels Group **17**
Kristoff **19**
Marco Polo **4**
Marshal **13**
Moskva **25**
Nevsky Forum **24**
Northern Lights **9**
Piter **1**
Pulford **16**
Pulkovskaya **27**
Radisson SAS Royal **22**
Rossiya **27**
Rus **15**
Sokos Hotel
  Palace Bridge **5**
St. Petersburg **12**

0   1/2 mi
0   0.5 km

Common terms and abbreviations

naberezhnaya/nab	*Embankment*
most	*Bridge*
ploshchad/pl	*Square or plaza*
prospekt/pr	*Avenue*
sad	*Garden*
ulitsa/ul	*Street*

lobby, while glistening in white marble, lacks any period style. The spacious guest rooms, many boasting wide windows, are decorated in warm woods that differ little in quality and style from the Astoria's. The view of St. Isaac's makes a street-facing room worthwhile; triple-paned windows keep the traffic roar to a light hum.

24 Malaya Morskaya Ulitsa. www.angleterrehotel.com. ℂ **812/494-5666.** Fax 812/494-5125. 193 units. From 20,000 rubles double; from 30,000 rubles suite. AE, DC, MC, V. Metro: Nevsky Prospekt. **Amenities:** Restaurant; concierge; executive-level rooms; health club; small indoor pool; room service; sauna; smoke-free rooms; spa; free Wi-Fi in lobby (350 rubles per hr.). *In room:* A/C, interactive TV w/ satellite, fridge, hair dryer, Internet 200 rubles per hr., minibar.

Moderate

Herzen House ★★ 🛋 Central, comfortable, and fairly priced for this neighborhood, the Herzen House should have lines out the door. It doesn't, fortunately, but welcomes a steady flow of regular-folk travelers tipped off to its value since it opened in 2007. No historical glamour here, just medium-sized rooms decked in lemon butter tones and wicker chairs. You can get free tea, coffee, and Russian pastries around the clock in the lobby, though you'll find no fridge. It's ecological by being economical (for example, it has showers only, no baths, in the minimalist bathrooms). The Hermitage and St. Isaac's Cathedral are among nearby sites, and the nearest metro is a 5-minute brisk walk. The street is a mish-mash of renovated apartment houses and a few still screaming to be fixed up, a true taste of today's St. Petersburg. The staff can tip you off to new restaurants and bars and find a professional to look after your children while you explore.

25 Bolshaya Morskaya Ulitsa. www.herzen-hotel.com. ℂ **812/571-5098.** Fax 812/315-5550. 20 units. Low season from 4,400 rubles double; high season from 5,700 rubles double. AE, DC, MC, V. Metro: Nevsky Prospekt. **Amenities:** Restaurant; concierge; babysitting. *In room:* A/C, satellite TV; free Wi-Fi.

Pulford Apartments ★ This British-Russian company offers serviced apartments all over town, but its prime spots are along the lanes between Palace Square and Nevsky Prospekt metro station. These are also its more expensive apartments, though they still cost less than most hotel options in the neighborhood. All apartments are renovated to Western standards, with fully equipped kitchens and bathrooms, and from one to several bedrooms. Rental is daily, weekly, or monthly. Maid service can be arranged as often as you like, as can other hotel-like services such as extra towels, theater tickets, cellphone rental, and visa help. It's a bit more isolated than hotel living, but English-speaking help is just a phone call away. Security is assured, but some apartments are in unguarded buildings, so avoid coming home alone late at night. The top locations offer perks such as a personal grocery-shopping service and delivery of DVDs.

www.pulford.com. ℂ **812/331-5877.** Fax 812/320-7561. 15 1-bedroom apartments, 4 2-bedroom apartments; 5 3-bedroom apartments. From 90 euros for 1-bedroom apartment; 130 euros for 2-bedroom; 150 euros for 3-bedroom. Longer term rentals available on enquiry. AE, MC, V. **Amenities:** Executive-level rooms; smoke-free rooms; tour arrangements and personal guides; transport services. *In room:* A/C, TV w/satellite, fridge, hair dryer, free Internet, kitchen.

Inexpensive

The Northern Lights Hotel ★★ 🛋 ☺ This quiet mini-hotel on the third floor of a 19th-century building is superbly located a stone's throw from St. Isaacs Square, and has attracted a following of independent travelers and families alike. As ever in St. Petersburg, don't judge a mini-hotel by its run-down entrance (plus there's no

family-friendly HOTELS

Russians dote on their kids but don't generally take them traveling to big cities, preferring to take them to a family *dacha* (country cottage) or *dom otdykha* (country resort) for vacations. Because Russia's newer hotels are aimed more at lucrative business clients than at families, child-friendly services remain rare. The international chains, now well-established in St Petersburg, have the most amenities for families. **Corinthia**

Hotel St. Petersburg stands out in this category, offering a children's playroom and babysitting at their fantastic Sunday brunch. If you pick carefully, smaller hotels have increasingly child-friendly attitudes—try the **Northern Lights Hotel**, the **Fifth Corner**, whose young staff is happy to babysit; and **Alexander House**, run by a couple ready with help and English advice on how to share St. Petersburg with your children.

elevator)–the contrast once inside could not be greater. Rooms are impeccably decorated in a classical style inspired by imperial St. Petersburg, and are equipped with comfortable beds and modern bathrooms. The deluxe room with a Jacuzzi is spacious and well worth paying the modest extra fee. The English-speaking staff are friendly and knowledgeable, and are happy to arrange add-ons such as babysitting or personal tour guides. There's an excellent continental breakfast included in the price and brought to your room.

50 Bolshaya Morskaya Ulitsa. www.nlightsrussia.com.com. © **812/570-0334.** Fax 812/570-6409. 5 units. From 57 euros for twin room with shared bathroom; from 102 euros suite. Prices include breakfast and 18% VAT. Extra bed 15 euros. AE, DC, MC, V. **Amenities:** Internet; room service; smoke-free rooms; tour arrangements and personal guides; transport services. *In room:* A/C in deluxe suite only, TV w/ satellite and free movies, fridge, hair dryer, free Internet.

UPPER NEVSKY PROSPEKT

The city's best hotel district, upper Nevsky Prospekt is the commercial heart of St. Petersburg and the richer end of its main thoroughfare.

Best For: Almost anyone. Those who reserve well ahead of time are in better stead than those who don't to find a spot near the city's top museums, shopping and restaurants.

Drawbacks: All housing options fill up quickly in this coveted neighborhood, especially around the White Nights—when the prices shoot up precipitously, too. It's not a quiet quarter.

Very Expensive

Corinthia Hotel St. Petersburg ★★ ☺ Hidden behind a 19th-century facade on Nevsky, this hotel has a glass-enclosed lobby and atrium lush with greenery that feels more like Sydney or Los Angeles than subarctic St. Petersburg. The five-star Corinthia Hotel opened in 1993 in two renovated neoclassical mansions, and completed upgrades in 2005 and an expansion in 2009. Geared more toward executives than tourists, the hotel offers a range of suites and thoroughly modern (if somewhat colorless) rooms. Even the smallest room has a bidet along with top-quality bathroom facilities. Staff is businesslike but not particularly effusive. In a nod to the building's history, the hotel houses a small theater museum, in honor of the Samoilov family of actors who lived on the property in the 1800s. Its prime location almost justifies its high prices. Though street-facing windows are well-fortified, Nevsky's constant buzz makes a courtyard-facing room more appealing. Their Sunday brunch, a smorgasbord of international cuisines, is worth a splurge. On-site are child-friendly entertainment, a playroom, and a babysitter.

57 Nevsky Prospekt. www.corinthia.com. ☏ **812/380-2001.** Fax 812/301-1937. 388 units. Double 160 euros mid-Oct to mid-May, from 260 euros mid-May to mid-Oct; suite from 600 euros mid-Oct to mid-May, 819 euros mid-May to-mid-Oct. AE, DC, MC, V. Metro: Gostiny Dvor. **Amenities:** 2 restaurants; 3 bars; cafe; babysitting; concierge; executive-level rooms; health club; Jacuzzi; room service; sauna; smoke-free rooms; spa, secure parking. In room: A/C, satellite TV, fridge, hair dryer, minibar, free Wi-Fi.

Expensive

Ambassador Hotel ★ ☺ Contemporary opulence on the banks of one of St. Petersburg's most famed canals, that's what on offer in this hotel opened in 2005. It's in a historic if not smack-dab-central part of town, neighbor to Yusupov's Palace and a crooked block away from the Mariinsky Theater. The rooms pale a bit compared to the Czech-glass chandeliers in the lobby, but their deep mattresses provide a welcome refuge. Unusual for Russian hotels, this one goes out of its way to help people with limited mobility, though showers are tiny. Kids, take note: You get undersized bathrobes and children's menus hard to find in most restaurants in town. More and more foreigners are catching on to the Ambassador's advantages and the prices are rising correspondingly, but good off-season deals can still be had. The narrow indoor pool is a plus, as is the view from the roof restaurant.

5-7 Rimsky-Korsakov Prospekt. www.ambassador-hotel.ru. ☏ **812/331-8844.** Fax 812/331-9300. 251 units. From 5,300 rubles double; from 11,000 rubles suite. Prices double in high season. AE, DC, MC, V. Metro: Sadovaya. **Amenities:** 2 restaurants; 2 bars; babysitting; concierge; health club; Jacuzzi; room service; sauna; spa. In room: A/C, interactive TV with satellite, hair dryer, Internet, international direct dial telephone, minibar.

Grand Hotel Europe ★★★ This hotel has every right to call itself grand. Grandeur seeps from its carpeting to its ceiling friezes, and it is one of the best places to stay in town. Originally opened in 1875, it served as a children's quarantine center during the Russian Revolution and as an evacuation center during World War II. Run by Orient Express, it was completely overhauled for a 1991 reopening, from the baroque facade to the Art Nouveau interiors. Its five floors surround a luscious winter garden and mezzanine cafe visible from inward-facing rooms. Even if you don't stay here, spend a lazy morning or rainy afternoon savoring tea from a silver samovar and listening to the harpist on the mezzanine. Previous guests included Tchaikovsky, Dostoyevsky, and Bill Clinton when he was U.S. president; its current clientele seems to be European tourists and international executives. Guest rooms are elegant, modern, and (except for the presidential suite) mid-size, while bathrooms are full-size and full-convenience.

1 Mikhailovskaya Ulitsa. www.grandhoteleurope.com. ☏ **812/329-6000.** Fax 812/329-6001. 301 units. From 9,000 rubles double; from 21,000 rubles suite. Rates 20% higher May–July. Extra bed 1,300 rubles. AE, DC, MC, V. Metro: Gostiny Dvor or Nevsky Prospekt. **Amenities:** 5 restaurants; 2 bars; babysitting; concierge; executive-level rooms; health club; Jacuzzi; room service; sauna; smoke-free rooms. In room: A/C, TV w/satellite and pay movies, fridge, hair dryer, minibar, free Wi-Fi.

Radisson Royal ★★ The stylish corner bar is among the most appealing things about this five-star hotel, along with its good location and larger-than-usual rooms. The elegance of the bar extends to the suites but not to the standard rooms, which don't have much character. Young, friendly staff is helpful in finding you the best room—except during the busiest season, or when large groups of business visitors fill up its floors. Opened in 2002, the Royal occupies a building that dates back to the 1730s. Courtyard-facing rooms are considerably quieter than street-facing ones, though they cost the same, and the view of Nevsky, while romantic at night, is just as well experienced from the hotel's Cannelle bar on the ground floor as from your room.

49/2 Nevsky Prospekt. www.radisson.ru/hotel-stpetersburg. ✆ **812/322-5000**. Fax 812/322-5001. 164 units. From 9,000 rubles double; from 18,000 rubles suite. Children 18 and under stay free in parent's room. AE, DC, MC, V. Metro: Gostiny Dvor. **Amenities:** Restaurant; bar and lounge; concierge; executive-level rooms; health club; room service; sauna; smoke-free rooms. *In room:* A/C, TV w/satellite, fridge, hair dryer, minibar, free Wi-Fi.

Moderate

Nevsky Hotels Group ★★ ◈ This company has six centrally located mini-hotels, and has recently opened a budget "Sky Hotel" and a hostel—and all are a big hit with American and European travelers. The prices and locations, with two hotels along Nevsky and four along Bolshaya Konyutchnaya Ulitsa near the Hermitage, are hard to beat. Staff is cheerful and always open to suggestions. Nevsky Express Hotel has the most basic services and the least appealing locale, just across from the exit to Moskovsky Train Station and its attendant grime. Nevsky Central Hotel is across busy Insurrection Square (Ploshchad Vosstaniya), on a posher section of the avenue. The mini-hotels all charge the same moderate rates, which are often discounted, for basic wood decor, plenty of greenery, and natural light, while the Sky Hotel, which has some shared bathrooms, and the Hostel, with dorms, both on Bolshaya Konyush-ennaya Ulitsa, are inexpensive. They also offer apartments with fully equipped kitchens and a range of business services for long-term guests. The company can arrange visas and translators, too. All in all, an excellent value choice.

Nevsky Hotel Moika 5: 5 Nabereshnaya Moika; *Nevsky Hotel Aster:* 25 Bolshaya Konyushennaya Ulitsa; *Nevsky Hotel Grand:* 10 Bolshaya Konyushnaya Ulitsa; *Nevsky Express Hotel:* 93 Nevsky Prospekt; *Nevsky Central Hotel:* 90 Nevsky Prospekt; *Nevsky Breeze Hotel:* 12 Galernaya Ulitsa; *Sky Hotel:* 17 Bolshaya Konyushennaya Ulitsa; *Nevsky Hostel Konyushennaya 11:* 11 Konyushennaya Ulitsa. www.hon.ru. ✆ **812/703-3860**. 297 units total. Double 3,300 rubles Oct-Apr, from 5,000 rubles May-Sept; from 6,800 rubles suite. Sky Hotel doubles from 2,500 rubles, hostel from 650 rubles for a dorm. DC, MC, V. Metro: Nevsky Prospekt or Ploshchad Vosstaniya. Amenities: Cafe in each hotel; executive-level rooms; Jacuzzi in suites; room service; sauna. In room: A/C (some units), TV w/satellite, hair dryer, free Wi-Fi.

Nevsky Forum ★★ This would be a choice hotel even without the Nevsky Prospekt address, which adds to its cachet and convenience. True, the city's biggest train station is just around the corner, but its attendant grime doesn't reach the Nevsky Forum and it means you don't need to take a taxi after you roll in on the overnight train from Moscow. And you have your pick of souvenir shops and restaurants of many flavors just outside the Nevsky Forum's door. Street-facing rooms are good for people-watching but even triple-paned windows can't keep out all the clamor. (Courtyard rooms cost the same.) It paints itself as a "business hotel," but it pulls in plenty of tourists out to discover the city on their own. Creamy upholstering meets somber alderwood in the guest rooms, and the shower-only bathrooms are a study in efficient use of space.

69 Nevsky Prospekt. www.nevskyforum.com. ✆ **812/333-0222**. Fax 812/333-0222. 29 units. From 5,000 rubles double; from 9,900 rubles suite. AE, DC, MC, V. Metro: Mayakovskaya. **Amenities:** Restaurant; bar; concierge; room service. *In room:* A/C, satellite TV, fridge, hair dryer, minibar, free Wi-Fi.

Somebody has to get the best room in the house. It might as well be you.

o You can start by joining the hotel's frequent-guest program, which may make you eligible for upgrades.

o A hotel-branded credit card usu-ally gives the owner "silver" or "gold" status in frequent-guest programs for free.

o Always ask about a corner room. They're often larger and quieter, with more windows and light, and they often cost the same as standard rooms.

o When you make your reservation, ask if the hotel is renovating; if it

is, request a room away from the construction.

o Ask about nonsmoking rooms; rooms with views; rooms with twin, queen- or king-size beds.

o If you're a light sleeper, request a quiet room away from vending machines, elevators, restaurants, bars, and discos.

o Ask for a room that has been most recently renovated or redecorated.

If you aren't happy with your room when you arrive, ask for another one. Most lodgings will be willing to accom-modate you.

LOWER NEVSKY TO SMOLNY CATHEDRAL

A more original and historically rich neighborhood than those listed above, lower Nevsky Prospekt and the streets north toward the river offer more reasonable prices and hidden discoveries beyond the package-tour itineraries.

Best For: Those less flush with cash, not drawn to downtown bustle and curious about the city's past. Good walking shoes or a car are crucial.

Drawbacks: You might have to hunt to find a store or restaurant near some of these hotels, or take a long walk.

Expensive

Marshal ★★   This one-story, 18th-century mansion doesn't look like most hotels, and that's a big part of why it has so many fans (myself included). Its corridors circle a courtyard that once sheltered the household cavalry of nearby nobility. The building was turned into a hotel in 2001, and houses a one-room museum to the first president of Finland, one-time cavalryman Duke Mannerheim. Guest rooms are spacious, and even the smallest singles have sunny furniture and spotless modern bathrooms (most with shower only). The rooms facing the army barracks feel so far from the rest of the hotel that they're almost isolated. One room offers a water bed. The small glass and chrome cafe offers a simple but satisfying breakfast, and coffee and snacks through-out the day. The Marshal's winning combination of charm and conveniences means it's increasingly popular among independent European tourists, which in turn means space is often limited. The nearby streets hold several unsung architectural and his-torical treasures. Big discounts are available via online booking sites.

41 Ulitsa Shpalernaya. www.marshal-hotel.spb.ru. ✆ **812/579-9955** or 812/579-7500. 26 units. From 5,300 rubles double; from 8,300 rubles suite. Breakfast included. AE, DC, MC, V. Parking. Metro: Chernyshevskaya. **Amenities:** 24-hr. restaurant; Jacuzzi; room service; sauna; smoke-free rooms. *In room:* A/C, TV w/cable, fridge, hair dryer, minibar, free Wi-Fi.

Moderate

Arbat Nord ★★   An inviting, peach-colored building on a quiet side street, the Arbat Nord is an elegant mix of antique desks and top-of-the-line laptop reservation terminals. Opened in 2004, it blends more carefully with St. Petersburg's 18th-century classicism than the hotels of the Soviet era. Staff is always ready to include personal touches, such as guidebooks in your native language or wine from your country left at the bedside. Its five stories hold mid- to large-size rooms of polished dark woods and sumptuous, firm bedding. The top-floor rooms have skylights that offer stunning views of the long summer sunsets and sunrises—though be sure the blinds close securely if you want to get any sleep during the White Nights. The neighborhood is so quiet it feels almost isolated, but it's just around the corner from Chernyshevskaya metro station and plenty of usual and unusual commerce.

4 Ulitsa Artillereiskaya. www.arbat-nord.ru. ✆ **812/703-1899.** Fax 812/703-1898. 33 units. 4,300 double Nov–Apr; 7,200 rubles double May–Sept. AE, DC, MC, V. Metro: Chernyshevskaya or Mayakovskaya. **Amenities:** Restaurant and bar; room service; smoke-free rooms. *In room:* A/C, satellite TV, fridge, hair dryer, free Wi-Fi.

IBIS St Petersburg Centre ★   This international three-star chain filled a gaping hole in the market when it opened in 2008, as it offered budget travelers an alternative to the huge Soviet-era hotels or mini-hotels. It's well located, especially for train travelers, as it's just a short walk from the Moskovsky Train Station, and although it's in a busy area the rooms are well sound-proofed. Rooms are modern and tastefully decorated with hardwood floors, well-equipped bathrooms and flatscreen TVs. Rooms with adjoining internal doors are available, which is handy for families. Add the all-you-can-eat breakfast, and the handy ATM machine in the lobby, and you have a reliable, familiar mid-range option.

54 Ligovsky Prospekt. www.ibishotel.com. ✆ **812/622-0100** or bookings 812/622-0100. Fax 812/622-0101. 221 units. From 4,100 rubles double. AE, DC, MC, V. Metro: Vladimirovskaya. **Amenities:** Restaurant; car hire service desk; disabled access; secure parking. *In room:* A/C, TV w/cable, hair dryer, free Wi-Fi.

Inexpensive

Moskva   A standard on the tour-group circuit since its appearance in the 1970s, the Moskva's most salient feature is its size. With 825 rooms rounding its semicircular facade overlooking the Neva River, the Moskva was made to accommodate Soviet-size congresses and conventions—and now its boosters say it's ideal for hosting "productive, solid business meetings." Today's guests include North American and European tour groups (especially Finns), groups from former Soviet republics, and a few contingents of Chinese businesspeople. At the bottom end of Nevsky Prospekt, the hotel is a few minutes on foot from dozens of restaurants and is on top of a metro station. The hotel was fully renovated in 2007, and the upgraded rooms, with their proper plumbing, comfortable toilet seats, and double beds, have banished memories of the dingy Communist era. The only echo of those times remains in the corridors, which are big enough to house a football field, reflecting Soviet disregard for property value. While the hotel is not charming or elegant, it's reasonably priced.

2 Alexander Nevsky Sq. (Ploshchad Alexandra Nevskogo). www.hotel-moscow.ru. © **812/333-2444.** Fax 812/274-2130. 825 units. From 3,200 rubles double; 5,000 rubles suite. Prices nearly double during the White Nights. AE, MC, V. Metro: Ploshchad Alexandra Nevskogo. **Amenities:** 4 restaurants; cafe; cinema; concierge; room service beauty salon; free Wi-Fi zones; Avis rent-a-car agency. *In room:* A/C, TV w/cable, fridge, Internet, minibar (in some rooms).

Rus An inexpensive and decent choice in an up-and-coming neighborhood, the Rus suffers the unfortunate drawback of a hideous design, which resembles a concrete spider. It was the ultimate in Soviet modernity when it opened in the 1970s. The hotel completed a full renovation in 2009, including of the antiquated barber shop, and in the process lost the "floor ladies" (a holdover from the Communist era), who were stationed outside the elevators and charged with keeping track of everyone staying on their floor. The dizzying floor layout may mean a long walk from the elevator. The hotel is not far from the lively neighborhood around Chernyshevskaya metro station and Taurida Gardens.

1 Ulitsa Artillereiskaya. www.hotelruss.spb.ru. © **812/579-5003.** Fax 812/579-3600. 146 units. From 3,000 rubles double; 5,800 rubles suite. MC, V. Secure parking. Metro: Chernyshevskaya or Mayakovskaya. **Amenities:** Restaurant; cafe; concierge; room service; sauna with swimming pool, spa; billiard club; free Wi-Fi in lobby. *In room:* A/C (in some units), TV w/cable, in some units: fridge, hair dryer, minibar.

SOUTH OF NEVSKY

The area stretching south of Nevsky Prospekt offers more affordable hotels and a glimpse at up-and-coming neighborhoods and St. Petersburg's modern-day style.

Best For: Those with a sense of adventure and good walking legs, and without an executive expense account.

Drawbacks: Distances to the metro and key museums can be far, so you need to factor that into your planning if you're only in town for a day or two.

Expensive

Alexander House ★★ ☺ This unbeatable hotel was born when a television journalist and his wife decided to switch careers and open a mini-hotel, using only environmentally friendly building materials and furniture. That's no easy task in Russia, and they remain St. Petersburg's most eco-friendly hoteliers. The project was clearly a labor of love. The rooms are named after different cities, and each is decorated uniquely. What they have in common are exposed brick and wood beams, double beds, and roomy wardrobes. There's no business center, but they can rent you a laptop and help you arrange for translators, tours, or other needs. They welcome kids and pets. The hotel inhabits a picturesque, tranquil spot overlooking the Krikova Canal, yet it's just down the street from Mariinsky Theater and within walking distance of St. Isaac's Cathedral and Palace Square. You'll need to walk about 10 minutes to reach much commerce or dining, but the intimate charm of this hotel makes it well worthwhile.

27 Naberezhnaya Krikova Kanala. www.a-house.ru. ©/fax **812/575-3877.** 19 units. From 6,500 rubles double; 7,900 rubles suite. AE, DC, MC, V. Metro: Sadovaya or Sennaya Ploshchad. **Amenities:** Cafe; concierge; room service; smoke-free rooms. *In room:* A/C, TV w/satellite, fridge, hair dryer, minibar, free Wi-Fi.

Moderate

Dostoyevsky Hotel ★   The Dostoyevsky Hotel feels worlds away from its name-sake's haunted, mildewed, 19th-century St. Petersburg, instead occupying a spotless modern building atop one of the city's toniest shopping malls. The name refers to the surrounding neighborhood, where Dostoyevsky lived the last years of his life and wrote *The Brothers Karamazov.* The hotel, meanwhile, is aimed squarely at the 21st-century middle-class consumer. The soft lighting of the rooms feels cozy and inviting and takes the edge off the gleaming exterior of the building. Downstairs, the Vladi-mirsky Passage hosts nearly 200 shops, from designer boutiques to souvenir stands. If the shopping bustle is overwhelming, ask for a courtyard-facing room on a higher floor for some peace. Breakfast and taxes are included.

19 Vladimirsky Prospekt. www.dostoevsky-hotel.ru. ℂ/fax **812/331-3200.** 207 units. Double Nov–Mar 124 euros; Apr–May and Aug–Oct 166 euros; June–July 216 euros. AE, DC, MC, V. Metro: Dostoyevskaya. **Amenities:** Restaurant; cafe; concierge; health club; room service; sauna; smoke-free rooms. *In room:* A/C, TV w/satellite, fridge, hair dryer, minibar, free Wi-Fi.

Fifth Corner (Pyaty Ugol) ★★ ☺   There's nothing historic about this fresh, roomy, and welcoming hotel—and that's just fine. Offering the best of modern conveniences at reasonable prices, Fifth Corner is three floors of rooms in an apartment building that opened as a hotel in 2003. The increasingly coveted neighborhood, called "Five Corners" because of its confusing intersection, hosts an array of casual cafes, jeans shops, music stores, and more. The hotel's biggest drawback is the three-story climb up a wide, orange staircase to reach the lobby—no elevator is available. You could look at it as a mini-gym, since the hotel has no health club of its own. The hotel attracts Russian and international visitors, but it's too small for tour groups. The young, eager staff are open to suggestions, and offer baby beds and babysitting. Some bathrooms have showers only, but they're all clean and spacious.

13 Zagorodny Prospekt. www.5ugol.ru. ℂ/fax **812/380-8181.** 49 units. From 2,500 rubles double; 5,000 rubles suite; 1,100 rubles extra bed. Breakfast included. AE, DC, MC, V. Metro: Dostoyevskaya or Vladimirskaya. **Amenities:** Restaurant and bar; babysitting; concierge; room service; smoke-free rooms. *In room:* A/C, TV w/satellite, fridge, hair dryer, minibar, free Wi-Fi.

Kristoff ★   Hotels such as this are ubiquitous in western European capitals—big-ger than a bed-and-breakfast but small enough to make guests feel cared for and part of the family. Russia still has relatively few such places, making Kristoff all the more precious. Housed in two renovated floors of an apartment building near the "Five Corners" neighborhood (described in the preceding review), the hotel is just far enough from Nevsky to escape the tourist crush but not so far as to feel isolated. Visitors range from students to seniors, first-time visitors to old Russia pros. The lobby is on the second floor, which is not immediately obvious from the street. Guest rooms are compact and decorated with plain but sturdy Russian furniture. The dou-ble rooms have king-size beds, a real rarity in Russia. All bathrooms have showers or bathtubs. There's often only one person on duty, but service is attentive and individ-ual. Breakfast is included.

9 Zagorodny Prospekt. www.kristoff.ru. ℂ **812/571-6643.** Fax 812/571-3692. 31 units. From 4,000 rubles double; extra bed 900 rubles. AE, DC, MC, V. Metro: Dostoyevskaya or Vladimirskaya. **Amenities:** Restaurant; concierge; room service; smoke-free rooms. *In room:* A/C, TV w/satellite, fridge, free Wi-Fi.

Rossiya   The Rossiya soars over a square set back from the Stalin-era pomp of Mos-kovsky Prospekt. Its architecture and generous scale reflect the bland modernism of the 1960s, but inside it's been updated to a fresher style. A favorite with tour groups, the hotel is offering more and more services expected by Western tourists, such as nonsmoking rooms and babysitting. If you're on a higher floor (sixth or above), ask for a room with a view of downtown or of Victory Park across the street, since they cost the same as the courtyard-facing rooms. The rooms are spacious, with firm mattresses and equipped, roomy bathrooms. The park across the street serves as a monument to the Soviet victory in World War II, and is great for a morning walk. The hotel is far from Nevsky but near Park Pobedy metro station and several buses that run to the center of town.

11 Ploshchad Chernyshevskogo. www.rossiya-hotel.ru. © **812/329-3932.** Fax 812/369-7215. 413 units. From 3,500 rubles double; from 5,000 rubles suite. AE, MC, V. Metro: Park Pobedy. **Amenities:** Restaurant; bar and dance club; cafes on most floors; concierge; health club; room service; sauna; smoke-free rooms; free Wi-Fi in lobby. *In room:* A/C, TV w/cable, fridge, minibar.

VASILEVSKY ISLAND & THE PETROGRAD SIDE

Crossing the Neva River opens a broader range of hotel options and a broader view on the city.

Best For: Those with more than a couple of days in St. Petersburg, and energy to explore. And those with good math—key streets are numbered unusually.

Drawbacks: You have to cross the river to get here, which means negotiating far-apart bridges or finding the nearest metro.

Expensive

Marco Polo ★★   One of many appealing hotels on Vasilevsky Island, this hotel stands out for its careful juxtaposition of modern art and 19th-century fireplaces. The staff pays individual attention to guests and to detail, and the hotel offers some unusual add-on services, such as professional photo sessions, and children's parties in the restaurant. Guest room furniture is unadventurous, but the art is intriguing. The bathrooms are large and fully outfitted. Two of the rooms have balconies, and the higher category rooms have king-size beds. All rooms are quiet because the hotel faces an unremarkable side street between the island's two main avenues. It's a long walk to the nearest metro, though compensation is the less-frequented sights nearby, such as the cathedral on the embankment; the icebreaker *Krasin* docked nearby; and the Mining Institute, one of Russia's first universities.

12 Liniya 27 (Vasilevsky Island). © **812/449-8877.** Fax 812/323-1867. www.mpolo-spb.ru. 47 units. From 5,100 rubles double; from 7,200 rubles suite; extra bed 1,300 rubles. AE, DC, MC, V. Metro: Vasileostrovskaya. **Amenities:** Restaurant; bar; concierge; room service; sauna. *In room:* A/C, TV w/satellite, minibar, free Wi-Fi.

Sokos Hotel Palace Bridge ★ 👔   St Petersburg's first purpose-built "spa hotel" opened in 2008 and is run by the Finnish Sokos chain. The spa facilities, which include eight different saunas, a range of treatment rooms, a swimming pool and a hydromassage pool, are unrivalled. The spa is free to hotel guests from 7am to 10am—a perfect start to a day's sightseeing. After 10am expect to pay around 500 rubles per day. A bowling alley and nightclub are further perks to this solid, upscale offering.

Birzhevoi Pereulok 2-4 (Vasilevsky Island). www.sokoshotels.fi. ✆ **812/335-2200.** Fax 812/335-2201. 319 units. From 5,500 rubles double; from 9,500 rubles suite; extra bed 800 rubles. AE, DC, MC, V. Metro: Vasileostrovskaya. **Amenities:** 2 restaurants; bar; cafe; concierge; health club; pub/night club/ bowling alley; room service; smoke-free rooms; spa; free Wi-Fi. *In room:* A/C, TV w/satellite, hair dryer, minibar, free Wi-Fi.

Moderate

Courtyard St. Petersburg Vasilievsky Run by the Marriott group, the Courtyard St. Petersburg Vasilievsky opened in 2009 in an attractive setting on the banks of the Neva. The river-facing rooms are a good vantage point for drawbridge activity during the White Nights. The Hermitage is a 20-minute walk away along the embankment, and other sights within walking distance include the Peter and Paul Fortress and the Russian Museum. Rooms are spacious and decorated in a Scandinavian style, equipped with comfortable beds and flat screen TVs. The breakfast is pricy for what you get, so consider eating out.

2 Liniya 61/30 (Vasilevsky Island). www.marriott.com. ✆ **812/380-4011.** Fax 812/380-4022. 202 units. From 4,000 rubles double (6,000 in high season); from 9,500 rubles suite. AE, DC, MC, V. Metro: Sportivnaya. **Amenities:** Restaurant; bar; concierge; health club; room service; free Wi-Fi; secure parking (1,000 rubles per day). *In room:* A/C, TV w/satellite, fridge, hair dryer, free broadband Internet, minibar.

NasHotel ★ This bright, welcoming hotel was built on the site of a Soviet vitamin factory (look for the outline of the warehouse building in the reconstructed facade). Opened in 2006, it's an example of the regeneration taking place across this formerly run-down, industrial area of Vasilevsky Island. For those who prefer a quieter location, it's ideally situated, only 5 minutes' walk from the metro and one stop away from Nevsky Prospekt. Staff are eager and attentive and the summer terrace cafe, open until 3am, is a plus during the White Nights. Rooms are large and well-decorated, as are the bathrooms. Only the higher-category rooms have baths; most have showers only. Also worth noting is the disabled access in some rooms, and that pets are allowed on request.

http://en.nashotel.ru. 50, 11ya Liniya. Vasilievski Ostrov ✆ **812/643-0081.** Fax 812/643-0082. 58 units. From 5,400 rubles double; from 7,200 rubles family room. AE, MC, V. Metro: Vasileostrovskaya. **Amenities:** Restaurants; bar; cafe (in summer); concierge; room service. *In room:* A/C, TV w/cable, hair dryer, minibar, free Wi-Fi.

NEAR THE AIRPORT

Pulkovskaya ★ Pulkovo Airport has no airport hotels in the traditional sense, although its first is planned for completion in 2013. The closest equivalent is the Pulkovskaya, 10 minutes north on a straight highway toward the city center. Free shuttles run from airport to hotel and back. Another Soviet-era giant, the hotel has been renovated to international standards. Russian and foreign tour groups fill up many rooms, but there are always plenty to spare. The marriage agency on the seventh floor aims at single male tourists, though the hotel also offers family-friendly holiday events and a dinner theater show. Guest rooms are mid-size, while generously spaced bathrooms offer showers and tubs alike.

1 Ploshchad Pobedy (Victory Sq.). www.parkinn.com/hotelpulkovskaya-stpetersburg. ✆ **812/740-3900.** 842 units. From 4,900 rubles double; from 6,900 rubles suite. AE, DC, MC, V. Secure parking.

Metro: Moskovskaya. **Amenities:** 4 restaurants; bar; concierge; health club; indoor pool; room service; 2 saunas; smoke-free rooms; free Wi-Fi. *In room:* A/C, TV w/satellite, fridge, free Wi-Fi in business category rooms.

PRACTICAL INFORMATION

The Big Picture

St. Petersburg's priciest hotels are mainly clustered on and around upper Nevsky Prospekt, such as the **Grand Hotel Europe** and the **Corinthia Hotel St. Petersburg,** while the huge Soviet-era hotel towers are farther from the center. Meanwhile choices elsewhere have expanded—and, now that most have upgraded from communist-era services, their quality is more consistent. Generally speaking, an excellent price-to-quality ratio and more individual service are found in the numerous "**mini-hotels,**" some of which have fantastic central locations (see "A City of Mini-Hotels," earlier in this chapter).

When choosing accommodations in St. Petersburg, bear in mind that it's a city of bridges that are drawn up in the wee hours to allow shipping traffic through. This means that if your late-night plans involve something on the other side of the Neva River from your hotel, you may be in for a long wait or a detour to get back—especially important during the parties of the White Nights. See chapter 17 for drawbridge schedules.

The larger international hotels generally offer car rentals, while most smaller hotels can arrange a car with a driver for a few hours or for the duration of your stay at a reasonable, sometimes negotiable price. Many hotels have a "transport desk" which offers something between a taxi and a limo service.

Suites in Russia (called *luxe* or *demi-luxe*) nearly always have two rooms, though size varies broadly. In older hotels a double will usually mean two single beds, while newer hotels offer the choice of one double bed for two people, or two single beds. Single rooms and single rates are nearly always available, so be sure to ask about them if you're traveling alone.

Men traveling alone should be braced for the possibility that prostitutes may call your room and offer their services, even in relatively upscale hotels. This is illegal in Russia, and it's worth calling to the management's attention. See "Nighttime Companionship" on p. 64.

Getting the Best Deal

Don't be alarmed by some high prices above—those listed are the official "rack rates," the highest official prices charged by hotels. Hotel websites often offer bargains or package deals, as do many traditional and online travel agencies.

The tourist season in St. Petersburg is much more pronounced than in Moscow, centering around the White Nights festivals in late June. Accommodations are at a premium from May to July, and reservations are essential. The rest of the year, particularly during the sleepy winter months, you'll have options and can often find deep discounts. See the "St. Petersburg Neighborhoods" in chapter 10 and neighborhood descriptions earlier in this chapter for the pros and cons of different districts.

Prices above are listed in rubles (see the "Currency Confusion at Your Hotel" box on p. 74) and do *not* include breakfast or 18% VAT unless noted; most travel agencies

Keep a hotel business card or brochure with you at all times, with the hotel's name and address written **in Russian**. You can show this to cab drivers or emergency workers to ensure you get home safely.

(online and traditional) *do* include VAT in their quotes. For more hotel hints, see "Tips on Accommodations" on p. 294.

Deep discounts are available on www.waytorussia.net and www.hotelsinrussia. com. Russian-language sites can offer deeper discounts, but beware of the extra fees some hotels charge for non-Russian taxpayers (see "Foreigner Tax" on p. 62).

You can also look for deals on online travel booking sites like **Travelocity, Expedia, Orbitz, Priceline,** and **Hotwire,** or you can book hotels through **Hotels.com, Quikbook** (www.quikbook.com), and **Travelaxe** (www.travelaxe.com).

It's not a good idea to arrive without a reservation, especially late at night or on holidays, when tourist agencies are closed.

Reservation Services

Most hotels require at least a day's deposit before they will reserve a room for you. In St. Petersburg, the only option is usually paying by credit card, either by phone, online, or with a travel agent. You can usually cancel a room reservation 1 week ahead of time and get a full or nearly full refund. A few hotel keepers will return your money up to 3 days before the reservation date, but some will take your deposit and never return it, even if you cancel far in advance. Mini-hotels are less generous about cancelled reservations, so make sure you know their rules before paying anything.

Among booking services, **Way to Russia** (www.waytorussia.net) is among the most upfront and reasonable, and rooms are almost always discounted. Its website and staff are responsive and seem to "get" what Western visitors are looking for—and don't automatically assume you're flush with cash or looking for a Russian wife, like some Russian agencies. **Hotels in Russia** (www.hotelsinrussia.com) also offers online-only reservation services for a range of budgets, though with a somewhat more Russian mindset. The best stop for mini-hotels is the **St. Petersburg Small Hotels Association** (✆ 812/335-2583; www.inn.spb.ru).

Alternative Accommodations

While the mini-hotels are unusual, they're so widespread in St. Petersburg that they're no longer really "alternative" options. Apartment stays are a good bet, especially for those staying for a long period, or with a family. The only drawback is the lack of a central reception desk and all the services it can render. Be sure to ask the apartment agency where to find food and essentials. Supermarkets are not always obvious and can be challenging if you don't speak Russian.

Serviced apartments come with basic kitchen facilities and varying levels of maid service. Some have minimum stays of a week, and monthly or even longer stays are available. **Pulford Apartments** (see p. 192) offer higher-end options with great locations. **Way to Russia** (www.waytorussia.net) provides help finding serviced apartments and homestays.

If you want to immerse yourself in Russia or Russian, or want to adopt a babushka (grandmother) of your own, try a **homestay.** It's not for those seeking privacy or neutral tones—you're likely to be showered with food and attention and surrounded by layers of books, tchotchkes, and Russian history. But you're certain to leave feeling you've experienced something special, and nothing like home.

WHERE TO EAT IN ST. PETERSBURG

S t. Petersburg's current dining scene reflects its seaside and river-crossed geography, with fresh- and saltwater fish on every menu. Its eye-on-Europe heritage means that traditional Russian dishes are often upstaged by French-inspired terrines and roasts, or by pastas and pizza. Cuisines from the former Soviet republics in central Asia and the Caucasus are well represented though less common than in Moscow. The sushi craze has definitely gripped the country's northern capital, too (see the "Sushi" box on p. 85).

best ST. PETERSBURG DINING BETS

- **Best Traditional Russian Cuisine:** To sample the victuals of tsarist-era nobility, or at least a 21st-century version, try **Demidoff,** where the sterlet is among the several sterling choices. For a gastronomic version of what Russians eat at home, **Restoran** is a top choice, with its rich zakuski collection and freshest of fish. For those on a budget, grabbing *bliny* at the **Teremok** street stands gives a quick taste of local fare. See p. 212, 217, and 211.

- **Best Romantic Dinner:** Reserve a quiet corner in **Staraya Tamozhnaya** and revel in the old-world decor as you select caviar and a bottle of Bourgogne Blanc. Or wrap yourself in the Italian-Russian aura of **Francesco,** with its summer terrace and sumptuous chocolate desserts, and the language of amore will erase memories of the anonymous crush of the metro crowds. See p. 213.

- **Best Quick Lunch:** Any one of the **Chainaya Lozhka** or **Yolki Polki** restaurants around central St. Petersburg will nourish you quickly and cheaply almost any time of day. For a more original meal, try a "**business lunch**" in any good restaurant, by definition faster and less expensive than the dinner service. See p. 211 and 216.

- **Best Place to Take Tea:** No setting is more calming than the atrium of the **Grand Hotel Europe,** and the full tea service can be copious enough for a midday meal. A more modest but more authentic Russian option is the **Marco Polo,** where the samovar takes center stage for the afternoon tea service. See p. 218.

Price Categories	
Very Expensive	$60 and up per person without alcohol
Expensive	$40 and up
Moderate	$20 and up
Inexpensive	Under $20

○ **Best for Families:** Feeding squirmy and selective eaters has gotten easier with the chain restaurants and the many buffets on hand (see "Best of the Buffets," later in this chapter), and such venues as the **Stroganoff Steak House,** which offers activities as well as a rich children's meal. See p. 210.

○ **Best Dinner on a Budget:** Head straight to **V Teple,** where you can fill up on sorrel soup and chicken and mushroom canneloni for a few rubles. Or for a funkier experience, choose **Idiot,** where a vegetarian meal costs less than the entry fee to the city's many museums. See p. 211 and 217.

○ **Best Splurge:** Most of the over-the-top St. Petersburg venues aren't worth the jaw-dropping prices, but **Palkin** is an exception. Pamper your tastebuds with homemade foie gras, or scallops and crab in coconut milk and ginger. Their website theme song? "Diamonds are a Girl's Best Friend." See p. 207.

○ **Best Caucasian Cuisine:** Immerse yourself in a Caucasus Mountains village at **Karavan,** complete with in-house 'rivers' and costumed waitstaff. **Kavkaz Bar** is less atmospheric but the food is so authentic you'll hear Georgian and Armenian spoken as much as Russian or English. See p. 214.

○ **Best Views:** Dining on the Neva River offers the best panoramas of this maritime city. The ship-restaurant **Flying Dutchman** has window seats on the water if you reserve in advance. Or grab a loaf of fresh bread and Baltic cheese and snack on any embankment to watch the mighty Neva rush past. See p. 217.

AROUND PALACE SQUARE & THE HERMITAGE

Expensive

NEP ★ RUSSIAN   Named after Lenin's New Economic Policy, an attempt at state-run capitalism in the 1920s that was crushed by Stalin's collectivization campaign, this restaurant is political only in name. Offering traditional Russian, European, and Thai cuisine, its prime location on the corner of Palace Square and the Moika River makes it rather touristy, but the fare is decent and filling and the prices are not as high as they could be in this locale. Play it safe and order the beef stroganoff—or go all out and try the venison filet with blueberry and juniper, a modern rendition of traditional northern Russian fare. Sadly, the restaurant doesn't offer a view of its surroundings, since it's in the basement, but the ambience is convivial. The service can be warm or cold depending on the day and the waitstaff. The Thai menu ranges from the predictable (spring rolls and fried noodles) to the more adventurous (carpaccio of duck, and tiger prawns in coconut sauce). An award-winning late cabaret show, followed by a discotheque, is included Wednesday through Saturday, with performances every day during high season.

Tea Traditions

The best tea is drunk in St. Petersburg, and generally throughout Russia. Since China has a common border with Siberia, tea need not be transported by water to reach Moscow or St. Petersburg. Sea voyages are very bad for tea.
　　　　　–Alexandre Dumas, *Dictionary of Cuisine*

Russian tea traditions date back to the 17th century, when Czar Mikhail I received a gift of tea leaves from the Mongol Khans. Herbal teas date back much farther, as Russians have long used drinks of boiled forest herbs to cure their ills. Today, tea—*chai* in Russian—remains Russians' hot drink of choice, and they're far more likely to quench thirst with a cup of tea than a glass of water. The tea bag and busier schedules have encroached on tradition, but tea—and its attendant cakes and sandwiches—is still the first thing you're offered upon entering any Russian home. In the countryside, the samovar remains as crucial a part of Russian kitchen culture as the tea it brews inside. If your time and budget allow it, take tea at a historic hotel while in Russia such as the **Astoria** or **Grand Hotel Europe.**

37 Naberejnaja Moiky. © **812/571-7591.** www.neprestoran.ru. Main courses 300–1,000 rubles. AE, MC, V. Sun–Tues noon–11.30pm; Wed–Sat noon–1am. Metro: Nevsky Prospekt.

Inexpensive

Hermitage Cafe RUSSIAN　This cafe is surprisingly small for the size of the museum, given that any visitor doing the museum justice will need a rest and a food stop at some point during the day. Once you get a seat (which can be a long wait), you'll see that the light, Art Nouveau hall is a pleasant place in which to eat. The cuisine is essentially Russian fast food, with limp mini-pizzas, roast chicken, and tasty little sandwiches. The Internet cafe across the hall offers hot drinks, sandwiches, and desserts, as well as dozens of terminals set up with links to museums of the world (along with regular Internet access).

Ground floor of Hermitage Museum in Winter Palace. Lunch plate 150–300 rubles. No credit cards. Tues–Sun 11am–5:30pm. Metro: Nevsky Prospekt.

UPPER NEVSKY PROSPEKT

Very Expensive

Palkin ★★★ FRENCH-RUSSIAN　If you want to splurge just once in St. Petersburg, do it here. The original Palkin opened in 1785 and became a mecca for aristocrats and intellectuals; today's reincarnation opened in 2002 on the same spot, displacing the movie theater that had stood here for decades. The interior today is at least as sumptuous as in the decadent days of Catherine the Great. A century after Catherine's reign, Tchaikovsky, Chekhov, and Dostoyevsky enjoyed generous servings and lively debates at Palkin. Today, members of Russia's 21st-century elite make it a frequent stop, including friends of St. Petersburg native (and Russian former president and current prime minister) Vladimir Putin. Chefs research menus of past centuries, including wedding feasts for grand princes, to create dishes like sterlet baked in white wine with a sauce of cepes and crayfish. More standard fare includes

St. Petersburg Restaurants

Backstage
  (Za Stsenoj) **14**
Bagrationi **30**
Black Cat, White Cat **29**
Chainaya Lozhka **22**
Demidoff **19**
Erivan **24**
Flying Dutchman **4**
Francesco **26**
Hermitage Museum
  Café **8**
Hermitage Restaurant **10**
Idiot **13**
Karavan **15**
Kavkaz Bar **28**
Kilikia **16**
Literary Café **18**
Lucky Shot **11**
Marco Polo **2**
NEP **9**
Onegin **23**
Palkin **27**
Park Giuseppe **20**
Pelmenny Bar **11**
Porto Maltese **25**
Restoran **6**
Russkaya Rybalka **1**
Russky Kitsch **7**
7:40 (Sem Sorok) **31**
Staray Tamozhnya **5**
Stray Dog Cellar **21**
Stroganoff
  Steak House **12**
Tinkoff **17**
Troitsky Most **3**

Common terms and abbreviations	
naberezhnaya/nab......	Embankment
most........................	Bridge
ploshchad/pl...............	Square or plaza
prospekt/pr.................	Avenue
sad.........................	Garden
ulitsa/ul...................	Street

a *pot-au-feu* of young chicken and vegetables cooked lightly enough to retain a rich flavor.

47 Nevsky Prospekt. © **812/703-5371.** Reservations required. restaurant@palkin.ru. Jackets preferred for men. Main courses 500–2,000 rubles. AE, DC, MC, V. Daily noon–1am. Metro: Mayakovskaya.

Expensive

Backstage (Za Ctenoy) ★ EUROPEAN   Billing itself as a "continuation of the Mariinsky Theatre's stage," this restaurant right by the theatre entrance claims to have a floor made of its reclaimed stageboards. The theatrical theme doesn't really come across in the elegant but rather bland interior, but it's still a quality choice for a night at the ballet or opera. Performers occasionally pop in, too, making it hard to get a table post-show. Service can be haughty, but the food, including European classics such as lobster soup and osso buco, is worth it.

18/10 Teatralnaya Ploschad © **812/327-0521.** www.elbagroup.ru/backstage. Main courses 800–1,300 rubles. AE, MC, V. Daily noon–midnight. Metro: Sadovaya/Sennaya.

Lucky Shot (Udachny Vystrel) ★ RUSSIAN   If you're feeling carnivorous, dedicate an evening to this urban version of a Russian hunting lodge. It offers a taste of the fruits of Russia's northern forests and its über-macho hunting culture. The reindeer and boar heads on the walls seem to encourage diners to regale their friends with tall tales of hunting adventures. The sauces made from wild mushrooms, nuts, bilberries, cranberries, and other forest delicacies are as good as—and sometimes better than—the meat. All ingredients are allegedly local, which means the meat menu varies by season. I had success with moose and boar, but it's always a good idea to ask your server or neighboring tables which meats are good that day. The "tender lard with fresh greens" is a delectable appetizer, despite its name. Lunchtime is calmer, with fewer tables of large, vodka-soaked parties.

3 Gorokhovaya Ulitsa. © **812/571-6949.** www.lucky-shot.ru. Reservations recommended. Main dishes 400–900 rubles. AE, DC, MC, V. Open noon until the last customer leaves. Metro: Nevsky Prospekt.

Stroganoff Steak House ★ INTERNATIONAL ☺   Like sushi before it, the steakhouse has become a culinary sub-genre in its own right in this city with a knack of assimilating international trends. Stroganoff Steak House is well-established, buzzing and centrally located—the food is a little pricey, but it's worth it for the dry-aged steaks imported from Argentina, Australia, and New Zealand. Fish steaks are also well represented with halibut from Murmansk, Norwegian salmon, and tuna. The wine cellar includes some Russian wines from the Krasnodar region alongside a good selection from both Europe and the New World. The children's room is an added bonus if you're *en famille*.

4 Konnogvardsky Bulvar. © **812/314-5514.** www.stroganoffsteakhouse.ru. Main courses 400–2,500 rubles. AE, DC, MC, V. Daily noon–midnight. Metro: Sadovaya/Sennaya or Nevsky Prospekt.

Moderate

Literaturnoye Café ★ RUSSIAN   The second floor of this 200-year-old standby is a tribute to the 19th-century literary giants who dined and philosophized here. Alexander Pushkin's name is closely associated with the cafe, and his favorite dishes are listed on a separate menu page—*shchi* cabbage soup and baked creamed mushrooms top the list, both quite good. The rest of the menu is a rundown of standard Russian fare,

Most street food in St. Petersburg is either inedible or risky, with one notable exception: the food at the triangular wooden shacks labeled ТЕРЕМОК (which looks like ТЕРЕМОК in Cyrillic, and means "little wooden house"). They sell Russian *bliny*, crepe-style pancakes made on the spot with a variety of fillings. Mushrooms with sour cream is a popular savory filling, and the numerous berry choices are winners for dessert. The huts are handy for satisfying midmeal cravings or snacks for energetic children for 100 rubles or less.

satisfying but not stunning. The green lampshades lend romance to the evenings, but any time of day the cafe is also a good, calm spot for a quick cup of tea, coffee, or *shiten*, a hot drink made from hot water, herbs, and honey. Residents still refer to the place as Beranger, the cafe's original 19th-century name. (The "literary" label came as a tourist draw much later.) On nice days, you can sit on the benches outside.

18 Nevsky Prospekt. ✆ **812/312-6057.** Main courses 350–1,000 rubles. AE, DC, MC, V. Daily noon–1am. Metro: Nevsky Prospekt.

V Teple ★ 🍴 RUSSIAN/INTERNATIONAL   Laid-back, friendly, and kitted out like a Russian home, this restaurant has become a word-of-mouth hit among travelers—so you'll find other Western visitors but also plenty of young, professional Russians among the clientele. At the weekday set lunch you can mix and match from soup, salad, a main course, and a side dish, and a combination of three of these won't set you back much over 200 rubles—a rare bargain in such a central place. Staff generally speak good English and the menu has something for everyone, with Russian classics, a good range of soups, salads, and pastas and a few Asian-inspired dishes. It's conveniently located for the Mariinsky Theater, but if you've fixed on a particular date, its popularity makes booking advisable.

45 Bolshaya Morskaya Ulitsa. ✆ **812/570-1974.** www.v-teple.ru. Main courses 250–850 rubles. Reservations recommended. AE DC MC V. Mon–Fri 9am–midnight; Sat 10:30am–1am; Sun 1pm–midnight. Metro: Sadovaya/Sennaya.

Inexpensive

Chainaya Lozhka (Teaspoon) ☺ RUSSIAN   A sort of Russian cafeteria, this chain serves cheap, quick fare with a Russian emphasis. The beet-and-carrot salad, creamy ham-and-potato salad, marinated mushrooms, and cabbage soup are hardly haute cuisine, but they can satisfy midday hunger at unbeatable prices. The children's menu includes pancakes with a choice of toppings. Nothing is written in English, but the food is displayed at the counter, so you can just point to what you want. Despite its name, the teas are mediocre bag teas and the coffee is either watery or grainy, but most drinks are around a dollar. The place can get crowded, but turnover is quick. This is a safe, convenient choice if you're wandering Nevsky any time of day. There are branches across the city, and several have Wi-Fi.

44 Nevsky Prospekt (among 45 other locations). ✆ **812/571-4657.** www.teaspoon.ru. Salads and main dishes 25–150 rubles. No credit cards. Daily 7am–11pm; weekends and June–Aug 24 hr. Metro: Nevsky Prospekt.

SQUARE OF THE ARTS UP TO SUMMER GARDENS

Expensive

Demidoff ★ RUSSIAN On the Fontanka embankment opposite the Mikhailovsky Castle, this luxurious restaurant sets out to re-create the Russia of the 18th century, both in terms of the interior, with its ceiling frescoes and tablecloths with folkloric prints, and the menu, with its "Old Russian recipies in the Petersburg tradition." The omnipresent influence of French cuisine is muted, with meats accompanied by traditional Russian sauces based on fruit and berries, although fans of beef stroganoff won't be disappointed. The house specialties, if you're on a splurge, are the sterlet in crab sauce or, if you're plumping for the full-on experience, fillet of young bear in a red wine sauce. For dessert there's even a Russian take on tiramisu featuring cherry sauce and black currants. On the drinks menu is a nostalgic choice that you seldom see these days—Soviet champagne (basically sweet, white sparkling wine), at a tenth of the price of the Moet and Dom Perignon alongside it. A Gypsy ensemble plays every evening.

14 Nabereshnaya Fontanki ✆ **812/272-9181.** http://en.restoran.ru. Main courses 400–1,600 rubles. AE, DC, MC, V. Daily noon until the last client leaves. Live music 8–11pm. Metro: Gostiny Dvor.

Park Giuseppe ★★ ITALIAN The main reason to come here is the environment: You're almost inside Mikhailovsky Gardens, with a view of the Mikhailovsky Castle and the candy-colored domes of the Church on the Spilled Blood. The cozy, compact pink building has an inviting shaded terrace and artsy attic room. It's hard to imagine that in Soviet times this pavilion was a public toilet. Thankfully there's no remnant of that era left, and the only scents wafting out are those of hot tea and fresh flowers. The cuisine is Russian-style Italian, meaning thin-crust pizzas, Caesar salad with salmon, and plenty of fish. The service can be slow, so don't come here in a rush.

---

family-friendly RESTAURANTS

Because St. Petersburg children are usually fed at home by Babushka (Grandma) until adolescence, and few tourists come with small kids, few restaurants have been motivated to accommodate families. This is changing, thanks largely to international hotel and restaurant chains but increasingly smaller restaurants are catching on by providing a children's room. The weekend brunch at **Corinthia Nevsky Palace** (p. 193) includes a playroom and kids' activities as well as many kid-palatable buffet options. The restaurant in the **Marco Polo** hotel takes younger diners seriously with a wide choice of dishes on its children's menu. **Russkaya Rybalka** has a children's play area and child's menu, and older kids may get a kick out of helping their parents fish off the pier. For quick food at all hours, Russian fast-food restaurant **BlinDonalt's** has a child's corner and familiar fare, with a focus on pancakes and mini-pies stuffed with jam, meat, or potatoes. **McDonald's, KFC,** and **Sbarro** are always safe bets for a highchair and baby-changing tables, though they don't generally have play equipment, and Americans will find them to be less spacious than their outlets in the U.S.

2 Canal Griboyedova, building B (entrance across from church). ℭ **812/571-7309.** www.park-restaurant.ru. Main courses 350–1,000 rubles. AE, MC, V. Daily 10am–3am. Metro: Gostiny Dvor.

Moderate

Stray Dog Cellar (Podval Brodyachy Sobaki) ★ RUSSIAN   This was a mecca for St. Petersburg's artistic and literary groundbreakers in the early 20th century, who considered themselves "stray dogs" shunted aside by proper aristocratic society. The basement cafe reopened in 2001 after years of disrepair, and is again hosting poetry readings, one-act plays, sculpture shows, and live music from 7pm every evening. Anna Akhmatova hid here during the Civil War, and fellow poets Vladimir Mayakovsky and Oscar Meyerhold frequented the cafe early in their careers. History aside, this is a convenient place for a bite to eat, offering average Russian fare and a few departures. Stick to the Russian favorites, such as sturgeon, fresh or smoked salmon, and meat-based soups; avoid the adventurous dishes with exotic fruits. The back rooms get smoky at night.

5/4 Square of the Arts (Ploshchad Isskustv). ℭ **812/312-8047.** Main courses 250–400 rubles. No credit cards. Mon–Sat 11:30am–10pm. Metro: Gostiny Dvor.

LOWER NEVSKY PROSPEKT UP TO SMOLNY CATHEDRAL

Expensive

Francesco ★ ITALIAN   In a city exceptionally well-served by Italian restaurants, this fine dining establishment, opened in 2009, is the cream of the crop. Decor is in the intimate style of an Italian country house, with wooden paneling, dressers and beams, candelabras and sumptuous velvet chairs. The creative, Mediterranean cuisine is courtesy of Sicilian-born chef Guiseppe Priolo, with dishes such as red mullet with fennel and coriander and veal in breadcrumbs. For dessert, try the semifreddo with almonds and chocolate sauce. In the summer months, ask for a seat on the terrace.

47 Suvorovsky Prospekt ℭ **812/275-0552.** www.restoran-francesco.ru. Main courses 500–3,500 rubles. MC, V. Daily noon until the last client leaves. Metro: Ploschad Vostaniya.

Moderate

Black Cat, White Cat (Chornaya Koshka, Bely Kot) ★ SERBIAN/RUSSIAN   This is a top choice for lunch or dinner in the once-neglected neighborhood around Chernyshevskaya metro station, which now boasts numerous antiques stores and historic buildings undergoing long-overdue renovations. Named after a Serbian film that won a cult following in Russia, the restaurant offers cuisine with a Serbian focus as well as plenty of Russian and international standards, including sushi. Tasty roasted meats are grilled on a spit in the middle of the hall. You can also sample rice-based salads and tangy sausages. At night the understated black-and-white hall turns disco, the black lights go on, and you can no longer tell what color your stuffed tomatoes are.

13/15 Ulitsa Pestelya. ℭ **812/579-7430.** Main courses 350–1,500 rubles. MC V. Daily noon–midnight. Metro: Chernyshevskaya.

Filling up on Zakuski

You'll notice that many Russian menus have a full page or two for "zakuski," or appetizers, yet just a handful of main dishes. These appetite-awakeners are where Russian cuisine excels and star at Russian parties, where most guests are uncomfortably full even before the main course arrives. In a restaurant, a good way to savor a range of flavors without stripping your wallet clean is to skip the entrees altogether and choose three or four zakuski instead. You can cover any food group that way: fresh and marinated vegetables, caviar on toast, salmon-stuffed crepes, smoked meats, garlic-cheese or walnut-based salads, to name just a sampling of my personal favorites. Do be warned that very few "salads" listed on menus are based on lettuce; and they're usually much more filling than you expect.

Kavkaz Bar ★★ GEORGIAN   For expats and visitors, this is St. Petersburg's most popular spot to sample cuisine from the former Soviet state of Georgia, which features Caucasus Mountain spices and fruits not usually found in Russian cooking. Cozy and tastefully decorated with Georgian pottery and tapestries, the restaurant is just a block north of Nevsky but the atmosphere is relaxed. Garlic is used liberally, so if you'd prefer a dish without it, be sure to ask. Try the enormous *khinkali,* spiced meat dumplings you're supposed to eat with your hands; the tandoor-style chicken (chicken *tabaka*); or the eggplant slices slathered in walnut-garlic paste. Meat dishes come with *tkemali,* a sweet and spicy sauce made from Georgian sour plums, plus you get stalks of fresh cilantro, dill, and lemony *cheremsha* to munch on. The food is reasonably priced, but the wines, mostly Georgian and French, cost more than they should. If you want to try Georgian wine, stick with the dry reds. Don't be turned off by Kavkaz's cheesy ads in the local magazines and brochures found at most hotels.

18 Karavannaya Ulitsa. ✆ **812/312-1665.** www.kavkazbar.ru. Main courses 300–3,000 rubles. MC, V. Daily 11am–1am. Metro: Mayakovskaya.

Porto Maltese ★ MEDITERRANEAN/SEAFOOD   The seafaring theme starts with the porthole in the door, which opens directly onto a fish counter spilling with octopus, lobster, sturgeon, and more. Though the restaurant is nominally Maltese and offers Mediterranean seafood, the menu favors fish caught in the rivers and lakes surrounding St. Petersburg, such as pikeperch and *som,* a kind of catfish. The octopus and squid are good but are shipped in and not as fresh as the local fare. The salad bar—a relative rarity in St. Petersburg—is also seafood-centered, with shellfish salads and several versions of Baltic herring. Fish is sold by weight and priced per 100 grams (3.8 oz.). Porto Maltese is one of the best dining options at this far end of Nevsky.

174 Nevsky Prospekt. ✆ **812/329 8972.** www.portomaltese.net. Main courses 300–2,300 rubles. DC, MC, V. Daily noon–11pm. Metro: Ploshchad Alexandra Nevskogo.

SOUTH OF NEVSKY
Expensive

Erivan ★★ ARMENIAN   From the Armenian chef and the traditional live music right down to the napkin holders designed by Armenian craftsmen, this restaurant is not only authentic, it has outstanding food, and service, with waitstaff keen to help you navigate the adventurous menu. If you're dining in a group, try the "tasting menu" based on meat, fish, or desserts, which contains a selection of chef's specialties. Dishes of note are the milk-based soups, and *tolma*—grape leaves stuffed with a variety of fillings. For dessert, try the dried fruits or halva—a kind of sweetmeat. There is a wide choice of drinks you won't find elsewhere, such as pomegranate wine, and a range of Armenian beers and cognacs. The business lunch on weekdays at under 500 rubles is worth a detour.

51 Naberezhnaya Fontanki (Fontanka Embankment). © **812/703-3820.** www.erivan.ru. Main courses 500-1,200 rubles. MC, V. Daily noon-midnight. Live music from Mon-Sat from 8pm. Metro: Sadovaya or Sennaya Ploschad.

Tinkoff ★★ ☺ INTERNATIONAL This is Russia's premiere version of the brewery-restaurant, successful on every front and better than many you'll find at home. The lively dinner spot is popular among hip, successful Russians and expats, with several halls offering an extensive Russian-German menu—and, of course, beer. Tinkoff's own brew comes in several unfiltered flavors and some filtered ones, from pale white to deep dark, and includes a nonalcoholic choice. The beer-based cocktails are potent stuff. If the Tinkoff brand doesn't impress you, try one of the German, Irish, or Japanese beers on offer. The restaurant also makes its own sausages and bakes its own bread. On weekdays, choose between a European or Japanese "business lunch," while there's a brunch at weekends. Children are well-catered to with their own menu, playroom, and entertainment. The place fills up fast on weekend nights.

7 Kazanskaya Ulitsa. © **812/458-7788.** www.tinkof.ru. Reservations suggested on weekends. Main courses 500-1,000 rubles. DC, MC, V. Sun-Thurs noon-11pm; Fri-Sat noon-2am. Seasonal closings. Metro: Sadovaya or Nevsky Prospekt.

Moderate

Karavan ★ CENTRAL ASIAN This little taste of central Asia is a fun way to escape a rainy day in Petersburg and immerse yourself in foliage, spices, and fruits. The little streams running through the hall are more evocative of St. Petersburg's canals than of Uzbekistan, but they're a nice touch. They must be crossed by tiny bridges, so watch your feet. Diners lounge on deep couches piled with brightly patterned pillows, in a variation of the platform-style seating arrangement common in central Asia. The menu includes several Azerbaijani and Georgian dishes as well as the Central Asian *manty* (steamed dumplings stuffed with spiced ground lamb) and *plov* (rice pilaf of lamb, carrots, and raisins). Try the yogurt drinks or the *cutaby*—pancake-shaped pies of cheese, chopped greens, or ground meat stuffed into ultra-thin dough. Russians generally order several appetizers and a selection of grilled meats for the whole table to share.

46 Voznesensky Prospekt. © **812/310-5678.** www.caravan2000.ru. Reservations necessary on weekends. Main courses 200-2,000 rubles. MC, V. Daily noon-midnight. Metro: Sadovaya.

Kilikia ★ ◢ ARMENIAN For a nourishing and leisurely dinner or hearty lunch, come to Kilikia. Even if you know nothing of Armenian cuisine, you're bound to find something familiar and satisfying. It resembles Middle Eastern cooking, with added fruits and spices found in the Caucasus Mountains. The grilled lamb and beef dishes are excellent, as is the stewlike *teva*. The vegetable-based appetizers can constitute a meal in themselves; try anything with eggplant or grape leaves. Don't tell the server it tastes like Turkish food, however—hostilities between the nations remain fierce

Best of the Buffets

Eating in St. Petersburg can be hard on the wallet for families. If you can't stand McDonald's or *salat stolichny* at Yolki Palki, head for the weekday buffet lunches at the Western hotels. The Holiday Club St. Petersburg's **Sevilla Restaurant** must be the city's best-kept secret, offering soup, salads (including delicious antipasti), hot dishes, desserts, water, and coffee for a very reasonable 800 rubles. The Novotel's **Cote** **Jardin** serves up an impressive range of salads, soup, hot dishes, and desserts for 750 rubles. It's open until 4pm, so dodge the queues with a late lunch. But the **Beerstube** business lunch buffet at the Corinthia Hotel St. Petersburg (490 rubles) from 1 to 5pm is the best value: salads, delicious main courses, and the best dessert selection by quite some margin.

nearly a century after the 1915 genocide of Armenians during the Ottoman Empire. The restaurant's name refers to a traditionally Armenian region that's now in Turkey. The restaurant is a favorite of St. Petersburg's extensive Armenian community. The 3-course business lunch at 139 rubles is a cheaper option than dinner and quite popular, so you may have to wait for a table if you come after 1pm.

26/40 Gorokhovaya Ulitsa. (℡) **812/327-2208.** Main courses 200–800 rubles. MC, V. Daily noon–midnight. Metro: Sennaya Ploshchad.

Inexpensive

BlinDonalt's RUSSIAN   The tacky name makes this place sound worse than it is. It's not really the Russian version of McDonald's; it's a cheap place to get quick food, for here or to go. Baked potatoes, small meat pastries, and the *bliny* (pancakes) that give the restaurant its name make this a low-budget way to try local fare. Don't expect friendly service or elegant presentation, but do expect to fill up fast. The *pelmeny* (meat ravioli) are a good cold-weather choice, steaming and heaped with the sauce of your choice (Russians prefer sour cream, or *smetana*). One of its easily reached locations is listed below.

186 Moskovsky Prospekt. (℡) **812/327-9755.** www.blindonalds.ru. Metro: Park Pobedy. Full meal 60–200 rubles. No credit cards. Daily 10am–10pm.

Idiot VEGETARIAN   This bohemian basement on the foggy banks of Moika Canal, named after one of Dostoyevsky's novels, attracts a fair share of brooding, philosophical types of all nationalities. It bills itself as a vegetarian restaurant, and there is indeed no meat on the menu, but most people come here to warm up with a glass of mulled wine or the complimentary welcome shot of vodka, or to chill out with a book and a cool drink in the back room. The food is homey and satisfying, especially anything with the wild mushrooms that Russians are so expert at preparing, as well as the miniature pies *(pirozhki)* stuffed with cabbage, apricots, or potatoes. Idiot is a great place to stop while wandering the Moika.

82 Moika Canal. (℡) **812/315-1675.** www.idiot-spb.com. Main courses 500–900 rubles. MC, V. Daily 11am–1am. Metro: Sennaya Ploshchad or Nevsky Prospekt.

VASILEVSKY ISLAND & THE PETROGRAD SIDE

Expensive

Flying Dutchman (Letuchy Gollandets) INTERNATIONAL   The most eccentric of the overpriced ship-restaurants along the north shore of the Neva, the Flying Dutchman has a 24-hour fitness center among its amenities so you can burn off your dinner, and a beauty salon to clean you up afterward. The top-floor restaurant, the dance club downstairs, and the gym have floor-to-ceiling windows with views of the Peter and Paul Fortress or of the river and the Hermitage on the opposite bank. In the summer months, you can eat at "Ponton," which is a restaurant on a pontoon moored on the Neva. In general, this is a good place for a big party or a special night out, but it's not very subtle or intimate. Though there's no official dress code, hosts may snub you in favor of better-dressed customers. Cuisine is all over the world map, from caviar on ice to duck à l'orange and the ubiquitous sushi. Quality is overall good, but mostly you're paying for location and atmosphere, not the food.

6 Mitnenskaya Naberezhnaya. *Ⓒ* **812/313-8866.** www.gollandec.ru. Reservations recommended weekends. Main courses 6,00–3,000 rubles. AE, MC, V. Different halls have different opening hrs, roughly 10am till the last guest leaves. Metro: Gorkovskaya.

Restoran ★★ RUSSIAN/SEAFOOD   This excellent restaurant achieves elegance in cuisine and decor through simplicity, a rare thing in this city of elaborate imperial tastes. The chefs focus on reinterpreting Russian classics with an emphasis on fish from the Baltic and nearby rivers. The unvarnished wood and the stone vaulted arches make the place feel medieval, but the food's presentation and preparation are fully modern. A table of homemade liqueurs made from cranberry, ginger, juniper, or garlic is the first thing you pass; farther along is a tea table with a samovar and homemade jams; and deeper inside is a salad bar focusing on marinated vegetables and pickled fish. The appetizers are extensive and can be combined to make a full meal. Otherwise, try the pike quenelles or the tender rabbit with braised vegetables. The staff is accommodating but not overbearing, and though they welcome tour groups, the restaurant doesn't feel at all touristy. There's live music on Friday nights.

2 Tamozhenny Pereulok. *Ⓒ* **812/327-8979.** Reservations recommended on weekends. Main courses 400–3,000 rubles. AE, DC, MC, V. Daily noon–midnight. Metro: Vasileostrovskaya.

Staraya Tamozhnya (Old Customs House) ★★FRENCH/RUSSIAN   This top-notch restaurant is as ornate as its neighbor Restoran (above) is austere. Scarlet and gold plates are carefully set upon gold-embroidered table linens, furniture is artfully carved and polished, and even the flowery menu is constantly redesigned. The restaurant celebrates French culinary traditions the way Russian aristocracy of the 18th and 19th centuries did. Today it's popular with well-to-do Russian and foreign executives and visitors on a splurge. The menu is updated according to seasonal availability. A special truffle menu comes out in January, and the *pot-au-feu* with lobster pops up a few times a year. Keep an eye out for the maigret of duck with pan-fried foie-gras.

Impressions

On the tray were herb-brandy, different kinds of vodka, pickled mushrooms, rye-cakes made with buttermilk, honey in the comb, still mead and sparkling mead, apples, plain nuts and roasted nuts, and nuts in honey . . . preserves made with honey and with sugar, a ham and a fowl that had just been roasted to a turn.

–Leo Tolstoy, *War and Peace*

The French cheeses and chocolate marquise are always divine. The wine cellar corner is cozy, and a light jazz ensemble plays most evenings.

1 Tamozhenny Pereulok. ☎ **812/327-8980.** www.old.concord-catering.ru/restaurants/old-customs. Reservations required for dinner. Main courses 1,200–2,700 rubles. Piano performances 1–5pm, jazz performances at 7pm. AE, DC, MC, V. Daily 1pm–1am. Metro: Vasileostrovskaya.

Moderate

Marco Polo ★ ☺ EUROPEAN   Exquisitely decorated like a 19th-century drawing room, this cozy but stylish restaurant, attached to the hotel of the same name (see review in Hotels chapter), has Italian, Scandinavian, and seafood specialties on the menu, while the chef's selection has traditional Russian classics such as borscht (beetroot soup), *pelmeni* (meat ravioli) and *kotleti* (meat patties). There's also a traditional Russian afternoon tea from 4pm, with a samovar taking pride of place in the center of the room. The children's menu has a wide and thoughtful selection, from mainstays like meatballs to the more adventurous beef stroganoff and chicken shashlyk. Try one of five distinct business lunch menus, (it changes every day of the week) for just 270 rubles.

12 Liniya 27 (Vasilevsky Ostrov). ☎ **812/449-8877.** www.mpolo-spb.ru. Main courses 400–700 rubles. DC, MC, V. Daily 7:30am–3am. Metro: Vasileostrovskaya.

Russkaya Rybalka (Russian Fishing Expedition) **★ ☺ RUSSIAN**   For a more hands-on dining experience, head to this island escape and catch your own meal. This restaurant harvests local fish that customers can reel in themselves, and its chefs then clean and prepare it to order. Catfish, eel, carp, crayfish, sterlet, and even sturgeon are among the offerings, but the choice depends on the season. In summer diners can sit out on the sunny terrace. Ducks and swans populate the ponds, too, but are not on the menu. Among the dozens of homemade sauces, the garlic-almond cream sauce is the standout. The restaurant is welcoming and offers a generous children's play area. In a taxi or car, it's just 10 or 15 minutes from the city center, but on public transport you have to walk a good 15 minutes from the nearest metro.

Krestovsky Island, 11 Yuzhnaya Doroga. ☎ **812/323-9813.** www.russian-fishing.ru. Reservations recommended, especially in summer. Fish sold by weight; main courses 200–600 rubles. MC, V. Daily noon–midnight. Fishing ponds heated in winter but selection is better Apr–Oct. Metro: Krestovsky Ostrov, then taxi (ask the driver for Russkaya Rybalka) or 15 min. on foot.

Russky Kitsch ★ RUSSIAN/INTERNATIONAL   This theme restaurant makes fun of wealthy New Russians and their extravagant tastes, and is a fun and picturesque place to stop for a bite. The menu is both creative (Japanese specialties and fondues) and traditional (beef stroganoff and "sala" (animal fat), which for a European twist is offered as a carpaccio). Many of the menu items and decorative details are jokes that may be lost on non-Russians, but others are universally silly: ceiling frescoes feature Russian pop icons and politicians (including, strangely, Arnold Schwarzenegger), and menus are presented in tomes of Lenin's works. Despite the faux-imperial atmosphere, prices are mostly reasonable. There's a stunning view across the Neva River toward the Winter Palace—ask for a seat on the glass-enclosed terrace overlooking the river. It feels airy and cheery even in the depths of winter. The corner room has raspberry-colored walls in homage to the favored shade of sport jacket preferred by an entire class of Russian thugs-turned-businessmen.

25 Universitetskaya Naberezhnaya. © **812/325-1122.** www.old.concord-catering.ru/restaurants/russian-kitch. Main courses 350–1,000 rubles. AE, DC, MC, V. Daily noon–1am. Metro: Vasileostrovskaya.

7:40 (Sem Sorok) ★★ JEWISH/GEORGIAN/RUSSIAN   Fun and tongue-in-cheeky, this family-run restaurant is a culinary and atmospheric treasure plunked in an unfortunately distant locale. The appetizers, including several versions of gefilte fish, have more character than the succulent but standard grilled lamb and beef on the main dish menu. The restaurant recently relaunched as kosher, and also added Georgian food to its repertoire, so look out for the *shashliki* (kebabs). Its name comes from a popular Russian-Jewish song about a 7:40 train from Odessa. The two floors are often busy but there's rarely a wait. Worth the extra money for a taxi to avoid the unreliable tram ride to get there.

108 Bolshoi Sampsionevsky Prospekt. © 812/492-3444. www.restoran740.ru. Main courses 500–8,000 rubles. MC, V. Sun–Thurs noon–11pm. Metro: Chornaya Rechka.

Inexpensive

Grand Café Troitsky Most (Trinity Bridge) VEGETARIAN   This small, local cafe chain specializes in clean living and meatless cuisine, regardless of which continent the food comes from. Indian, Italian, Georgian, and even Russian dishes make it to the menu, but no alcohol is served. The whole place is smoke-free, which is extremely rare in St. Petersburg. Try the fresh pastas or the mushroom lasagne. The house specialty is a strange potato-tofu-cheese casserole. Decor is pseudo-Indian, the atmosphere is laid-back to the extreme, and the prices are low. Troitsky Most has several other locations across the city, but Zagorodny Prospekt is the flagship branch.

Zagorodny Prospekt 38. © **812/933-0085.** Metro: Pushkinskaya. Main courses 70–120 rubles. No credit cards. Daily 9am–11pm.

PRACTICAL INFORMATION

Round-the-clock cafes and restaurants of all genres and calibers abound in the center of town. The farther you venture from **Nevsky Prospekt,** the cheaper your options will be—but they'll also be more limited and less likely to have menus in English. Exceptions are the ship-restaurants that line the north side of the Neva River, most of which are gaudy and overpriced but very tourist-friendly. Overall, though, St. Petersburg restaurants have a very good quality-to-price ratio, with something for everyone on most menus. Keep an eye out for "**business lunches,**" a good way to get a reasonably priced meal and quick service at midday. Also try a place in one of the surprising clutches of elegant restaurants on up-and-coming Vasilevsky Island.

Nonsmoking sections are becoming more and more common in St. Petersburg, but they are not yet a rule. Call ahead to check, if smoke concerns you. Hotel restaurants are spacious enough that you'll usually be able to find a table away from the smokers.

Restaurants serve continuously from lunch through dinner, though few are open for breakfast. **Families** will be well served by most hotel restaurants and chains, but less so by the top-end restaurants. An exception are the luxury hotels that offer Sunday brunches, such as the **Corinthia Hotel**—these offer an all-you-can-eat bounty sure to please any palate, and often children's entertainment, too.

Make sure you know what currency is being cited on the menu before you order. Sometimes they are listed in rubles (as they are in this guide), but some menus list prices in dollars or euros. When the check comes, you pay in rubles at the current exchange rate. See the "Currency Confusion at Your Hotel" box on p. 74 for a fuller explanation. Most larger restaurants will accept credit cards, but they are rarely accepted at small or inexpensive cafes.

Most restaurants listed here have menus in English. For those that don't, see the glossary of menu terms in chapter 18. For an overview of Russian cuisine and dining customs, see chapter 2. For tips for vegetarians and picnicking, refer to chapter 5.

RESTAURANTS BY CUISINE

ARMENIAN
Erivan ★ (South of Nevsky, $$$, p. 214)
Kilikia ★ (South of Nevsky, $$, p. 215)

CENTRAL ASIAN
Karavan ★ (South of Nevsky, $$, p. 215)

EUROPEAN
Backstage ★ (Upper Nevsky, $$$$, p. 210)
Marco Polo ★ (Vasilevsky Island, $$, p. 218)

FRENCH/RUSSIAN
Palkin ★★★ (Upper Nevsky, $$$$, p. 207)
Staraya Tamozhnya ★★ (Vasilevsky Island, $$$, p. 217)

GEORGIAN
Kavkaz Bar ★★ (Lower Nevsky-Smolny, $$, p. 214)

INTERNATIONAL
Flying Dutchman (Vasilevsky Island, $$$, p. 217)

Stroganoff Steak House ★ (Upper Nevsky, $$$, p. 210)
Tinkoff ★★ (South of Nevsky, $$$, p. 215)

ITALIAN
Francesco ★ (Lower Nevsky-Smolny, $$$, p. 213)
Park Giuseppe ★★ (Square of the Arts, $$$, p. 212)

JEWISH/GEORGIAN/ RUSSIAN
7:40 ★★ (Vasilevsky Island, $$, p. 219)

MEDITERRANEAN/ SEAFOOD
Porto Maltese ★ (Lower Nevsky-Smolny, $$, p. 214)

RUSSIAN
BlinDonalt's (South of Nevsky, $, p. 216)
Chainaya Lozhka (Upper Nevsky, $, p. 211)
Demidoff ★ (Square of the Arts, $$$, p. 212)

KEY TO ABBREVIATIONS:
$$$$** = Very Expensive   **$$$** = Expensive   **$$** = Moderate   **$ = Inexpensive

Hermitage Cafe (Around Palace Square, $, p. 207)

Literaturnoye Café ★ (Upper Nevsky, $$, p. 210)

Lucky Shot ★ (Upper Nevsky, $$$, p. 210)

NEP ★ (Around Palace Square, $$$, p. 206)

Russkaya Rybalka ★ (Vasilevsky Island, $$$, p. 218)

Stray Dog Cellar ★ (Square of the Arts, $$, p. 213)

RUSSIAN/INTERNATIONAL

Russky Kitsch ★ (Vasilevsky Island, $$, p. 218)

V Teple ★ (Upper Nevsky, $$, p. 211)

RUSSIAN/SEAFOOD

Restoran ★★ (Vasilevsky Island, $$$, p. 217)

SERBIAN/RUSSIAN

Black Cat, White Cat ★ (Lower Nevsky-Smolny, $$, p. 213)

VEGETARIAN

Grand Café Troitsky Most (Vasilevsky Island, $, p. 219)

Idiot (South of Nevsky, $, p. 216)

EXPLORING ST. PETERSBURG

S t. Petersburg is a coherent and carefully planned city, and the value of its individual buildings is best appreciated when you take a step back and view the ensemble to which the buildings contribute. Sculpted parks and curving canals are part of the plan, and well worth a detour—though be sure to have a map in English *and* in Russian, because off the main roads, street signs are usually in the Cyrillic alphabet only.

The city is Russia's principal port, and its geography and history make it immediately distinguishable from Moscow. St. Petersburg did not grow gradually from provincial backwater to major metropolis like its southern rival, and it was never the capital of world Communism—this city was built up from the bogs, fast and furious, to be an imperial capital, and it served as such for 2 centuries. St. Petersburg is better at celebrating the past than at choosing a direction for the future, which means that museums, palaces, and ballet and opera houses are where its strengths lie; daring modern art and architecture are not. The Hermitage is a crucial stop but far from the only museum you should visit on this trip.

St. Petersburg's relative youth and the secular ideas of its founder, Peter the Great, mean that cathedrals play a less crucial and less religious role here than in 850-year-old Moscow. Still, your visit should include a church or two; the ones listed below are architecturally or historically notable. Some cathedrals remain museums as they were in Soviet days, but many are again functioning churches and hold services throughout the day. For hints on avoiding offense while visiting Orthodox cathedrals, see the box "Visiting Churches" on p. 109.

Museum entrance fees are often higher for foreign visitors than for Russians, although this practice is becoming less common. In general, fees are comparable with those in western Europe. When visiting the main tourist sites such as the Peter and Paul Fortress or the Russian Museum, look out for combined ticket deals that will get you entrance to several adjacent attractions. Be prepared to surrender your coat or jacket at the coat check any time of year (see the box "Cult of the Coat Check" on p. 115). Be aware that many museums are closed 1 day a month for "sanitary days"—especially important to note if you're in town for only a few days.

THE siege OF LENINGRAD

Nearly everyone in St. Petersburg today has a family member who lived through the 900-day siege of the city by Nazi forces, and mere mention of the humanity-crushing blockade still brings tears to the eyes of those who survived it. About one million people died during the siege of the city then known as Leningrad, most of them civilians who wasted away of hunger, cold, and disease. From September 1941 to January 1944, residents of this former imperial capital were reduced to eating leather belts, stray dogs, and even human corpses to survive. Antique furniture was stuffed into stoves to survive three winters without heat or electricity. All the while, shells from German aircraft rained down on the city's monuments, accompanying Leningraders' descent into desperation. The only source of supplies to the city was the Road of Life, a rough and remote ice road cut across Lake Ladoga during the first winter of the siege. Though Russians credit Stalin with breaking the back of Nazi forces, the Soviet dictator is also blamed for prolonging Leningrad's suffering by not doing more to end the blockade or to boost supplies to the city.

Today the politics of this period are largely forgotten, and the siege is viewed as evidence of the city's resilience and endurance. St. Petersburg has several museums about the *blokad,* as Russians refer to it, and monuments to victims of the siege; three are listed in this chapter. Even if you don't visit one (they're not for the weak-kneed), keep an eye out for shell wounds on city monuments such as St. Isaac's Cathedral, or for plaques around town showing residents which sides of city streets to favor to avoid shelling. Harrison Salisbury's book *The 900 Days* remains the most vivid and respected chronicle of the blockade in English, 40 years after it was first published.

I did not on this day forget
The bitter years of oppression and of evil
But in a blinding flash I understood
It was not I, but you who suffered and waited
...
My Motherland with the wreath of thorns
And the dark rainbow over your head
I love you—I cannot otherwise—
And you and I are one again, as before.

–Olga Berggolts, St. Petersburg poet, writing on the day of the German invasion, June 22, 1941, of her love for her country despite having been imprisoned in Stalin's purges of the 1930s

HERMITAGE & ENVIRONS

The State Hermitage Museum and the Winter Palace ★★★ The Winter Palace would be a museum itself even if it didn't hold the Hermitage Museum, one of the world's largest and most valuable collections of fine art. The patterned parquet flooring, dazzling chandeliers, and extravagant and turbulent history of the 1750s-era palace almost distract from the riches on display—but not quite. Most of the Hermitage's masterpieces lie in warehouses or the museum basement, but they're hardly missed; it's exhausting enough to view the permanent collection, which, among other treasures, includes more French artworks than any museum outside France. Hall nos. 185 to 189 are worth a glance even if their labels, RUSSIAN CULTURE and PALACE

Exploring St. Petersburg

Monetnaya ul.

ul. Mira

Posadskaya ul.

⑤ ul. Kuybysheva ⑥

Troitskaya
pl.

Troitsky
most

Pirogovskaya nab.

Petrogradskaya nab.

Nevka

Sampsonievsky prospekt

ul. Kom. Smirnova

ul. Akademika Lebedeva

Klinicheskaya

Finland
Station

ПЛ. ЛЕНИНА
pl. Lenina

pl. Lenina

ul. Komsomola

Arsenalnaya ul.

Kondratevsky pr.

Sverdlovskaya nab.

Neva

⑳30

Smolnaya nab.

Orlovskaya ul.

ul. Smolnovo

pl. Proletarskoy
Diktatury

㉙29

Tulskaya ulitsa

Arsenalnaya nab.

Liteyny
most

nab. Robspera

Zakharevskaya ul.

ulitsa Chaykovskovo

ЧЕРНЫШЕВСКАЯ
Chernyshevskaya Ⓜ

Kirochnaya ulitsa

ul. Ryleeva

Shpalernaya ulitsa

Potemkinskaya ul.

Tavrichesky
sad

Paradnaya nab.

Tavricheskaya ul.

Kavalergardskaya ul.

Sinopskaya nab.

LOWER NEVSKY/
SMOLNY CONVENT

Sampsonievsky
most

⑤ ⑥

Troitskaya
pl. Petrovskaya nab.

Neva

nab. Kutuzova

Gagarinskaya ul.

Suvorovskaya
pl.

Letny
sad ⑲19

Marsovo
Pole

Dvortsovaya nab.

Milonaya ul.

nab. reki Moika

Church of the Savior
on the Spilled Blood

Moika

⑰17

nab. reki Fontanki

Liteyny prospekt

ul. Radishcheva

ul. Vosstaniya

ulitsa Mayakovskovo

ulitsa Nekrasova

8-ya ul.

ulitsa Moseenko

Grechesky prospekt

Suvorovski prospekt

5-ya ul.

Sovetskaya ul.

Novgorodskaya ul.

Neva

Russian State
Museum

⑱18

pl. Iskusstv

Italyanskaya ul.

most
Belinkovo

⑳20

⑳21

⑳22

ul. Zhukovskovo

2-ya

Mytninskaya ul.

most
Aleksandra
Nevskogo

Narodny
most

Kazanskaya
pl. ⑯16

ulitsa Sadovaya

Griboedova

Konyushennaya ul.

Nevsky Prospekt

Anichkov
most

НЕВСКИЙ ПРОСПЕКТ
ГОСТИНЫЙ ДВОР
Nevsky Prospekt-
Gostiny Dvor Ⓜ

Vladimirsky pr.

ploshchad
Vosstaniya

prospekt Bakunina

Khersonskaya ul.

⑳26

САДОВАЯ-
СЕННАЯ ПЛ.
СПАССКАЯ.
Sadovaya-
Sennaya pl.-
Spasskaya Ⓜ

Sadovaya ul.

Lomonosova

Pushkin-
skaya

Kuznechny per.

Moscow
Ⓜ **Station**

ПЛ. ВОССТАНИЯ
МАЯКОВСКАЯ
pl. Vosstaniya-
Mayakovskaya

㉓23

㉔24

㉕25

Nevsky Prospekt

pl. Aleksandra
Nevskogo

pr. Obukhovsky

㉗27

Sennaya pl.

Gorokhovaya ul.

nab. reki Fontanki

ДОСТОЕВСКАЯ-
ВЛАДИМИРСКАЯ
Dostoyevskaya-
Vladimirskaya Ⓜ

Razezhaya ul.

Marata

Kolomenskaya ul.

ЛИГОВСКИЙ ПРОСПЕКТ
Ligovsky Prospekt Ⓜ

ul. Chernyakhovskovo

ПЛ. АЛЕКСАНДРА НЕВСКОГО
pl. Aleksandra Nevskogo

Obukhovsky
most

Moskovsky prospekt

Zagorodny prospekt

Pionerskaya

ul. Marata

ulitsa Pravdy

ПУШКИНСКАЯ
ЗВЕНИГОРОДСКАЯ
Pushkinskaya-
Zvenigorodskaya Ⓜ

Borovaya ulitsa

ul. K. Zaslonova

Ligovski prospekt

nab. Obvodnovo Kanala

Vitebsky
Station

Tekhnologicheskaya
pl. Ⓜ

ТЕХНОЛОГИЧЕСКИЙ
ИНСТИТУТ
Tekhnologichesky
Institut

Maloddetskoselsky pr.

nab. Obvodnovo Kanala

Kurskaya ulitsa

Tambovskaya ulitsa

Dnepropetrovskaya

ОБВОДНЫЙ КАНАЛ
Obvodny Kanal Ⓜ

㉖26

Common terms and abbreviations	
naberezhnaya/nab......	*Embankment*
most............................	*Bridge*
ploshchad/pl................	*Square* or *plaza*
prospekt/pr..................	*Avenue*
sad..............................	*Garden*
ulitsa/ul......................	*Street*

0   1/2 mi

0   0.5 km

St. Petersburg Metro

Blue
- Parnas
- Prospekt Prosvechnia
- Ozerki
- Udelnaya
- Pionerskaya
- Chernaya Rechka
- Petrogradskaya
- Gorkovskaya

Red
- Devyatkino
- Grazhdansky Prospekt
- Akademicheskaya
- Politekhnicheskaya
- Ploshchad Muzhestva
- Lesnaya
- Vyborgskaya
- Ploshchad Lenina *(Finland RR Station)*
- Chernyshevskaya

Purple
- Komendantskiy Prospekt
- Staraya Derevnya
- Krestovskiy Ostrov
- Chkalovskaya
- Sportivnaya

Green
- Primorskaya
- Vasileostrovskaya

Nevsky Prospekt/ Gostiny Dvor

Mayakovskaya/ Ploshchad Vosstania *(Moscow RR Station)*

Vladimirskaya/ Dostoevskaya

Yellow
Sadovaya/ Sennaya Ploshchad/ Spasskaya

Ligovsky Prospekt

Pushkinskaya/ Zvenigorodskaya *(Vitebsky RR Station)*

Ploshchad Aleksandra Nevskogo I & II

Tekhnologichesky Institut I & II

- Novocherkasskaya

- Baltiskaya *(Warsaw RR Station) (Baltic RR Station)*
- Narvskaya
- Kirovsky Zavod
- Avtovo
- Leninsky Prospekt
- Prospekt Veteranov

Red

- Frunzenskaya
- Moskovskiye Vorota
- Electrosila
- Park Pobedy
- Moscovskaya *(Bus to Airport)*
- Zvezdnaya
- Kupchino

Blue

- Obvodny Kanal
- Volkovskaya

Purple

- Elizarovskaya
- Lomonosovskaya
- Proletarskaya
- Obukhovo
- Rybatskoye

Green

- Ladozhskaya
- Prospekt Bolshevikov
- Ulitsa Dybenko

Yellow

INTERIORS, don't enthrall you. The Pavilion Hall, with mosaic tables and floors, marble fountains, engineering marvels, and a wraparound view, is a favorite for the whole family. The Impressionist and more recent works, including two rooms of early Picassos, are a must-see, though they're in plainer rooms on the third floor, which can be stuffy and crowded in summer. Crowds are thinner in the Antiquities halls on the ground floor, which include relics from early, pre-Slavic tribes as well as riches from the Greeks, Romans, and Egyptians. Italian, Dutch, and Spanish masters are well represented, though Russia's greatest art is housed in the Russian Museum across town. Planning is key to any Hermitage visit, and an online tour can be a great preparation. Mornings tend to be full of Russian school groups except in July and August, which tend to be full of European tour groups. The audioguide is quite helpful, but the official English-speaking guides hovering around the entrance can offer more detail and nuance. Be sure to ask if you can set your own itinerary or if they will show you only specific rooms. It's worth checking the museum website before you go in order to get a sense of what you want to focus on, and to see which halls are closed for renovations. A bank machine and post office are available on the ground floor. Spread around the city are four other parts of the Hermitage Museum complex: the General Staff Building, Menshikov Palace, Winter Palace of Peter the Great, and the Museum of Lomonosov Porcelain Factory. Allow yourself a full morning or afternoon in the Hermitage itself—or a full day, if you can spare it. You won't regret it.

2 Palace Sq. Entrance to Hermitage main collection: through courtyard of Winter Palace, from Palace Sq. © **812/710-9079.** www.hermitagemuseum.org. Admission to Hermitage Museum 400 rubles for adults, free for students and those 16 and under. Free for all individual visitors on the first Thurs of the month. For English tours for up to 5 people by official museum guides call © **812/571-8446.** Admission to other buildings in the Hermitage collection is 300 rubles for each one. Main museum Tues–Sat 10:30am–6pm; Sun and Russian holidays 10:30am–5pm. Ticket office closes 1 hr. before museum closing. Metro: Nevsky Prospekt.

AROUND PALACE SQUARE

The Winter Palace forms just one element of the magnificent architectural ensemble of **Palace Square (Dvortsovaya Ploshchad)** ★★★, the city's most important plaza. Shaped like a truncated piece of pie, this square isn't large by Russian standards, but it is certainly grand. It was not part of Peter's original plan for the city, but grew up over the 18th and 19th centuries to accommodate the Winter Palace and the curved General Staff Headquarters, while opening up at an angle toward the Admiralty and the Neva beyond. It achieves a perfect sense of balance despite its unusual form, and offers a stunning—and intentional—vista of the city's elegant lines from any given point. Its architectural beauty did little to protect it from the city's political upheavals, and the square became a center of fermenting dissent in the century leading up to the Russian Revolution. The unrest culminated in the Bolshevik seizure of the Winter Palace via the square that quashed all hope of retaining aristocratic rule. For decades after the seat of Russian power was moved to Moscow, Palace Square was the staging ground for obligatory displays of Communist solidarity and might—until the end of the Soviet regime saw it again become a forum for antigovernment expression. Politics rarely touch the square today; instead, it fills with in-line skaters and tour buses. For a calmer experience of the square, show up early in the morning. Stand in front of the Alexander Column—a 600-ton monolith topped by a cross-carrying angel, built under Czar Alexander II to celebrate the Russian victory over Napoleon—and imagine all that this square has seen.

The square's chief element after the Winter Palace is the **General Staff Building (Generalny Shtab;** © 812/571-8446). Its facade, bending around the square for nearly half a mile, was designed to enclose several facilities, the army's General Staff Headquarters being just one of them. The czarist-era Ministry of Finance and Foreign Ministry were housed on the left as you look from Palace Square, linked to the General Staff Building by an unusual, three-piece triumphal arch celebrating Russia's victories against Napoleon, Turkey, and Sweden. The Library of the General Staff is

Exploring St. Peter and Paul Fortress

Boathouse of
  Peter the Great **6**
Casemates
  (Gun Openings) **3**
Commandant house **7**
Engineer's yard **9**

Former political prison **1**
Guard House **8**
Kronverkskiye Gates **5**
Nikolskiye Gates **4**
Peter the Great Gates **10**
Turrets **11**

Vasilievskiye Gates **2**
Yoannovskiye Gates **12**

still housed there and is closed to the public; its collection was once considered among the world's best military libraries. The left wing is now part of the Hermitage and houses temporary exhibits. The city hopes to link the buildings with the Winter Palace via an underground passageway, and the Guggenheim Museum hopes to open a St. Petersburg museum in the General Staff Building in the future. The building itself is closed for restoration until 2014, and meanwhile its exhibits are on loan to the Hermitage.

Overlooking Palace Square from a distance to the west is the **Admiralty (Admiralteistvo)** ★★, once a fortified shipyard. It is now a naval academy that sadly is not open to the public. It's such a crucial St. Petersburg monument, however, that it's worth spending a few minutes admiring its 61m-high (200-ft.) spire, topped by a weather vane in the shape of a ship. Stand on the plaza beneath the spire and look toward the city: You're at the nexus of three major avenues—Nevsky Prospekt, Gorokhovaya Ulitsa, and Voznesensky Prospekt—that shoot out from the Admiralty like a trident. This is no accident, and is one example of the city's careful design. The building was one of the first in St. Petersburg, built to feed Peter the Great's dream of making Russia into a naval power.

CATHEDRALS, MONASTERIES & MORE

Alexander Nevsky Monastery and Cemetery (Lavra Aleksandra Nevskogo) ★
The reason most visitors come to this complex is for its two cemeteries, which hold

PETER & PAUL fortress (PETROPAVLOVSKAYA KREPOST)

Reserve a morning or afternoon for a visit to the fortress that overlooks the Neva's busy traffic and was originally meant to serve as the city's nucleus. Although today's St. Petersburg is centered on the south bank of the Neva River, Peter had planned to base it on the north side, and the Peter and Paul Fortress was one of his greatest masterpieces. The citadel occupies small Hare's Island (Zaichy Ostrov) across from the Winter Palace, and contains a notable cathedral, the Museum of City History, a mint, an old printing house, a former political prison, and a long stretch of sandy beach packed with bathers in the summer. **Peter and Paul Cathedral ★★★**, named after the city's patron saints and erected in 1723, was St. Petersburg's first stone church. The spire made the cathedral the city's tallest building until the 20th century. It became the burial place of all Russian czars and their families from Peter's day until the end of the Romanov empire. The remains of Czar Nicholas II and his family, executed by the Bolsheviks in 1918, were moved here in 1997 from the Siberian city where they were killed, after painful debate over whether the remains were authentic. In another cruel chapter from Russia's history, the Trubetskoi Bastion housed political prisoners for centuries, including Peter the Great's son Alexei, Fyodor Dostoyevsky, Leon Trotsky, and Vladimir Lenin's brother.

The fortress can be reached from bridges on either side, though the ticket office is closer to the eastern bridge, just inside the gates on the right. Two highlights are **walking along the fortress's southern walls** (it costs a nominal fee that can be paid as part of a combined ticket at the main ticket desk); and watching (and hearing) the **daily cannon blast** at noon. The city museum is rather disappointing and not enough exhibits are explained in English. In summer the sandbar on the Neva side of the island hosts a sand sculpture competition. In winter ice fishermen camp out on the shore—and a few brave souls plunge into the icy water to cure their ills. On the facing embankment is the small house where Peter lived while building his capital.

The fortress is on **Zaichy Ostrov (Hare's Island; ✆ 812/230-0329;** metro: Gorkovskaya). Entrance to the fortress grounds, which are open daily from 6am to 10pm, is free. A joint admission ticket to the cathedral and all the museums on the grounds costs 600 rubles; 350 rubles students with ID; free for under 16s. Separate admission tickets are 200 rubles for the Cathedral and 150 rubles for each of the museums. The museums and cathedral are open Thursday to Tuesday from 10am to 6pm, apart from the Trubetskoi Bastion that is open every day. The Cathedral is occasionally closed for religious ceremonies, so check ahead.

the remains of some of Russia's leading cultural figures, whose gravestones are works of art themselves, often reflecting the trade of those buried beneath. The monastery was built in 1710, named by Peter after the 13th-century Grand Duke Alexander Nevsky, who defeated the Swedes in a decisive 1240 battle. Nevsky's remains were brought here; his grave was later joined by those of Dostoyevsky and Tchaikovsky; fellow composers Rimsky-Korsakov, Glinka, and Mussorgsky; the architects of St. Petersburg's key monuments; and the brilliant and remarkable founder of Russia's first universities, Mikhail Lomonosov. Cross the bridge over tiny Chornaya Stream to the central monastery courtyard, before you visit the incongruously cheerful Church of the Annunciation. The churches here are more baroque and neoclassical than the medieval monasteries in Moscow. The ticket desk is just inside the arched entrance; ask for a map of the cemeteries. Allow at least an hour and a half to see the grounds and Lazarus and Tikhvin cemeteries (also known as the Cemetery of Masters of Art).

1 Naberezhnya Reki Monastirka. © **812/274-1702.** www.lavra.spb.ru. Free admission. Grounds daily 5:30am–11pm. Cathedrals daily 6am–8pm (9pm in summer). Metro: Ploshchad Alexandra Nevskogo.

Buddhist Temple (Budisky Khram)   The red portico of this temple immediately catches your eye as you drive along the otherwise nondescript avenue. At once eastern and western, it is a blend of Tibetan Buddhist features and Russian Art Nouveau, built in 1909. Construction was led by Czar Nicholas II's personal doctor, a Buddhist, who rallied funds from open-minded sponsors in Russia and even from the Dalai Lama. It has enjoyed renewed attention in Russia in recent years thanks to the eclectic Russian rock legend Boris Grebenshchikov, a devout visitor. It's now run by monks from Buryatia, one of Russia's primarily Buddhist republics, near Lake Baikal. Inside, the red-and-yellow prayer hall and smell of incense transport you far from 21st-century St. Petersburg.

91 Primorsky Prospekt. © **812/430-9740.** Free admission. Daily 10am–7pm; services at 10am and 5pm. Metro: Staraya Derewnia.

Chesma Cathedral and Monastery   This Gothic, candy-cane cathedral is worth a visit only if you're already in the neighborhood around Victory Park (Park Pobedy), since it's well south of the city center. Architecture buffs will be fascinated by the cathedral's pink-and-white vertical stripes and unusual column construction. The monastery across the street is now an aviation construction institute, where students perform lab work in the former monks' cells. The church was abandoned in Soviet times, and children climbed through broken stained glass to romp through its chapels. It's now a functioning church once again.

12 Lensoveta St. © **812/373-6114.** Free admission. Daily 9am–7pm.

Church of the Savior on the Spilled Blood (Tserkov Spasitelya Na Krovi) ★ St. Petersburg's most-photographed church, this cathedral is a mountain of blindingly bright, beveled domes topped by glistening gold crosses. Its architects sought to revive medieval Russian architectural styles, but the cathedral's bold cheeriness lacks the brooding mysticism of similar churches in Moscow, instead reflecting the renewed nationalism and material prosperity of late-19th-century Russia. It was built on the site where Czar Alexander II was assassinated in 1881, prompting residents to come up with the Spilled Blood reference. Its official name is Church of the Resurrection of Christ. Alexander II was the forward-thinking czar who finally freed Russia's serfs in 1861, but he grew conservative in his later years and was targeted by a group of revolutionaries demanding more reform. The church's interior mosaics were created by Russia's top artists of the day, including Art Nouveau master Mikhail Vrubel.

2b Naberezhnya Kanala Griboyedova (embankment of the Griboyedov Canal). © **812/315-1636.** Admission 250 rubles adults, 150 rubles students with ID, free for children 7 and under. Audio guide in English 100 rubles. Daily 10am–6pm; Thurs–Tues also evening opening 6:15–10pm, 350 rubles for all. Metro: Nevsky Prospekt or Gostiny Dvor.

Kazan Cathedral (Kazansky Sobor) ★★   This prominent landmark on Nevsky Prospekt is an example of nontraditional Russian Orthodox architecture adapted to

It was always known in advance when the students would riot in front of Kazansky Cathedral. Every family had its student informer. The result was that these riots were attended—at a respectful distance to be sure—*by a great mass of people.*

–Osip Mandelstam, St. Petersburg poet and author who fell victim to Stalin's secret police

13

EXPLORING ST. PETERSBURG

Cathedrals, Monasteries & More

satisfy church tradition. To fit with the city's careful design, the cathedral's columned, curved facade faces Nevsky—but Orthodox custom requires that the nave run east–west, so the entrance to the cathedral is actually around the side. Completed in 1811, the cathedral was partly inspired by St. Peter's Basilica in Rome. Its centered single dome, horizontal line, and gray color scheme have little in common with the more vibrant, vertical cathedrals typical of previous centuries. The cathedral was named after the icon of Our Lady of Kazan, whose intriguing tale is the first item in church brochures. For more than 60 years it housed the State Museum of Atheism and Religion, and for a while in the 1990s it managed to be simultaneously a functioning church and a museum to godlessness. The museum has since moved and dropped the "Atheism" from its name.

2 Kazanskaya Ploshchad. ℂ **812/318-4528.** www.kazansky-spb.ru. Free admission. Mon–Sat 9am–8pm. Services every day at 10am and 6pm. Metro: Nevsky Prospekt.

St. Isaac's Cathedral (Isaakevsky Sobor) ★★ St. Isaac's mighty, somber facade rose only in the mid–19th century but has become an indelible part of St. Petersburg's skyline since then. Critics of the day called it "The Inkwell" because of its boxy shape topped by a single enormous gray dome, in contrast to the multilayered and multicolored domes and towers of most Orthodox churches. Its massive hall can accommodate 14,000 people, though it probably never has. More popular with tourists than believers, the church earned residents' respect during World War II, when it endured Nazi shelling and its grounds were planted with cabbage to help residents survive the 900-day Nazi blockade. Its interior is as awesome as its exterior, with columns made of single chunks of granite, malachite, and lazurite; floors of different-colored marble; and never-ending frescoes. If the viewing balcony around the dome is open, it's well worth a climb for the view of the city and of the cathedral from on high. However, ticket prices for this activity are rising at an alarming pace. Allow an hour, more if you visit the balcony.

Isaakevskaya Ploshchad. ℂ **812/315-9732.** www.cathedral.ru. Admission 250 rubles adults, 150 students with ID and children 8 and older. To climb colonnade, an additional 150 rubles adults, 100 rubles students and children. Audioguide 100 rubles. Thurs–Tues 10am–7pm (closed Wed); colonnade closes 6pm. Metro: Nevsky Prospekt.

St. Petersburg Mosque (Mechet) Built in 1910, the mosque's enormous blue-tiled roof was modeled after the striking complex of tiled buildings in Samarkand, Uzbekistan, housing the mausoleum of medieval Muslim conqueror and thinker Tamerlane. The mosque was a gift to St. Petersburg from the emir of the Silk Road city of Bukhara, then part of the Russian empire. Closed down by the Bolsheviks, it was used as a medical equipment warehouse during World War II. It was the largest mosque in the Soviet Muslim world—even larger than the Uzbek ones it emulated—

and is still a major symbol for Russia's 20 million–plus Muslims. Its gray granite walls contrast vividly with the sky-blue mosaics covering the dome and minarets. Inside, columns of green marble break up the vast prayer spaces.

Kamennoostrovsky Prospekt. © **812/233-9819.** Free admission. Daily 10am-6pm, daily services at 2:30pm, with major service on Fri. Metro: Gorkovskaya.

Smolny Cathedral and Convent (Smolny Sobor) ★ You're unlikely to wander past the vibrant robin's-egg blue walls of the Smolny complex, because of its distant location in a barren district tucked in a curve in the Neva. But it's worth a visit if you have a guide who can interpret its architecture and history, or if you can attend one of its organ and chamber music concerts. The convent was originally designed in the 18th century for Peter the Great's daughter Elizabeth, but she later abandoned her plans for monastic life and became empress after a palace coup. It is one of the masterpieces of Italian architect Bartolomeo Rastrelli, also responsible for the Winter Palace. Unfortunately, most of the grounds are closed to the public (having been converted into insurance offices and city government annexes) or under renovation. Allow a couple of hours if you have a guide.

3/1 Ploshchad Rastrelli. © **812/710-3159.** Admission 150 rubles, 100 rubles students and children 7 and over. Bell tower 100 rubles. Oct-Apr Thurs-Tues 11am-5pm; May-Sept daily 10am-6pm. Concert tickets available at cathedral ticket office. Metro: Kropotkinskaya.

Synagogue (Sinagoga) This Moorish temple was consecrated in 1893, during a lull in the pogroms that were decimating Jewish populations elsewhere in Russia. Even more remarkable than its construction was its survival throughout the next century, when atheist (and anti-Semitic) Soviet leaders razed cathedrals and other architectural monuments with impunity. The dome and corkscrew-like towers are covered with handmade carvings. Services are held in the red-brick Small Synagogue (Malaya Sinagoga). The Grand Synagogue (Bolshaya Sinagoga) is reserved for festivals, but through the doors you can see its yellow-and-white interior. It's located in a neighborhood behind the Mariinsky Theater called Kolomna, which housed many prominent Jewish families at the turn of the 20th century. Only the most highly educated and professionally trained Jews were allowed to live in St. Petersburg during that period; the rest were banished to the Pale of Settlement, a zone stretching from Poland to western Russia. If you visit, skullcaps are required for men, and are available at the shop at the entrance.

2 Lermontovsky Prospekt. © **812/713-8186.** Free admission. Sun-Thurs 10am-7pm; Fri 10am-6pm, services at 10am. Closed on Jewish holidays. Metro: Sadovaya.

MAJOR MUSEUMS

Blockade Museums Two exhibits, both of them eye-opening and tear-jerking, trace the city's experience enduring 900 days of siege and isolation by Nazi forces from 1941 to 1944 (see the box "The Siege of Leningrad" earlier in this chapter). Try to squeeze in an hour-long visit to one of these sobering museums. The **Memorial Museum of the Leningrad Siege** ★ is the more commonly visited, hosting tour groups in the afternoons and Russian school groups in the mornings. The small two-story museum gets crowded leading up to Victory Day on May 9, when Russians celebrate the victory over Nazism. Less frequented but no less impressive is **"Leningrad During the Great Patriotic War"** ★★, a permanent exhibit at the **St.**

Petersburg History Museum in a riverside mansion. The hall of children's photos and diaries is especially moving. The exhibits aren't marked in English, but each room has a panel in English describing its contents. The last hall shows a video in English and Russian about the blockade, with plenty of chairs to rest in while you watch. Exhibits include posters for Shostakovich's Seventh Symphony, composed and first performed during the siege; a chronicle of the Road of Life; and a metronome that played on Leningrad radio during the blockade, its speed indicating the level of danger of shelling on a given day. Both exhibits gloss over Stalin's role in exacerbating the city's struggle and the country's wartime losses, but even the Soviet propaganda doesn't overshadow the very real horrors presented by the museums. For an even more powerful but less intimate way to remember the blockade victims, see the Piskarevo Cemetery review in the "Monuments, Memorials & Squares" section below.

Memorial Museum of Leningrad Blockade. 9 Solyanoi Pereulok.(℃ **812/275-7208.** Admission 80 rubles adults, 30 rubles students and children 8 and over. Thurs–Tues 10am–4pm. Closed last Thurs of each month. St. Petersburg History Museum. 3 Petropavlovskaya Krepost.(℃ **812/230-6431.** Admission 150 rubles, 40 rubles students and children 8 and over. Thurs–Tues 10am–5pm. Closed last Thurs of every month. Metro: Sportivnaya.

Kunstkamera ☺

Officially called the Peter the Great Museum of Anthropology and Ethnography, this museum was created back in Peter's day to study the human body and fight superstition rampant in 18th-century Russia. The 300-year-old building itself is in a rather sorry state, with its stone staircases uneven from wear, and moldings flaking off. The real reason people visit is the repulsion and attraction of its "naturalia" collection of anatomical specimens, including deformed animals, bottled human body parts, and diseased babies preserved in jars for nearly 300 years. This is not for those with weak stomachs, or for very young or sensitive children (older ones love the gross-out factor of the exhibits). It was aimed at advancing Peter's fascination with modern science, which struck horror in most Russians at the time. Many of today's scientists credit Peter with laying the groundwork for the institutions that later produced Dmitry Mendeleyev (creator of chemistry's periodic table) and the Nobel Prize–winning scientists of the 20th century. The museum also holds a collection of coins and artifacts from around the globe, which were more remarkable when Russia remained largely cut off from the rest of the world, but are still impressive for their variety.

3 Universitetskaya Naberezhnaya (entrance from Tamozhenny Pereulok). (℃ **812/328-0812.** www. kunstkamera.ru. Admission 200 rubles adults, 50 rubles students and children 8 and over. Tues–Sun 11am–6pm (until 7pm June–Aug). Closed last Tues of every month. Metro: Vasileostrovskaya.

Museum of Arctic and Antarctic (Muzei Arktiki I Antarktiki)   This curious collection of artifacts brought back from polar expeditions is not for everyone, but if you're fascinated by snow, northern cultures, or geology, stop in. It's also a nice way to cool off (at least mentally) on a hot afternoon. It's only logical that Russia, whose northern border spans much of the Arctic, would have a museum dedicated to the Far North—especially now that it's jockeying for authority over the region's oil reserves. The Antarctic exhibits were added after a series of Soviet-era expeditions there. Housed in an early-19th-century church, the museum has a dome inlaid with a mosaic map of Antarctica engraved with the Soviet-sounding phrase CONTINENT OF PEACE AND FRIENDSHIP. The English-language brochures are good but not free. Canadians in particular seem to appreciate this museum. Allow an hour.

24a Ulitsa Marata. ✆**812/571-2549.** www.polarmuseum.sp.ru. Admission 150 rubles adults, 50 rubles students and children 8 and over. Wed–Sat 10am–6pm. Sun 10am–5pm. Closed last Fri of the month. Metro: Dostoyevskaya.

Museum of Musical Instruments (in the Sheremetev Palace) ☺ If you play a musical instrument and have a free hour or so, this museum is a fun opportunity to discover inventive ways Russians and others have made music over the centuries. If you're lucky, one of the museum guides will let you use the computer program that reproduces the sounds of the museum's instruments. One of Tchaikovsky's pianos stands in a second-floor hall packed with harpsichords, early mechanical pianos, and spinets. Note the elegant display of the evolution of harp design from the 16th to the 20th century, and the Arctic tribal instruments. Children with some knowledge of music will enjoy the quirkier exhibits, such as the glass harmonica on the first floor, a piano-size contraption of glass cups stacked horizontally and played with wet hands to produce an airy, wind instrument sound. The museum's setting, the resplendent 18th-century Sheremetev Palace by architect Savva Chevakinsky, is part of the reason to visit.

34 Naberezhnaya Fontanka. ✆**812/272-4441.** Admission 250 rubles adults, 30 rubles students and children 8 and over. Audioguide 100 rubles. Wed–Sun noon–6pm. Closed last Wed of each month. Metro: Mayakovskaya.

Pushkinskaya 10 ★ Anyone interested in modern art, experimental performance, or alternative music should visit this art complex. It calls itself a "non-museum;" its galleries showcase artists who use a wide variety of media, and its performance spaces host lectures, "sound experiments," and other hard-to-define modern cultural events. See the website for listings. The alley leading up to it is covered in graffiti, mostly of questionable artistic merit, but past the dodgy courtyard, the art center is a haven of creativity. The gift shop is a good source of unusual gifts.

10 Pushkinskaya Ulitsa (entrance from 53 Ligovsky Prospekt, through the arch). ✆**812/764-5371.** www.en.p-10.ru. Admission varies with exhibit or performance. Galleries and museum Wed–Sun 3-7pm. Metro: Ploschad Vosstaniya.

Russian Museum (Russky Muzei) ★★★ This museum should be on every visitor's itinerary, even those who know or care little about Russian art, despite its hefty admission fee. It's as much an introduction to Russian history, attitudes, and vision as it is a display of artistic styles. Housing 32,000 artworks from the 12th to the 20th century, the museum is best viewed with a tour guide or by using the English-language audioguide to ensure that you get the most out of its collection before you drop from exhaustion. The most popular rooms are in the Benois Wing, where works by Avante-Garde artists Malevich and Kandinsky attract international crowds. Chronologically, they're at the end of the exhibit, so save time and energy if you want to see them. The Old Russian Wing deserves a good look, too, offering perspective on the evolution of Orthodox icon painting that helps you better appreciate any cathedrals you visit later. The rural scenes of Russian village life by Alexei Venetsianov and the soothing forestscapes of Ivan Shishkin, both on the ground floor, are often unfairly overlooked. Note the Art Nouveau paintings and sketches of set designs for Diaghilev's Ballet Russe. Take a few moments to appreciate the museum's exterior before you go in. It was built in the 1820s for the brother of Czar Alexander I and Czar Nicholas I, Grand Duke Mikhail. The museum owes many of its riches to private collections seized by the Soviets, or "volunteered" by wealthy collectors hoping to avoid persecution. Allow at least 2 hours, more if you have an enthusiastic guide.

4/2 Inzhenernaya Ulitsa. ✆ **812/595-4248.** www.rusmuseum.ru. Admission 350 rubles adults, 150 rubles students with ID and children aged 7 to 16, free for children 6 and under. Permission for photographs or videos 250 rubles. English-language tour for up to 5 with official museum guide 1,500 rubles plus entrance fee. Combined ticket including exhibits in the Marble Palace, Stroganoff Palace, and St. Michael's Castle 600 rubles adults, 300 rubles students and children aged 7-16. Wed-Mon 10am-5pm (closed Tues). Metro: Gostiny Dvor or Nevsky Prospekt.

PARKS & GARDENS

Summer Gardens (Letny Sad) ★★   This is the place to rest on a bench after a day of visiting museums, or to escape from the crush of city sidewalks—or to imagine how Peter the Great spent his summer afternoons. The lush greenery (at least for a few months of the year) almost makes you forget that these gardens were entirely planned, designed for Peter's pleasure walks and adhering to the city's rules of classicism. Peter brought in marble Renaissance-era statues from Italy to give the park a more European feel. He and his successors threw grand receptions here with dancing, drinking, and fireworks under the endless sun of the White Nights. The statues and fountains serve as landmarks in case you get disoriented. The shrubbery was once carefully trimmed but now its groomers allow trees to take on more abundant forms. The Summer Palace is open to visitors, its rooms re-created as they would have been in Peter's time. The small two-story building was not heated, so it was a summer treat. Glance inside the Coffee House and the Tea House, too. The park closes for a few weeks in spring, usually in April, for a "drying out" period as the slush melts.

Entrance from Kutuzov Embankment (Naberezhnya Kutuzova) or Panteleimon Bridge (Panteleimonovsky Most). Park daily 10am-8pm; admission charged during festivals. Summer Palace Wed-Sun 10am-6pm. Tickets 350 rubles adults, 150 rubles children 8 and up. Metro: Gostiny Dvor or Gorkovskaya.

Taurida Gardens (Tavrichesky Sad)☺   This park is gradually returning to its past splendor, when its ponds were thronged with boaters, and aristocratic families strolled its winding lanes and rolling hills. Now it's one of the few good places to take kids near the city center, with a skating rink and sledding slopes in winter, a carousel and other rides, and plenty of woodland to frolic in. Some of the grounds are in disrepair, with chipped alleys and rusted fences. The park, originally a private garden for Catherine the Great's adviser and lover Grigory Potemkin, reflects Catherine's informal landscaping style, in contrast to the rigidity of Peter's Summer Gardens. The gardens host open-air jazz festivals during the White Nights and other concerts throughout the summer.

2 Ulitsa Potemkinskaya. Daily 7am-10pm. Metro: Chernyshevskaya.

Victory Park (Park Pobedy)☺   Built to celebrate the victory over Nazi Germany in World War II, this extensive city park is far from the city center but has its own metro stop. If you're staying nearby or are traveling with children, it's worth a visit. It suffers from the forced triumphal feeling of many Soviet parks, but if you ignore the massive monuments, the many outdoor attractions make it feel human-sized again. Its ponds offer skating and sledding in winter, and boating and water bikes in summer (though they're rather rickety). Elsewhere you can find tennis courts, flower gardens,

island PURSUITS

For a taste of nature within St. Petersburg that few foreign tourists seem to know about, venture out to the three island-parks north of the Neva. The nobility used them for outdoor pursuits in the 18th century, but they were opened to the proletariat in the 20th. Today Russians of all classes wander their peaceful paths.

The most pleasant of the three is **Yelagin Island (Yelaginsky Ostrov)**, officially named the Central Park of Culture and Rest (entrance 100 rubles for adults, 50 rubles for children). Stroll its traffic-free, oak- and chestnut-lined roads, float in a canoe on its boating ponds, and tour its classical royal palace. Yelagin Palace, built in 1812, was the first major building by Carlo Rossi, who later left his mark on much of the city. Note the patterned parquet floors and mahogany doors with gilded fittings. **Yelagin Palace Museum** (© 812/430-1130) is open Wednesday through Sunday from 10am to 5pm. Watching the sun set on the far west end of the island, over the Gulf of Finland, is an honored tradition, though it's a long walk. Several rides and other attractions for children are available, some sturdier than others. To get to Yelagin Island, head to metro station Krestovsky Ostrov, then walk over one of the footbridges or take bus no. 411 or no. 416 to the end of the line.

Kamenny Island (Kamenny Ostrov) became a private refuge of the nobility soon after it was forcibly relocated to Peter the Great's new capital in the 1700s. Catherine the Great bought it for her son at one point, and commissioned a palace for him on its eastern point. The neoclassical **Kamennoostrovsky Palace** is now a veterans' hospital that is largely off-limits to visitors. The west side of the island is more accessible and once housed the summer mansions of the aristocracy, and later the Soviet elite (particularly top KGB generals). It now is home to Russia's nouveau riche. Seeking security, they've built fences so high that the elaborate homes are not visible to outsiders. A few of the older homes are still visible and worth admiring. The main pursuit here, however, is wandering the tranquil, wooded roads. This can be combined with a visit to one of the other islands. To get to Kamenny Island, get off at the Chernaya Rechka metro station and walk south across the river (about 10 min.).

Krestovsky Island (Krestovsky Ostrov) is the largest and least romantic of the three. It's more a sporting center, with tennis courts, yacht clubs, and enormous Krestovsky Stadium. Seaside Victory Park (Primorsky Park Pobedy) was planted by survivors of the World War II siege of Leningrad in memory of those who died, and in celebration of the victory over the Nazis. Two popular restaurants are boosting the island's reputation—Russkaya Rybalka (p. 218) and the German-style beer hall Karl I Friedrich—though they're hard to reach without a car. To get to the island, take the metro to Krestovsky Ostrov. Most of the sights are west of there, reachable on foot or by bus no. 134 from the metro.

and an amusement park. On a sobering note, the park was built on the site of a brick factory whose ovens were used to burn corpses of victims of the 900-day Nazi siege.

Moskovsky Prospekt. Daily 10am–9pm. Free admission to park, with small charge for park rides. Metro: Park Pobedy.

MONUMENTS, MEMORIALS & SQUARES

St. Petersburg is full of unforgettable architectural moments, if you take a minute—or 15—to stop and look around. Of the city's chief monuments, at the top on your list should be the **Bronze Horseman (Medny Vsadnik)** ★★. This most famous of St.

> ### Impressions
>
> *Behind him, to the darkness wedded,*
> *Lit by the moon's pale ray and slight,*
> *One hand in warning raised, the dreaded*
> *Bronze Horseman galloped through the night.*
>
> —Alexander Pushkin,
> *The Bronze Horseman,* 1833

Petersburg's monuments is best viewed from a boat in the Neva River, where you can feel the ferocity of Peter the Great and his stallion rising above you and the city he created. It's worth visiting on foot, too, to enjoy a walk through Decembrists' Square and watch newlyweds pay their respects to the city's founder. Commissioned by Catherine the Great in honor of her grandfather-in-law and designed by French sculptor Etienne Falconet, the monument was unveiled in 1782. It depicts Peter in control of his wild steed (representing Russia), his hand reaching out over his masterpiece of a metropolis. The rearing horse is perched on a wavelike chunk of granite, its hoof stepping on the snake of Treason. The monument took on a deeper and more sinister significance for St. Petersburg residents after Pushkin's epic poem "The Bronze Horseman," in which the unfortunate protagonist imagines the statue coming to life and pursuing him.

Pushkin himself is the subject of another monument, at the center of the **Square of the Arts (Ploshchad Isskustv)** ★★. The square is the real architectural masterpiece here, forming a nucleus of cultural institutions, while the Pushkin statue, built in 1957, is little more than a landmark. Originally designed by Carlo Rossi, an Italian-Russian architect, the square acquired many of its buildings in later years, but they all adhered to his original vision. Take a moment on one of its benches to appreciate its lines, and then walk around the square to take in Mikhailovsky Palace (now the Russian Museum), the Ethnography Museum delicately and elegantly added later, the Mussorgsky Theater, the Operetta Theater, and the Philharmonic. The closest metro stop is Gostiny Dvor.

Ostrovsky Square (Ploshchad Ostrovskogo) ★ rests at the heart of another of St. Petersburg's impressively planned districts, and is an ideal spot at which to rest your feet after exploring Nevsky. The square separates Pushkin Theater from Nevsky Prospekt, allowing the theater to line up and incorporate with Lomonosov Square on the Fontanka River beyond. The square, designed by the ever-present Italian Carlo Rossi, centers around a statue of Catherine the Great, represented at her most elegant and regal. The base of the statue is carved with Catherine's advisers, envoys, and consorts, some silly enough to be caricatures. Look behind the Pushkin Theater at **Rossi Street (Ulitsa Zodchego Rossi)**, an example of St. Petersburg's relentless sense of proportion: It is 22m (72 ft.) wide and 220m (722 ft.) long, and it's flanked by matching buildings 22m (72 ft.) tall.

Anyone interested in naval history or ship construction should visit the **Cruiser Avrora,** moored on the embankment on the Petrograd side across from the St.

Petersburg Hotel. The cruiser, built in 1897, took part in the Russo-Japanese war of 1905. It has been a city landmark since the Russian Revolution, when the ship bellowed out a blank shot to announce the Bolshevik storming of the Winter Palace in 1917. It's now a free public museum and training ground for cadets. In Soviet times the city's Pioneers, a sort of Communist Boy Scouts (and Girl Scouts), were brought here for their swearing-in ceremonies. The exhibits are mostly in Russian, but the cadets speak some English and can serve as informal tour guides. The decks are a bit treacherous in icy weather and the stairs are quite steep. Spend half an hour here before continuing along the embankment for more ship-gazing. Admission is free. The cruiser is open Wednesday to Sunday 10:30am to 4pm (metro: Gorkovskaya).

In sharp contrast to the reverent, almost decadent monuments in the center of town is **Piskarevo Park and Memorial Cemetery (Prospekt Nepokorionnikh)** ★, open daily sunrise to sunset. The mass graves in this vast and somber park hold the bodies of about half a million people who died during the 900-day Nazi siege of Leningrad during World War II. Most were civilians who died of cold, starvation, and disease. St. Petersburg residents, nearly all of whom have a relative who perished during the blockade, come here regularly to lay flowers and remember. It's far from the center and most tourist sights, but several tours include a stop here. The long central alley leads to a Soviet-style statue of a grieving woman representing the Motherland, and the rest of the graves are uniform and extend far into the park. An exhibit of photographs and documents related to the siege is housed in a pavilion; for a fuller story, visit the St. Petersburg History Museum's blockade exhibit (see description earlier in this chapter). It's far from public transport, so take a taxi if you're on your own. Allow 2 hours with transport time.

LITERARY ST. PETERSBURG

Anna Akhmatova Museum ★★ One of St. Petersburg's most eloquent and prolific chroniclers, Akhmatova watched her city survive revolution, civil war, political terror, and world war. From the 1920s to the 1950s, she lived in this apartment in the "Fountain House" (Fontanny Dom), a former palace with a history as troubled as her own. The four-room museum is rich in detail despite its small size, and English-language printouts in each room provide the depth and context you need to make this a worthwhile visit. The audioguide provides more ambience but not much more information. The museum is hard to find: Enter through the arch on Liteiny Prospekt and head for the small park; turn left and head to the apartment entrance at the southwest corner of the park. Akhmatova struggled here to write freely under the budding Soviet state while avoiding arrest. From here she prepared the care packages she sent to her son when he was imprisoned for political reasons, some of which are on display.

Her tangled love triangle with Nikolai Punin and his wife played itself out here, with all three sharing the apartment at one point. The most vivid part of the museum is the photo album through which visitors can leaf, showing Akhmatova and her family growing up through the turbulence of early-20th-century Russia. The building, which once belonged to the family of Count Sheremetev, was transferred to the state after the revolution. It became an Arctic research institute, and though some residents were allowed to continue living here, they could enter only with special ID cards. Akhmatova's is shown here, with the renowned poet's profession listed simply as "resident." Allow an hour for the visit.

53 Liteiny Prospekt. © **812/579-7239.** www.akhmatova.spb.ru. Admission 200 rubles adults and children 8 and over. English-language audioguide 100 rubles. Closed Mondays. Tues 10:30am–6:30pm. Weds 1–9pm. Thurs–Sun 10:30am–6:30pm. Last entrance 1 hr. before closing. Metro: Mayakovskaya.

Dostoyevsky House Museum ★   Fyodor Dostoyevsky's native city, which obsessed and oppressed him, was a central theme in his work; it's only logical to honor him by visiting one of the houses where he lived. This corner house in a gentrifying neighborhood is one of the best-displayed and most tourist-friendly of the city's many house museums. This is because Dostoyevsky is perhaps the most world-famous of the legions of poets and writers who sprang from the intellectual and political ferment of 19th-century St. Petersburg, even if Alexander Pushkin is more fondly admired within Russia. For followers of the desperate characters of *Crime and Punishment* and *Notes From Underground*, Dostoyevsky's house may seem unusually middle-class and almost cheery. Closer examination reveals signs of the ups and downs that beset the writer throughout his career, from debts to imprisonment for revolutionary activity. After finishing the *Brothers Karamazov* in his study, with his wife Anna's unwavering assistance, Dostoyevsky died here of lung disease. In an unsettling reference to his demise, the exhibit includes cigarettes that he rolled himself. A note from one of his sons slid under the door while the author was at work strikes a chord with any busy parent: "Daddy, give me a candy. –Fedya." Take advantage of the English-language audioguide, which lasts about an hour.

> ## Impressions
>
> *I make no claim
> on this illustrious house,
> But it has turned out that almost
> all my life
> I have spent under the notable roof
> Of the Fontanka Palace . . . I destitute
> Came and destitute leave . . .*
> —Anna Akhmatova, *Sochineniye v Dvukh Tomakh (Works in Two Volumes)*

5/2 Kuznechny Pereulok. © **812/571-4031.** Admission 160 rubles adults, 80 rubles students and children 8 and over. Audioguides in English 100 rubles. Tues–Sun 11am–5:30pm. Closed last Wed of the month. Metro: Dostoyevskaya.

Nabokov Museum ★   Vladimir Nabokov lived here from his birth in 1899 to 1917, when he fled the revolution with his family, first for Crimea and ultimately for the United States. The museum is a small but revealing look at the man who produced some of the 20th century's most searing, daring works (and not just *Lolita*). The family once occupied all three floors of this neoclassical building, but now their remaining belongings are crowded into the ground floor (the upper floors host a local newspaper office). Exhibits include some of Nabokov's first poems, penned in his school years, and notes or gifts from family visitors such as H. G. Wells.

47 Bolshaya Morskaya Ulitsa. © **812/315-4713.** Admission free. 100 rubles to take photos or video. Tues–Fri 11am–6pm; Sat–Sun noon–5pm.

ESPECIALLY FOR KIDS

St. Petersburg doesn't seem like a child-friendly place at first, with its business-oriented service industry and surfeit of strip clubs and casinos, but a little perseverance can make your child's visit unforgettable. Russia's world-famous **circus** traditions wow children and adults alike, particularly the acrobatics, though anyone sensitive to animal rights should probably stay away. **St. Petersburg Circus** (Tsirk; © 812/314-8478) performs at 3 Naberezhnya Fontanki (Fontanka Embankment). Tickets cost 400 to 2,000 rubles. The closest metro station is Gostiny Dvor. Performances are at 3 and 7pm, ticket office open 11am to 7pm.

St. Petersburg Zoo, 1 Alexandrovsky Park (© **812/232-8260;** metro: Gorkovskaya), is a perennial child-pleaser, though it's in need of an upgrade. It costs 350 rubles for adults, 100 for children over 6, 50 rubles for children under 6, and is open Tuesday through Sunday from 10am to 9pm.

Boat rides along the Neva River or the city's canals (see "Organized Tours" below), or simply boat-watching along the embankment, are good ways to give kids a sense of the city's marine geography and history. The **Peterhof** palace and grounds (p. 270) are well worth the journey if you're with kids and it's summertime. They can play in the musical fountains, explore the grotto beneath the main cascade, and clamber through the extensive park. For older kids with an interest in science or just in being grossed out, visit the **Kunstkamera** (reviewed earlier in this chapter), with its bottled body parts. **Victory Park's** many attractions include a Ferris wheel and other rides, though some are in sorry repair. Victory Park and **Taurida Gardens** (both covered earlier in this chapter) also offer skating rinks in winter and paddle boats in summer.

ORGANIZED TOURS

The best tours of St. Petersburg are those done by **boat.** The smaller boats that cruise the canals give a closer view of the city's insides than the ferries that go up and down the Neva River. The ferries and hydrofoils are the ideal mode of transport to visit out-of-town sights such as **Peterhof** and **Pushkin/Tsarskoye Selo** (see chapter 16 for details). Water cruises are of course available only when the city's waterways aren't iced over, roughly May through October. You can pick up a canal tour on Griboyedov Canal just north of Nevsky Prospekt, and on the Fontanka River just north of Nevsky Prospekt; prices run 100 to 200 rubles for a 1-hour tour. River cruises to Peterhof and along the Neva and Finnish Gulf start from the embankment in front of the Winter Palace. The **Vodokhod** company (Dvortsovaya Naberezhnaya; © **812/740-5885;** www.vodohod.com) is cheaper, but **Russian Cruises** (Nevsky Prospekt 51; © **812/ 325-3341;** www.russian-cruises.ru) offers more enthusiastic service and English-speaking staff. Most companies offer a special White Nights tour in late evening during June and July.

English-language tours of museums or other city sights are often organized by the hotels. Companies to seek out for individual or group tours are **Davranov Travel,** which runs bus trips to the key sights out of town and offers several museum tours

(17 Italianskaya Ulitsa; ✆ **812/312-4662;** www.davranovtravel.ru); and **Eclectica,** offering tours of the city and outskirts (44 Nevsky Prospekt; ✆ **812/610-0540;** www.eclectica-guide.ru).

OUTDOOR PURSUITS

See the "Parks & Gardens" section earlier in this chapter for more suggestions.

Biking

Biking is a daring undertaking anywhere in Russia, where drivers are unaccustomed to sharing the road with nonmotorized vehicles and bike paths are nonexistent. Half the year the roads are too slushy or icy for pleasant biking, but in summer, a cruise along any one of the city's embankments is delightful for experienced bikers. Try **Skatprokat** (7 Goncharnaya Ulitsa, inside the Kitsport store; ✆ **812/717-6838;** www.skatprokat.ru). Bikes are available from 500 rubles per day; bike tours are also available.

Boating

This is a city of canals and rivers, and in the months when they're not iced over they offer a variety of boating options. See "Organized Tours," above. Numerous private boats also ply the canals, offering rides for groups from 2 to 10 people. Rates are negotiable and vary widely, from about $25 to $125 an hour, usually set in dollars or euros, so it's worth your while to bargain or find a Russian speaker to help out. Safety features are generally good in the big tourist ferries and hydrofoils, but they can be negligible in the smaller boats.

Fishing

Ice fishing is the sport of choice for Russian men of a certain age and temperament in the winter. You can catch a glimpse of them sitting motionless on the Gulf of Finland. Unless you have lots of ice fishing experience, this is a better spectator sport than participatory one.

Gyms

St. Petersburg is just catching on to the gym concept, and only the biggest hotels have a Western-style health club. If your hotel doesn't, **Planeta Fitness** is a Russian chain with branches around town offering daily passes (✆ **812/315-7175;** www.fitness. ru); day passes start from 600 rubles.

Ice-Skating

Russian children often skate before they can read. Watching a determined grandfather guide his grandkids along an icy pond in the winter can be just as fun as watching a big tournament. Any pond turns into an informal rink during the freezing season. Victory Park and Taurida Gardens (both covered earlier in this chapter) have real rinks as well, and rent basic skates.

Jogging

A White Nights jog along the Neva River is an unforgettable experience—but your feet may never forgive you. St. Petersburg's stone streets, treacherously crooked and cracked sidewalks, and drivers unused to dodging speedy pedestrians make jogging a challenge. Your best bet is to hit the larger parks, such as Victory Park; even the smaller parks closer to the center of town such as Taurida Gardens or Summer Gardens can make for pleasant runs. Running during daylight hours is recommended, which is not a problem during the long days of spring and summer. Russians are not big on casual jogging, viewing it as the domain of athletes and not amateurs, so be prepared for perplexed looks.

Paragliding

For thrill-seekers, tandem paragliding flights are available at the Uglovo airfield for a bargain 1,300 rubles (✆ **812/298-3751;** www.glide.ru).

Skiing

The forests around St. Petersburg are a paradise for cross-country skiers, but downhill options are limited to resorts a few hours out of town. Some dedicated city residents skate-ski through the lanes of the bigger city parks, such as Victory Park. Cross-country ski rentals are available adjacent to the palace at Tsarskoye Selo, for royal rural sightseeing (see chapter 16 for details).

SPECTATOR SPORTS

In addition to the venues mentioned below, check the schedules of **Yubileiny Sports Palace,** 18 Prospekt Dobrolyubova (✆ **812/498-6033;** metro: Sportivnaya) for a variety of sporting events throughout the year. In 2012, the "New Zenit" stadium on Krestovsky Ostrov (island; metro: Krestovsky Ostrov) hosting matches of FC Zenit St. Petersburg is due to open.

Figure Skating

Russia is one of the world's premier figure skater factories and St. Petersburg has produced many of the country's top skaters. Check out the schedule at the **Ice Palace (Ledovy Dvorets)**, 1 Prospekt Pyatiletok (✆ **812/718-6620;** www.newarena. spb.ru; metro: Ledovy Dvorets). Otherwise, come during one of the figure skating tournaments, which are held in January and February. See the International Skating Union website for details (www.isu.org).

Hockey

Ice hockey is a crucial sport in this northern city. Viewing the big matches became a lot more pleasant with the construction of the Ice Palace/Ledovy Dvorets (see above for contact information) for the 2000 Hockey World Cup. For more casual viewing pleasure, come in winter and visit the bigger city parks, where a match is nearly always underway on the ponds. Tickets for the Ice Palace are available at the palace itself or at theater ticket kiosks around town (called *kassa,* spelled КАCCA in Russian).

Soccer

Soccer is Russians' favorite sport. St. Petersburg's premier soccer club, Zenit, is finally emerging from the shadows of its Moscow rivals. If you're in town during a Zenit match, head for **Petrovsky Stadium,** 2 Petrovsky Prospekt (✆ **812/275-0330;** metro: Sportivnaya), and be prepared for some raucous behavior. City parks host

informal soccer (called *futbol* here) matches year-round—even in the snow
uefa.com for European League matches in St. Petersburg.

Tennis Tournaments

The St. Petersburg Open, held at rather run-down **Peterburgsky Sport Co...ex,** 8 Ulitsa Gagarina (*©* **812/388-2164;** www.spbopen.ru; metro: Park Pobedy), is the main venue at which to catch top-ranked Russian ATP stars on their homeland's courts. The Davis Cup also sometimes comes here (www.daviscup.com).

WALKING TOUR: **ST. PETERSBURG HIGHLIGHTS**

Start:	**Palace Square.**
Finish:	**Gostiny Dvor.**
Time:	**About 2 hours.**
Best Times:	**Any weekday or Sunday morning, when the crowds are thinner.**

This tour links key St. Petersburg sights with less important ones. The side streets and embankments are just as crucial to understanding the city as are the palaces, so look at everything, even between stops.

1 Palace Square

Stand at the Alexander Column in the center and turn around slowly, a full 360 degrees. Each building on the asymmetrical square emerged in a different era, but they combine to create a flawless ensemble. Nothing in this view, or this city, is accidental. Imagine the royal equipages pulling into the square, the czarist army processions, the revolutionaries' resentment of all that the square stood for—and the Communist-era appropriation of the square for holiday parades. The column itself is not attached to the ground—its weight keeps it upright.

Walk north from the column to the courtyard of the:

2 Winter Palace

The palace's now tranquil courtyard bustled with court activity in Empress Elizabeth's and Catherine the Great's days, and with revolutionary activity 150 years later. It was closed to visitors until recently, visible only from inside the Hermitage Museum. You can pick up a museum plan while you're here, though a visit to the Hermitage deserves at least an afternoon or a full day to itself.

As you leave the courtyard, take in the view of the curved General Staff building across the square.

Head left toward the Moika Canal, then turn right and follow it down to Nevsky Prospekt. Note the uniformity of the buildings along the canal, all in various shades of yellow, and the odd proportion of the wide bridges crossing the narrow waterway. Cross Nevsky and head left, until you reach the columned gray facade of:

3 Kazan Cathedral

Walking the length of the cathedral's concave colonnade gives you a stepped-back view of Nevsky on one side and a sense of the cathedral's scale on the other. Its modern, secular lines are almost reminiscent of the Capitol Building in Washington, built just 2 decades earlier. Compare this to other Orthodox churches you see around Russia. Marshal Kutuzov, who led the Russian victory over Napoleon, is buried here. Even if you don't go in, note that the church's entrance is on the east side instead of facing the street, to satisfy Orthodox church canon.

Cross the avenue again and stop at the corner of Nevsky and Griboyedov Canal to admire:

4 Dom Knigi

This Art Nouveau treasure is just another building along Nevsky, but worth noting are its glass dome and mystical mosaics. It once belonged to the Singer sewing machine company, whose name is still engraved on the facade, between the second and third floors. For decades it was Dom Knigi, or House of Books, Leningrad's main bookstore. After a recent renovation, it now houses the bookstore on the first floor and an upscale shopping mall on the higher levels.

Cross Griboyedov Canal and head north along it, past the boatmen hawking canal tours, toward the dizzying domes of the:

5 Church of the Savior on the Spilled Blood

Built 7 decades after Kazan Cathedral, this church sprang from an entirely different era and worldview. Though constructed during Russia's industrial and economic boom of the late 19th century, the Church of the Savior harkens back to the piled, etched, color-coated domes of medieval Russian churches, and is slathered with gold and precious stones—a much more Russian style of church-building than the reasoned lines of European-style Kazan Cathedral. Inside the Church of the Savior, note the spot where Czar Alexander II was assassinated by a revolutionary. This politicized location is part of the reason for the church's nationalist design.

Walk around the cathedral along the outer edge of Mikhailovsky Gardens, stopping to study the undulating patterns of the cast-iron fences surrounding the gardens. This could be a good moment for coffee, or something more substantial.

6 Park Giuseppe ☕

The one-story pink pavilion in Mikhailovsky Gardens was once a public toilet, but don't let that deter you. The Park Giuseppe restaurant (☎ 812/571-7309) now has a splendid terrace overlooking the gardens and the Church of the Savior. Good pizzas (by Petersburg standards), strong coffee, and a good selection of teas and desserts are the menu highlights.

Continue to follow the fence around to the entrance to the gardens.

7 Mikhailovsky Castle & Gardens

The warm coral of the castle's exterior makes it look almost inviting despite its grim history. The paranoid Czar Paul I had it built because the Winter Palace made him feel too exposed to threats from without and within his court. (Paul was right about the threats, but not about the security of his new home: He was assassinated by advisers soon after he moved in.) Compare the high fences enclosing the gardens and the inaccessibility of this castle courtyard to the more sociable Winter Palace, facing the Neva River and opening onto Palace Square. Mikhailovsky Castle was later an engineering school and is now the Engineering Museum.

1 Palace Square
2 Winter Palace
3 Kazan Cathedral
4 Dom Knigi

5 Church of the Savior on the Spilled Blood
6 Park Giuseppe
7 Mikhailovsky Castle and Gardens

8 The Russian Museum
9 Shostakovich Philharmonic
10 Gostiny Dvor
11 Grand Hotel Europe

Circle the palace and turn right onto Italianskaya Ulitsa, heading straight until you reach the Square of the Arts. Take a rest on a bench in this small rectangular plaza, then wander its circumference to study its components:

8 The Russian Museum

This museum is housed in the triumphantly classical Mikhailovsky Palace (Dvorets), not to be confused with the Mikhailovsky Castle (Zamok) that you just saw. The optimism of the period when the palace was built (1819–25) is reflected in the mock war trophies that top its gates and victorious frieze. The royal family made it a museum in 1898, as their belated effort to create a gallery of Russian art to rival Moscow's Tretyakov Gallery.

Walk around the square past the Mussorgsky Theater (check out its repertoire of ballet and opera performances on the way), around the Grand Hotel Europe and across Mikhailovskaya Ulitsa to the:

9 Shostakovich Philharmonic

Built in the 1830s, Russia's premier music hall has staged the country's leading works, from Tchaikovsky's concertos to Rachmaninoff's symphonies. It has hosted giants including pianist Sviatoslav Richter and cellist Mstislav Rostropo-vich, and does great justice to the composer who gave it a name, Dmitry Shostakovich.

Continue down Mikhailovskaya Ulitsa to Nevsky Prospekt. Turn around and look at the Square of the Arts one more time from this perspective. Then turn left down Nevsky and continue to the underground walkway at the next intersection. Cross Nevsky through this passage, noting its lively commerce in pirated CDs, DVDs, and software. You'll emerge at:

10 Gostiny Dvor

This 19th-century shopping mall has gone through several incarnations. Picture its early years, when it was a gathering place for the nobility looking for gifts to take to balls at the Winter Palace. It was also a place to come after lighting a candle at an icon at Kazan Cathedral. Its current customers include the city's new middle class, as well as some members of the nouveau riche who made fortunes in the privatizations and economic chaos of the 1990s.

11 Grand Hotel Europe ☕

To stay in an aristocratic, 19th-century mood after this walk, stop at the mezzanine of the Grand Hotel Europe, back on Mikhailovskaya Ulitsa (✆ 812/329-6000). The plush arm-chairs in this peaceful atrium make you feel like an escapee from modern St. Petersburg, especially when the harpists play. Tea, pastries, and small sandwiches are available.

SHOPPING IN ST. PETERSBURG

Shopping in St. Petersburg can produce precious porcelain or a bag full of cheap lacquer boxes, depending on your energy level, resourcefulness, and pocketbook. The matryoshka nesting dolls are so plentiful and ubiquitous that you probably won't be able to leave without one. For more original ware, visit Lomonosov Porcelain Factory, which has a museum and shop featuring imperial china patterns along with striking new designs.

Soviet banners and Red Army gear are a draw for some, though Moscow features more of a selection, since St. Petersburg prefers to emphasize its royal heritage rather than its Soviet past. Amber from the Baltic region is a bargain compared to what you'd pay in countries farther from the source, and the selection is much broader. St. Petersburg is fast on its way to competing with Moscow as a luxury shopping capital, with plenty of French, Italian, and local haute couture aimed at the nouveau riche. Multinational retail chains are slowly discovering the city, for better or for worse. Tips on purchasing traditional Russian gifts are outlined below; for more on Orthodox icons, *matryoshka* dolls, Russian linen, and the porcelain style known as Gzhel, see chapter 7.

THE SHOPPING SCENE

The chief challenge in finding unique souvenirs and gifts in Russia is in determining whether you're allowed to bring them home. See "Customs" in chapter 17 for an explanation of the export regulations of Russia's Culture Ministry, which affect Orthodox icons, samovars, and many artworks.

Hotel gift shops and the souvenir stands on Nevsky have higher prices than elsewhere. The outdoor markets are a better bet, such as the one across from the Church of the Savior on the Spilled Blood (see "Vernisazh" later in this chapter). Be ready to bargain, and beware of counterfeiting. If something sounds suspiciously cheap, there's a reason. The monasteries and cathedrals have the richest selection of icons.

Several of the city's souvenir stores are grouped under one umbrella, with fairly standard and relatively high prices. Still, their selection beats most others around, and quality is guaranteed. You can see a sampling of their wares (and even make purchases) online at www.souvenirboutique. com, but the selection and price range is much broader in the stores. Two

St. Petersburg Shopping

Monetnaya ul.

ul. Mira

Posadskaya ul.

ul. Kuybysheva

Nevka

Pirogovskiy prospekt

Sampsoniyevskiy prospekt

ul. Kom. Smirnova

ul. Akademika Lebedeva

Arsenalnaya ul.

Kondratevsky pr.

Sverdlovskaya nab.

Neva

Smolnaya nab.

Klinicheskaya

Sampsonievskiy most

Finland Station

ПЛ. ЛЕНИНА pl. Lenina

pl. Lenina

pl. Komsomola

Arsenalnaya nab.

Orlovskaya ul.

ul. Smolnovo

Troitskaya pl.

Petrovskaya nab.

Neva

nab. Kutuzova

Liteyny most

nab. Robspera

Shpalernaya ulitsa

Potemkinskaya ul.

Tavricheskaya nab.

Kavalergardskaya ul.

pl. Proletarskoy Diktatury

Tulskaya ulitsa

Troitsky most

Zakharevskaya ul.

ulitsa Chaykovskovo

ЧЕРНЫШЕВСКАЯ Chernyshevskaya

Kirochnaya ulitsa

Tavrichesky sad

Shpalernaya ul.

Suvorovskaya pl.

Letny sad

Marsovo Pole

Dvortsovaya nab.

Milionnaya ul.

nab. reki Moika

Moika

Church of the Savior on the Spilled Blood

ul. Ryleeva

ul. Radishcheva

Paradnaya nab.

LOWER NEVSKY/ SMOLNY CONVENT

ulitsa Moseenko

Novgorodskaya ul.

Sinopskaya nab.

Neva

Gagarinskaya ul.

Russian State Museum

most Belinkovo

nab. reki Fontanki

Fontanka

Liteyny prospekt

ul. Mayakovskovo

ulitsa Nekrasova

ul. Zhukovskovo

Grechesky prospekt

Ligovsky prospekt

8-ya Sovetskaya

Suvorovski prospekt

7-ya

6-ya

5-ya Sovetskaya ul.

Mytninskaya ul.

Church of the Savior on the Spilled Blood 19

Moika

9

pl. Iskusstov

italyanskaya ul.

Nevsky Prospekt

10

11

12

13

14

15

16

17

18

20

21

22

23

24

25

26

27

28

29

30

31

32

33

34

35

36

Narodny most

Konyushennaya ul.

Kazanskaya pl.

Kanal Griboyedova

Sadovaya ul.

Lomonosovskaya ul.

Anichkov most

2-ya

Vladimirsky pr.

НЕВСКИЙ ПРОСПЕКТ- ГОСТИНИЙ ДВОР Nevsky Prospekt- Gostiny Dvor

САДОВАЯ- СЕННАЯ ПЛ.- СПАССКАЯ Sadovaya- Sennaya pl.- Spasskaya

Sennaya pl.

Gorokhovaya ul.

nab. reki Fontanki

ДОСТОЕВСКАЯ ВЛАДИМИРСКАЯ Dostoyevskaya- Vladimirskaya

ul. Marata

Kuznechny per.

Pushkin- skaya ul.

ploshchad Vosstaniya

Moscow Station

ПЛ. ВОССТАНИЯ- МАЯКОВСКАЯ pl. Vosstaniya- Mayakovskaya

Nevsky Prospekt

Khersonskaya ul.

prospekt Bakunina

most Aleksandra Nevskogo

Neva

pr. Obukhovsky

ПЛ. АЛЕКСАНДРА НЕВСКОГО pl. Aleksandra Nevskogo

pl. Aleksandra Nevskogo

Moskovsky prospekt

Obukhovsky most

Pionerskaya pl.

Zagorodny prospekt

ul. Pravdy

Razezhaya ulitsa

Kolomenskaya ul.

ul. Marata

ЛИГОВСКИЙ ПРОСПЕКТ Ligovsky Prospekt

ПУШКИНСКАЯ- ЗВЕНИГОРОДСКАЯ Pushkinskaya- Zvenigorodskaya

Vitebsky Station

Borovaya ulitsa

ul. K. Zaslonova

ul. Chernyakhovskovo

Ligovsky prospekt

Tekhnologicheskaya pl.

ТЕХНОЛОГИЧЕСКИЙ ИНСТИТУТ Tekhnologichesky Institut

Malodetskoselsky pr.

nab. Obvodnovo Kanala

Kurskaya ulitsa

Borovaya ulitsa

Petropavlovskaya ulitsa

Tambovskaya ulitsa

Dnepropetrovskaya ulitsa

ОБВОДНЫЙ КАНАЛ Obvodny Kanal

Common terms and abbreviations	
naberezhnaya/nab.........	*Embankment*
most.............	*Bridge*
ploshchad/pl.................	*Square* or *plaza*
prospekt/pr..................	*Avenue*
sad.........................	*Garden*
ulitsa/ul....................	*Street*

0 ... 1/2 mi

0 ... 0.5 km

box THAT UP

Lacquer boxes are a staple of Russian souvenir shops, and while they can look all alike from afar, with a little context they take on a greater meaning. The practice of painting on papier-mâché boxes started in the village of Danilovka outside Moscow in the 1700s, and quickly spread to surrounding towns. Today, the towns of Palekh, Fedoskino, and Mstera are among the leading lacquer-art producers. The boxes sold now are made of several layers of papier-mâché pressed together, cut, and oven-dried. Generally painted on a black background, the colors are primarily scarlet- and gold-based, and the finished product is lacquered in clear varnish, often in multiple layers, for radiance and durability. The images usually represent scenes from Russian fairy tales or legends, and can vary widely depending on the artist's interpretation. Study several before buying a lacquer box. The box should be lightweight, and the detail should be impeccable, since the better artists spend up to 2 months painting them using special magnifying glasses.

For a gift for a whole family, buy a lacquer box together with the English-language translation of the fairy tale depicted (on sale at many souvenir shops and bookstores).

---

of the group's stores, **Babushka** and **Katarina,** are listed below. Another, Onegin, is widely advertised in St. Petersburg but has higher prices for the same goods.

St. Petersburg has no sales tax, but be clear with the vendor about what currency is being cited. In shops most prices will be printed in rubles. Street vendors will sometimes cite prices in dollars or euros, though they're technically forbidden from accepting anything but rubles. VAT is always included in the price, but it is not refundable at the border as it is in some European countries.

If you want to ship home large items such as paintings or carpets, try **DHL,** 4 Izmailovsky Prospekt (© **812/326-6400**), which can take care of any Customs clearances you need. Also, some of the stores listed below, including Babushka and Katarina, can arrange Culture Ministry approvals of valuable artwork and ship it to you, for a fee.

Credit cards are not accepted as widely as you might expect. Shops and shopping centers are generally open 7 days a week from around 10 or 11am until 7 or 8pm, and a very few still take an hour off for lunch between about 1 and 2pm. Most are closed on Russian holidays.

GREAT SHOPPING AREAS

Nevsky Prospekt is the city's commercial lifeline, offering an almost repetitive abundance of souvenirs, clothing, and snacks. **Gostiny Dvor** shopping arcade concentrates all of Nevsky's riches in one two-story pre-revolutionary mall. The facades on Nevsky tell only part of the story, since many lead back into passages of luxury boutiques, discount clothing stores, or jewelry shops. Commerce thins out at Nevsky's extremities. **Upper Nevsky** holds the posher shops, while **Lower Nevsky** (east of Moskovsky Train Station) is calmer and less pretentious. Souvenir and art stands clog the thoroughfare and adjacent courtyards, and seem to multiply in summer.

The area from St. Isaac's to Palace Square is a shopper's wasteland but an architectural paradise. The Summer Gardens and adjacent areas are similarly commerce-barren, except for the **Vernisazh**—the city's most convenient, reliable, and extensive gift bazaar.

With Nevsky so saturated, the area around Chernyshevskaya metro station is emerging as a calmer, less expensive shopping alternative. Several antiques shops have opened here, along with an increasing number of hotels and cafes centered around Ulitsa Pestelya, in this neighborhood north of Lower Nevsky.

Russians do much of their shopping at **farmers' markets** and **open-air bazaars,** most of which are outside the center of town. These lively and pungent markets offer a fun if intense way of experiencing the real Russia, and quickly make you forget those Gorbachev-era images of bread lines and shortages. In the food markets, pomegranates and kiwis spill from fruit stands, rows of lamb carcasses line the meat stalls, and familiar American coffees and candies rise high in the dry goods section. In the nonfood markets (which Russians call the "things" market, or *veshchevoi rynok*) you can find fur coats, Turkish leather jackets, 20¢ Russian-made underwear, Chinese-made plastic chess sets, and just about anything else, at prices below what shops charge. Two food markets near the center worth checking out are **Vladimirsky Rynok** (Kuznechny Pereulok, just outside Vladimirskaya metro station) and **Maltevsky Rynok** (Ulitsa Nekrasova, not far from Chernyshevskaya metro station). Both are cleaner and slightly more expensive than average. The main "things market" downtown is **Apraksin Dvor** (Sadovaya Ulitsa, south of Nevsky Prospekt and near Gostiny Dvor metro station), with throngs of shoppers morning to night, 7 days a week. Pickpocketing is common, so keep one eye on your wallet.

SHOPPING CENTERS

St. Petersburg's premier shopping center since the 1760s has been **Gostiny Dvor (Guest Courtyard)**, a triangular arcade of shops on two floors on Nevsky Prospekt. In the Soviet era the long, doorless corridors were flanked by shop after shop carrying the same limited selection of gray suits, uncomfortable shoes, and two-ring binders. Today the shopping center holds just about everything, though most of it is priced beyond the means of the average Russian. Boutiques selling 25,000-ruble dresses abut shops with Italian briefcases and French fountain pens. At the back edge of the arcade, facing Ulitsa Lomonosova, are a few cheaper shops that are your best bet for clothing in the heart of town. Souvenir shops are sprinkled throughout the center, as are several little cafes that offer cheap Russian-style open-faced sandwiches and savory pies for an energy boost and a chance to rest your feet.

St. Petersburg's other shopping centers fall into two categories. The *passazh*, an enclosed row of shops leading back from a main street, is a concept left over from the pre-revolutionary years when they were usually reserved for the aristocracy and could be closed off to the general public. Today some have been beautifully restored and house designer boutiques and posh beauty salons—and admission is open to anyone. Start with the one called simply **Passage** (48 Nevsky Prospekt); the view of inside and out from the second-floor cafe is exceptional. Nearby is the newer **Grand Palace** (44 Nevsky Prospekt), with rows of Italian and French couture boutiques and a staggeringly expensive chocolate shop. Only slightly less decadent is **Vladimirsky Passage** (19 Vladimirsky Prospekt). The less appealing but more affordable type of shopping center is the *torgovy tsentr.* These glass-and-chrome constructions have sprung up around Russia in recent years, feeding Russians' hunger for consumer goods. The most convenient, clean one for most tourists is **DLT** (see listing below), though it's often quite crowded. There's little historic or unique about these centers, but they're your best bet for basic needs such as shampoo, camera batteries, or umbrellas, and they offer a way to see how average city residents spend their money.

SHOPPING A TO Z

Amber

The Baltic Sea coast, from Kaliningrad through Lithuania, Latvia and up toward St. Petersburg, holds nearly all of the world's amber. This strange gem of petrified tree sap is ubiquitous in Russia's imperial capital. Rings, necklaces, brooches, cigar holders, pens, and other souvenirs made of varied hues of amber are widely available. Although they're not cheap, they cost much less than in other countries farther from the source. Any souvenir market, crafts store, or jewelry shop is bound to have a decent selection (see reviews below). Keep an eye out for the more unusual shades of pale green or yellow.

Amber House (Yantarny Dom)   A broad and reliable but pricey selection of jewelry made from amber and Siberian stones can be found here. The really unusual items are usually the better buys. 24 Nevsky Prospekt. ✆ **812/571-8810.** Metro: Nevsky Prospekt.

Antiques & Collectibles

Abim Plus   This spacious and eclectic gallery on the Fontanka embankment offers paintings, china, and knickknacks. 5 Fontanka Naberezhnaya. ✆ **812/314-0080.** Metro: Gostiny Dvor.

Belazh   This is an old standby on Nevsky, whose prices are higher because of its location but whose quality and selection of artworks and porcelain remain good. 57 Nevsky Prospekt. ✆ **812/310-6688.** Metro: Gostiny Dvor.

Panteleimonovsky   Paintings, furniture, and tabletop collectibles may be found here, with an emphasis on Art Nouveau objects. 13/15 Ulitsa Pestelya. ✆ **812/579-7235.** Metro: Chernyshevskaya.

Russkaya Starina   Its focus is on Russian crafts and antiques, as opposed to the western European collectibles carried by most other antiques shops. 27 Baskov Pereulok. ✆ **812/273-1847.** www.rusant.ru. Metro: Chernyshevskaya.

Art

Art Modus   This informal market in front of the Lutheran Church on Nevsky has been almost institutionalized in its many years parked here. A broad selection of paintings, watercolors, sketches, and photos is on display by the artists. The more original and less expensive pieces are usually displayed at the booths in the back. Prices are negotiable, and range broadly. Vendors speak English. 32-34 Nevsky Prospekt. ✆ **921/871-7973.** Metro: Nevsky Prospekt.

Gallery D-137   This small gallery houses works by several daring and respected local artists, in a renovated brick basement. 90/92 Nevsky Prospect. ✆ **812/275-6011.** Metro: Mayakovskaya.

Hermitage Museum Store   While not as extensive as they could be, the various stalls in the Hermitage sell art prints and postcards of many sizes, as well as other museum memorabilia. Palace Sq. ✆ **812/710-9079.** Metro: Nevsky Prospekt.

Pechatnaya (Printing Press)   This unusual gallery is tucked in the Peter and Paul Fortress, offering customers a view of artists working on woodcuts, etchings, and other works. You can also buy a finished product of a former imperial printing press. Prices range broadly, from overinflated to some surprising deals. Peter and Paul Fortress, Zaichy Ostrov. ✆ **812/238-4742.** Metro: Gorkovskaya.

Pushkinskaya 10   One of the functions of this all-purpose arts center is to sell art, though it doesn't seem obvious at first from its chaotic, countercultural atmosphere. Galleries hold rotating exhibits featuring local artists, whose styles range from naturalism to nihilism. See the review for Pushkinskaya 10 on p. 234. 10 Pushkinskaya Ulitsa. ✆ **812/764-5371.** www.pushkinskaja-10.spb.ru. Metro: Mayakovskaya.

Books

Most hotels and museums also have books about the city in English.

Anglia British Bookshop   The Anglia has the best selection of books in English, with an emphasis on travel guides, picture albums, and classic and modern fiction. However, it's more expensive than its Russian counterparts selling all of the above. 38 Fontanka. ✆ **812/579-8284.** Metro: Mayakovskaya or Gostiny Dvor.

Dom Knigi   The relocated "House of Books" still has a good selection of English-language books and is open until midnight daily. 62 Nevsky Prospekt. ✆ **812/570-6546.** Metro: Mayakovskaja.

DVK (Dom Voyennykh Knig)   One of the world's few 24-hour bookstores, this three-story emporium has replaced the landmark Dom Knigi as the city's premier bookstore. Though the name means "house of military books," this store has every kind of reading material imaginable, with a small selection of English-language guides and novels on the first floor, near the main entrance. 20 Nevsky Prospekt. ✆ **812/312-3946.** Metro: Nevsky Prospekt.

China & Porcelain

Lomonosov Porcelain Factory   An exceptional and recommended gift is china from this factory, which you can buy at stores around town or at the source. Or you can view the wares here, note your choice, and order home delivery on the Internet. The factory was opened in 1744 by Peter the Great's daughter, Empress Elizabeth I. Its craftspeople designed china for the royal family and nobility. After the revolution it was nationalized and produced plates with Constructivist Soviet art and propaganda slogans. Today it's been reprivatized, and sells both imperial and Soviet patterns. Check out the factory museum while you're there, which is part of the Hermitage Museum's holdings. 151 Prospekt Obukhovskoi Oborony. ✆ **812/326-1744.** www. ipm.ru. Metro: Lomonosovskaya.

Chocolate

Russian chocolate has come a long way from the waxy stuff sold in Soviet shops, though it's still sweeter than what you'll find in Switzerland or Belgium. A few ounces of these chocolates in their cheerful, Russian-lettered wrappings are a sure way to please any underage friends or family back home (though you might want to sample them first, since a few are made with liqueurs). The big supermarkets also usually have small wrapped chocolates for very reasonable prices. Try **Belochka,** 28 Sredny Prospekt, on Vasilevsky Island (✆ **812/323-1763;** metro: Vasileostrovskaya); or **Nevskiye Berega,** 32 Naberezhnaya Makarova (✆ **812/323-5919;** www.cake.spb. ru; metro: Vasileostrovskaya).

Crafts

See the review for Vernisazh under "Gifts/Souvenirs," below.

Discount Shopping

Apraksin Dvor This 200-year-old shopping mall has lost its aristocratic elegance and become a jumble of cheap clothing stalls, seedy gaming halls, electronics markets, and lowbrow bars and cafes. It's slated for a cleanup, but in the meantime it has plenty of low-priced clothes, shoes, toys, and CDs. Watch your pocket. 30 Sadovaya Ulitsa. Metro: Gostiny Dvor.

Fashion

CHILDREN'S

DLT This shopping center is full of shops selling imported and Russian goods with an emphasis on children's stores. 21/23 Bolshaya Konyushennaya Ulitsa. ✆ **812/312-2627.** Metro: Nevsky Prospekt.

WOMEN'S & MEN'S

Gostiny Dvor This arcade has mostly international brands but in a Russian atmosphere. They offer discount cards for heavy shoppers. See description under "Shopping Centers" earlier in this chapter. Hours are daily 10am to 10pm. 35 Nevsky Prospekt. ✆ **812/710-5408.** www.bgd.ru. Metro: Gostiny Dvor.

Pryalka (Spinning Wheel) This store, styled like a cottage hut for the new rich, offers original clothes and gifts, largely handmade from natural products, including goat down sweaters and blouses of Russian linen as well as standard and unconventionally designed accessories. Prices are higher than you'll find in department stores but the selection and quality are quite good. 1st Line, Vasilevsky Island. ✆ **812/323-1021.** Metro: Vasileostrovskaya.

Tatyana Parfionova Arguably St. Petersburg's most famous fashion designer, Parfionova creates unforgettable, original clothes and accessories. Her shows are the hottest ticket in town and her pieces are displayed in the Russian Museum. For something you definitely won't find at home, stop at her boutique. Excellent service. 51 Nevsky Prospekt. ✆ **812/713-1415.** Metro: Mayakovskaya.

Food

Lenta This local hypermarket offers a staggering selection of goods at reasonable prices and is increasingly popular among Petersburg's middle class. Its stores are in the not-so-convenient edges of town, and best reachable by car, but you'll find just about anything you could imagine here, including vodka and even reliable caviar at the best prices in town. Both of the following are open 24 hours. 11 Vyborgskoye Shosse, near metro Ozerki. ✆ **812/336-4800.** www.lenta.com. Also at 33 Pulkovskoye Shosse, on the way to the airport. ✆ **812/703-3000.**

Stockmann   This Finnish-Russian supermarket chain sells a range of reliable international products, at prices higher than you'll find in the bazaars but lower than in the hotels. 114 Nevsky Prospekt ℂ **812/313-6000**. www.stockmann.ru. Metro: Nevsky Prospekt.

Gifts/Souvenirs

Babushka   This homey, stylized store (its name means "grandma") is part of a group of souvenir stores around town offering a large selection of lacquer boxes, amber and other jewelry, nesting dolls, and many other, more original gifts. Prices are relatively high, but quality is assured and it makes an easy all-around shopping destination. 33 Naberezhnaya Leytenanta Shmidta. ℂ **812/321-1477.** www.souvenirboutique.com. Metro: Vasileostrovskaya.

Katarina   Part of the same chain as Babushka (above), this store has a similar selection plus some Russian filigree and Fabergé eggs. Prices and quality are slightly higher. 46 Angliiskaya Naberezhnaya. ℂ **812/312-7072.** www.souvenirboutique.com. Metro: Nevsky Prospekt.

Vernisazh   This is your best one-stop souvenir shopping bet in town, a compact but rich outdoor market across from the Church of the Savior on the Spilled Blood. Hand-painted tea sets, mountains of lacquer boxes and *matryoshka* dolls, Soviet maps, wooden Christmas ornaments, decorative eggs, hand-knit wool shawls, fur hats, malachite chess sets, flasks with the hammer and sickle, and amber brooches are among the multitude of wares here. In sharp contrast to the market's haphazard, earlier days, the vendors now are neatly organized and registered, and many take credit cards. Prices, often quoted in dollars, are very negotiable. Vernisazh is run by the Center for the Support of Art and Entrepreneurship. 1 Canal Griboyedova. No phone. Metro: Nevsky Prospekt.

Icons

Also see chapter 7 for history and advice on Orthodox icons.

Russian Icon   An extensive array of icons is on display in this convenient boutique. They're all recently made, meaning you'll have no problem taking them out of the country, but they follow the same rules icon painters have adhered to for centuries. The icons are more expensive than those at the monasteries, but the selection is larger. 15 Bolshaya Konyushennaya. ℂ **812/314-7040.** Metro: Nevsky Prospekt.

Jewelry

See also review under "Amber" and the reviews for Babushka and Vernisazh under "Gifts/Souvenirs."

Ananov   This exclusive shop exhibits some original designs using unusual stones and gems, at high prices. 7 Michurinskaya Ulitsa. ℂ **812/235-8338.** www.ananov.com. Metro: Gorkovskaya.

Music

Iceberg   This new chain offers a range of international artists, modern and classical at reasonable prices. 10 Zagorodny Prospekt. ℂ **812/315-5843.** www.icebergspb.ru.

Severnaya Lira   This treasure trove of cheap sheet music emphasizes Russian composers. 26 Nevsky Prospekt. ℂ **812/312-0796.** Metro: Nevsky Prospekt.

The Russian version of the lacy, open-work metal design known as filigree makes for a precious souvenir to bring home. It's one of the few things you can really find only in Russia, as it's not widely sold at Russian-themed stores abroad. Top suggestions include a silver filigree box with a Russian lacquer lid, silver filigree necklaces embedded with Siberian stones, and Russian-themed filigree Christmas ornaments. Smaller items from rougher metal can cost as little as 300 rubles; more elaborate or delicate items can cost hundreds of dollars.

Tsentr Design You'll find a great selection of classical, choral, and Russian folk music, mostly labeled in English as well as Russian. Instruments on sale, too. 2 Mikhailovskaya Ulitsa. ℂ **812/710-4428.** Metro: Nevsky Prospekt.

Toys

See **DLT,** listed above under "Fashion," for modern, international toys. **Vernisazh,** listed above under "Gifts/Souvenirs," offers more original toys like wooden Russian puppets and unusual chess sets.

Vodka & Wine

See **Stockmann** and **Lenta** above under "Food." Both have good, inexpensive selections of Russian vodkas and wines from Georgia, Crimea, and Moldova that you're unlikely to find at home. The spirits sold in the ubiquitous kiosks around town are sometimes counterfeit and not worth risking despite their lower prices. Another to try is this:

Monopol Extensive selection of wines, vodkas, brandies, and other liquor from around the world. 9 Konnogvardeisky Bulvar. ℂ **812/312-0319.** Metro: Gostiny Dvor.

ST. PETERSBURG AFTER DARK

M ost of St. Petersburg's liveliest and richest cultural events take place during the magical summer weeks when there is no "after dark," under the soft, elongated sunset of the White Nights. Its 18th-century palaces throw open their doors for midnight music concerts, its regal parks and squares host open-air jazz festivals, and much of the city seems to be wandering the bridges and quays or floating down the canals until morning.

Of course, this city that considers itself Russia's cultural capital is alive with performances the rest of the year as well, and city boosters increasingly fill the calendar with events to even out the tourist flow, and to remind visitors that its northern latitude is not the only reason to visit St. Petersburg.

What was known for decades as the Kirov Ballet and Opera Company has again adopted its pre-revolutionary name of the Mariinsky Company, and performs at the magnificent Mariinsky Theater when it's not touring internationally. Its reputation, funding, and talent suffered during the decade following the Soviet Union's collapse, as many of its best dancers went abroad. But it's enjoying a revival, and its standards remain world-class. Meanwhile, the city has benefited from growing competition by smaller companies. See chapter 8 for tips on buying Russian theater tickets.

The city's club and bar scene hasn't quite reached the superlative debauchery of Moscow's, but St. Petersburg's dance clubs and bars still offer plenty to shock and stimulate a Western visitor.

English-language listings for theater, music, and movies are best found in *The St. Petersburg Times* (www.sptimes.ru). Bar and club reviews can be found in the free, bilingual listings magazines found at restaurants and hotels.

THE PERFORMING ARTS

This is the city where Maurice Petipa invented ballet, so it would be a shame not to pay homage by watching some of the world's top stars interpret this most classical of dance forms. Yet watching *The Nutcracker* in a Russian theater or hearing a Shostakovich concerto in a Russian symphony hall are only the most obvious ways to appreciate St. Petersburg's

WHERE TO GO DURING white nights

Several festivals claim to be St. Petersburg's "official" White Nights event, but in fact there are so many entertainment options that it doesn't matter who's more official than whom. The city government defines the period as the 50 days when the sun never gets more than 9 degrees below the horizon, roughly from late May to mid-July. The biggest events run for 2 weeks in late June around the summer solstice. Some festivals with the name "White Nights" in them start as early as May, so even if you're not in town on the longest day of the year, you have plenty of performances to choose from. See the Mariinsky Theater website (www.mariinsky.ru) for details of its **Stars of the White Nights** festival, considered the most prestigious in town. For schedules of the **White Nights Jazz** festival, another top draw, see www.jazz.ru/eng. The Shostakovich Philharmonic hosts a June music festival. Film festivals, fashion festivals, and beer festivals fill up any space left on the White Nights calendar. Once you arrive, consult your hotel concierge or the English-language *The St. Petersburg Times* for more listings.

The main all-night, outdoor party scene is along a stretch of **Angliiskaya Naberezhnya (English Embankment)** on the south bank of the Neva, not far from the Hermitage, with street musicians, food stands, and throngs of people. Elsewhere, most official events are held in the evening, starting around 8 or 9pm, except at the dance clubs, where the partying starts and ends much later. Outdoor music festivals fill up stages at the **Summer Gardens** and **Taurida Gardens,** good for walks and picnics before or after the concerts. The imperial palaces outside St. Petersburg put on summer music performances, with the festival at **Peterhof** especially impressive, including concerts around the fountains and in the ballrooms. The towns of Vyborg and Tsarskoye Selo (Pushkin) also host music concerts; see chapter 16 for details. A few cruise companies and dozens of private boats ply St. Petersburg's canals in the wee hours during the White Nights, offering an excellent way to celebrate the city's overall beauty.

performing arts. Flawless dancing and searing melodies grace lesser-known works, too. St. Petersburg offers you an opportunity to explore operas and ballets less common outside Russia, such as Tchaikovsky's *Eugene Onegin* or Rimsky-Korsakov's *Imperial Bride.* Classical music venues are conservative in their repertoires but produce consistently rigorous performances—at surprisingly low prices. **Take note:** Most theaters close down after the White Nights until the season reopens in September, so if you're here in late July or August, your performance options will be slim. See "The Performing Arts" in chapter 2 for a brief history of Russian ballet, opera, theater, and classical music.

Dance

Alexandrinsky Theater Also called the Pushkin Theater, the Alexandrinsky hosts performances by the acclaimed Russian Ballet and visiting dance companies, as well as dramatic plays (in Russian only). It is an impressive alternative to the Mariinsky if tickets there are not available or are out of your price range. Designed in the 1820s by Carlo Rossi, the Alexandrinsky is an important part of the surrounding architectural ensemble. Sip champagne at intermission on the columned balcony for the full experience. It's one of the rare theaters that stay open in summer, offering top-quality performances when other theaters are shuttered or the troupes are on tour. 2 Ploshchad Ostrovskogo. ℂ 812/710-4176. www.alexandrinsky.ru. Ticket desk open noon–7pm. Metro: Gostiny Dvor.

Hermitage Theater   This exclusive viewing hall created for Catherine the Great is an intimate way to appreciate some of the world's top dancers and musicians. The hall's small size means tickets are expensive and limited, but the splurge is worthwhile. Tickets are available at the Hermitage Museum ticket office. 34 Dvortsovaya Naberezhnya (Neva River side of the Winter Palace). ℂ **812/579-0226.** Metro: Nevsky Prospekt.

Mariinsky Theater   Viewing anything in this theater makes you feel regal, even if the performance is limp and you're in sneakers. The sea-green exterior encloses a five-tiered theater draped, embroidered, and gilded in blue and gold. Top-floor seats have a dimmer view of the performers but a close-up view of the ceiling frescoes that draw you right into their pillowy clouds and floating angels. The snack bar offers champagne and small, cheap, open-faced sandwiches topped with caviar or smoked salmon. The reason visitors come, however, is to see the renowned and rigorous Mariinsky (formerly Kirov) Ballet. Director Valery Gergiev still prefers the classics, such as *Sleeping Beauty* and *La Bayadere,* but the repertoire includes the occasional anthology or less well-known Russian ballets. The higher balconies can get stuffy in summer, and the restrooms are well below the standards of the rest of the building. The theater closes in August and early September, though visiting troupes occasionally perform during this period. Tickets purchased at the box office are cheaper than those bought through your hotel, but availability is often limited, since travel agencies buy up huge blocks of tickets in advance. 1 Teatralnaya Sq. ℂ 812/326-4141. www.mariinsky. ru. tickets@mariinsky.ru. Ticket office open 11am–7pm. Metro: Sadovaya or Sennaya Ploshchad.

Mussorgsky Theater (aka Maly Theater or State Academic Opera and Ballet Theater)   A cultural landmark since its first performance in 1833, this theater's repertoire includes Russian classics such as *The Nutcracker* and Prokofiev's *Romeo and Juliet,* international favorites *Barber of Seville* and *Carmen,* and a few small anthology-style performances. The theater itself is an only slightly less grand version of the Mariinsky, with the same open orchestra surrounded on three sides by four levels of balconies, all of which offer good views. A faithful miniature model of the theater next to the ticket office, aside from being a work of art, is useful for determining which seats you want. Much more convenient than the Mariinsky, this theater is right on the elegant Square of the Arts. It is closed late July to early September. 1 Sq. of the Arts (Ploshchad Isskustv). ℂ **812/595-4305.** www.mikhailovsky.ru. Metro: Gostiny Dvor.

Nikolayevsky Palace   The "Feel Yourself Russian" folk show at this 18th-century palace is aggressively promoted at many hotels, and is extremely tourist-oriented. The traditional costumes are superb, if overly bright, and the dancers are strong, but the whole performance is almost stereotypical. It's cheery and accessible to non-Russian speakers, and unlike many similar shows around town that toss in a topless number at the end, this one is family-friendly. Buffet food is included in price. 4 Ploshchad Truda. ℂ **812/312-5500.** www.folkshow.ru. Ticket desk open 11am–showtime, with shows at 7pm and 9pm. Metro: Sadovaya.

Classical Music

St. Petersburg Conservatory (Rimsky-Korsakov St. Petersburg State Conservatory)   This training ground for classical musicians across from the Mariinsky was

St. Petersburg Nightlife

long a coveted and cosseted institution. Today the theater needs renovations, the musicians need to be better paid, and the ticket office could be friendlier, but performances here are still impressive. If you buy directly from the ticket office, you'll pay less than you would through your hotel. Primarily Russian composers and performers are featured. 3 Teatralnaya Sq. ☎ 812/312-2519. www.conservatory.ru. Metro: Mayakovskaya.

Shostakovich Philharmonic   This is an unforgettable place to hear symphonies, solo piano concerts, international festivals, and competitions, featuring music by both Russian and international composers. It holds two halls, the Grand and the smaller Glinka. The Grand Hall is home to the St. Petersburg Philharmonic but shares its stage with visiting performers. Both halls boast ornate and intricate interiors and superb acoustics, though they're in need of renovation. The building itself contributes to the elegant ensemble of the Square of the Arts. 2 Mikhailovskaya St. ☎ 812/312-9871. www.philharmonia.spb.ru. Ticket desk open 11am–8pm. Bookings also by e-mail: bzfzakaz@philharmonia.spb.ru. Metro: Gostiny Dvor.

Smolny Cathedral and Convent   The acoustics of the central cathedral in what was once an elite convent make for unforgettable organ and chamber music concerts. They're staged several nights a week at varying times; some start in mid- or late afternoon. Concert tickets are available at the Cathedral ticket office. See p. 232 for more details on the Smolny complex. 3/1 Rastrelli Sq. ☎ 812/710-3159. Metro: Chernyshevskaya.

State Academic Kapella   Housed in a classical building just across the canal from Palace Square, this music academy houses a renowned chorus and symphony orchestra. It hosts international music festivals, including excellent organ festivals. In 2005, it underwent a much-needed renovation of its 18th-century stage and practice halls. 20 Moika Embankment. ☎ 812/314-1058. www.glinka-capella.ru. Ticket desk open noon–7pm. Metro: Nevsky Prospekt.

Opera

Mariinsky Theater   The city's premier opera and dance venue has a repertoire including international favorites such as *The Marriage of Figaro* and *Carmen* performed in their original languages, as well as Russian favorites *Sadko* (a colorful and whimsical interpretation of a Russian fairy tale) and Mussorgsky's historical opera *Boris Godunov*, about the family dramas and tumultuous politics of 16th- and 17th-century Russia. See the listing under "Dance" above. Closed late July to early September. Shows at 11:30am, 7pm, and 8pm. 1 Sq. of the Arts (Ploshchad Isskustv). ☎ 812/326-4141. Metro: Gostiny Dvor.

Mussorgsky Theater (aka Maly Theater)   A recommended place to see and hear strong performances of international and Russian opera classics, especially if you can't get tickets to the Mariinsky. Operas are performed in their original languages

Beyond the White Nights

Some festivals to watch out for during the off season include the **Autumn Marathon Jazz Festival** in October, run by the city Jazz Philharmonic; the **White Days** festival in January, with performances at all the major ballet and concert halls; and the **New Year's Festival** of dance and music late December to early January.

and sets are elaborate. Best to buy them in advance (ticket desk open 10am–showtime) to avoid last-minute price hikes, especially in summer. See the review of theater under "Dance," above, and description of the Russian opera scene in chapter 8. Closed late July to early September. 1 Sq. of the Arts (Ploshchad Isskustv). 𝄫 **812/595-4305.** www.mikhailovsky.ru. Metro: Gostiny Dvor.

St. Petersburg Chamber Opera   This talented company stages a range of Russian and international operas in an atmospheric 18th-century mansion. It's more intimate and generally less expensive than the Mariinsky, and its singers and musicians are as rigorously trained as any in town. 33 Galernaya Ulitsa. 𝄫 **812/312-3982.** www.spbopera.ru. Ticket desk open noon–showtime. Metro: Sadovaya.

Theater

English-language theater performances are rather rare in St. Petersburg, though the choices multiply during the White Nights. See *The St. Petersburg Times* (www.sptimes.ru) for listings.

THE CLUB & MUSIC SCENE

Someone is playing live music or spinning dance tracks somewhere in St. Petersburg any time of day, any time of the year. The city claims to be the birthplace of Russia's post-Soviet rock scene, spawning such bands as **Pep-see, Tequilajazz,** and the raspy, raunchy **Leningrad,** which went on to spawn others. Dance clubs run the gamut from freaky to haute couture to retro. Even the most mainstream of nightclubs or bars is bound to have topless entertainment, which has become such a staple of Russian nightlife that most Russians don't seem to watch.

St. Petersburg's jazz clubs are a treasure, but there aren't enough of them to go around. Petersburgers cultivate a keen interest in the genre, celebrating world-renowned musicians and those who practice the searing notes of the particular form of Russian jazz. The White Nights Jazz Festival is one of the highlights of the summer season, not to be missed if you're here that time of year. See www.jazz.ru for details and listings.

Dance Clubs & Discos

Griboedov   The sort of place that can produce a memorable evening, Griboedov bills itself as an "underground center of culture and relaxation," and the atmosphere is like a rather haphazard house party. It was founded in 1996 in an abandoned bomb shelter, and consists of "Griboedov Hill," a music cafe hosting DJs, cultural events, and live music sessions, and the quieter "Amsterdam Bar" which has a summer terrace. The program is a roll call of every conceivable variety of dance music. Their retro nights have a loyal following. Drop in and see what's happening. 2a Voronezskaya Ulitsa. ☎ 812/764-4355. www.griboedovclub.ru. Cover 300–400 rubles. Tickets for some concerts are cheaper bought in advance. Metro: Ligovsky Prospekt.

Metro St Petersburg's biggest dance club, Metro is huge and spread over three levels, with long bars and seating areas separate from the action, making conversation possible as well as dancing. The first level has Russian dance music, the second level R&B, and the third European dance music. The third floor is where you'll find, for a change, an all-male dance show. The clientele is young and local. All in all, this is a winner for people-watching. 174 Ligovsky Prospekt. ☎ 812/766-0204. www.metroclub.ru. Cover from 280 rubles. Metro: Livogsky Prospekt.

Nevsky 106 At the lower end of Nevsky Prospekt, this club-restaurant puts on popular theme nights and has live music in the early evening. Dancing kicks off at 10:30pm with DJs. This is a good place to have a night off the vodka, as the Mojito bar on the first floor offers non-alcoholic cocktails, and nonsmokers will appreciate the smoke-free room. It's also a good anytime option as it's open 24 hours, with a breakfast menu available from 9am to, thoughtfully, 2pm. 106 Nevsky Prospekt. ☎ 812/273-2966. www.nevsky106.spb.ru. Metro: Mayakovskaya, Ploschad Vosstaniya.

Rock & Pop

Konyushenny Dvor A hillbilly bar with an urban edge, this bar attracts Russian yuppies and foreign tourists who have little in common with the cowboy paraphernalia on its walls. Its small dance floor gets packed by midnight and music is mainstream but always dance-friendly. The balcony seats are much more fun, but watch out for the crooked, dim stairwell if you've been sampling Russian vodka. Daily 7am to 6am. 5 Canal Griboyedova. ☎ 812/315-7607. www.kondvor.ru. Metro: Nevsky Prospekt.

Liverpool The Beatles had an especially devoted following in the Soviet Union, where their music made it to the masses only through bootleg LPs and underground fan clubs. At the Liverpool pub, live (Russian) bands play Beatles covers and other music of their era most nights. This is a weird and worthwhile stop for any Beatles fan, with food available all day. Daily noon to 1am. 16 Ulitsa Mayakovskaya. ☎ 812/579-2054. www.liverpool.ru. Metro: Mayakovskaya.

Money Honey One of the more democratic clubs in town, this place can be rough and rowdy on weekend nights. Live rockabilly music is on offer nearly every night, along with cheap beer. 28 Sadovaya Ulitsa. ☎ 812/310-0549. www.moneyhoney.ru. Cover 150–400 rubles for major shows. Metro: Sadovaya.

Rossi's Once you get past the scary metal dragon-bird skeleton gateway and the metal detector, Rossi's is a lively and welcoming basement bar and music club. The low, vaulted ceilings of exposed brick and wood beams mean the place gets smoky at night. If that's a problem, make it an early evening stop for a beer or cocktail. 1/3 Ulitsa Zodchego Rossi. ☎ 812/710-4016. www.rossis.ru. Entrance is 150–500 rubles depending on the day of the week. Men and women have separate entrance tariffs—men pay slightly more. Women get in free Mon–Wed before 11pm. Metro: Gostiny Dvor.

Jazz & Blues

Jazz Philharmonic Hall For more traditional shows, head to St. Petersburg's jazz shrine, whose large hall offers balconies and a nostalgic atmosphere. Performances are consistently excellent, with classically trained performers. Shows start at 7pm daily. Check out the Museum of Petersburg Jazz on the second floor. 27 Zagorodniy Prospekt. ℂ **812/764-8565.** www.jazz-hall.spb.ru. Tickets 500–850 rubles. Metro: Vladimirskaya.

JFC Elegant yet relaxed, this venue features Russian and foreign musicians and is a favorite among expats and Russian jazz connoisseurs. 33 Shpalernaya Ulitsa. ℂ **812/272-9850.** www.jfc-club.sp.ru. Cover 200–300 rubles. Metro: Chernyshevskaya.

Jimi Hendrix Blues Club This basement bar inhabits a building that Russians know better as the house of poet Sergei Yesenin. It's the best place in town to hear blues, both authentic (by visiting U.S. performers) and with a Russian twist. Despite the exposed brick walls and torn posters, the place would have been too classy for Hendrix, but the atmosphere is pretty laid-back, the food is good, and the prices are reasonable. 33 Liteiny Prospekt. ℂ **812/579-8813.** Cover 200 rubles. Shows at 7:30pm. Metro: Chernyshevskaya.

Red Fox Jazz Club Live jazz 7 nights a week, tasty food and tempting drinks— this is an excellent place to wind down after a busy day of sightseeing. Check out their website for listings of their broad selection of bands, from Cuban to New Orleansean to homegrown Russian rhythms. 50 Mayakovskaya. ℂ **812/275-4214.** www.rfjc. ru. Cover 60–100 rubles. Metro: Chernyshevskaya.

Folk & Alternative

Cynic (Tsynik) This fun and funky venue stayed hip even after expanding to a three-room space with room enough to dance (unlike its minuscule original locale). Students, expats, and anyone with steam to blow appreciate its spontaneous shows by underground bands and its cheap beer and food. It's famous for its *grenki*, garlic toast, but you get used to the smell fast. Open Sunday through Thursday from noon to 3am; Friday and Saturday from noon to 6am. 4 Antonenko Pereulok. ℂ **812/312-9526.** Metro: Sennaya Ploshchad.

Fishfabrique Part of the Pushkinskaya 10 art complex (p. 234), this is the hippest and most creative place for alternative bands, though perhaps the smallest. It's called "Fishka" by locals. Check out the gallery of experimental sound and other wonders in this countercultural cavern of performance and gallery spaces. Open daily from 3pm to 6am; concerts usually take place Thursday through Saturday. 10 Pushkinskaya Ulitsa. ℂ **812/164-4857.** Cover 100–300 rubles for concerts. Metro: Ploshchad Vosstaniya.

Nightclubs & Cabaret

Unfortunately, most nightclubs in St. Petersburg have become synonymous with bordellos, and the stage shows are little more than strip acts. The nightclubs in the more expensive hotels are somewhat cleaner, though they tend to be stale and not worth the high drink prices. The bars and dance clubs are a better way to feel the city's nighttime pulse. One exception, perhaps the only cabaret in town, is the **Chaplin Club,** which puts on pantomime shows, comedy shows, or jazz performances at 7:30pm every night for about 100 rubles. The shows are in Russian but visually enjoyable, and the atmosphere is relaxed and arty with a vaudevillian feel. During the day, children's parties are staged. It's at 59 Chaikovskogo Ulitsa (ℂ **812/272-6649;** metro: Chernyshevskaya).

THE BAR SCENE

St. Petersburg's bar scene is less extensive than Moscow's, but it's more compact— with many bars jammed up along Nevsky Prospekt—and perhaps more creative.

Nevsky's bar-restaurants are open until the wee hours, or all night. During the White Nights, the taps flow steadily till dawn. The brewing industry has blossomed in and around St. Petersburg in recent years, and many of the country's favorite brands are based here. Be sure to try out local beers Tinkoff, Baltika (no. 7 is the most accessible), and Nevskoye at some point during your stay.

Baranka This laid-back bar-restaurant has an airy feel, and does a wide range of food and cocktails. It's also open for breakfast—try the homemade cranberry juice and omelette. Open daily 8am to 1am. 5 Ulitsa Chapaeva. ℰ **812/934-8979**. Metro: Moskovskaya.

Pivnaya Bochka (Beer Barrel) Russian beer on tap and basic Russian cuisine at reasonable prices are the main draws here. This is a good after-dinner spot but it stays open only until midnight. 30 Bolshaya Pusgkarskaya. ℰ **812/232-8760.** Metro: Sportivnaya.

Prokhodimets Beerhouse This is a friendly spot for porter, lager, and unfiltered beer in the section of town known as the Five Corners (Pyat Uglov). Its name translates as something like "rascal." Daily 1pm to 1am. 8 Ulitsa Rubinshteina. ℰ **812/517-1243.** Metro: Vladimirskaya.

Shamrock Bar This Irish pub is handy to get a bite to eat or drink on the square near the Mariinsky Theater. It's cozy and friendly, and about as culturally distant from the imperial ballet theater as you can get. There's live Irish music most nights, and lots of beer on tap. Daily 9am to 2am. 27 Ulitsa Dekabristov (Teatralnaya Sq.). ℰ **812/570-4625.** www.shamrock.spb.ru. Metro: Sadovaya.

Shelter Pub and Whisky Bar This bar's interior is inspired by English private members clubs, and it bills itself as a comfortable haven from the bustle of the city. It has over 50 kinds of whisky and a good range of draught beers, as well as a bar menu featuring steaks and grills. Just down the road from the Russian Museum, it attracts a mixed crowd of tourist and locals. Open daily from 11am until the last guest leaves. 29 Italyanskaya Ulitsa. ℰ 812/570-0868. www.pubshelter.ru.

Tinkoff This brewery houses a lively sports bar, sushi bar, and music club, and is among the city's most consistently popular hangouts. See review for Tinkoff restaurant on p. 215. 7 Ulitsa Kazanskaya. ℰ **812/458-7788.** www.tinkof.ru. Metro: Sadovaya or Sennaya Ploshchad.

GAY & LESBIAN NIGHTLIFE

The gay scene in Petersburg, as elsewhere in Russia, really emerged only over the past decade or so after Soviet-era laws against homosexuality were scrapped. Now the city's gay club scene is like its counterparts in any major metropolis: fickle. Today's hot spot may be too mainstream—or may have gone straight—by next season. Many of the city's top dance clubs have gay nights, and nearly all clubs are gay-friendly. See www.gay.ru/english for up-to-date listings.

Sinners (Greshniki) Four floors of an old mansion host one of the city's best mixed party spots. Sometimes it's gay-dominant, sometimes simply gay-friendly, but it's always good for dancing. Paint and brushes are often available for body art. 28/1 Canal Griboyedova. ℰ 812/570-4291. Cover 200 rubles men; 500 rubles women. Metro: Nevsky Prospekt.

Tri El (Three Ls) St. Petersburg's—and perhaps Russia's—first lesbian club, this hip and friendly place is slowly opening up to a broader public, although it's women only. Its cozy lounge and inexpensive bar draw in visitors as much as its

St. Petersburg's high-brow history didn't keep out the flood of gaudy gambling establishments embraced by post-Soviet Russia. Slot machines are found in places you least expect them, including upscale restaurants and shops. Casinos however were shut down in 2009 in an effort to clean up the shady business that often goes hand-in-hand.

lesbian strip shows and drag acts. The club runs themed fancy dress nights with reduced entry price (200 rubles) for anyone who makes the effort. 107-109 Moscovsky Prospekt. ✆ **812/387-1150.** www.triel.spb.ru. Cover 400 rubles. Women only Sat–Wed. Metro: Moscovskiye Vorota.

MORE ENTERTAINMENT

Billiards

See "More Entertainment" in chapter 8 for a description of Russian *piramida* vs. English billiards and American pool.

Panda and Kartathena This nightspot houses a casino favored by St. Petersburg's nouveau riche, as well as billiards and pool tables. No informal dress is allowed, but if you want an atmospheric way to shoot some balls, come here. 26 Griboyedov Canal. ✆ **812/312-8896.** Tables 90-200 rubles per hr. Metro: Nevsky Prospekt.

Sapsan This entertainment center on the 4th floor of the Galeria entertainment centre has Russian billiards (weekdays 300 rubles per hr., weekends 450 rubles per hr.) and American pool (weekdays 240 rubles per hr., weekend 360 rubles per hr.). Booking advised at weekends. Open daily 10am to 6am. 30a Ligovsky Prospekt. ✆ **812/600-0331.** Metro: Ligovsky Prospekt.

Bowling

To prepare for the trendy disco atmosphere of most Russian bowling alleys, see "More Entertainment" in chapter 8.

Bowling Park ☺ This chain of entertainment centers has a branch in the "Sennaya" shopping center with 36 bowling lanes, 20 of which are equipped for children to use. Monday to Friday 11am to 6am, Saturday and Sunday 10am to 6am. 3, Ulitsa Yemifova. ✆ **812/380-3005.** www.bowlingpark.ru. Lanes 300 rubles per hr. and up. Metro: Sennaya/Sadovaya.

M-111 This multistory amusement zone offers some of the hippest bowling in town, with black light and club music after 9pm. Daily noon to 6am. 111 Moskovsky Prospekt. ✆ **812/441-3000.** Lanes 400-1,200 rubles per hr., depending on time of day (around midnight on weekends the price peaks). Metro: Moskovskiye Vorota.

SIDE TRIPS FROM ST. PETERSBURG

A nywhere you go outside St. Petersburg will give you new perspective on the city's geography and its place in Russia's history. Whether you want to breathe fresh air, delight in country palaces of the nobility, or see rural architecture, branching out from the city is well worth a day or so of your trip.

Peterhof, Pavlovsk, and Pushkin (also known as Tsarskoye Tselo—home of the ill-fated Amber Room) house three of the most spectacular summer estates of the Romanov czars and most tour groups and individual tourists visit at least one of them. I recommend the same, though best to avoid them on rainy days. The extensive, landscaped parklands around the palaces are as much a part of the trip as the overly gilded interiors. The towns, charming in their own right, nevertheless remind you why Peter chose to base his capital elsewhere, on the river-crossed delta opening to the Baltic Sea.

The other destinations listed here reflect entirely different chapters in Russian history. Vyborg is a 13th-century town that has been Swedish, Finnish, and Karelian (an ethnic group based in what is now northwest Russia and eastern Finland) as well as Russian, and its architecture and mind-set are nothing like those of Peter the Great's Enlightenment-era capital. Kronshtadt is an island fortress that once served as a Viking rest stop but later became a major Soviet naval base closed to outsiders. It's now open to tourists and makes for a fascinating day trip.

All these destinations are best appreciated with a tour guide unless you know a lot about them before you go. Peterhof and Kronshtadt are fairly easy to reach on your own, and both can be accessed by boat in the warmer months. The other destinations require multiple modes of transportation if you're not with an organized tour.

PETERHOF (PETRODVORETS) ★★★

30km (19 miles) W of St. Petersburg

Unquestionably the number-one day trip from St. Petersburg, Peterhof lures visitors with its Versailles-inspired palace, which overlooks a cascade of fountains and gardens opening onto the Baltic Sea. This scene is much better appreciated from April to October, when the Grand Cascade is flowing and the park is in bloom. Going to Peter the Great's summer palace by ferry or hydrofoil enhances the pleasure of the experience, giving you a sense of Peter's maritime ambitions and of the region's role as Russia's western frontier. The boat ride and extensive park make this a great summer outing for kids.

Essentials

You'll get much more out of Peterhof if the weather is clear, since a major part of the experience is seeing the fountains (Apr–Oct) and wandering the grounds. The trip can easily be handled on your own, though organized tours are readily available. Tours offer two main advantages: no worries about transport, and detailed descriptions of the sights. The disadvantages are that you may be stuck in a crowded, touristy restaurant for lunch, and you won't get to explore the grounds freely. Tour costs are not much higher than paying for transport and museum tickets on your own. Check with your hotel about tours, or try **Davranov Travel** (17 Italianskaya Ulitsa; © **812/312-4662;** www.davranovtravel.ru).

Boat trips are the best way to get here from mid-May to early October, not least because of the breathtaking view of the palace as you pull up to the Peterhof pier.

Two companies run hydrofoils from the docks on the Neva River in front of the Winter Palace. **Russian Cruises** (© 812/325-6120; www.russian-cruises.ru) is the better equipped and offers English-language commentary. The **Vodokhod** company (© 812/740-5858) is cheaper but more rudimentary. The 45-minute trip takes you along the forested banks of the Baltic Sea. Boats run several times a day. When you disembark, head up the canal for the palace; the entrance is on the opposite side. Organized tours will often take you there on a boat and back home on a bus.

From October to May the best way to go is by bus. Russian vendors hawk trips on direct buses from Nevsky Prospekt metro station. They cost about 600 rubles round-trip and take an hour and a half.

The more adventurous and well-heeled can now take a **helicopter,** providing the weather's fair. They take off from Peter and Paul Fortress (see p. 229) three times a day, and the ride costs about 1,200 rubles per person.

What to See & Do

The palace and grounds offer enough to fill a day, or at least an afternoon. Start with the **Great Palace,** and be prepared to squint at all the gold inside. The rooms run in a long line facing the park, which can make for bottlenecks if visitors reverse direction or when there are large groups. Many visitors say the palace feels too magnificent to live in—and Peter felt the same, preferring **Monplaisir,** a small baroque bungalow close to the water's edge that was the first building in the Peterhof complex.

Peter chose Peterhof's location for his summer residence based on its proximity to Kronshtadt, the island fort that housed his fledgling Russian navy (see review later in this chapter). Built in 1715 by Jean Baptiste Leblond, the Great Palace came to be known for its grand summer fetes, in which everyone was invited to explore the czar's domain. The palace was occupied by the Nazis during World War II and suffered severe damage; its painstaking renovation became the region's pride. Note the Throne Room, with its dizzying light and portraits of the Romanovs; the neighboring Ladies-in-Waiting Room; and the intricate wooden floors of the Western Chinese Study.

In the lush park, the Monplaisir house, the small red-and-white Hermitage, and the **Marly Palace** (with a carved wood desk that Peter himself made) are well worth exploring, too, and more atmospheric than the Great Palace. Before heading down into the park, spend a moment on the palace balcony to take in the view of the greenery and the **Grand Cascade** from above. If it's open, explore the **grotto** beneath the fountain to see the 18th-century engineering feats that helped pipe in water from springs in the surrounding Ropsha Hills and make the cascade's 64 water jets work in synchronicity.

The most elaborate statues and fountains are along the axis from the palace to the pier. Be sure to see **Samson Fountain,** with the biblical strongman tearing apart the jaws of a lion, symbolizing Peter's victory over Sweden in 1709. Off to one side are the musical staccato fountains that shoot up at unpredictable intervals, where children love to drench themselves in warm weather while trying to guess which one will go off next. The park also includes a labyrinth of paths and ornate iron footbridges, as well as several small pavilions and gazebos. Park pavilions have opening days and admission fees different from those of the palace; weekends are the only time everything is open.

Peterhof (Petrodvorets) Palace and Park is at 2 Razvodnaya Ulitsa (© 812/450-5287; www.peterhofmuseum.ru). Admission to the palace costs 520 rubles adults, 250 rubles college students and children; admission to the park alone costs 400 rubles adults, 200 rubles students and children. After the fountains are turned

Baltic Sea

Ferry to St. Petersburg

Marly Palace

Marly Pond

Hermitage

Morskaya alleya

Berezovaya alleya

Marlinskaya

alleya

Monplaisir Palace

ul. Morskogo Desanta

Sandy Pond

Samson Fountain

Grand Cascade

Nikolskaya alleya

Zolotaya ul.

Proletnaya ul.

Prudovaya ul.

Great Palace

Eykhenskaya ul.

Razvodnaya ul.

Pravlenskaya ul.

Kalininskaya ul.

Aleksandriyskoe shosse

Red Pond

Sankt-Petersburgskiy prospekt

| 0 | 1/4 mi |
| 0 | 0.25 km |

Olga Pond

off, the price drops to just 50 rubles for the palace and park. The palace is open Tuesday through Sunday from 10:30am to 7pm (closed last Tues of each month). Monplaisir, the grotto beneath the palace, and other buildings on the grounds have different hours and in some cases extra admission fees.

Where to Eat

The most convenient dining options are on the grounds of the park itself. **Imperatorsky Stol,** in the orangerie near the Triton Fountain, is a cozy place for tea, snacks, or a full meal of decent and inexpensive Russian-European cuisine (© **812/450-6106**). The **Standart** restaurant (© **812/450-6281**), at the center of the Lower Park near the canal, has more elegantly and expertly prepared Russian fare, for a higher price. It's housed in the former Illumination Yard, which was used to store pyrotechnic equipment for the palace's extravagant balls. Outside the grounds are a few restaurants playing up the town's imperial heritage for the benefit of rich Russian and foreign tourists, with servers in period costume and ornate dining halls. One of these is **Ofitserskoye Sobraniye** (25 Ulitsa Konstantinovskaya; © **812/427-4903**), housed in a former club for pre-revolutionary royal officers. Its extensive appetizer selection is more successful than the main courses.

16 TSARSKOYE TSELO (PUSHKIN)

25km (16 miles) S of St. Petersburg

For an intimate view of imperial country living during St. Petersburg's rise to world prominence, visit the baroque Catherine's Palace at Tsarskoye Tselo (formerly called Pushkin). This is almost always viewed together with a trip to nearby Pavlovsk to see Czar Paul I's classical castle and sculpted gardens (see the next section). It was here that Russian engineers laid the country's first railway line, connecting these two royal resort towns, in order to shuttle nobles between palaces for summertime balls. Today anyone can ride the train, a 5-minute, 20-ruble ride, and view a model of the original train that took Czar Nicholas I and his family on their first ride. The world-famous **Amber Room**—gutted by the Nazis and recently meticulously reconstructed—is the major draw at Catherine's Palace; the rest of its rooms are marginally less impressive.

Essentials

Tsarskoye Tselo and Pavlovsk each can be visited on its own, but their proximity to each other and convenient transport between them make for a pleasant dual-destination trip. Nearly all organized tours combine the two. You could fit both into 1 day, extend the trip over a weekend, or visit each separately. If you're visiting both, it makes most sense to hit Tsarskoye Tselo in the morning, then head to Pavlovsk for a picnic lunch in the park before visiting the palace there.

Many St. Petersburg hotels offer tours, as do **Davranov Travel** (17 Italianskaya Ulitsa; ✆ 812/571-8694; www.davranovtravel.ru) and **Frigate Tours** (✆ 812/331-3333). You can also get a riverboat to Tsarskoye Tselo from the pier in front of the Winter Palace in St. Petersburg during the warmer months. Getting there on your own is not too difficult, but getting around once you're there requires a great deal of walking. A good tour guide or detailed book about the palaces (available at bookstores in St. Petersburg; see "Books" in chapter 14) is recommended. Organized tours usually take you by bus to Tsarskoye Tselo first, then to Pavlovsk.

If you're on your own, Russian tour buses run direct to Tsarskoye Tselo from in front of Nevsky Prospekt metro station; the trip takes about 40 minutes and costs about 750 rubles round-trip. You can also take a suburban train (*elektrichka*), which leaves Vitebsk station in St. Petersburg for Tsarskoye Tselo, then continues on to Pavlovsk. The ride costs about 200 rubles and takes about 45 minutes, then another 5 minutes to Pavlovsk, but you must be able to read the names of both towns in Russian to make sure you don't miss your stop (see chapter 18 for Cyrillic alphabet guide). The train station at Tsarskoye Tselo is a sight in itself, with its Art Nouveau sweep and murals showing stations along the route, as well as the Royal Waiting Room upstairs. The walk to the palace takes a good 15 minutes, or you can hire a taxi.

What to See & Do

The town's original name, Tsarskoye Tselo (Tsar's Village), comes from the palaces and parks built by empresses Catherine I (Peter the Great's second wife) and Elizabeth I (their daughter). The electric-blue, white, and gold **Catherine's Palace (Yekaterinsky Dvorets)**—the world's longest palace, at nearly 300m (984 ft.)—is the town's central star. In the Soviet era, the town was named after the adored Russian poet Alexander Pushkin, who studied at the *lycée* here for 6 years in the early 19th century and later had a *dacha* (country house) in town. The Pushkin-related sights are worth visiting only if you speak Russian. The town has since readopted its pre-revolutionary name, but many Russians and much literature about the town still refer to it as Pushkin.

Although the palace was named after Catherine I, it was Catherine II (the Great) who was responsible for much of its interior design. It was built in stages, each of which reflects the character of the empress in charge at the time. Its baroque, festive features come from Elizabeth's favored court architect Bartolomeo Rastrelli, who later designed St. Petersburg's Winter Palace, while the simpler, neoclassical interiors came from Catherine the Great's English architect Charles Cameron. The facade of the palace is as sunny as the muted green face of the Winter Palace in Petersburg is misty, and much of the interior of Catherine's Palace glares even more brightly than its exterior. The gold cupolas of the palace church rise above one end of the facade, and a flowery, ornamental "E" (the Russian initial for Yekaterina) tops its entrance.

The palace's masterpiece, the **Amber Room,** is a crucial part of every tour. Museum guards sometimes restrict visitors' time there to control crowds. Its unrivalled concentration of amber, its unusual concept, and its dramatic history make it worth all the hype. The room actually feels small compared to others in the palace. It takes you a moment to realize that its walls are lined in amber panels, using nearly a ton of stone (or technically, petrified sap). Florentine mosaics portraying the five

THE amber ROOM

Originally constructed in 1701–1709 within the Charlottesburg Palace, the panels of what was to become Tsarskoye Tselo's Amber Room were give by the Prussian King Friedrick Wilhelm I to his then ally Peter I in 1716. They were not unpacked and installed until 1755, however: a task that required some eight tons of amber and that took 10 years to complete. Attempts to protect it from the German invasion of 1941 proved futile: the panels were too fragile to move, and its disguise (under wallpaper) was discovered by the Nazis in less than 36 hours. Initially transferred to Konigsburg (now Kaliningrad), the original panels have never been recovered, and rumors of their current locations abound. Some claim they were destroyed in the Allied bombings of Konigsburg, others that they were torpedoed in transit. A group of German treasure hunters claimed to have found evidence of them near the Czech border in early 2008. Reconstruction of the new Amber Room began in 1979 (with financial support from Germany), and it opened in 2003.

senses combine a staggering array of shades of amber, from milky green to deep rust brown. Furniture inlaid with amber occupies the room. Many of the works, however, are copies of long-lost originals. The original engraved wall panels were a gift to Peter the Great from the king of Prussia in 1716, then were stolen by Nazis who occupied the palace during the siege of Leningrad. One of the mosaics, *Smell and Touch,* is an original, discovered in private hands in Bremen, Germany, in 1997. The palace itself suffered even more widespread damage when the Nazis retreated—they blew up many of its masterpieces on their way, and the reconstruction took decades.

The other chief highlight of the palace is the **Great Hall,** a grand ballroom lined with two tiers of windows interspersed with mirrors, much like Versailles's Hall of Mirrors. When the sun shines, the hall sparkles with reflections off the mirrors—perfect for balls on sunny midsummer nights. The palace holds chamber music concerts during the White Nights. The Grand Hall's ceiling painting runs nearly the length of the room, and depicts Russian military victories and accomplishments in the sciences and arts.

Similarly luxurious halls elsewhere in the palace are the **Agate Pavilion,** a bathhouse of polished Siberian stone; and the **Blue Drawing Room, Blue Chinese Room,** and **Choir Anteroom,** all of which have intoxicating silk wall coverings. The **Green Dining Room** is one of the first imperial rooms in Russia to incorporate a fireplace and marble mantelpiece; until then, the preference had been for Dutch-tiled corner ovens.

Leave plenty of time to explore the grounds, in particular the **Marble Bridge** over the Great Pond, and the **Pyramid,** where Catherine the Great's favorite dogs were buried. The pavilion on the island was built for the musicians who accompanied royal boat trips on the pond.

Catherine's Palace (Yekaterinsky Dvorets) is located at 7 Ulitsa Sadovaya, Pushkin (© 812/465-9424; www.tzar.ru). Admission to the park is 100 rubles for adults, 50 rubles for students, children free; admission to the palace costs 320 rubles for adults, 160 rubles for students, and 100 rubles for children. The park is open daily sunrise to sunset; the palace is open Wednesday through Monday from 10am to 6pm (closed last Mon of each month).

Where to Eat

Cafe Tsarskoye Tselo in the palace itself is the most convenient but least interesting lunch option in the vicinity, with hot and cold drinks and small open-faced sandwiches. (Its entrance is opposite the *lycée*; © **812/470-1349**). A more picturesque spot is the **Admiralty (Admiralteistvo)**, on the second floor of the pavilion of the same name on the shore of the Baltic Sea, at the other side of the Great Pond from the palace (Yekateriinsky Park; © **812/465-3549**). The cuisine is primarily Russian, and service is friendly. Slightly farther from the palace, along the park's edge, is **Staraya Bashnya (Old Tower)** restaurant, concealed in the cluster of buildings called Fyodorovsky Gorodok (14 Akademichesky Pereulok; © **812/466-6698**). Russian items such as garlicky beef dumplings *(pelmeni)* and beef stroganoff are particularly worthwhile. The restaurant is small, so reservations are a good idea before you make the trek out there.

PAVLOVSK

30km (19 miles) S of St. Petersburg

The park at Pavlovsk outshines even its impressive palace, and is perfect for picnicking on a clear day. Several enclaves dot the grounds, representing more human-size architecture of the 18th and 19th centuries. The town is named after the palace's original ruler, Czar Paul I (Pavel in Russian). In a reflection of their characters, Paul's summer home is as restrained and classical as his mother Catherine the Great's summer getaway at Tsarskoye Tselo is extravagant and baroque. Comparing the two is a key reason to combine visits to them in a single day.

Essentials

This trip is often combined with a journey to Tsarskoye Tselo (see review above). If you want to view it separately, you can try to arrange an individual tour through your hotel or a travel agency. Otherwise, you can take a suburban train *(elektrichka)* from St. Petersburg's Vitebsk Station. The train takes about 50 minutes, and goes through Tsarskoye Tselo first; Pavlovsk is the next stop. You must be able to read the name in Russian (see chapter 18 for Cyrillic alphabet guide). The trip through town to the palace is about a 15-minute walk or ride on a local bus; it's not marked, but any resident can direct you.

What to See & Do

Here, as in Tsarskoye Tselo, the town's palace is the central attraction. More an imitation of a Roman villa than a royal residence, the yellow-and-white Grand Palace at Pavlovsk was built in 1782 on a bluff overlooking the Slavyanka River. The Nazis also occupied this palace, but curators managed to save many of its masterpieces by hiding them in niches behind false walls.

A who's-who of Russian imperial architects had a hand in the palace's interiors, including Charles Cameron, Jacomo Quarengi, and Carlo Rossi. You'll notice the split personality this produced in the contrast between the extravagant **Throne Room** and the simple, dignified **Corner Drawing Room,** lined in lavender marble and Karelian birch furniture. Note the table settings in the **Dining Room,** ready for imperial guests. **Paul's Library** includes tall tapestries given to him by Louis XVI soon before the French Revolution.

Paul's wife Maria Fyodorovna lived here another 27 years after his death, and her quarters constitute a separate little museum within the palace. The **Dowager Empress Rooms,** as they're named, feel lived-in, unlike the rest of the palace, with its cold ornamentation. The rooms especially come alive after you look at palace portraits of Maria and at her own artworks.

The 607-hectare (1,500-acre) park is a winding labyrinth of wooded lanes, shady glades, and pavilions, but it's well planned enough that you never feel lost no matter how far you wander. Highlights include the Circle of White Birches at the end of the Rose Pavilion Alley, Centaur Bridge, and the partly crumbled Apollo Colonnade on the riverbanks on the palace side.

Admission to the **Grand Palace (Veliky Dvorets)**, 20 Ulitsa Sadovaya (© 812/ 452-1536; www.pavlovskmuseum.ru) and grounds is 500 rubles for adults, 300 rubles for students, children free; to see the grounds alone costs 150 rubles for adults, 50 for students, children free. You'll pay an additional 100 rubles to visit the Dowager Empress Rooms. The palace is open daily from 10am to 6pm (closed 1st Mon of each month).

Where to Eat

The grounds here are so ideal for picnicking that the best dining suggestion is to stop in the **Great Column Hall (Bolshoi Kolonny Zal)** restaurant and order food to go. (You can even get a bottle of champagne—or technically, Russian sparkling wine.) Housed in the former servants' quarters, the restaurant has a cafeteria-style section and a full-menu section as well, in case the weather is dreary. The Russian dishes are more successful, though you can order international favorites like Caesar salad. Another charming but basic option in the park is **Cafe Slavyanka,** across Centaur Bridge from the palace and to the left.

For an enthusiastic, satisfying, and almost kitschy taste of Russian country dining, stop at **Podvorye** restaurant (16 Filtrovskoye Shosse; ✆ **812/466-8544**) on your way to or from Pavlovsk. The hunting-lodge-style restaurant is on the main highway leading to St. Petersburg, so you need a bus or taxi to get there. Wild boar steak, elk cutlets, and even bear meat are among your options; vegetarians should try the pickled garlic and mushrooms, or pretty much anything with garlic or wild mushrooms. Guests are greeted with free vodka samples. A milder drink choice is *mors,* a delicious cranberry juice made from stewed local berries.

KRONSHTADT

30km (19 miles) SW of St. Petersburg

For a place that was closed to outsiders just a decade ago, this island is remarkably accessible today, and is perhaps the easiest day trip outside St. Petersburg. The island was first mentioned as a 12th-century rest stop for Viking expeditions to Greece, later became a fortress buttressing Peter the Great's new capital from attack, and later still became a key Cold War naval outpost. Today it's open for tourist business but still appears to be casting about for its modern role. Head here to wander the carefully planned harbor, the immaculate boulevards, the neo-Byzantine Naval Cathedral, and the naval history museum—or simply to gaze at the restless Baltic Sea around you.

Essentials

Kronshtadt is one of the few side trips manageable without a group or a tour guide. If you prefer a tour, check with your hotel; most places can arrange an individual or group tour. You can also try travel agencies such as **Davranov Travel** (17 Italianskaya Ulitsa; ✆ **812/571-8694;** www.davranovtravel.ru) and **Frigate Tours** (✆ **812/331-3333**).

The most appropriate way to travel to a naval outpost is, of course, by boat. From May to October, ferries head here several times a day from the piers behind the Hermitage Museum and from in front of Kunstkamera Museum on the other side of the Neva River. The ride takes about 1 hour and costs about 200 rubles.

You can also take a bus. Russian vendors hawk group bus trips at the corner of Nevsky Prospekt and Griboyedov Canal for about 500 rubles round-trip (the ride takes about an hr.). Or take minibus no. K-405 from metro station Chernaya Rechka, for about a 40-minute ride that costs just 45 rubles. Access to the **fortress** costs 300 rubles for adults, 100 rubles for students and children 8 and over (✆ **812/236-4713**).

Once you arrive, it couldn't hurt to buy a map from a newspaper kiosk. They're not always available, but the island is too small for you to get lost. The map helps you focus on specific spots and saves you time wandering through the bleaker neighborhoods of Soviet apartment blocks.

What to See & Do

The chief sights are the Naval Cathedral, which houses a good naval history museum, and the harbor. Much of the architecture and port infrastructure dates from Peter the Great's time, when he ordered a base built on Kotlin Island for Russia's fledgling navy, to block enemies from approaching his new capital. After victory over Sweden in the decisive Battle of Poltava in 1709, Peter launched large-scale construction of the island, and the first harbor and adjacent warehouses appeared. Some chronicles suggest Peter originally wanted to put the new capital on the island, but he never went further than building one of his many palaces here. It later burned down, but the palace of his chief adviser Alexander Menshikov still stands—it's an impressive Italian-designed mansion on the southern shore. The town itself is clearly planned, in the style of St. Petersburg, with broad, straight avenues and large squares. The **harbor** still feels more like a utilitarian military base than a romantic island boardwalk, but it's worth a wander nonetheless, if only to see the aging warships and port infrastructure.

The broad, etched dome of the **Naval Cathedral** dominates the skyline and looms over otherwise empty Yakornaya Ploshchad (Anchor Sq.). The anchor is incorporated into the cathedral's door carving, and pops up around town in grillwork, signage, and restaurant decor. Built in 1902 in a pseudo-Byzantine style, the cathedral is covered with intricate carvings and seems out of place in this otherwise rational, reserved city. The church's interiors have largely been turned over to the **Kronshtadt Museum of Naval History,** which is worth a visit if you have an English-speaking guide; otherwise, it may prove frustrating since most exhibits are in Russian only. The museum is packed with models of ships, weaponry through the centuries, seascapes by Russian artists, and unusual items such as antisubmarine netting. While it recounts the history of the island, the museum is rather awkward in its handling of the bloody mutiny that most Russians have come to associate with the name Kronshtadt. When the island's entire battalion staged an uprising against repressive Bolshevik leaders in 1921, the Soviet government responded swiftly and fiercely, massacring almost the whole battalion. The city remained a closed naval base for the rest of the Soviet era, and was opened only in 1996. The museum (© **812/311-4713**) is open Wednesday to Sunday from 11am to 5pm.

Where to Eat

Kronshtadt has no bustling beach boardwalk, but it has several mediocre restaurants within walking distance of the cathedral, museum, or harbor. None is particularly outstanding or particularly risky, though few have English-language menus. This is starting to change, and any place with a menu in English will be more expensive and probably offer somewhat better food and service. One pleasant spot for lunch is **Stary Gorod (Old Town),** 7 Ulitsa Grazhdanskaya (© **812/236-2238**), offering Russian and European standards such as borscht and baked salmon in a simple, homey setting. Seafood dishes are in the majority, though the selection is not as broad as you'd expect for an island town. The "business lunch" is just 160 rubles. Decent Russian beer is on tap.

VYBORG

130km (81 miles) NW of St. Petersburg

For a journey into an entirely different era and mind-set from St. Petersburg and the imperial estates on its outskirts, head to Vyborg. This 13th-century, cobblestoned city near the Finnish border has less glamour but more depth than Peter the Great's capital. Vyborg's architecture reflects its history, which tossed it back and forth among Swedes, Russians, Finns, and Karelians native to the region. The couple of hours it takes to get there can be thought of as journeying into Scandinavia for a day; then the trip doesn't seem so long at all. The distance is a good reminder of how close to the edge of his empire Peter the Great based his new capital.

Essentials

Organized tours to Vyborg are rarer than those to Peterhof or Pavlovsk, but a hotel concierge or tour guide can help you find one. Vyborg is on the main highway between St. Petersburg and Finland, which can get clogged on Russian holiday weekends and on which traffic slows down considerably during the blustery winter months. A summer weekday is an ideal time to go if you're in a car or on a tour bus. Trains also run three times a day from St. Petersburg's Finlandsky Vokzal Station; the trip takes 2 hours one way.

For a provincial city, Vyborg is unusually international, with menus in several languages and service staff usually eager to speak English. That's largely because of its proximity to Finland, and its popularity among Finnish tourists who come to buy cheap vodka, beer, and cigarettes. Russian vendors may speak to you in Finnish before they try English. If you're traveling on your own, buy a map at a newspaper kiosk; the city can be unwieldy if you don't know where you're going.

What to See & Do

The city inhabits a peninsula and several small islands on the northeast Baltic coast. The area was initially a trade settlement of Karelians, an ethnic group native to a region in what is now eastern Finland and northwest Russia. The Swedes came along and founded a city here in 1293 to use as a base for raids into neighboring Russia. Peter the Great conquered the city in 1710 during his 40-year war with Sweden. A century later, in 1811, it went to the Grand Duchy of Finland under Russian sovereignty. The city and surrounding region were part of the fledgling, independent nation of Finland from 1917 to 1940, and Vyborg (called Viipuri in Finnish) was Finland's second-largest city. The Winter War between Finland and the Soviet Union left Vyborg again in Russian hands, where it has remained since. Karelians remained the primary inhabitants until World War II, when many were evacuated to western Finland or forced out by Soviet troops.

Vyborg Castle, on a rocky island in the center of town, was the Swedes' first major project here, built in the 1290s. The stone castle saw many additions in subsequent centuries, and now houses a small museum whose exhibits include archaeological finds from the area and some curious items confiscated by 20th-century border guards. The island itself is an almost mystical outpost that lends itself easily to imagining what it looked like 700 years ago. The castle hosts St. Petersburg's White Nights events such as jazz or classical music concerts. The castle (© **813/782-1515**) is open Tuesday through Sunday from 10am to 5pm.

Be sure to wander through the **Old Vyborg district,** which boasts architecture from the 14th to 17th centuries that is markedly more Scandinavian in style than the Russian palaces that later popped up around town. Catholic and Protestant churches are more plentiful than Orthodox ones. **Market Square (Rynochnaya Ploshchad)** includes the only remaining tower of the 16th-century fortress wall built by the Swedes; the market itself dates from 1905 and shows hints of the Russian obsession with Art Nouveau. The **Central Library,** designed by Alvar Aalto in the 1930s, is a highlight of Finnish design during this fruitful architectural period. The architectural and nature reserve at **Monrepos Park** is well worth a stroll or picnic if the weather is fine. The romantic landscaping of the island park includes gardens and sculptures favored by the aristocracy and architects of Peter the Great's day. **Progonnaya Ulitsa (Driving St.),** once used for driving sheep and cows to pasture, now boasts several unusual buildings as it stretches toward the Gulf of Finland.

Where to Eat

Cheap restaurants and beer halls abound in Vyborg, largely aimed at Finnish students and bargain hunters who come for the day or weekend. Two better-than-average places to eat are Kruglaya Bashnya and Atlantik. **Kruglaya Bashnya** (Round Tower), located in a former watchtower next to the castle (© **813/782-1729**; www.roundtower.ru), describes itself as a bistro with fusion cuisine, which means its primarily Russian menu includes international standards such as chicken curry. It's open around the clock for those taking night trains to or from Finland, and the atmosphere is friendly and lively. Near the castle, **Nika** in the Hotel Atlantik, 9 Ulitsa Podgornaya (© **813/954-1513**), is in a drab stone building that conceals a cozy, wood-dominated interior. It offers mostly Russian standards with an emphasis on Baltic Sea fish—fresh, smoked, or pickled. The restaurant fills up with groups on weekends.

PLANNING YOUR TRIP TO MOSCOW & ST. PETERSBURG

Russia vaults across two continents and spans eleven time zones, yet its territorial vastness is easily forgotten in the crush of rush-hour metro rides and in crowded urban apartments. This chapter helps you figure out how to tackle your trip: where and when to go; how to get there; what precautions to take; and how to save money.

Moscow is almost a country unto itself, a metropolis of 12 million people enjoying the fruits of Russia's booming oil economy. Despite Russians' innate conservatism, today's Moscow is a 24-hour city that pulses with change, from the ruthlessly competitive restaurant and club scenes to the volatile financial markets and the clamor for the latest top-of-the-line cellphone. In the background, tented spires and golden cupolas of medieval cathedrals beckon, Stalin's neo-Gothic skyscrapers soar, and the imposing authority of the Kremlin lords over it all.

St. Petersburg occupies a world of architectural order forged out of a swamp at a forbidding latitude. Peter the Great's invention cost the lives of thousands of workers sent to make the Baltic Sea delta inhabitable 300 years ago. But his vision lives on—even new buildings adhere to the symmetry and classicism of Peter's day. The sea-green Winter Palace overlooking the Neva River houses the Hermitage Museum's staggering collection of fine art, and sumptuous royal estates dot the surrounding forests. St. Petersburg's reputation as Russia's intellectual and cultural center has not brought the city the prosperity that today's Moscow enjoys, but Petersburg has better hotel choices and a restaurant scene nearly as vibrant as the capital's.

GETTING THERE: MOSCOW

By Plane

Russia's chief international carrier remains Aeroflot, the former Soviet behemoth. Delta is the only major U.S. airline that flies into Russia, though all major European carriers serve Moscow and St. Petersburg. You can often find good deals through British Airways, Air France, and KLM. For a cheaper option, try the Eastern European airlines, such as Poland's LOT or Hungary's Malév, or Asian carriers such as Air India that use Moscow as a fueling stop.

For internal flights in Russia, such as between Moscow and St. Petersburg, the luggage weight limit is 20 kilograms (44 lb.); sometimes carry-ons are weighed as well. Above that weight, you'll have to pay a fee, usually at a separate cash desk apart from the check-in counter.

LONG-HAUL FLIGHTS: HOW TO STAY COMFORTABLE

o Your choice of airline and airplane will definitely affect your legroom. Find more details about U.S. airlines at www.seatguru.com. For international airlines, the research firm Skytrax has posted a list of average seat pitches at www.airlinequality.com.

o Emergency exit seats and bulkhead seats typically have the most legroom. Emergency exit seats are usually left unassigned until the day of a flight (to ensure that someone able-bodied fills the seats); it's worth checking in online at home (if the airline offers that option) or getting to the ticket counter early to snag one of these spots for a long flight. Many passengers find that bulkhead seating offers more legroom, but keep in mind that bulkhead seats have no storage space on the floor in front of you.

o To have two seats for yourself in a three-seat row, try for an aisle seat in a center section toward the back of coach. If you're traveling with a companion, book an aisle and a window seat. Middle seats are usually booked last, so chances are good you'll end up with three seats to yourselves. And in the event that a third passenger is assigned the middle seat, he or she will probably be more than happy to trade for a window or an aisle.

o To sleep, avoid the last row of any section or the row in front of an emergency exit, as these seats are the least likely to recline. Avoid seats near highly trafficked toilet areas. Avoid seats in the back of many jets—these can be narrower than those in the rest of coach. Or reserve a window seat so you can rest your head and avoid being bumped in the aisle.

o Get up, walk around, and stretch every 60 to 90 minutes to keep your blood flowing. This helps avoid **deep vein thrombosis,** or "economy-class syndrome." See the box "Coping with Jet Lag,'" p. 285.

o Drink water before, during, and after your flight to combat the lack of humidity in airplane cabins. Avoid caffeine and alcohol, which will dehydrate you.

GETTING INTO TOWN FROM THE AIRPORT

The main port of entry for international flights is **Sheremetevo-2 Airport** (© **495/ 956-4666** or 495/578-9101; www.sheremetyevo-airport.ru), 30km (19 miles) north of downtown. Built for the 1980 Olympics, it has recently undergone a partial renovation and is now split between a dingy gray terminal and a gleaming, well-marked new terminal. The passport control lines can be formidable. Luggage carts are free, though they sometimes run short in number, so grab one as soon as you see the baggage carousel. A currency exchange booth and ATM are available after you've cleared Customs; rates are better in town if you can afford to wait. An information desk with English-speaking personnel is in the main arrivals hall, along a row of car-rental desks and airline ticket offices. Package tours generally include transport to and from Russia's airports.

If you're on your own, your best bet is the **Aeroexpress train** to Savyolovsky Train Station, which runs once an hour and takes 40 minutes compared to the 1-to-2-hour car ride (© **800/700-3377;** www.aeroexpress.ru). It costs 250 rubles for adults. Tickets are available in the airport after you emerge from Customs.

In the old terminal, be prepared for the odorous herd of taxi drivers in the arrivals hall. If you prefer taxis, better to reserve in advance. **Moscow Taxi** (www.mymoscow taxi.com) and **Taxi Blues** (© **495/925-5115;** www.taxi-blues.ru) offer good English-speaking services. Women travelers, try **Pink Taxi** (© **495/662-0003;** www. womantaxi.ru) with exclusively women drivers and passengers. If you arrive without a ride, push your way to the official taxi desk near the exit. Official cabs are either yellow or have TAXI written in big letters in English and Russian. Rates are determined by a zone map, and a ride to the city center runs about 1,500 rubles. The freelance cabbies will try to convince you that $100 (or even 100 euros) is your cheapest option.

Buses leave from the airport parking lot and stop at Rechnoi Vokzal metro station (bus no. 851) or Planernaya metro station (bus no. 517). The fare, about 30 rubles, must be paid in rubles to the driver. Allow yourself at least an hour to reach downtown in a taxi, and at least 90 minutes by bus or metro.

A few European airlines now arrive at the bright, renovated **Domodedovo Airport** (© **495/933-6666** or 495/720-6666; www.domodedovo.ru), 50km (31 miles) south of the center. Domodedovo has all the same services as Sheremetevo but in a friendlier setting. It runs a train direct to Paveletsky station, just south of the city center, and it has a clear, fair, and computerized taxi service greeting passengers as they exit. The taxis aren't cheap but make sense if you are in a small group. Taxis from Domodedovo to the center take about an hour (it could be more than 2 hr. in heavy traffic) and cost around 2,300 rubles. The train ride to Paveletsky is 40 minutes and costs 200 rubles (see schedule at www.aeroexpress.ru). Two metro lines meet at Paveletsky station, where taxis are also available. Private buses run from Domodedovo to the nearest metro station, Domodedovskaya, every 15 minutes for just 80 rubles. Look for the buses labeled **Scania.** It takes about 30 minutes depending on traffic.

Flights to Moscow from St. Petersburg usually arrive at **Sheremetevo-1** (© **495/ 232-6565**), adjacent to Sheremetevo-2 but smaller. Taxis from there cost slightly less than from the international terminal. Other domestic Russian flights come into **Vnukovo** (© **495/436-2813**), 30km (19 miles) southwest of the city. Taxis to the center of the city cost about 1,500 rubles. Vnukovo also runs a train directly to Kievsky Station close to the city center that costs 100 rubles. The train runs every hour between 7am and 9pm; the trip takes about 40 minutes.

By Bus

Several European tour companies offer bus trips to Moscow, usually departing from Germany. However, the journey is long (2 days from Berlin) and along poorly maintained highways, and the waits at the borders are significant. For any trip traveling through or originating in Ukraine or Belarus, you may need a transit visa from those countries. Buses arrive at **Tsentralny Avtovokzal (Central Bus Terminal)** at 2 Uralskaya Ulitsa (© **495/468-0400**). The Shcholkovskaya metro station is adjacent. Taxis from the terminal take about 30 minutes to reach the center at a rate of about 450 rubles.

Jet lag is a pitfall of traveling across time zones. If you're flying north–south and you feel sluggish when you touch down, your symptoms will be the result of dehydration and the general stress of air travel. When you travel east-west or vice-versa, your body becomes confused about what time it is, and everything from your digestive system to your brain is knocked for a loop. Traveling east is more difficult on your internal clock than traveling west because most peoples' bodies are more inclined to stay up late than to fall asleep early.

Here are some tips for combating jet lag:

o **Reset your watch** to your destination time before you board the plane.
o **Drink lots of water** before, during, and after your flight. Avoid alcohol.
o **Exercise and sleep well** for a few days before your trip.
o If you have trouble sleeping on planes, **fly eastward on morning flights.**
o **Daylight** is the key to resetting your body clock. At the website for **Outside In** (www.bodyclock.com), you can get a customized plan of when to seek and avoid light.

By Car

For those rare arrivals by car, take the vehicle straight to your hotel and inquire about secure parking. Unfortunately, no current maps in English indicate one-way streets or other such crucial details for drivers. The Travellers Yellow Pages map in English, otherwise quite good, is available at www.infoservices.com and at major Moscow hotels. Do not underestimate Moscow traffic, which has mushroomed in the past decade and can leave visitors trapped in a labyrinth of jammed one-way streets, especially from 8 to 10am and 5 to 8pm. Watch out, too, for the traffic police, who, always eager for pocket money, can stop you just to make sure your documentation is in order. Garages are rare despite rising demand. Muscovites park on sidewalks and in doorways if they can't find free spaces, but because theft is not uncommon, this is not advised. There are also an increasing number of guarded parking areas, usually just a strip of parking places commandeered by a private company with a fare collector hanging out on the corner. Rates are usually fixed regardless of how long you stay parked. Renting a car with a driver is a more reliable and often cheaper option than driving yourself.

For information on car rentals and gasoline (petrol) in Moscow and St. Petersburg, see "Getting Around by Car," later in this section.

By Train

The St. Petersburg–Moscow train route is the country's best-maintained and most romantic. An overnight ride on a sleeper brings you into Leningradsky Station and costs 1,200 to 3,500 rubles, depending on the train's class and hour. The pricier rides come complete with slippers, in-cabin television, and a late-night meal. Two fast day trains, the Express and the Aurora, make the trip in about 5 hours, with a seat running 2,300 to 4,500 rubles. Leningradsky, like all of Moscow's train stations, is conveniently located on the Circle Line of the metro. Western European trains generally arrive in Belorussky Station, barely north of the city center and within walking distance of the hotels on busy Tverskaya Street. A second-class ticket in a sleeping car from Warsaw takes 24 hours and costs about $70; from farther west the time and cost rise accordingly. Most European trains travel through Ukraine or Belarus, both of which require a transit visa. Contact the Ukrainian or Belarusian embassy in your country for details, or pick a route through the Baltic states or Scandinavia. The train from Beijing takes 5 days and costs about $250. *Note:* Rail passes that serve the rest of Europe do not serve Russia.

GETTING AROUND MOSCOW
Visitor Information

Moscow has lacked a network of official tourist offices since the demise of the Soviet era. **Intourist,** formerly the government tourist agency, can be useful and has offices in the Kosmos Hotel at 150 Prospekt Mira (© **495/730-1919;** www.intourist.ru) and other sites closer to downtown, including one at 10 Leontevsky Pereulok (© **495/234-9509**). Hotel concierges and tour desks are likely to have as much information as Intourist, or more. Most hotels and many newspaper kiosks in the center of town sell maps in English (ask for a *karta na angliiskom,* pronounced "*kar*-ta na ahn-*glees*-kom"). Pick up a copy of the free English-language daily *The Moscow Times* for weather, exchange rates, entertainment listings, and more. The newspaper is not sold at newsstands, but most of the hotels listed in chapter 4 (particularly the high-end ones) carry copies.

CITY LAYOUT
At Moscow's heart and nearly its geographical center lies the Kremlin, from which the rest of the city has expanded in roughly concentric circles: the Boulevard Ring, the Garden Ring, and the Third Ring. The last circle, the Moscow Ring Road, is the bypass around the city limits. The expansion continues apace and Moscow is now an unwieldy megalopolis of 12 million people encompassing 1,000 sq. km (386 sq. miles)—nearly 10 times bigger than Paris or Manhattan.

 Map Confusion

Beware of maps and guidebooks printed before the mid-1990s, which may include the Soviet-era names of many streets and metro stations instead of the new ones.

The Moscow and Yauza rivers curve through the city, delineating neighborhoods. Visitors are often struck by Moscow's broad boulevards and vast squares, as well as the city's large swaths of green space (which turn to white space during the winter). Yet housing remains largely concentrated in cramped apartment blocks.

All major airports are well out of town (see above). Train stations are scattered around a circle that generally corresponds to the Garden Ring Road and the metro system's Ring Line. Trains from the west arrive at Kievsky Station or Belorussky Station on the northwest side of town, and trains from the north arrive at Leningradsky Station or Rizhky Station on the northeast side.

By Public Transportation

The **Moscow Metro** is an attraction unto itself (see the review on p. 110), and well worth a visit just to view a few stations even if you have other transport. It's generally clean and efficient, with trains running every 90 seconds or so during the day. Station entrances are marked with a letter M. The Circle Line runs around the center, with nearly a dozen radial lines crossing it. Color-coded maps are posted at every station entrance and in every train car, and most are now printed in English as well as Russian. The signs in the stations directing you to platforms are in Russian, however, so it helps to know what the name of your station looks like printed in the Cyrillic alphabet. The system is slowly expanding but has not kept up with population growth. Trains are nearly always crowded, and stops are too few and far between. Opening and closing times vary from station to station but are roughly 5:30am to 1am.

Paper tickets with a magnetic strip are sold in each station, for one trip (22 rubles), two trips (44 rubles), five trips (105 rubles), or 10 trips (200 rubles). No senior or student discounts are available for foreigners. You scan the ticket across the sensor on the machine's front and walk after the light changes from red to green.

Trams are second-best to the metro if there's a tram route near your hotel or destination. The stops are on the sidewalk, even where the tram tracks are in the middle of the street. Three of the best lines (A, 3, and 39) run along the picturesque Boulevard Ring before crossing the Moscow River, offering a stunning view of the Kremlin and winding toward Moscow State University and Danilovsky Monastery, among other sights. **Trolley buses,** attached to electrical lines overhead, are a good option for travel around the Garden Ring Road or along Novy Arbat Street. Rush hour is crowded and the timing between trolley buses is unpredictable. **Buses** are the least convenient and most overcrowded form of public transport.

Tickets for trams, trolley buses, and buses cost 20 rubles if bought from street ticket booths and 25 rubles if purchased from the driver. You validate your ticket while entering the bus at the machine and walk through a turnstile when you see the green light. Maps are posted inside the vehicles, and routes are often listed at the stops, but in Russian only. Bus stops are marked by signs with the letter A, trolley stops with the letter T, and tram stops with the letters TP. Some stops serve all three. Waiting time can be from 5 to 40 minutes, depending on the hour and the traffic. The three forms of transportation run from 6am to midnight.

A **monorail system** serves northern Moscow, between metro station Timiryazevskaya and Sergei Eisenstein Street. It serves the All-Russian Exhibition Center (see p. 117) and the Ostankino Estate. It's well beyond the center of town but worth a cruise along the full route (allow 40 min.) if you are in the neighborhood, for a view of a corner of Moscow that few visitors reach. Prices are the same as on the metro.

Route taxis, or *marshrutky,* are minivans that take up to 10 people along several routes that bigger buses don't serve. Fares vary but are generally not more than a couple of dollars. The destinations are marked on the front of the van in Russian only. To get off, yell "Stop!" to the driver. The minivans are more convenient than buses, trams, or trolleys, but the drivers are often reckless and there are no seat belts.

Getting Around Russia
BY TRAIN
The most pleasant, romantic, and historic way to travel around Russia is by train. The Moscow–St. Petersburg route is the most frequented and best maintained. Travelers choose between a leisurely 8-hour night trip in a comfortable sleeping compartment (about 1,125 rubles per person in a four-bed cabin; 2,125 rubles per person in a two-bed cabin), and a 5-hour day trip (same price). A snack and beverages are included

CLOTHING SIZE conversions

Russian clothing and shoe sizes are similar to—but not always exactly the same as—continental European standards. Items in Russian clothing stores are labeled in European sizes, Russian sizes, or both, usually depending on the country where the item was manufactured. It is always worth asking a vendor for advice if you have any doubt, especially if you are buying a gift for someone else.

Women's Clothing

AMER.	CONT.	BRIT.	RUSS.
6-8	36-38	8-10	42
8-10	38-40	10-12	44
10-12	40-42	12-14	46
12-14	42-44	14-16	48
14-16	44-46	16-18	50
16-18	46-48	18-20	52
18-20	48-50	20-22	54

Women's Shoes

AMER.	CONT.	BRIT.	RUSS.
5	36	4	35
6	37	5	36
7	38	6	37

Women's Shoes

AMER.	CONT.	BRIT.	RUSS.
8	39	7	38
9	40	8	39
10	41	9	40

Children's Clothing*

AMER./BRIT.	CONT./RUSS.
1 year	74
2 years	92
3 years	98
4 years	104
5 years	110
6 years	116
7 years	122
8 years	128
9 years	134
10 years	140

*Note that American and British clothing manufacturers tend to size children's clothing by age, while European and Russian children's clothing is usually sized by height in cm.

in the price, though you sometimes have to pay the conductor for the bed linens (about 50 rubles).

Trains from Moscow to St. Petersburg leave from Moscow's Leningradsky Station and arrive at St. Petersburg's Moskovsky Station. Both are in the center of town and easily accessible. Arranging train tickets before you arrive, for example through your travel agent at home, is the safest way to go, but is often more expensive. Most hotels can arrange train tickets to major cities. It's cheaper to buy from the train stations themselves, though the lines are chaotic and interminable.

Commuter trains (called *elektrichkas*) with hard benches and rock-bottom prices serve many of the country estates and other sights just outside the big cities.

BY PLANE

Given Russia's size, plane travel is crucial for reaching more distant destinations such as Lake Baikal or Vladivostok. The Russian airlines Aeroflot and Pulkovo dominate the Moscow–St. Petersburg route, and prices for a one-way ticket run 1,750 to 3,000 rubles. Flights on this route are nearly all on large, sturdy Soviet-era jets (not the flimsy twin-propeller Soviet planes that crash with alarming frequency), and although

Children's Shoes

AMER.	CONT.	BRIT.	RUSS.
8	24	7	23
9	25	8	24
10	27	9	26
11	28	10	27
12	29	11	28
13	30	12	29
1	32	13	31
2	33	1	32
3	34	2	33

Men's Shirts

AMER.	CONT./RUSS.	BRIT.
14½	37	14½
15	38	15
15½	39	15½
16	41	16
16½	42	16½
17	43	17
17½	44	17½
18	45	18

Men's Suits

AMER.	CONT./RUSS.	BRIT.
34	44	34
36	46	36
38	48	38
40	50	40
42	52	42
44	54	44
46	56	46
48	58	48

Men's Shoes

AMER.	CONT.	BRIT.	RUSS.
7	39½	6	38½
8	41	7	40
9	42	8	41
10	43	9	42
11	44½	10	43½
12	46	11	45
13	47	12	46

the upholstery is badly outdated, the service is steadily improving. See www.aeroflot.ru, www.pulkovo.ru, or www.eastline-tour.ru.

BY CAR

If you're not on a tour bus, renting a car can be a reasonable way to get around Moscow or St. Petersburg. However, a strongly recommended alternative is to rent a car with a driver. It can cost no more than a standard rental, and you don't have to worry about the challenges presented by Russian driving. Roads are riddled with holes, signage is often poor, and gas stations and services are sparse. Russian drivers are ruthless, especially with the indecisive. Moscow's traffic is overwhelming much of the day, and traffic police are hostile to anyone behind the wheel and rely heavily on on-the-spot "fines" for their incomes. Most sidewalks or walkways are fair game for parking, and there are very few parking garages. Knowledge of the Cyrillic alphabet is strongly recommended for anyone driving in Russia, in order to decipher street signs.

For rental without a driver, see Avis (www.avis.com), Hertz (www.hertz.com), or Europcar (www.europcar.com). For cars with drivers, try www.mymoscowtaxi.com.

BY BUS

Russian-run tourist buses offer day trips to cities on the Golden Ring outside Moscow and several sights around St. Petersburg, and are generally comfortable. Vendors often hawk tours on loudspeakers at central spots such as St. Petersburg's Nevsky Prospekt metro station and Moscow's Red Square. Otherwise, hotels can often arrange bus tours.

GETTING THERE: ST. PETERSBURG

By Plane

All international flights into St. Petersburg land at Pulkovo-2 Airport (✆ 812/704-3822 for Pulkovo-1 [domestic flights] or ✆ 812/704-3444 for Pulkovo-2 [international flights]; www.pulkovo.ru), which is friendlier and more manageable than Moscow's Sheremetevo-2 Airport. Pulkovo also has the advantage of a 2003 renovation that opened up the halls and lightened up the atmosphere, making the long lines for security and passport control much more tolerable.

Use of luggage carts is free. The airport money-exchange booths offer poorer rates than downtown; a better bet are the airport ATMs, which give rubles at the official Central Bank exchange rate. Internet access is available. The arrivals hall has an information desk with English-speaking personnel, car-rental desks, and airline ticket offices.

Tour groups won't have to worry about transfers to and from the airport, which is 16km (10 miles) south of the city limits or about a 45-minute ride to the center of town. If you're an individual traveler, arrange a taxi in advance from Pulkovo-2 by calling the **official airport cab company** at ✆ 812/312-0022. Otherwise, you can negotiate a ride upon arrival. Official cabs are often scarce, and charge about 800 to 1,000 rubles to Nevsky Prospekt. Official cabs are either yellow or have TAXI written in big letters in English and Russian. The ubiquitous independent cabbies rarely go below 1,300 rubles for the same trip. Public bus no. 13 takes you to the Moskovskaya metro station, south of the city center. Tickets are just 18 rubles, purchased aboard. No trains serve the airport.

Domestic flights into St. Petersburg, from Moscow for example, come into the neighboring **Pulkovo-1 Airport** (✆ 812/704-3822). The facilities are similar to those of Pulkovo-2, though more basic. Taxi service is the same as at Pulkovo-1, and public bus no. 39 takes you to the Moskovskaya metro station. To book your transfer by Internet, go to www.saint-petersburg.com/transfers/index.asp.

By Train

Entering St. Petersburg by overnight train from Moscow is one of the most romantic things you can do in Russia. The Moscow-based trains arrive at, appropriately, **Moskovsky (Moscow) Station,** right on Nevsky Prospekt, within walking distance of several major hotels and adjacent to the Ploshchad Vostanniya and Mayakovskaya metro stations. The official taxis in front of the station set their own prices, which are invariably higher at the train station than elsewhere in town.

Another easy train connection is from Helsinki, 5½ hours away (plus a 1-hr. time difference). The trip ends at St. Petersburg's **Ladoga Station** (Ladozhsky Vokzal, Zanevsky Prospekt 73; ✆ 812/436-5310). Taxis from there to Nevsky Prospekt cost

Important Visa Information

Passengers who participate in St. Petersburg shore excursions or arrange for private transportation through the ship's shore-excursions desk do not need to obtain a visa. Those who wish to go ashore on their own, however, do have to obtain a tourist visa prior to departure. To receive a Russian visa, you must have a valid passport that remains valid at least 30 days past the last day of the cruise. For more information on obtaining a visa, see "Visas," later in this chapter.

about 600 rubles. Three daily trains run to and from the Finnish capital, both stopping in Vyborg to clear Customs.

From Poland, Germany, and the Baltic states, trains arrive at Vitebsky Terminal (Vitebsky Vokzal), metro station Pushkinskaya, 52 Zagorodny Prospekt. If you are entering Russia from a European Union member country, you will need only a Russian visa. But if you enter through Belarus or Ukraine, you will need transit visas for those countries. Be aware, too, that rail passes that serve the rest of Europe do **not** include Russia.

By Bus

A few tour companies offer bus tours to St. Petersburg from Scandinavia on top-class Finnish coaches. From Helsinki the ride takes about 6 hours, including the long stop to clear Customs. Ordinary, nontour buses, which are cheaper than the train, are also available to and from Helsinki. If you travel on your own, you must take care of your Russian visa yourself. The road from Helsinki is relatively well maintained, unlike many others in the region. Buses arrive at **St. Petersburg Bus Station** (Avtobusny Vokzal; 36 Naberezhnaya Obvodonovo Kanala; ✆ **812/766-5777**).

By Boat

Many Scandinavian cruises include a stop in St. Petersburg, at the major commercial port 20 minutes north of the city center, at 1 Morskoy Slavy Sq. (✆ **812/322-6052;** metro: Primorskaya and Vasileostrovskaya). Minibuses to the metro (K-47, K-128, K-129, K-183, K-273, K-310, K-349, K-359, and K-690) run frequently and cost around 25 rubles.

Most cruises include an organized bus trip to the center. This is the most convenient option, since the metro is a long walk and the minibuses are often overcrowded. The official taxis serving the port charge more than elsewhere; expect to pay about 500 rubles to Nevsky Prospekt in the city center.

By Car

A few intrepid travelers come to St. Petersburg by car from Finland. Not including the long lines for Customs and document check at the border, the 370km (230-mile) drive from Helsinki is about 6 hours. Once in St. Petersburg, head straight to your hotel and settle the parking question. It's easy to park in St. Petersburg, since nearly any sidewalk or embankment is fair game, though underground garages are extremely scarce in this city built on swampland. It's harder to guarantee secure parking, however. Existing maps in English do not indicate one-way streets or other crucial driving details, though the Russian-language pocket-size *Atlas of St. Petersburg Roads* (*Atlas*

drawbridge DILEMMA

The drawbridges that span the Neva are both a charming attraction and a logistical consideration for St. Petersburg's tourists. They remain down during the day for automobile and foot traffic, but lift in the middle of the night in a carefully synchronized performance to allow shipping traffic from the Baltic Sea into Russia's inland rivers. That means you want to be sure to be on the same side of the river as your hotel when night falls, or else you may be stuck for a few hours.

The main bridges are up at roughly the following times, with minor adjustments each year:

Volodarskiy: 2 to 3:45am and 4:15 to 5:45am

Alexandra Nevskogo: 2:20 to 5:10am

Liteiny: 1:50 to 4:40am

Troitskiy: 1:40 to 4:50am

Dvortsovy: 1:25 to 4:55am

Blagoveshchenksy (formerly Leytenanta Shmidta): 1:25 to 2:45 and 3:10 to 5am

Birzhevoy: 2 to 4:55am

Tuchkov: 2 to 2:55 and 3:35 to 4:55am

Finlyandsky: 2 to 5:30am

Bolshoi Okhtinsky: 2 to 5am

Dorog Peterburga) is quite useful. Traffic in St. Petersburg has gone from a trickle to a substantial rush-hour event over the past decade. Be sure to have all of the car's documentation in perfect order, as the ever-hungry traffic police will quickly spot and fine any infraction. Renting a car with a driver is easier and often cheaper than driving on your own.

GETTING AROUND ST. PETERSBURG
Visitor Information

The **St. Petersburg City Tourist Office** is quite modest for such a significant city, with not much more to offer than most hotels. Still, it's worth a visit to find out about festivals or special events that you might otherwise miss. The main offices are at 14 Sadovaya Ulitsa (✆ **812/310-2822**), open Monday to Friday from 10am to 7pm.

Maps are available free in most hotels, and for a low price at bookstores and newspaper stands, though sometimes they're only in the Cyrillic alphabet. An easy-to-read and richly detailed map to look out for is the bilingual "St. Petersburg Guide to the City." Avail yourself of the numerous free listings magazines at nearly all hotels and many restaurants. Most are in English and Russian and are heavy with ads but are full of information. Pick up a copy of *The St. Petersburg Times,* a twice-weekly English-language newspaper, for local and international news.

CITY LAYOUT

Peter the Great built his dream city on a cluster of islands in the marshland of the Gulf of Finland. To make sense of this boggy site, he designed a network of canals and bridges whose grueling construction cost the lives of many of the city's builders. The gift they left later generations is a city of remarkable logic and beauty despite the irregularity of its land.

The Neva River folds around the city center in a rounded number 7, taking in water from the city's dozens of canals before flowing out to the Baltic Sea. The city's main land artery is Nevsky Prospekt, a 4km-long (2½-mile) avenue that slices across the city center roughly northwest to southeast. The city retains a coherent center even as it has expanded north, east, and south in recent decades. (The sea stops it from expanding westward.) Museums, hotels, and shopping are conveniently concentrated in and around Nevsky and the historical downtown. Train and bus stations are all attached to the subway system, which is fast and efficient even though the city has outgrown its overcrowded four lines.

Today's St. Petersburg houses five million residents and, like Moscow, is both dense and territorially large. That means a lot of walking even within the city center, but St. Petersburg is not nearly as unwieldy or overwhelming as its southern sister.

Addresses in Russia are often perplexing, so don't be afraid to ask for detailed directions. (See "Address Advice" on p. 295.) It's also a good idea to carry your hotel business card with you, to show taxi drivers the name written in Russian to avoid misunderstandings.

By Public Transportation

The **St. Petersburg Metro** is a fast, cheap, and extraordinarily deep subway system that every visitor should try out at least once. Station entrances are marked with a big blue letter *M*. The four-line system is easy to follow, with each line color-coded and transfers clearly marked—though usually in Russian only. This is where it's highly useful to learn the Cyrillic alphabet (see alphabet lesson and glossary in chapter 18).

THE WORLD underground

The *perekhod,* or underground walkway, is one of those things that leaves you thinking: "Only in Russia. . . ." Soviet city planners built the walkways to allow passage across the extrawide boulevards they so favored, without disrupting aboveground traffic. Post-communism, the *perekhods* turned into thriving commercial centers lined with kiosks, shops, buskers, pharmacies, and cafes. They also provide shelter on blustery days or during rainstorms, and are often used as wintertime meeting places ("Meet me under Pushkin Square at 8pm"). They're invariably crowded but are often useful: for getting rubles at a currency exchange booth, for buying a cool drink or quick snack, or for finding an emergency umbrella (or shampoo, or batteries, or aspirin, or a DVD, or a bunch of wildflowers, or a fur hat . . .). As a pedestrian, you're bound to encounter plenty of them in Moscow and St. Petersburg. When trying to cross major avenues, you may have to walk some distance to find the next *perekhod,* but making the extra journey is much wiser than trying to jaywalk across an eight-lane road clogged with fearless Russian drivers. The busiest *perekhods* are at central intersections or along major thoroughfares such as Moscow's Tverskaya Street and St. Petersburg's Nevsky Prospekt. Many also serve as auxiliary entrances to metro stations, though the thicket of kiosks sometimes makes it hard to find the metro doors. There's nothing sinister about this underground world during the day, but after the shops shut down at night, some *perekhods* attract drug dealers and drunken brawls. Avoid them after dark if you're alone.

Trains run from 5:45am to 12:15am. Each train car has a metro map inside to consult, though it's a good idea to carry one with you (they're available free at all ticket counters). The trains run quite frequently but the system is insufficient for the size of the city and doesn't serve many of the key tourist attractions. It can also be crowded at any time of day, and you can find yourself in a waddling mass squeezing onto the fast, steep escalators. Most platforms are enclosed and resemble a long hall full of elevator-like doors. You can't see the train as it approaches, but you hear a tone and suddenly the doors open—and there's a train on the other side.

One ride costs the same no matter how far you're going. The city is phasing out metro tokens, replacing them with paper cards using a magnetic strip. For the time being, every metro station sells tokens, which cost 20 rubles, or they sell cards for 5, 10, or more trips that get cheaper the more you buy.

The blue plastic tokens are dropped into machines with marked slots. The cards are slid into machines with slots on the side and pulled out on the other end before you can cross.

Trams are a pleasant way to see the city, but only a few lines are convenient for hotels and tourist sights. Two lines worth trying are the no. 14, which runs from the Mariinsky Theater up through the center of town and across the Neva, and the no. 1, which runs through Vasilevsky Island, including a stop just outside the Vasileostrovskaya metro station. **Trolley buses** run along Nevsky Prospekt and some other large avenues.

Tickets for trams and trolley buses cost 18 rubles and are available from a conductor in a yellow vest who roams the vehicle selling them. Maps are posted inside the vehicles, and routes are often listed at the stops, but in Russian only.

By Taxi

Reliable companies to try are the official **Petersburg Taxi** (✆ **068**—that's right, just 3 digits) or **Taxi Park** (✆ **812/265-1333**), or Khoroshee Taxi (✆ 812/700-0000) or New Yellow Taxi (Novoye Zholtoye Taxi; ✆ **812/600-8888**). All work 24 hours.

By Car

Some rental companies to try are these:

Hertz/Travel Rent: Pulkovo Airport-1 and 2, arrivals halls. ✆ **812/326-4505,** 326-4501. www.hertz.com. Rents cars with or without drivers.

Europcar: Pulkovo-2, arrivals halls. ✆ **812/703-7733.** www.europcar.com. Rents with or without drivers.

Rolf-Neva: 17/10 Vitebsky Prospekt. ✆ **812/320-0010.** Rents with or without drivers.

By Bus

Several European tour companies offer bus trips to St. Petersburg, usually from Finland. The Helsinki–to–St. Petersburg journey takes about 7 hours and is often included on Scandinavian-based tours.

By Cruise Ship

St. Petersburg, one-time capital of imperial Russia and the second-largest city in Russia, is the country's largest port. It's also become a popular cruise ship destination. Shore excursions to St. Petersburg include visits to top sights like the Hermitage Museum, which has one of the richest art collections in the world (p. 223); the Peter

& Paul Fortress, the burial place of the Romanov dynasty (p. 229); and St. Isaac's Cathedral, the fourth-largest cathedral in the world (p. 231). Cruise lines also typically offer nighttime shore excursions to see ballet, opera, folk performances, or circuses.

TIPS ON ACCOMMODATIONS

Hotel options in Russia have come a long way from the days of the state agency Intourist's monopoly on serving foreigners, but the country still has far too few mid-range hotel rooms to satisfy demand. Luxury chains were quick to recognize this new market and opened several top-class hotels in the 1990s, some opting for renovating elegant old hotels while others started from scratch. The most active chains in the luxury market are Marriott, InterContinental, Radisson, Sheraton, and Renaissance (now part of the Marriott chain). Holiday Inn (now part of the InterContinental hotel group) and Best Western have also entered the scene with somewhat cheaper offerings.

Even the highest-end locations sometimes offer deep discounts through online or traditional travel agencies or their own websites, up to 60% off the official or "rack" rate. It definitely pays to shop around. Most package tours rely on well-established Soviet-era hotels, usually enormous, architecturally bleak buildings offering the key services tourists need but with limited enthusiasm. The good news is that several of these hotels are renovating one floor at a time, and the increased price for the new rooms is usually well worth the fresh plumbing and improved service.

The best Russian hotel development in recent years is the flowering of the "minihotel" market in St. Petersburg. Dozens of hotels of 12 to 30 rooms have opened up, often occupying a few renovated floors of an apartment building. Most are centrally located and inexpensive, and offer eager, individual service that the big hotels lack. Unfortunately, Moscow's powerful hotel industry has kept this phenomenon largely at bay in the capital.

 Address Advice

Finding addresses in Russia can be challenging, especially for buildings tucked in a courtyard or down a footpath. Russians usually list the house number after the street name. The number may include dashes or slashes or have an addendum like "building 2" or "wing 3." Big apartment buildings rarely have one central entrance; instead, apartments are reached by separate entrances called *podyezdy*, making it crucial to know which entrance you need.

Don't be alarmed if you see a slash in your address, such as 5/2. Pay attention to the number before the slash, which corresponds to the street number. The number after the slash usually refers to an annex, or wing. So for example, 5/2 Tverskaya Ulitsa will be on the odd-numbered side of the street, somewhere between No. 3 and No. 7. It may be adjacent to No. 5, or tucked into a courtyard behind No. 5. (Successive waves of reconstruction may mean that there's no 5/1—but don't let that worry you!)

For example, to find Kutuzovsky Prospekt 21/4, building 3, entrance 1, apartment 16: Locate no. 21/4 between nos. 19 and 23 (ignore the "/4"), walk through the parking lot, and search for building no. 3. Then find entrance no. 1 and check the list in the elevator to locate apartment no. 16's floor.

Hostels and traditional bed-and-breakfasts are rare though growing. Several companies rent out furnished apartments at rates much lower than the hotel rates. Quality varies widely, with some offering warm and helpful English-speaking hosts, others offering daily maid service and hotel-style assistance, and still others offering nothing but a key. Get the opinions of previous guests through websites such as www.frommers.com or www.virtualtourist.com before booking.

Russian hotels tend to be emptier in winter and busier in summer, especially around St. Petersburg's White Nights festival from late June to early July. Rates usually reflect this. Be aware of any big festivals or holiday events that might fill up hotels (see the "Calendar of Events" in chapter 2 for guidance).

Neither Moscow nor St. Petersburg offers an official reservations service, and your chances of just showing up and getting a room are slim, even in hostels. You are strongly recommended to reserve in advance by phone or online; the cost is usually lower that way as well. Another advantage of reserving ahead is that most hotels will arrange for your visa, and register it once you arrive (see "Entry Requirements" earlier in this chapter).

Hotels often have "floor monitors" employed round-the-clock who in the Soviet era often acted as KGB informers; now they're basically nosy chambermaids and sometimes they'll make guests tea.

Russia's star-rating system is only gradually adjusting to the international standard and is an unreliable source of judging quality.

Homestays & Apartment Rentals

Opting for less conventional accommodations can inject your trip with individuality and flexibility—or it could tangle you in scams and unfulfilled promises. If you choose wisely, these options can offer comfort, charm, and a convenient location at a reasonable price. Be aware that they lack many of the security features and financial guarantees of big hotels, and that rates and quality vary widely.

Russia lacks what most people understand as a "bed-and-breakfast." Russian tourism gurus have taken the term to mean just about anything: an upscale urban hotel, a room in a student dormitory, a spotless apartment serviced by a real estate agency, or a cramped room in a family's apartment vacated just for the duration of your stay. There is no single body regulating who or what can call itself a B&B. The website www.bnb.ru, for example, is a portal for Russian accommodations of any category, from high-end Marriott hotels to long-term real estate deals. The main thing to keep in mind is that in Moscow and St. Petersburg, bed-and-breakfasts are urban experiences, not village cottages with fruit fresh from the orchard. More common are "**mini-hotels**," which usually occupy a single floor of an apartment building. St. Petersburg has many more of these than Moscow. Some were once communal apartments, with entire families sharing single rooms and the whole floor sharing a single bathroom and kitchen, but today they are entirely renovated and quite comfortable. To help you avoid misunderstanding, the reviews in chapter 4 ("Where to Stay in Moscow") and chapter 11 ("Where to Stay in St. Petersburg") are as thorough as possible.

Renting a **private apartment** for your stay is also popular, opening up more options in price and location than the hotel industry can. This is especially convenient during high seasons, such as the White Nights in St. Petersburg, when hotels fill up fast. The safest bet is to use a real estate agency that services the apartment and is available for assistance at all hours in case of emergency. Many individual apartment owners also advertise rentals online or hover around international airports and train stations, but most of these are risky propositions.

If you're seeking a closer look at day-to-day Russian existence, or want to learn or practice Russian, a **homestay** can be a good option. The ideal homestay is an apartment with a family history and a family member eager to tell you about it, as opposed to someone merely renting out a room for extra cash. Your room will probably be packed with the family's stuff, a library's worth of books, and a few generations' worth of knickknacks. Your host will clear out a shelf in the overstuffed closet for your belongings, but little more. The best way to determine what you're getting into is to call your hosts before you reserve, or at least before you pay. (This is also a good way to check how well they speak English.)

Note: With any of the above options, be sure to find out *before you reserve* whether they can arrange your **visa invitation.** If not, you'll need to find a reputable travel agency to take care of that for you, which could cost up to 5,000 rubles more and takes at least 2 weeks. See the visa advice at the beginning of this chapter for details.

In addition to the reviews in the "Where to Stay" chapters, the following companies can help you with less traditional accommodations.

o **Russian Travel Service** (www.123russia.com): This service arranges homestays in St. Petersburg with English-speaking or Russian-only hosts. Rates start at 500 rubles per night. They'll ask you about your animal and food allergies and arrange your visas.

o **Host Families Association** (www.hofa.ru): This service arranges homestays in both Moscow and St. Petersburg, with either Russian or English-speaking hosts. Rates start at 625 rubles per night.

o **City Realty** (www.cityrealtyrussia.com): This company provides serviced apartments of all categories in Moscow and St. Petersburg, from 1,250 rubles per night.

VISAS & CUSTOMS

Visas

International visitors' first experience of Russia is usually the costly, sometimes frustrating process of getting a visa. Brace yourself, and remember that the rest of your Russian experience—the exhilarating White Nights, the gilded bell towers, the salmon tartlets following iced vodka—will be worth the hassle.

All visitors to Russia need a valid passport and visa, with the exception of residents of a few former Soviet republics. Package tours usually take care of visas, though you will need to give the travel agency your passport for submission to the nearest Russian embassy or consulate.

I strongly recommend going through some kind of visa service if you are on your own, to limit troubles and misunderstanding. For independent travelers, visa applicants must provide proof of hotel reservations in an official letter from a hotel or travel agency. Travelers staying in private homes need an official invitation from a Russian organization. Three places that offer this service for a fee are www.waytorussia.net; www.travelinrussia.com (in the U.S., © **253/550-7816**); and Sindbad's Hostel in St. Petersburg, www.sindbad.ru (© **812/331-2020**). Fees for the visa (in addition to any fees for the invitation) range from $30 to $350, depending on your nationality, how quickly you need it, how long you need it, and how many times you want to enter the country. For example, a single-entry, 3-month tourist visa costs $140 in the United

States. Start the process several weeks before you leave. If you do not live near a Russian embassy or consulate, you can apply by mail, but you will have to send your passport to them via Federal Express. Anyone applying for a visa for more than 3 months must provide proof of a recent HIV test, a discriminatory and futile effort to cope with Russia's growing AIDS/HIV problem.

Once you get your visa, which is generally a sticker affixed to your passport, make a copy of it in case of emergency. You will need the original visa to leave the country as well as to enter it, and for as long as you're in Russia. While in Russia you will also need to **register your visa** with the local authorities. Most hotels will do this automatically for you the first day, but ask to be sure. If they don't offer this service, check with the visa agencies listed above.

Contact your nearest Russian embassy for rules in your country:

UNITED STATES: Embassy: 2650 Wisconsin Ave. NW, Washington, DC (✆ **202/ 939-8907 or 8918;** www.russianembassy.org). Consulates:

o 9 E. 91st St., New York, NY (✆ **212/348-0926**);

o 2790 Green St., San Francisco, CA (✆ **415/928-6878**);

o 2322 Westin Building, 2001 6th Ave., Seattle, WA (✆ **206/728-1910**).

AUSTRALIA: 78 Canberra Ave., Griffith, Canberra, ACT 2603 (✆ **02/6295-9474;** http://canberra.rusembassy.org).

BRITAIN: 5 Kensington Palace Gardens, London W8 4QS (✆ **0870/005-6972;** www.rusemblon.org).

CANADA: 52 Range Rd., Ottawa, Ontario K1N 8G5 (✆ **613/594-8488;** www. rusembcanada.mid.ru).

IRELAND: 186 Orwell Rd., Rathgar, Dublin (✆ **01/492-3492**).

For an up-to-date, country-by-country listing of passport requirements around the world, go to the "Foreign Entry Requirement" Web page of the U.S. State Department at http://travel.state.gov/foreignentryreqs.html.

Customs
WHAT YOU CAN BRING INTO RUSSIA

Visitors can bring in most things other than weapons, drugs, and livestock. If you have cash in any currency worth more than $1,500; anything antique; or valuable jewelry, laptop computers, cameras, or other electronics, then fill out a Customs declaration form upon entry and go through the **Red Channel** at airport Customs. That way you won't have any problem taking the items home with you when you leave. The declaration form will be stamped and returned to you, and you must present it again upon departure. You can take up to $10,000 if you declare it. Otherwise, you can pass through the **Green Channel** without filling out any forms. If you go through the Red Channel, be aware that if the amount of cash you take out of Russia is larger than the sum you declared upon entry, you may be questioned on suspicion of abetting capital flight.

WHAT YOU CAN TAKE HOME FROM RUSSIA

Be careful when shopping in Moscow or St. Petersburg, because some souvenirs are illegal to export, such as antiques, certain icons and artwork, and caviar. Overfishing has shriveled the population of Caspian Sea sturgeon, the main source of the world's black caviar. Travelers are currently allowed to take 250 grams (10 oz.) of red caviar out of the country, though Americans should be aware that U.S. customs forbids importing fish products. The rules on artwork and antiques change with puzzling frequency.

Some items cannot be exported at all; others can be exported only with special Culture Ministry certification. Fortunately, most vendors can complete the export certification for these items for you.

You will generally not need an export permit for: contemporary souvenirs, electric samovars, or any books, posters, or reproductions produced within the last 50 years. You may export up to 250g of red caviar. Export of black caviar is forbidden.

You will need an export permit for any of these items, regardless of when they were made: icons, paintings (even recent works), carpets and rugs, traditional samovars (non-electric).

Most galleries and auction houses will assist in obtaining export clearance. If you need independent advice in Moscow, contact the Assessment Committee of the Ministry of Culture (Neglinnaya Ul. D. 8; © **495/692-1532**) or refer to the Moscow Service for the Preservation of Cultural Property at © **495/244-7675** (www.culture-expert.ru). The Customs Service has advice desks at Both Sheremetyevo II and Domodedovo airports in Moscow (www.eng.customs.ru). If you need independent advice in St. Petersburg, contact the Ministry of Culture at Malaya Morskaya Ulitsa d. 17 (© **812/117-3496**), or the St. Petersburg Assessment Committee (© **812/310-1454**). The Customs Service has an advice desk at Pulkovo airport, terminal II.

Export applications cost about $10, but duties can run up to 100% and the process is tedious. Demand receipts when buying anything valuable, even items from open-air markets.

Until recently, visitors were prohibited from taking rubles out of the country. Now a small amount can be taken, but the limit is indexed to the official minimum wage and therefore changes often, so stick to small sums to be safe. Bear in mind that you may have a hard time exchanging them for dollars when you get home, since the ruble only recently became internationally convertible and is still not traded in most banks.

HEALTH
GENERAL AVAILABILITY OF HEALTHCARE

Soviet healthcare was universal and nearly free, though clinics were chronically short of equipment. State subsidies shriveled in the 1990s and shortages worsened; doctors remain dismally paid and depend heavily on bribes from patients. But competition is slowly emerging, and Moscow and St. Petersburg have several private clinics that offer high-standard care and English-speaking personnel, though at high prices.

No vaccinations are necessary to visit Russia, though there have been cases of diphtheria and cholera in provincial areas in recent years, and tuberculosis is a major problem in prisons. Most visitors' biggest health challenges are digestive, either from St. Petersburg's bacteria-ridden water or dubiously prepared street food. Bottled water is cheap and widely available. HIV is a growing problem, and prevention and public information campaigns are sorely inadequate.

Bring any prescriptions with you, and Imodium or other anti-diarrhea medication. All-night pharmacies are common in Moscow and St. Petersburg, and over-the-counter medications are easily available, though generics are rarer. Foreign brands are often of better quality and always more expensive than their Russian equivalents. For the bold, even penicillin and IUDs can be purchased without a prescription.

Contact the **International Association for Medical Assistance to Travelers** (**IAMAT**; *✆* 716/754-4883 or, in Canada, 416/652-0137; www.iamat.org) for tips on travel and health concerns in the countries you're visiting, and for lists of local, English-speaking doctors. The United States **Centers for Disease Control and Prevention** (*✆* 800/311-3435; www.cdc.gov) provides up-to-date information on health hazards by region or country and offers tips on food safety. **Travel Health Online** (www.trip prep.com), sponsored by a consortium of travel medicine practitioners, may also offer helpful advice on traveling abroad. You can find listings of reliable medical clinics overseas at the **International Society of Travel Medicine** (www.istm.org).

COMMON AILMENTS

DIETARY RED FLAGS Moscow's water is potable but can be risky for foreigners. St. Petersburg's water contains the bacteria *giardia lamblia* and should be avoided (beware of tooth-brushing and iced drinks). Many St. Petersburg hotels have their own water filtration system. Cheap bottled water is widely available. Avoid fried meat pies sold on the street and meat sold outdoors. Vegetarians are finding more and more options in Russia, mainly at restaurants that specialize in Japanese or American cuisine. However, nearly all restaurant soups are made with meat stock, and vegetable side dishes are often prepared in lard. Although Russia has substantial Muslim and Jewish minorities, very few restaurants cater to those with religious dietary restrictions.

RESPIRATORY ILLNESSES Tuberculosis, virtually wiped out by Soviet health campaigns, has resurfaced in recent years, largely among prison populations. The disease is treatable but some strains have grown resistant to standard medicines. Another respiratory challenge is air quality, which is dismal in most Russian cities. Fuel emissions are restricted but the restrictions are barely enforced.

EXTREME WEATHER EXPOSURE Though Russia is no doubt a cold place, most travelers do not spend enough time outdoors in the winter to risk hypothermia or its milder cousin, frostbite. Visitors engaging in a lot of outdoor winter activity should carry many layers of clothing and thermoses of warm liquid.

WHAT TO DO IF YOU GET SICK AWAY FROM HOME

Any foreign consulate can provide you with a list of area doctors who speak English. If you get sick, consider asking your hotel concierge to recommend a local doctor—even his or her own. You can also try the emergency room at a local hospital. Finding doctors or all-night pharmacies can be hard in Moscow and St. Petersburg if you know no Russian, and is much easier with a Russian helper or hotel concierge. You will pay as you go no matter where you seek help, and prices can vary from a few dollars in a public clinic for emergency care to hundreds of dollars in a private one. Foreigners are sometimes charged more just because they are assumed to have more money than Russians.

For travel abroad, you may have to pay all medical costs upfront and be reimbursed later. Medicare and Medicaid do not provide coverage for medical

---

Healthy Travels to You

The following government websites offer up-to-date health-related travel advice.

- **Australia:** www.dfat.gov.au/travel
- **Canada:** www.hc-sc.gc.ca/index_e.html
- **U.K.:** www.dh.gov.uk/policyand guidance/healthadvicefortravellers/fs/en
- **U.S.:** www.cdc.gov/travel

costs outside the U.S. Before leaving home, find out what medical services your health insurance covers. To protect yourself, consider buying medical travel insurance.

Very few health insurance plans pay for medical evacuation back to the U.S. (which can cost $10,000 and up). A number of companies offer medical evacuation services anywhere in the world. If you're ever hospitalized more than 150 miles from home, **MedjetAssist** (✆ **800/527-7478;** www.medjetassistance.com) will pick you up and fly you to the hospital of your choice virtually anywhere in the world in a medically equipped and staffed aircraft 24 hours day, 7 days a week. Annual memberships are $225 individual, $350 family; you can also purchase short-term memberships.

If you suffer from a chronic illness, consult your doctor before your departure. For conditions like epilepsy, diabetes, or heart problems, wear a **MedicAlert identification tag** (✆ **888/633-4298;** www.medicalert.org), which will immediately alert doctors to your condition and give them access to your records through MedicAlert's 24-hour hot line.

Pack **prescription medications** in your carry-on luggage, and carry prescription medications in their original containers, with pharmacy labels—otherwise they won't make it through airport security. Also bring along copies of your prescriptions in case you lose your pills or run out. Don't forget an extra pair of contact lenses or prescription glasses. Carry the generic name of prescription medicines, in case a local pharmacist is unfamiliar with the brand name.

We list additional **emergency numbers** in the "Fast Facts" section, below.

FAST FACTS: MOSCOW

Area Codes   Moscow's area codes are either 495 or 499. See "Telephone" below for details on making calls.

Car Rental   See "Getting There by Car," earlier in this chapter.

Cellphones   See "Mobile Phones," later in this section.

Crime   See "Safety," later in this section.

Customs   See "Visas & Customs," earlier in this chapter.

Disabled Travelers   Most disabilities shouldn't stop anyone from traveling. There are more options and resources out there than ever before. That said, Russia remains a formidable destination for anyone in a wheelchair. Only the biggest and priciest hotels and restaurants are accessible. Many of Moscow's wide streets can be crossed only underground without ramps. Even some tourist destinations that claim to be accessible have a few stairs leading up to the cash desk, or into the church. Call every place you plan to visit before you go and be sure it can accommodate you.

Organizations that offer a vast range of resources and assistance to travelers with disabilities include **MossRehab** (✆ **800/CALL-MOSS** [2255-6677]; www.mossresourcenet. org); the **American Foundation for the Blind** (**AFB;** ✆ **800/232-5463;** www.afb.org); and **SATH** (**Society for Accessible Travel & Hospitality;** ✆ **212/447-7284;** www.sath.org). **AirAmbulanceCard.com** is now partnered with SATH and allows you to preselect top-notch hospitals in case of an emergency.

Access-Able Travel Source (✆ **303/232-2979;** www.access-able.com) offers a comprehensive database on travel agents from around the world with experience in accessible travel; destination-specific access information; and links to such resources as service animals, equipment rentals, and access guides.

Many travel agencies offer customized tours and itineraries for travelers with disabilities. Among them are **Flying Wheels Travel** (© **507/451-5005**; www.flyingwheelstravel.com) and **Accessible Journeys** (© **800/846-4537** or 610/521-0339; www.disabilitytravel.com).

Flying with Disability (www.flying-with-disability.org) is a comprehensive information source on airplane travel. **Avis Rent a Car** (© **888/879-4273**) has an "Avis Access" program that offers services for customers with special travel needs. These include specially outfitted vehicles with swivel seats, spinner knobs, and hand controls; mobility scooter rentals; and accessible bus service. Be sure to reserve well in advance.

Also check out the quarterly magazine *Emerging Horizons* (www.emerginghorizons. com), available by subscription ($16.95 a year in U.S.; $21.95 outside U.S.).

The "Accessible Travel" link at **Mobility-Advisor.com** (www.mobility-advisor.com) offers a variety of travel resources to persons with disabilities.

British travelers should contact **Holiday Care** (© **0845-124-9971** in U.K. only; www. holidaycare.org.uk) to access a wide range of travel information and resources for seniors and persons with disabilities.

Doctors   The following facilities offer Western-standard medical care and English-speaking staff who can help with everything from a broken limb to a bad flu. They are private clinics whose services are expensive and may not be covered by your insurance company, so be sure to check with your insurer before you go: **American Medical Center Moscow,** 26 Prospekt Mira (© **495/933-7700**; http://amcenter.ru/en); **European Medical Center,** 5 Spiridonievskiy Pereulok 5, building 1 (© **495/933-6655**; www.emcmos.ru); **International SOS Clinic,** 7 Orlovskiy Pereulok, 3rd floor. At ZAO International Medical Clinic. (© **495/937-5760**; www.internationalsos.ru/ru/index.htm). Also see "Hospitals," later in this section.

Drinking Laws   The official drinking age in Russia is 18, but it is almost never enforced. Drinking in public is acceptable (despite a recent law against it), and seeing teenagers clutching beers on their way home from school is common. Beer, wine, and liquor—primarily vodka, but also such cocktails as gin and tonic in a can—are available at all supermarkets and most street kiosks. Beware of cheap vodka from kiosks, since it's often watered down or of stomach-wrenching quality. Bars with special licenses can serve alcohol all night, and many do. Some stores are closed on Sunday, but those that are open sell liquor then as well as every other day.

Driving Rules   See "Getting Around," earlier in this chapter.

Electricity   Russia operates on 220-volt AC, like the rest of Europe. Bring converters if you have electrical equipment from North America, since they're harder to find in Russia. Most modern hotels use plugs with two thick prongs, as in continental Europe; some older hotels will need plugs with two thinner prongs. Small plastic adapters for these old plugs are available in Russian hardware stores, or often from the hotel staff. To guard against electricity surges for items like laptops, bring a stabilizer, too.

Embassies   All embassies are located in Moscow, the capital, with consulates for several countries in St. Petersburg as well.

- **United States**: 8 Bolshoi Devyatinsky Pereulok; © 495/728-5000; emergency after hours 495/728-5025.
- **Australia**: 10A/2 Podkolokolny Pereulok; © 495/956-6070.
- **Britain**: 10 Smolenskaya Naberezhnaya; © 495/956-7200.
- **Canada**: 23 Starokonyushenniy Pereulok; © 495/925-6000; night line 495/925-6055.
- **Ireland**: 5 Grokholsky Pereulok; © 495/937-5911.

Emergencies For fire, dial 01; police, 02; ambulance, 03. For medical emergencies, see the "Doctors" listing, above. In extreme cases, the international clinics will send you to a better-equipped Russian hospital with a translator.

Eyeglass Repair Almost any eyeglass store, called *optika*, will make minor repairs, often for free.

Family Travel Russia can be a daunting place with kids but an unforgettable experience for them. A major challenge is the Cyrillic alphabet—but you can turn that into a family game by setting out to learn its 33 letters together (many are the same as in English), and then sounding out street signs together ("Look, РЕСТОРАН means restaurant!"). Travel with small children is difficult, since few restaurants have highchairs, and nothing is stroller-friendly—even the pharmacies have steps and unwieldy doors. Because Russians travel infrequently with their children, there are few hotels with specifically kid-friendly services, though that doesn't mean they're hostile to families. Also be prepared for unsolicited child-rearing advice from well-meaning Russian grandmothers, who always seem to think that children are underdressed no matter what the temperature. Russian **circuses** are world-renowned, and the **Moscow Zoo** (p. 120) and **Gorky Park** (p. 115) are good family destinations. For attractions without concerns about animal rights, there are several puppet theaters in Moscow and St. Petersburg.

Recommended family travel websites include **Family Travel Forum** (www.familytravel forum.com), a comprehensive site that offers customized trip planning; **Family Travel Network** (www.familytravelnetwork.com), an online magazine providing travel tips; and **TravelWithYourKids.com** (www.travelwithyourkids.com), a comprehensive site written by parents for parents, offering sound advice for long-distance and international travel with children.

To locate accommodations, restaurants, and attractions that are particularly kid-friendly, look for the "Kids" icon throughout this guide.

Gasoline Please see "Getting There By Car," earlier in this chapter.

Health See "Health," earlier in this chapter.

Hospitals Some doctors speak English, but most of the Russian hospital staff is unlikely to, so try to get a translator if you need hospitalization. Ask your hotel for translator suggestions. These are some of the biggest and (relatively) good hospitals:

  o **Botkin City Hospital**, 5 Second Botkinsky Proyezd; ℂ 499/945-0033; www. botkinmoscow.ru.
  o **City Hospital No. 1** (Pirogovksy), 8 Leninsky Prospekt; ℂ 495/236-8066; http://gkb-1.ru.
  o **Morozovskaya Children's Hospital,** 1/9 4th Dobryninskiy Pereulok; ℂ 495/959-8904; www.mosgorzdrav.ru/mdgkb.

Internet & Wi-Fi Internet cafes are increasingly available in downtown Moscow. Many hotels have free or paid Wi-Fi, either in-room or in the lobby. Hotel business centers offer online access, for a fee. Try 24-hour **Time Online** on the bottom floor of the Okhotny Ryad shopping center next to the Kremlin (1 Manezhnaya Ploshchad; www.time online.ru), or **CafeMax,** a chain of cafes around town. Two convenient ones are at 25 Pyatnitskaya, building 1, near Novokuznetskaya metro station; and at 3 Novoslobodskaya Ulitsa, near Novoslobodskaya metro station. See www.cafemax.ru for other locations.

Language Russian is the principal language, a Slavic tongue that uses the Cyrillic alphabet. English is becoming more common but is not as widespread as in western Europe. In most hotels, at tourist sites, and in central Moscow and St. Petersburg visitors should have no trouble communicating in English. Younger people are far more likely to speak it well than their elders. The main challenge is the Russian alphabet. Despite efforts to print signs in the Latin alphabet (the one used for western European languages), most streets and metro stations are labeled in Cyrillic. It is well worth it to learn the 33-letter alphabet, which is very phonetic and shares many letters with English. See chapter 18 for a quick alphabet lesson and list of useful words and phrases. When buying a phrase book, make sure it has good phonetic transliterations of Russian words ("spa-see-ba" is "thank you," for example).

Legal Aid   Contact your local embassy or consulate in case of any legal trouble. For legal advice, in Russian, dial ☎ 065 (the line is open from 9am to 8pm and there is a charge for services). See "Embassies," earlier in this chapter.

LGBT Travelers   Soviet statutes barring homosexual acts were at last lifted in 1993, and Russia's gays and lesbians have been celebrating ever since. Still, Russia's conservative society remains suspicious of same-sex couples, and openly gay public figures remain rare outside the performing arts. Russian women, regardless of sexual preference, often hold hands and embrace in public, but public intimacy between gay men can provoke taunts or worse. Gay-friendly venues, including clubs, restaurants, business groups, and public pickup spots, are numerous in Moscow and St. Petersburg.

The website www.gay.ru is a solid starting place for gay and lesbian visitors to Russia, with accommodations suggestions and extensive club listings. **The International Gay and Lesbian Travel Association (IGLTA;** ☎ 800/448-8550 or 954/776-2626; www.iglta.org) is the trade association for the gay and lesbian travel industry, and offers an online directory of gay- and lesbian-friendly travel businesses and tour operators.

Many agencies offer tours and travel itineraries specifically for gay and lesbian travelers. **Above and Beyond Tours** (☎ 800/397-2681; www.abovebeyondtours.com) are gay Australia tour specialists. San Francisco–based **Now, Voyager** (☎ 800/255-6951; www. nowvoyager.com) offers worldwide trips and cruises, and **Olivia** (☎ 800/631-6277; www. olivia.com) offers lesbian cruises and resort vacations.

Gay.com Travel (☎ 800/929-2268 or 415/644-8044; www.gay.com/travel/outand about or www.outandabout.com) is an excellent online successor to the popular *Out & About* print magazine. It provides regularly updated information about gay-owned, gay-oriented, and gay-friendly lodging, dining, sightseeing, nightlife, and shopping establishments in every important destination worldwide.

The Canadian website **GayTraveler** (www.gaytraveler.ca) offers ideas and advice for gay travel all over the world.

The following travel guides are available at many bookstores, or you can order them from any online bookseller: *Spartacus International Gay Guide, 35th Edition* (Bruno Gmünder Verlag; www.spartacusworld.com/gayguide); and the *Damron* guides (www. damron.com), with separate, annual books for gay men and lesbians.

Mail   Russia's postal service is underfunded and unreliable. Postcards are a safe bet, though they may not arrive until you're back home. Postcards and letters to western Europe and North America cost about 30 rubles. Both should be addressed Russian-style, which is in reverse order of what's used in the U.S. and Western Europe; see examples posted up in the post office. Shipping packages through the regular post is not recommended, because there's nothing you can do if it gets lost or damaged, and because of the complex Customs rules. Several international shipping companies serve Russia, such as **FedEx** (☎ 495/788-8881), **DHL** (☎ 495/956-1000), and **UPS** (☎ 495/961-2211), though their services are not cheap.

Medical Requirements   See "Health," earlier in this chapter.

Mobile Phones   Mobile phones are widely used in Russia and leading companies **MTS** (☎ 495/766-0177; www.mts.ru) and **Bee-Line** (☎ 495/974-8888; www.beeline.ru) offer the full range of GSM services. **GSM** (Global System for Mobile Communications) is a big, seamless network that makes for easy cross-border cellphone use throughout Europe and dozens of other countries worldwide. GSM phones function with a removable plastic SIM card, encoded with your phone number and account information. If your cellphone is on a GSM system, and you have a world-capable multiband phone such as many Sony Ericsson, Motorola, or Samsung models, you can make and receive calls around much of the globe. Just call your wireless operator and ask for "international roaming" to be activated on your account. Unfortunately, per-minute charges can be high—up to $5 in places like Russia.

For many, **renting** a pay-as-you-go phone is a good idea. MTS and Bee-Line (see above) offer this service. While you can rent a phone from any number of overseas sites, including kiosks at airports and at car-rental agencies, I suggest renting the phone before you leave home. North Americans can rent one before leaving home from **InTouch USA** (✆ **800/872-7626;** www.intouchglobal.com) or **RoadPost** (✆ **888/290-1606** or 905/272-5665; www.roadpost.com). InTouch will also, for free, advise you on whether your existing phone will work overseas; simply call ✆ **703/222-7161** between 9am and 4pm EST, or go to www.intouchglobal.com/travel.htm.

For trips of more than a few weeks spent in one country, **buying a phone** becomes economically attractive, as Russia and many other countries have cheap, no-questions-asked prepaid phone systems. Once you arrive at your destination, stop by a local cell-phone shop and get the cheapest package; you'll probably pay less than 2,500 rubles for a phone and a starter calling card. Local calls may be as low as 2 rubles per minute, and with some Russian providers incoming calls are free.

Money & Costs   Frommer's lists prices primarily in the local currency. The currency conversions provided were correct at press time. However, rates fluctuate, so before departing consult a currency exchange website such as www.oanda.com/currency/converter to check up-to-the-minute rates.

Though capitalism has brought Russia more in line with the economies of the West, money matters continue to vex visitors. Red caviar, symphony tickets, and haircuts can barely dent your wallet; rubbery pizza and roach-ridden hotels can drain it. Russia can be quite cheap, though visitors on escorted tours may not notice, as accommodations are often overpriced and tour operators charge a premium. Cash is by far the most popular form of payment among Russians, but credit cards are increasingly accepted. ATMs are widely available in Moscow and St. Petersburg and are generally reliable.

Russia's **ruble** is still making the transition to becoming a truly "hard" currency, which means very few banks abroad will sell you rubles (in cash or traveler's checks) before you leave home or buy them back from you when you return. The U.S. dollar was the de facto second currency in the 1990s as the ruble lost all credibility among Russians. In recent years the ruble has remained quite stable, even stronger than the dollar, and inflation has calmed down considerably, though Russians still prefer to keep their savings in dollars or euros. If you're not queasy about carrying cash from home, change it at the currency exchange booths found at all airports, hotels, and most street corners. Note that prices listed on menus and in shops are often in dollars or euros, though only rubles are accepted as payment. This is a remnant of the 1990s, when the ruble's value plunged daily. For an explanation of the "monetary units" used on some price lists, see the "Currency Confusion at Your Hotel" box on p. 74.

Exchange booths *(obmen valyuty)* are found in every hotel, at many restaurants, and near all major metro stations. Many are open 24 hours, and most are well-guarded, reliable places to change cash. Rates are better than in most banks, and they're competitive, so shop around. Most don't charge a commission, and when they do, it's low—around a dollar. Make sure your U.S. bills or euros are new and untainted; crinkled or pre-1995 bills will be rejected. Exchange booths have signs out front with four figures: the buy and sell rates for U.S. dollars, and the buy and sell rates for euros. To exchange other currencies, try the banks, the underground passage next to Arbatskaya metro station, and the booth on the corner of Pokrovka Ulitsa and Pokrovsky Bulvar.

The easiest way to get cash in Moscow and St. Petersburg is from an ATM. The **Cirrus** (© **800/424-7787;** www.mastercard.com) and **PLUS** (© **800/843-7587;** www.visa.com) networks span the globe; look at the back of your bank card to see which network you're on. Most Russian ATMs accept both. Be sure you know your personal identification number (PIN) before you leave home, and be sure to find out your daily withdrawal limit before you depart. Also keep in mind that many banks impose a fee every time a card is used at a different bank's ATM; that fee can be higher for international transactions than for domestic ones. On top of this, the Russian bank from which you withdraw cash may charge its own small fee. For international withdrawal fees, ask your bank. To limit these charges, take out as much money as you're comfortable with at once.

You can also get cash advances on your credit card in dollars or rubles at an ATM at banks or ATMs, provided you know your PIN. If you've forgotten yours, or didn't even know you had one, call the number on the back of your credit card and ask the bank to send it to you. It usually takes 5 to 7 business days, though some banks will provide the number over the phone if you tell them your mother's maiden name or some other personal information. Credit card companies try to protect themselves from theft by limiting the funds you can withdraw outside your home country, so call your credit card company before you leave home. And keep in mind that you'll pay interest from the moment of your withdrawal, even if you pay your monthly bills on time.

Credit cards are welcome in nearly all Russian hotels and many restaurants, but many museums and train stations take only cash. Cards most commonly accepted in Russia are American Express, Visa, MasterCard, and Eurocard. Places that take Diners Club are rare, and those that take Discover are nearly nonexistent.

Beware of hidden credit-card fees while traveling. Check with your credit or debit card issuer to see what fees, if any, will be charged for overseas transactions. Reform legislation in the U.S., for example, has curbed some exploitative lending practices. But many banks have responded by increasing fees in other areas, including fees for customers who use credit and debit cards while out of the country—even if those charges were made in U.S. dollars. Fees can amount to 3% or more of the purchase price. Check with your bank before departing to avoid any surprise charges on your statement.

Few places in Russia accept traveler's checks outside major hotels and restaurants, and those that do usually accept only American Express. If you have checks from elsewhere, call your hotel in advance to see if they're accepted. Currency exchange booths in the major hotels generally accept traveler's checks, but most other exchange booths do not.

You can buy traveler's checks at most banks. They are offered in denominations of $20, $50, $100, $500, and sometimes $1,000. Generally, you'll pay a service charge ranging from 1% to 4%. Be sure to keep a record of the traveler's checks' serial numbers separate from your checks in the event that they are stolen or lost. You'll get a refund faster if you know the numbers.

For help with currency conversions, tip calculations, and more, download Frommer's convenient Travel Tools app for your mobile device. Go to www.frommers.com/go/mobile and click on the Travel Tools icon.

THE VALUE OF THE RUBLE VS. OTHER POPULAR CURRENCIES

Ruble	Aus$	Can$	Euro (€)	NZ$	UK£	US$
100A	$3.30	C$3.41	€2.39	NZ$4.16	£2.10	3.40

WHAT THINGS COST IN RUSSIA (IN RUBLES)

Taxi from airport to center of Moscow	1,000–3,000
Bus ride within the center	25
Double room at Moscow's Ritz Carlton (Very Expensive)	21,000
Double room at St. Petersburg's Angleterre (Expensive)	12,000
Double room at Moscow's Volga Hotel (Moderate)	4,500
Double room at St. Petersburg's Bed and Breakfast (Inexpensive)	1,700
Lunch for one, no wine, at Moscow's Taras Bulba (Moderate)	400
Lunch for one, no wine, at Moscow's Kitezh (Expensive)	600
Dinner for one, no wine, at St. Petersburg's Idiot (Inexpensive)	350
Dinner for one, no wine, at Moscow's Il Patio (Moderate)	700
Dinner for one, no wine, at St. Petersburg's Lucky Shot (Expensive)	1,200
Dinner for one, no wine, at Moscow's One Red Square (Very Expensive)	1,800
Glass of wine in a cafe	200
Glass of soda in a cafe	60
Cup of espresso	60
Admission to Hermitage Museum	350
Mariinsky Theater ballet ticket	350–1,500

Multicultural Travelers The Soviet Union was one of the most ethnically diverse places on the planet, and Russia is still home to hundreds of nationalities. Few Russians can claim to be 100% Slavic, after centuries of mingling with people of Turkic, Nordic, and Mongol blood. However, the two recent wars in Chechnya have fueled a blanket suspicion of people from the Caucasus region, and there have been sporadic incidents of skinhead violence against ethnic minorities in recent years, especially immediately following a terrorist attack. St. Petersburg, despite its cultured reputation, has seen some of the worst attacks, largely targeting vendors and transient workers from Central Asia or the Caucasus. These workers are crucial to the local economy, yet with the Slavic population aging and shrinking, some fringe groups see the migrant workers as a threat to Russia's identity. Foreigners with "southern" features—dark eyes and hair and olive skin—very occasionally suffer reluctant service and suspicious looks, unless it's clear that you're a tourist and not a terrorist. Africans from fellow socialist states were welcomed in the Soviet era, but periodic waves of nationalist sentiment in the post-Soviet era have resulted in backlashes against anyone with black skin, usually in the bleak suburbs where jobless young white men target their even poorer African and Asian neighbors. The majority of Russians do not share this hostility and tourists only very rarely suffer from it, especially those traveling in groups.

Most Russians are eager to criticize the U.S. government for something, but the comments are purely political—a way of making conversation and demonstrating their knowledge of world events, as opposed to a personal attack. Most interlocutors are happy to talk to a foreigner about current events, even if your views differ, and you'll find pro-Western sentiment as common as anti-Western sentiment.

Newspapers & Magazines *The International Herald Tribune, Financial Times*, and other English-language publications are on sale at the chain hotels and some of the larger Russian hotels, but they're not available at newsstands around the city. The English-language daily *The Moscow Times* (www.themoscowtimes.com) is the most comprehensive and even-handed reference for news and entertainment listings in English. The *eXile* exists online only as www.exiledonline.com, but no longer focused on Russia, is known for its raunchy commentary and detailed bar, restaurant, and club listings. For Russian speakers, *Vedomosti* and *Kommersant* newspapers are the most respected; *Afisha* is the weekly magazine of note for entertainment, dining, and shopping advice.

Packing Bring warm-weather gear for any season but June and July, and even in those months a jacket and umbrella are suggested. Bring llightweight clothes in summer, too, as temperatures can swing wildly and summer temperatures can be sweltering in a place with rare air-conditioning. Some clubs and cabarets require jackets and refuse anyone in sports shoes. For more helpful information on packing for your trip, download our convenient Travel Tools app for your mobile device. Go to www.frommers.com/go/mobile and click on the Travel Tools icon.

Passports All visitors to Russia need a valid passport and visa. See "Visas," below, for more information.

o **Australia** **Australian Passport Information Service** (© 131-232, or visit www.passports.gov.au).

o Canada Passport **Office,** Department of Foreign Affairs and International Trade, Ottawa, ON K1A 0G3 (© **800/567-6868;** www.ppt.gc.ca).

o **Ireland** **Passport Office,** Setanta Centre, Molesworth Street, Dublin 2 (© **01/671-1633;** www.foreignaffairs.gov.ie).

o **New Zealand** Passports Office, Department of Internal Affairs, 47 Boulcott St., Wellington, 6011 (© 0800/225-050 in New Zealand or 04/474-8100; www.passports.govt.nz).

o United **Kingdom** Visit your nearest passport office, major post office, or travel agency or contact the **Identity and Passport Service (IPS),** 89 Eccleston Sq., London, SW1V 1PN (© **0300/222-0000;** www.ips.gov.uk).

o **United States** To find your regional passport office, check the U.S. State Department website (travel.state.gov/passport) or call the **National Passport Information Center** (© **877/487-2778**) for automated information.

Petrol Please see "Getting Around by Car," earlier in this chapter.

Pharmacies The number of pharmacies, called *apteka* and marked by a blue cross, is growing rapidly in Russia's cities. One good chain is called **36.6** (http://366.ru), with branches all over Moscow; another is **Dr. Stoletov** (http://stoletov.ru). Check with your hotel concierge for the all-night pharmacy nearest you.

Police Call 02.

Safety The notorious Russian "mafia" makes for good movie villains, but its reputation is rather exaggerated and it is not a serious threat to foreign visitors. The victims of most organized crime are Russian millionaires and powerful tycoons who have much more to lose than the average Western tourist. Pickpockets and over-friendly drunks are the main annoyances to today's traveler; you can avoid both by being alert, traveling in groups, and sticking to well-lit areas after dark. Prostitution and drug use are illegal but widespread, and not worth a run-in with the Russian police. Drunk-driving laws are strict, forbidding drivers from having even one drink, but traffic police (unfortunately) readily accept pay-offs for overlooking minor infractions. Women on their own are not advised to travel on the metro, or in underground walkways, at night. Catcalls are the most likely threat but aggression is also possible. Police do not widely speak English and can seem forbidding when you ask for their help, though in times of emergency are generally reliable. If you are robbed or are otherwise in danger, seek security help from a hotel concierge (even if it's not your hotel) or staff at tourist sites, which often have their own security staff.

Senior Travel   Russians have great respect for their elders, but the country's modern history has been brutal to them, wiping out their savings, shriveling the value of their pensions, and leaving them without cheap healthcare just when they need it most. Russians over 60 qualify for discounts everywhere, including reduced admission on public transport and to many museums and other attractions. However, many tourist sites offer this discount only to Russians, and charge all foreigners a separate, inflated price. Also note that Russian sightseeing requires a lot of walking and ubiquitous stairs.

Many reliable agencies and organizations target the 50-plus market. **Road Scholar** (© **800/454-5768;** www.roadscholar.org) arranges worldwide study programs for those age 55 and over. **ElderTreks** (© **800/741-7956** or 416/558-5000 outside North America; www.eldertreks.com) offers small-group tours to off-the-beaten-path or adventure-travel locations, restricted to travelers 50 and older.

Recommended publications offering travel resources and discounts for seniors include the quarterly magazine *Travel 50 & Beyond* (www.travel50andbeyond.com) and the best-selling paperback *Unbelievably Good Deals and Great Adventures That You Absolutely Can't Get Unless You're Over 50, 2007–2008, 16th Edition* (McGraw-Hill), by Joann Rattner Heilman.

Smoking   Russians smoke heavily, and nonsmokers are rarely catered to. Expensive hotels and an increasing number of restaurants offer nonsmoking options, so don't be afraid to ask. Bars are universally smoky. Smoking is forbidden on public transport and in museums. Crude Russian cigarettes cost about 40 rubles a pack, while Russian-made Marlboros, available at any street kiosk, cost slightly more. Imported brands cost 90 rubles and up.

Student Travel   Students are granted discounts in most museums, on train tickets, and sometimes theater tickets. However the discounts sometimes only apply to Russian students. Basic Russian skills are usually enough to allow foreign students to talk their way in for a Russian student price.

Taxes   VAT (value-added tax) of up to 18% is always included in the list price of store items and restaurant bills, though not always in hotel rates. It's a good idea to ask if you're unsure. The VAT cannot be refunded upon departure as it is in European cities. There is no sales tax in Moscow.

Taxis   See "Getting Around," above.

Telephone   While cellphone service is quite advanced, Russia's traditional phone service remains so basic that many of those cell owners are still on waiting lists for land lines. Not so long ago, you had to order all international calls in advance. Today you can dial directly, but poor connections and disconnections are common on land lines.

To call Russia: If you're calling Russia from the United States:
1. Dial the international access code 011.
2. Dial the country code 7.
3. Dial the city code (495 or 499 for Moscow, 812 for St. Petersburg) and then the seven-digit number. So the whole number you'd dial would be 011-7-495-000-0000.

To make international calls: To make international calls from Russia, first dial 8, then wait for a tone, then dial 10, then dial the country code (U.S. or Canada 1, U.K. 44, Ireland 353, Australia 61, New Zealand, 64). Next, dial the area code and number. For example, if you want to call the Russian Embassy in Washington, D.C., you would dial 8 (tone) 10-1-202-298-5700. If you are calling from a hotel, you may have to dial 9 before dialing the 8, depending on hotel policy.

To call from city to city within Russia: First dial 8, then wait for a tone, then dial the city code and the number. For example, calling St. Petersburg from Moscow would look like this: 8 (tone) 812-777-1000.

To call within Russian cities: Just dial the five- to seven-digit number. Local calls are free.

For directory assistance: Dial 07 if you're looking for a number inside Russia, but only if you speak Russian.

For operator assistance: If you need operator assistance in making an international call, dial 8, then wait for a tone, then dial 194. You can also try 077. If you need help calling a number in Russia, dial 08, but few operators speak English.

Toll-free numbers: You cannot phone a 1-800 number in the United States from Russia, so be sure to have standard toll numbers for all your credit card companies and travel agencies before you leave.

Pay phones: Russia has largely phased out its coin-operated phones for card-operated ones. The coin-run ones rarely work and should be avoided. If you get stuck with one, they accept 1-, 2-, and 5-ruble coins. Cards for the other phones can be purchased at most metro stations and at many hotel kiosks in Moscow and St. Petersburg. Not all phones accept all kinds of phone cards, and not all phone cards allow international calls. The most common is Moscow City Telephone Service, known as MGTS by its Russian initials. Most cards provide instructions in English, though the phones use only Russian and internationally recognizable symbols.

International calling cards: Direct access numbers for AT&T in Moscow are ✆ 495/755-5042 and 325-5042; MCI is ✆ 495/747-3322; BT Direct is ✆ 10-80-01-10-1044 (dial 8 first and wait for the tone); Canada Direct is ✆ 495/755-5045 or 747-3325.

Time   Moscow used to be 3 hours ahead of Greenwich Mean Time from October to March until President Dmitry Medvedev switched the country to daylight saving time for the entire year, putting Moscow 4 hours ahead of GMT all year long. That means it's usually 3 hours ahead of London, 8 hours ahead of New York, and 11 hours ahead of San Francisco. To check the current time from any fixed-line phone, dial 100 (Russian only). For help with time translations, and more, download our convenient Travel Tools app for your mobile device. Go to www.frommers.com/go/mobile and click on the Travel Tools icon.

Tipping   Restaurants generally include service charges in the bill, though small tips are welcome. Taxis usually set the rate before you head out, so no tip is expected. Baggage handlers and coat-check staffers should be tipped the ruble equivalent of a dollar or so. In hotels, leave the equivalent of $2 per bag to bellhops, and $1–$2 per day to the chambermaid. For help with tip calculations, currency conversions, and more, download our convenient Travel Tools app for your mobile device. Go to www.frommers.com/go/mobile and click on the Travel Tools icon.

Toilets   You can find public toilets or restrooms in hotel lobbies, restaurants, museums, department stores, and railway and bus stations. The quality and cleanliness are better at large hotels than train stations. Museums and restaurants generally reserve their restrooms for patrons. A few outdoor public toilets are available, but are generally poorly maintained and can be dangerous at night.

VAT   See "Taxes" earlier in this section.

Visas   Nearly all visitors to Russia need visas. See "Visas & Customs," earlier in this chapter.

Water Tap water in Moscow is generally safe to drink—though not in St. Petersburg (See "Fast Facts: St. Petersburg," below). Bottled water is widely available and reliable.

Wi-Fi See "Internet & Wi-Fi," earlier in this section.

Terrorism Concerns

This is a sadly pertinent question for travel almost anywhere in this post-9/11 world. Russia's experiences with terrorism date back to the 19th century, when revolutionary bombers assassinated Czar Alexander II. The source of more recent terrorist attacks has been the war in Chechnya, where a conflict between Russian troops and Chechen guerrillas has simmered for nearly 2 decades. Two major terrorist attacks outside Chechnya in recent years—the Moscow theater siege in 2002 and the Beslan school massacre in 2004—terrified the world and hardened Russian opposition to the Chechen cause. With no end to the conflict in sight, the Chechen problem will continue to cast a shadow over Russia's post-Soviet progress.

The provinces in the Northern Caucasus Mountains neighboring Chechnya are at the most risk of spillover violence that could affect tourists. Moscow—1,000km (621 miles) to the north—is sheltered from everyday Chechnya-related violence, but as the seat of Russia's government, it is at risk of rare attacks like the theater siege. Like terrorist acts in other European cities, these are nearly impossible to predict and avoid. Most experts judge the terrorism risk in Moscow as no higher than in other major capitals, though if an attack occurs, Russian security services are likely to handle it more ruthlessly than their European counterparts would. St. Petersburg is considered at low risk for terrorism.

See the U.S. State Department's Advisory website (www.travel.state.gov) for recent warnings, though be aware that they tend to be more alarmist than the travel advisories posted by other governments. If you notice a suspicious abandoned bag on the metro or in a public place, report it to the nearest metro official or police officer.

FAST FACTS: ST. PETERSBURG

Area Codes St. Petersburg's area code is 812. See "Telephones" below for details on making calls.

Car Rental See "Getting There by Car," earlier in this chapter.

Cellphones See "Mobile Phones," in Fast Facts: Moscow.

Crime See "Safety," in Fast Facts: Moscow.

Customs See "Visas & Customs" earlier this chapter.

Disabled Travelers See "Fast Facts: Moscow" earlier this chapter.

Doctors For Western-standard medical care and English-speaking staff, try these private clinics. They'll help you deal with emergencies, allergy attacks, or general health problems. Their services are expensive and may not be covered by your insurance company, so be sure to check with your insurer before you go.

- American Medical Clinic and Hospital, 78 Naberezhnaya Moyky (✆ 812/740-2090; www.amclinic.com).
- Euromed, 60 Suvorovsky Prospekt (✆ 812/327-0301).
- Scandinavia, 55a Liteyny Prospekt (✆ 812/600-7777).

Also see "Hospitals," later in this section.

Drinking Laws See "Fast Facts: Moscow" earlier this chapter.

Driving Rules See "Getting Around," earlier in this chapter.

Electricity See "Fast Facts: Moscow" earlier this chapter.

Embassies and Consulates St. Petersburg has consulates for many countries, though the embassies are in Moscow (see "Fast Facts: Moscow," above, for embassy addresses in Moscow). Some consulate addresses:

- **United States:** 15 Furshtadskaya Ulitsa (℡ 812/331-2600).
- **Britain:** 5 Ploshchad Proletarskoi Diktatury (℡ 812/320-3200).
- **Canada:** 32 Malodetskoselsky Prospekt (℡ 812/325-8448).

Emergencies For fire, dial 01; police, 02; ambulance, 03. For medical emergencies, see the "Doctors" listing, above. In extreme cases, the international clinics will send you to a better-equipped Russian hospital with a translator.

Family Travel See "Fast Facts: Moscow" earlier this chapter.

Gasoline Please see "Getting There By Car," earlier in this chapter.

Health See "Health," earlier in this chapter.

Hospitals Most Russian hospital employees speak little or no English, except for the top doctors. These are some of the bigger and relatively reliable hospitals:

- **City Children's Hospital no. 1,** 14 Avangardnaya Ulitsa (℡ 812/735-9736)
- **Hospital no. 20,** 21 Gastello Ulitsa (℡ 812/708-4033)
- **Mariinsky Hospital,** 56 Liteyny Prospekt (℡ 812/275-7446).

Internet & Wi-Fi You won't have to look too far for free Wi-Fi in cafes, bars, and hotels. You can also connect to a 4G network with a Yota account (www.yota.ru), with weekly or monthly plans available. If you're traveling without a laptop, try Quo Vadis, at 24 Nevsky Prospekt; or Café Max at 90/92 Nevsky Prospekt. Both are open 24 hours. Café Max also has a branch inside the Hermitage Museum.

Language See "Fast Facts: Moscow" earlier this chapter.

Legal Aid See "Fast Facts: Moscow" earlier this chapter.

LGBT Travelers See "Fast Facts: Moscow" earlier this chapter.

Mail The main city post office (Glavny Pochtamt) is at 9 Pochtamtskaya Ulitsa (℡ 812/315-8022). See "Fast Facts: Moscow" earlier this chapter for advice on sending packages, postcards and letters.

Medical Requirements See "Health," earlier in this chapter.

Mobile Phones European GSM or North American tri-band phones will work in St Petersburg, but be sure to check roaming rates in advance with your provider. If you're staying for any length of time, you could buy a Russian SIM card with some talk time included. Megafon and MTS offer good coverage and have a wide network of shops across the city. Megafon is at 32 Nevsky Prospect. See "Fast Facts: Moscow" earlier this chapter for more information.

Money & Costs See "Fast Facts: Moscow" earlier this chapter for more information. To exchange currencies other than dollars or euros, try the bigger banks, or the exchange booths in the underground walkway at Gostiny Dvor, or big banks.

Multicultural Travelers See "Fast Facts: Moscow" earlier this chapter.

Newspapers & Magazines The twice-weekly English-language newspaper *The St. Petersburg Times* (www.sptimes.ru) is the best and pretty much only worthwhile source of local news and entertainment listings in English. *The International Herald Tribune*, *Financial Times*, and other international publications are sold at the chain hotels and some of the Russian hotels, but not at city newsstands. The many bilingual guidebooks offered free at hotels and tourist offices are good for listings and museum reviews. For Russian speakers, *Afisha Petersburg* is the best weekly magazine for entertainment, dining, and shopping advice.

Because the Russian language uses the Cyrillic alphabet, confusion often abounds when Russian names are translated—or more precisely, transliterated—into the Latin alphabet. There are several accepted systems for transliterating into English, as well as a French and German system. In this book I've stuck to the Revised American system, with a few exceptions made to aid pronunciation. Famous names such as Tchaikovsky and Gorbachev are spelled as they're most commonly known, not as they would be properly transliterated. See chapter 18, at the back of this book, for the Russian spelling and pronunciation of several key words, phrases, place names, and menu items.

Packing   See "Fast Facts: Moscow," earlier in this chapter.

Passports   All visitors to Russia need a valid passport and visa. See "Visas," below, for more information.

Petrol   See "Getting Around by Car," earlier in this chapter.

Pharmacies   St. Petersburg has an ever-growing number of pharmacies, called *apteka*, many of which are open 24 hours. Look for a blue or green cross. Check with your hotel concierge for the all-night pharmacy nearest you.

Police   Call 02.

Safety   See "Fast Facts: Moscow," earlier this chapter.

Salons   St. Petersburg residents make salons a part of their routine, and you can find the simpler *parikmakherskaya* (barber shop/hair salon) or the more elaborate *salon krasoty* (beauty salon) just about anywhere. Quality and prices are higher in the center. If you've got a night on the town, two central places to try (for both men and women) are Prestige, 56 Naberezhnaya Moiki (✆ 812/314-7521), and the fancier Adamant-Caprice, at 90/92 Nevsky Prospekt (✆ 812/272-7514).

Senior Travel   See "Fast Facts: Moscow," earlier this chapter.

Smoking   See "Fast Facts: Moscow," earlier this chapter.

Student Travel   See "Fast Facts: Moscow," earlier this chapter.

Taxes   See "Fast Facts: Moscow," earlier this chapter.

Taxis   See "Getting Around," above.

Telephone   See "Fast Facts: Moscow" earlier this chapter for full details. In St. Petersburg, phone cards for public phones can be purchased at any metro station, post office, and many hotel kiosks. Not all phones accept all kinds of phone cards, and not all phone cards allow international calls, so make sure that you check the card will work for the country you want to call. Most cards and card phones provide instructions, though very basic, in English. If you're calling home, using an international pre-paid phone card will almost certainly be cheaper than using a landline in your hotel room or rented apartment.

Time   St. Petersburg is in the same time zone as Moscow, 4 hours ahead of Greenwich Mean Time all year long. That means it's usually 3 hours ahead of London, 8 hours ahead of New York, and 11 hours ahead of San Francisco. To check the current time from any fixed-line phone, dial 100 (Russian only). For help with time translations, and more, download our convenient Travel Tools app for your mobile device. Go to www.frommers.com/go/mobile and click on the Travel Tools icon.

Tipping   See "Fast Facts: Moscow" earlier this chapter.

Toilets St. Petersburg has far too few public restrooms for its size, and the ones it has are odorous and often no more than a hole in the floor. Look out for the portable toilets in vans parked at tourist sites such as Palace Square; these charge a small fee. Bring toilet paper everywhere. In a pinch, dive into any hotel or restaurant restroom—many will charge a small fee for non-clients.

VAT See "Taxes" earlier in this section.

Visas See "Visas & Customs," earlier this chapter.

Water Tap water in St. Petersburg is not safe to drink. Most hotels have their own clean water supply, or use filtered water, because of St. Petersburg's often bacteria-infected groundwater. It's a good idea to ask before brushing your teeth with tap water. Numerous brands of locally bottled spring water are good cheap sources of clean water. Some safe brands are Saint Springs (Svyatoi Istochnik) and Natalia. Make sure you ask for *voda bez gaza*—literally, water without gas—unless you want the carbonated kind.

Wi-Fi See "Internet & Wi-Fi," earlier in this section.

USEFUL RUSSIAN TERMS & PHRASES

I f you do one single thing to prepare for your trip to Russia, make it learning the Cyrillic alphabet. It scares off most tourists, and that's a great shame. The 33-letter alphabet is really not hard to learn, since many of the letters are the same as in English. Knowing how to read those dizzying signs will make your trip through Russia much less mysterious and more comfortable. Kids are remarkably quick at picking out the new letters, and can turn the learning process into a family game of who can read that street sign faster. If you have any experience with college fraternities or sororities, you'll note that Cyrillic shares many letters with Greek, too.

Most Russians in hotels, restaurants, and shops will speak some English, especially those of the younger generations. Any effort to speak Russian will be welcomed, and in smaller establishments even a few words of Russian may get you out of a bind or improve service. Below is a rough guide to the alphabet, with phonetic English equivalents, followed by useful words and phrases with which to navigate Russian streets and restaurant menus. Words are printed in Russian followed by a pronunciation guide.

ALPHABET

Russian	Pronunciation
А а	ah
Б б	b
В в	v
Г г	g (hard g)
Д д	d
Е е	yeh
Ё ё	yö
З з	z
Ж ж	zh (like "s" in measure)

Russian	Pronunciation
И и	ee
Й й	ee (slightly harder than above)
К к	k
Л л	l
М м	m
Н н	n
О о	o
П п	p
Р р	r (rolled r, like the Spanish or Scottish)
С с	s
Т т	t
У у	u
Ф ф	f
Х х	kh (guttural)
Ц ц	ts
Ч ч	ch
Ш ш	sh
Щ щ	shch (like "fresh cheese")
Ъ ъ	hard sign (always silent)
Ы ы	between "y" and "we"
Ь ь	soft sign (always silent)
Э э	eh
Ю ю	yu
Я я	ya

BASIC VOCABULARY
Key Words

English	Russian	Pronunciation
Yes/No	да, нет	da, nyet
Hello	здравствуйте	*zdras*-tvoo-tye
Hi	привет	pree-*vyet*
Good morning	доброе утро	*do*-bro-ye *oo*-tra
Good day	добрый день	*do*-bry dyen
Good evening	добрый вечер	*do*-bry *ve*-cher
Good-bye	до свидания	*da* svi-da-nya
See you later	пока	pa-*ka*
Thank you	спасибо	spa-*see*-ba
Please/You're welcome	пожалуйста	pa-*zha*-li-sta
Excuse me	извините	eez-vee-*nee*-tye
Sorry	простите, пожалуйста	prah-*stee*-tye, pa-*zha*-li-sta

English	Russian	Pronunciation
How are you?	**как дела?**	kak deh-*la*
Fine, good	**хорошо**	kho-ro-*sho*
Bad	**плохо**	*plo*-kha
When	**когда**	ka-*gda*
Today	**сегодня**	se-*vohd*-nya
Yesterday	**вчера**	vche-*ra*
Tomorrow	**завтра**	*zav*-tra
Open	**открыто**	ot-*kree*-ta
Closed	**закрыто**	za-*kree*-ta
Watch out	**осторожно**	os-toh-*rozh*-no
Help!	**помогите**	pa-ma-*gee*-tye
Stop	**стоп, стой**	stop, stoi
Entrance	**вход**	vkhod
Exit	**выход**	*vy*-khod
Danger	**опасно**	o-*pas*-no
Hospital	**больница, госпиталь**	bol-*nee*-tsa, *gos*-pee-tal
Police	**милиция**	mee-*lee*-tsee-ya
Fire	**пожар**	po-*zhar*
Ambulance	**скорая помощь**	*sko*-ra-ya *po*-moshch
Pharmacy	**аптека**	ap-*teh*-ka
Currency exchange	**обмен валюты**	ob-*men* vah-*lyoo*-tee
Bank	**банк**	bahnk
ATM/cash machine	**банкомат**	bahnk-o-*mat*
Ticket	**билет**	bee-*lyet*
Post office	**почта**	*poch*-ta
Postage stamp	**марка**	*mar*-ka
Postcard	**открытка**	ot-*kreet*-ka
Airport	**аэропорт**	ah-air-o-*port*
Subway/metro	**метро**	me-*tro*
Bus	**автобус**	av-*toh*-bus
Tram	**трамвай**	tram-*vai*
Taxi	**такси**	tahk-*si*
Shop	**магазин**	ma-ga-*zeen*
Museum	**музей**	moo-*zay*
Park	**парк**	park
Church	**церковь, храм**	*tser*-kov, khram
Embassy	**посольство**	pah-*sohl*-stva
Coat check	**гардероб**	gard-yeh-*robe*
Admission fee	**вход**	vkhod
Free of charge	**бесплатно**	bes-*plaht*-no

Handy Phrases

English	Russian	Pronunciation
Do you speak English?	**Вы говорите по-английски?**	vy go-vo-*ree*-te po ang-*lee*-skee?
I don't speak Russian	**Я не говорю по-русски**	ya nee guh-vuh-*ryoo* pa-*roo*-skee
I speak a little Russian	**Я немного говорю по-русски**	ya ne-*mno*-go guh-vuh-*ryoo* pa-*roo*-skee
How much does it cost?	**сколько стоит?**	*skol*-ka *sto*-it?
Expensive	**дорого**	*do*-ra-ga
Cheap	**недорого**	ne-*do*-ra-ga
Where is . . .	**Где находится . . .**	gde na-*kho*-dee-tsa . . .
a hotel	**гостиница**	gos-*tee*-nee-tsa
the metro station	**станция метро**	*stan*-tsee-ya me-*tro*
the rest-room/WC	**туалет**	tua-*let*
To the right	**направо**	na-*pra*-vo
To the left	**налево**	na-*le*-vo
Straight ahead	**прямо**	*prya*-mo
What time is it?	**сколько времени?**	*skol*-ka *vre*-me-nee?
I would like to order . . .	**мне, пожалуйста . . .**	mnye, pa-*zha*-li-sta
I would like the check, please	**принесите счет, пожалуйста**	pree-ne-*see*-te shyot, pa-*zha*-li-sta
Service charge/tip	**за обслуживание**	za ob-*sloo*-zhee-va-nee-ye
VAT (tax)	**НДС (налог)**	en-de-es (nah-*lohg*)

Some Key Place Names

English	Russian	Pronunciation
Moscow	**Москва**	mosk-*vah*
Kremlin	**Кремль**	kreml
Red Square	**Красная площадь**	*kras*-nay-a *ploh*-shchad
Tverskaya Street	**улица Тверская**	*oo*-li-tsa tver-*sky*-ah
St. Petersburg	**Санкт-Петербург**	sankt pe-tehr-*burg*
Hermitage	**Эрмитаж**	er-mee-*tazh*
Nevsky Prospekt	**Невский проспект**	*nev*-ski pros-*pekt*

English	Russian	Pronunciation
Palace Square	Дворцовая площадь	dvar-*tsoh*-va-ya *ploh*-shchad
Street	улица	*oo*-li-tsa
Avenue	проспект	pros-*pekt*
Boulevard	бульвар	bool-*var*
Embankment	набережная	*na*-ber-ezh-nya
Lane	переулок	peh-reh-*oo*-luk
Underground walkway	переход	peh-reh-*khod*

Numbers

English	Russian	Pronunciation
1	один	ah-*deen*
2	два	dva
3	три	tree
4	четыре	chuh-*tee*-reh
5	пять	pyat
6	шесть	shest
7	семь	syem
8	восемь	*voh*-syem
9	девять	de-vyat
10	десять	de-syat
11	одинадцать	ah-*deen*-uh-tsat
12	двенадцать	dve-*na*-tsat
13	тринадцать	tree-*na*-tsat
14	четырнадцать	chuh-*teer*-nah-tsat
15	пятнадцать	pyat-*na*-tsat
16	шестнадцать	shest-*na*-tsat
17	семнадцать	syem-*na*-tsat
18	восемнадцать	voh-syem-*na*-tsat
19	девятнадцать	de-vyat-*na*-tsat
20	двадцать	*dva*-tsat
30	тридцать	*tri*-tsat
40	сорок	*so*-rok
50	пятьдесят	pyat-deh-*syat*
60	шестьдесят	shest-deh-*syat*
70	семьдесят	*sem*-deh-syat
80	восемьдесят	*voh*-syem-deh-syat
90	девяносто	deh-vya-*no*-sta
100	сто	sto
1,000	тысяча	*ty*-sya-cha

Days

English	Russian	Pronunciation
Monday	понедельник	pon-e-*del*-nik
Tuesday	вторник	*vtor*-nik
Wednesday	среда	sre-*da*
Thursday	четверг	chet-*vairg*
Friday	пятница	*pyat*-nee-tsa
Saturday	суббота	soo-*bo*-ta
Sunday	воскресенье	vos-kre-*seh*-nya

Months

English	Russian	Pronunciation
January	январь	yan-*vahr*
February	февраль	fev-*rahl*
March	март	mart
April	апрель	ah-*prel*
May	май	ma-ee
June	июнь	ee-*yoon*
July	июль	ee-*yool*
August	август	ahv-*goost*
September	сентябрь	sent-*yahbr*
October	октябрь	ahkt-*yahbr*
November	ноябрь	no-*yahbr*
December	декабрь	dek-*yahbr*

RUSSIAN DINING SAVVY
Basics

English	Russian	Pronunciation
menu	меню	men-*yoo*
breakfast	завтрак	*zahv*-trak
lunch	обед	o-*byed*
dinner	ужин	*oo*-zhin
smoking/nonsmoking	курящий/некурящий	koo-*rya*-shee/ne-koo-*rya*-shee
appetizers	закуски	za-*koo*-skee
salad	салат	sa-*laht*
soup	суп	soop
first courses	первые блюда	*per*-vee-yeh *blyoo*-da
main dishes	вторые блюда	vto-*ree*-yeh *blyoo*-da
dessert	десерт	deh-*sairt*
bread	хлеб	khleb
butter	масло	*mas*-lah

English	Russian	Pronunciation
salt	**соль**	sol
pepper	**перец**	*pe*-rets
sugar	**сахар**	*sah*-khar
honey	**мед**	myod
jam	**варенье**	var-*en*-ye
mustard	**горчица**	gar-*chee*-tsa
ketchup	**кетчуп**	*keh*-choop
cold	**холодный**	kho-*lohd*-nee
hot	**горячий**	go-*rya*-chee

Soup (СУПЫ)

English	Russian	Pronunciation
borscht	**борщ**	borshch
cabbage soup	**щи**	*shchee*
cold sorrel soup	**зеленые щи**	zel-*yon*-i shchee
tangy stew (meat- or fish-based)	**солянка**	sol-*yan*-ka
fish-based stew	**уха**	*oo*-kha
broth	**похлебка**	pokhl-*yob*-ka

Dairy Products (МОЛОЧНЫЕ ПРОДУКТЫ)

English	Russian	Pronunciation
milk	**молоко**	ma-la-*koh*
cream	**сливки**	*sleev*-kee
sour cream	**сметана**	sme-*tah*-na
cheese	**сыр**	syr
farmers' cheese	**творог**	*tvor*-ug
kefir	**кефир**	keh-*feer*
eggs	**яйца**	*ya*-ee-tsa
hard-boiled egg	**крутое яйцо**	kroo-toh-ye ya-ee-*tsò*
soft-boiled egg	**яйцо в смятку**	ya-ee-*tso* v *smyat*-koo
scrambled eggs	**омлет**	om-*lyet*

Meat (МЯСО)

English	Russian	Pronunciation
beef	**говядина**	gov-*ya*-dee-na
pork	**свинина**	svee-*nee*-na
chicken	**курица**	*koo*-ree-tsa
lamb	**баранина**	ba-*ra*-nee-na
veal	**телятина**	tel-*ya*-tee-na
ham	**ветчина**	vet-chee-*na*
cold cuts, sausage	**колбаса**	kohl-ba-*sa*
hot dog–type sausage	**сосиска**	sah-*see*-ska

English	Russian	Pronunciation
ground meat grilled on skewer	кебаб	ke-*bahb*
chunks of meat, usually lamb, grilled on skewer	шашлык	shash-*leek*
duck	утка	*oot*-ka
turkey	индейка	in-*day*-ka
ground meat–filled dumplings	пельмени	pel-*me*-nee
ground-meat cutlets	котлеты	kot-*leh*-tee
rabbit	кролик	*kroh*-leek
liver	печень	*pe*-chyen
aspic	студень	*stoo*-dyen
rare	с кровью	s *kroh*-vyoo
medium	прожаренный	pro-*zhar*-eh-nee
well-done	хорошо прожаренный	kho-ro-*show* pro-*zhar*-eh-nee

Fish (РЫБА)

English	Russian	Pronunciation
caviar (black)	икра (черная)	eek-*ra* (*chor*-na-ya)
beluga/sevruga/osetra	белуга/севрюга/осетра	beh-*loo*-ga/sev-*roo*-ga/o-*set*-ra
red caviar (salmon roe)	красная икра	*kras*-na-ya eek-*ra*
salmon	лосось-семга	lah-*sohs*, *syom*-ga
sturgeon	осетрина	ah-se-*tree*-na
trout	форель	fa-*rel*
pikeperch	судак	soo-*dak*
herring	сельдь	syeld
catfish	сом	som
tuna	тунец	too-*nets*
eel	угорь	*oo*-gor
crayfish	раки	*ra*-kee
sterlet	стерлядь	*ster*-lyad
sushi	суши	su-shi

Vegetables (ОВОЩИ)

English	Russian	Pronunciation
tomato	помидор	po-mee-*dor*
cucumber	огурец	ah-goo-*rets*
cabbage	капуста	ka-*poo*-sta
carrots	морковь	mar-*kov*
potatoes	картошка	kar-*toh*-shka
lettuce	салат	sa-*laht*
radish	редиска	reh-*dee*-ska

English	Russian	Pronunciation
mushroom	грибы	gree-*bee*
beets	свекла	*svyo*-kla
eggplant/aubergine	баклажан	bah-klah-*zhan*
spinach	шпинат	shpee-*nat*
sweet pepper	перец	*pe*-rets

Fruit (ФРУКТЫ)

English	Russian	Pronunciation
apple	яблоко	*ya*-blo-ko
banana	банан	bah-*nahn*
orange	апельсин	ah-pel-*seen*
plum	слива	*slee*-va
peach	персик	*pear*-seek
strawberry	клубника	kloob-*nee*-ka
cherry	вишня	*vee*-shnya
wild cherry	черешня	che-*re*-shnya
raspberry	малина	mah-*lee*-na
grape	виноград	vee-no-*grad*
currant	смородина	smo-*ro*-dee-na
melon (usually a sweet cantaloupe)	дыня	*dee*-nya
watermelon	арбуз	ar-*booz*
grapefruit	грейпфрут	grayp-*froot*

Desserts (ДЕССЕРТ)

English	Russian	Pronunciation
ice cream	мороженое	mo-*ro*-zhe-no-ye
cake	торт	tort
cookies	печенье	pe-*che*-nye
candy	конфеты	kon-*fyet*-ee
pie (savory or sweet)	пирог	pee-*rog*
bliny (crepelike pancakes)	блины	blee-*nee*
minipancakes	оладьи	oh-*la*-dee
chocolate	шоколад	sho-ko-*lad*

Drinks (НАПИТКИ)

English	Russian	Pronunciation
tea	чай	chai
coffee	кофе	*ko*-fye
water	вода	vah-*da*
still/sparkling	без газа/с газом	bez-*ga*-za / s *ga*-zom

English	Russian	Pronunciation
juice	сок	sok
milk	молоко	ma-la-*koh*
vodka	водка	*vohd*-ka
beer	пиво	*pee*-va
red wine	красное вино	*kras*-no-ye vee-*no*
white wine	белое вино	*bel*-o-ye vee-*no*
brandy	коньяк	kon-*yak*
whiskey	виски	*vis*-kee
cocktail	коктейль	kok-*tail*
Coca-Cola (or any cola-type drink)	кока-кола	ko-ka-*ko*-la
any sweet carbonated drink	лимонад	li-mo-*nad*

Index

See also Accommodations and Restaurant indexes, below.

General Index

A

Abim Plus (St. Petersburg), 252
Above and Beyond Tours, 303–304
Academic trips, 39
Access-Able Travel Source, 301
Accessible Journeys, 301
Accommodations, 39, 294–296.
See also Accommodations Index
Moscow and environs, 55–76
near the airport, 73–74
alternative accommodations, 75–76
Arbat, 67–68
best, 3, 6, 55–57
currency exchange, 74
family-friendly, 60
foreigner tax, 62
around The Kremlin and Red Square, 57–61
outside the Garden Ring Road, 70–73
Peredelkino, 171
Petrovka and The Ukrainian Quarter, 63–66
prices, 55, 75
prostitution, 64
reservations, 75
south of Moscow River, 68–70
Suzdal and Vladimir, 166
Tverskaya Street and environs, 61–63
St. Petersburg and environs, 187–204
near the airport, 201–202
best, 187–189
family-friendly, 193
around the Hermitage Museum and Palace Square, 189–193
landing the best room, 196
Lower Nevsky to Smolny Cathedral, 196–198
mini-hotels, 188
practical information, 202–204
prices, 187, 202–203
South of Nevsky, 198–200
Upper Nevsky Prospekt, 193–195
Vasilevsky Island and The Petrograd side, 200–201
Addresses, finding, 295
Admiralty (Admiralteistvo; St. Petersburg), 228
Admiralty (St. Petersburg), 181
Aeroexpress train (Moscow), 284
Agate Pavilion (Tsarskoye Tselo), 274
AirAmbulanceCard.com, 301
Air Force Museum, Russian (Moscow), 112–113
Air travel, 289
Moscow, 282–284
St. Petersburg, 289–290
staying comfortable in long-haul flights, 283
Akhmatova, Anna, 28
Museum (St. Petersburg), 238–239
Aktsia (Moscow), 136
Akunin, Boris, 28
Alexander Gardens (Alexandrovsky Sad; Moscow), 48, 107
Alexander I, Czar, 20
Alexander II, Czar, 16–17, 20, 182, 230, 244
Alexander III, Czar, 20
Alexander Nevsky Monastery and Cemetery (Lavra Aleksandra Nevskogo; St. Petersburg), 228–230
Alexandra, Empress, 19
Alexandra Nevskogo Bridge (St. Petersburg), 292
Alexandrinsky Theater (St. Petersburg), 258–259
All-Russian Exhibition Center (formerly VDNKh; Moscow), 117, 121
Alphabet, Russian, 315–316
Amber House (Yantarny Dom; St. Petersburg), 252
Amber Room (Tsarskoye Tselo), 273–274
American Foundation for the Blind (AFB), 301
American Medical Center Moscow, 301
American Medical Clinic and Hospital (St. Petersburg), 311
Ananov (St. Petersburg), 255
Andrei Rublev (film), 109
Andropov, Yuri, 21
Anglia British Bookshop (St. Petersburg), 253
Angliiskaya Naberezhnya (English Embankment; St. Petersburg), 258
Angliisky Podvorye (English Courtyard; Moscow), 125, 148
Anna Akhmatova Museum (St. Petersburg), 238–239

Antikvariat na Bronnoi (Moscow), 136
Antiques and collectibles
Moscow, 136
St. Petersburg, 252
Apartment rentals, 295–296
Moscow, 76
St. Petersburg, 203
Apraksin Dvor (St. Petersburg), 251, 254
Apshu (Moscow), 153
Arbat district (Moscow), 41, 48–49
accommodations, 67–68
restaurants, 89–91
shopping, 134
Arbatskaya Lavitsa (Moscow), 140
Archangel Gabriel, Church of the (Moscow), 128
Architecture, 23–25
best, 7–8
"Seven Sisters" (Moscow), 24
Shchusev Museum of Architecture (Moscow), 24
Arctic and Antarctic, Museum of (St. Petersburg), 233–234
Area codes, 301, 311
Aristocratic estates, Moscow, 117–118
Arkhangelskoye, 167–168
Armed Forces, Museum of (Moscow), 112
Armed Forces Day (Defenders of the Motherland Day), 35
The Armory Museum (Moscow), 102
Aromatny Mir (Moscow), 142
Art galleries
Moscow, 136–137
Central House of Artists (Tsentralny Dom Khudozhnika), 115
St. Petersburg, 252–253
Art Garbage (Moscow), 152
Art Modus (St. Petersburg), 252
Art MUSEON (Moscow), 110, 112
Art museums
Moscow
Art MUSEON, 110, 112
Museum of Private Collections, 114
New Tretyakov Gallery/ Museum of Modern Art (Novaya Tretyakovka), 115
Patriarch's Palace and Cathedral of the Twelve Apostles, 102
Pushkin Museum of Fine Arts (Muzei Izobratitelnykh Isskustv imeni Pushkina), 114